Creating the global company

THE HENLEY MANAGEMENT SERIES

Series Adviser: Professor Bernard Taylor

Creating the global company

Successful internationalization

Colin Coulson-Thomas

McGRAW-HILL BOOK COMPANY

London · New York · St Louis · San Francisco · Auckland
Bogotá · Caracas · Hamburg · Lisbon · Madrid · Mexico
Milan · Montreal · New Delhi · Panama · Paris · San Juan
São Paulo · Singapore · Sydney · Tokyo · Toronto

Published by
McGRAW-HILL Book Company Europe
Shoppenhangers Road, Maidenhead, Berkshire SL6 2QL, England
Telephone 0628 23432
Fax 0628 770224

British Library Cataloguing in Publication Data

Coulson-Thomas, Colin
  Creating the Global Company : Successful
  Internationalization. – (Henley Management
  Series)
  I. Title II. Series
  658

ISBN 0-07-707599-4

Library of Congress Cataloging-in-Publication Data

Coulson-Thomas, Colin.
  Creating the global company : successful internationalization/
  Colin Coulson-Thomas.
    p. cm. — (Henley management series)
  Includes bibliographical references and index.
  ISBN 0-07-707599-4
    1. International business enterprises—Management.   I. Title.
  II. Series.
HD62.4.C68 1992   92-16115
658'.049—dc20

12345 CUP 95432

Typeset by BookEns Ltd, Baldock, Herts,
and printed and bound at the University Press, Cambridge.

For Susan and Trystan

Contents

Preface

The purpose of this book is to assist senior management in the review of how a company should cope with changes in the international business environment. In view of the critical importance of people for effective responses, it is especially relevant to managers and directors with personnel and training responsibilities.

The book is designed to be of value both to the corporation that has established international operations and to a company that is moving for the first time into the international arena. *All* companies are having to reassess their organization and operations in the light of multiple challenges. Ford of Europe, for example, has needed to consolidate and rationalize its long-established presence in Europe in the light of the emergence of a single market.

The focus of the book is upon the management of internationalization and aims to spread understanding of what companies *are* doing, are *planning* to do and *ought* to do in order to respond effectively to the internationalization of markets and the changing requirements of customers within them. It is not intended to be a technical guide. References to legal matters, such as employment or competition law and national or EC legislation, are made by way of examples to illustrate the range of management issues to be considered. Legal and technical requirements are subject to revision and change so those for whom particular measures and conditions are important should seek appropriate and up-to-date professional advice.

The book aims to offer balanced advice, based upon the experience and judgement of practising managers. It draws almost exclusively upon recent questionnaire and interview surveys of corporate practice and aspiration, rather than the views of those who reflect 'off the field of battle'.

In addition, interviews and discussions were held with directors and managers in over 50 companies that are confronting the international market-place with varying degrees of success. Some of these additional interviews arose in the context of surveys that have been subsequently published (see Appendix I), while others have been carried out exclusively for this book.

The major source survey among those profiled in Appendix I is *Human Resource Development for International Operation*, an Adaptation survey sponsored by Surrey European Management School.[1] In total this survey covers organizations with a combined turnover of some £320 billion, employing over 2.7 million people. In addition, over one million people are individual members of the professional associations that participated in the survey. The exercise was itself international in scope and, in particular, major European multinational companies are well represented among the survey respondents.

Most of the company's examined have been multinationals rather than transnationals, but many of the multinationals have transnational ambitions:

background

- the multinational company may operate in many countries, but it tends to regard one as the home base and so many of its attitudes and values will reflect those of this country of origin – hence it is possible to speak of the 'US' or 'Japanese' multinational and nationals of the home country are likely to dominate the ranks of senior management, but, equally, profit opportunities may be sought in national markets and the company's senior staff may be concerned with national competitiveness
- the company that is referred to as transnational or pan-global tends to operate with an international perspective and to be free of attitudes associated with a particular home country, so the company might be quoted on several stock exchanges around the world, its management team may be drawn from various nationalities, profit opportunities may be sought on a global basis and the company's senior staff may be concerned with the company's own global competitiveness *vis-à-vis* other global players.

The book that results from all this research is not intended to be an academic text and, hence, is not littered with references to academic works. The views expressed are my own. Whether or not the collective responses of those surveyed and interviewed and the conclusions drawn correspond with the hobby horses of individual gurus or an academic consensus is purely coincidental. On occasion the reader who is seeking definitive answers and a 'blueprint' may be frustrated. A conscious attempt has been made to avoid presenting the findings of interviews and discussions in the form of standard packages. Instead, the emphasis is upon equipping you with a perspective that will help you to develop your own individual and tailored response.

Accordingly, early sections of the book concentrate upon the more distinctive features of the international environment and how some understanding of international society and international relations can assist the assessment of international risks and opportunities. International human resource development strategy needs to reflect the nature of international opportunities and business development strategy.

Subsequent sections examine the organization and skills that are necessary for effective international operation. Following these such traditional human resource areas as recruitment, remuneration and mobility are addressed. The internationalization of both directors and managers is then considered. Finally, some next steps are presented, along with the main characteristics of the form of network organization that is most likely to lead to international success.

Colin Coulson-Thomas

1
Introduction

Perspectives

I'm not global or local – I'm me and I run a company that I regard as unique. I want representatives from suppliers who can meet my requirements, whether or not these extend beyond the UK.

Chairman and Chief Executive, UK-based industrial group

The international dimension isn't an alternative, it's another dimension. We still need to be seen as an insider in each of the markets in which we operate.

Chief Executive, UK agricultural products company

All over the world people love their children and like to have pictures of them. The drive for happiness is universal – how could we operate on anything other than an international basis?

European Representative of Japanese company

The engineering technology comes from Norway, the electronics from the US. No society has a complete monopoly of ideas.

Founder Chairman, innovative European high-tech company

Expectations determine what is global and what is local. Wherever you go in the world you will find common elements. Our guests know what to expect. At the same time they expect some differences and they like to feel they have been abroad. We build in a local or regional flavour according to what is known about the expectations of our guests.

Director, international hotel company

Internationalization is a label. It's an adjective, a word our managers keep putting in front of things. These days it's international this and that – but attitudes have not changed.

German-based European Managing Director of packaging company

Our product is a commodity and all over the world it's bought by local customers. For me the European and international dimension are items called 're-allocated overheads' that wipe out my profits or put up my prices. When I read of the latest international taskforce, I wonder how much it is going to cost me.

Managing Director, European subsidiary of US multinational corporation

1

We invest in the US and the EC to become insiders and avoid protectionist pressures. We invest for supply or sourcing reasons in basic production facilities in Asia and South America.

Director, Japanese manufacturing company

1.1 The changing business environment

Organizations today face an unprecedented range of challenges and opportunities. Internationalization is but one of these. Many of the changes that are occurring are not just of degree, not merely incremental steps forward from what is familiar and understood, they are sudden and dramatic, taking people by surprise. Our responses are demanding leaps into the unknown. Frameworks are changing. Many old assumptions no longer apply:

old	new
– incremental adjustment	– radical transformation
– continuity	– change
– planning	– coping with the unexpected
– cartels, barriers and oligopolies	– competition
– barriers to entry	– freedom of choice
– national borders	– freedom of movement
– restrictions and constraints	– access and opportunity
– uninformed customers	– demanding customers
– consumer protection	– consumer power
– standard 'commodity' products and services	– differentiated products and services
– track record	– relevance of contribution
– scale and security	– flexibility, responsiveness and speed
– diversification	– focus and segmentation
– expansion	– prioritization
– static structure	– dynamic flows
– hierarchy	– relationships
– procedures	– processes
– individuals	– project groups and teams
– single discipline	– multidisciplinary
– facts and theories	– values and feelings
– quantity	– quality
– absolutes	– relative and contextual
– knowledge	– competence
– information	– understanding
– automation	– adding value

old	new
– management	– facilitation
– instruction	– learning

Competition and choice are becoming more widespread. Privatization, liberalization and deregulation became global phenomena during the 1980s. A multinational company such as IBM now finds itself facing several thousand competitors.

Traditionally, the ranks of the key players in the global market-place have been dominated by US multinational companies. Throughout the 1980s there was a steady increase in the number of Japanese companies with substantial international operations and they began to outspend US companies on overseas investments. During the 1990s they are likely to be joined by international players from a wider spread of countries.

Cartels, barriers and oligopolies are being eroded by market forces or swept away, creating new opportunities for companies and their competitors to penetrate national markets. Barriers that do remain can change in nature overnight, depending upon the outcome of international trade negotiations or as a result of political changes. For example, within Europe at the start of the 1990s:

- the dismantling of the command economies of Eastern Europe and what was the Soviet Union created new uncertainties and opportunities as these countries, for many companies, were no longer no go areas
- after almost 60 years of social democracy, the Swedish electorate in 1991 returned Carl Bildt as a Prime Minister with a programme to end the collectivism of the 'Swedish model' and introduce a deregulated free-market economy
- agreement between the European Community (EC) and the European Free Trade Association (EFTA) to set up in 1993 a European Economic Area (EEA) offers the prospect of a free trade zone covering 43 per cent of world trade (the EEA embraces 19 countries with a combined population of some 380 million people).

Similar changes have occurred elsewhere in the world. For example:

- India has sought transition from an environment of bureaucracy and licensing to one of freer competition in the market-place and a minority government announced in 1991 that areas of the market would be opened up to direct foreign participation
- in the same year, South Korea announced it would open its market to the extent that it would allow foreign companies to acquire a stake in domestic companies (the South Korean telecoms market is among those that have been opened to competition)

- Brazil has also sought to open up hitherto protected markets, such as information technology (IT), to allow greater foreign participation in previously closed industrial sectors and, as a result, various foreign companies sought to participate in the privatization and opening up of the Brazilian telecoms market and the transfer of the steel industry out of public control
- the private sector has grown rapidly within China and the country entered the 1990s with the intention of joining the General Agreements on Tariffs and Trade (GATT) and playing a more significant role in international trade
- negotiations in North and South America and the Pacific Rim raised the prospect of the emergence of common markets in these regions and, were these regional groupings to pursue protectionist trade policies, the consequences for countries excluded from them would be severe.

The telecommunications sector is one that has felt the impact of privatization and deregulation around the world. Information can be processed and transferred more quickly and developments in information technology mean that suppliers can reach individual customers from any point on the globe. The multiplication of media allows these customers to be better informed. They are more aware of the extent to which they have a choice.

The international spread of quality programmes has raised customer expectations. Complete performance and reliability is becoming the norm – a minimum requirement for being a market player rather than an end objective. Customers are becoming more demanding and exerting their greater bargaining power. Even in traditional mass consumer markets they are requiring individually tailored products and services:

- the US company Personics Systems supplies personalized tapes with an individualized selection of songs
- the pharmaceutical market is fragmenting as new drugs are developed to cope with particular diseases and conditions
- markets for cars are fragmenting into social and other segments, both within and across national markets and design centres such as that of Toyota recognize the need to reconcile the benefits of large-scale production with the flexibility to tailor to particular customer requirements.

At the same time, global advertising and communications programmes enable consistent messages to be put to audiences of hundreds of millions:

- Unilever has established the Food Executive, an international coordinating body, to identify opportunities to launch international food products and ensure greater consistency of global strategy

- names such as Chanel, Gucci and St Laurent are recognized by affluent consumers in cities all over the world
- franchising has enabled global mass markets to be reached by fast food chains such as McDonald's and Burger King (the actual range of products offered by McDonald's in Japan may be different from that available in the US, but the name is instantly recognizable)
- such is the global reach of a product like Coca Cola that I will never forget the shock of being told by an elderly waiter at the Carlton Club, St James, London, 'Sir, we have no drink of that name'.

A company such as Mars can promote the profitable brand on a pan-European basis. In other sectors, companies offering standard products and services are struggling to avoid joining the ranks of 'commodity' suppliers, whose margins are squeezed to the limit of survival profitability.

The development of many areas of technology is moving way ahead of our ability to determine useful applications. Technology and knowledge are less of a differentiator when they are equally available to all and both are fast becoming international commodities. The skill and competence to develop applications that add value for particular customers is emerging as a crucial source of competitive edge.

1.2 Spurs to internationalization

Fewer companies are able to satisfy customer requirements by themselves. Links and relationships along supply chains are being forged with both customers and suppliers.[2] Within these new networks of relationships, each organization has to assess how it might make the greatest added value contribution.

Companies are focusing, segmenting and prioritizing, determining core activities in order to build upon their strengths and enter into complementary arrangements and alliances. Many of the linkages that are emerging cross national borders:

- in response to changes in the telecommunications sector, the French company Alcatel has been implementing a programme of both acquisitions and disposals in order to focus upon core opportunity areas, such as public switching equipment, and arrangements entered into include those with Italtel of Italy; a merger with Telettra, a subsidiary of Fiat; an acquisition from Rockwell International in the US; and joint venture initiatives in Eastern Europe
- the US company AT&T has global ambitions – it has established over 30 manufacturing and support centres around the world, is focusing

upon long-distance calls and network equipment and it entered the 1990s with some two dozen strategic arrangements with various companies around the world.

The importance of establishing clear differentiation from available alternatives is a challenge for both individuals and organizations and is becoming more difficult to achieve as innovations and improvements spread with greater rapidity. A possible reason for internationalization could be a search for additional arenas in which to differentiate.

Other fundamental concerns could also be a spur to internationalization. Many of the challenges and opportunities facing organizations today are international in nature and scope. For example:

- environmental issues and problems tend to be global – most of them cannot be tackled within the framework of the nation state acting in isolation
- demographic trends and changing expectations are also international phenomena as population explosions tend to occur on a continental rather than a national basis.

The emergence of regional groupings of states is blurring the distinction between the national and international dimension. A regional grouping of states, such as the EC, can be a home market for some purposes but not for others. Certain customers will want to buy at a national level, others at a regional level and some at an international level. This complicates the analysis of opportunities and, therefore, the organization of responses.

What constitutes the 'national' level can change overnight as political entities fragment – as in the cases of what was the Soviet Union and Yugoslavia. *New* states can emerge, as we have seen with Estonia, Latvia and Lithuania, so an international company should be on the alert for potential fragmentation. For example, to what extent could a country the size of India be held together in the face of strong separatist pressures?

1.3 Markets and the international dimension

Given the various spurs to internationalization, Kenichi Ohmae has written of the global market-place as a 'borderless world'.[3] The extent to which the market environment is perceived as borderless varies accross companies and business sectors. The French Groupe Havas does not, according to its Chairman Pierre Dauzier, see one global communications market, 'but a multitude of markets, each of which must be defined differently for each business area, taking into account specific cultural and national features'.

When focusing upon what is being liberalized or opened up, it is sometimes easy to forget that certain developments can be the exception rather than the rule. For example:

- many markets remain heavily regulated and, at the start of the 1990s, trade barriers and restrictions on direct investment still protected many national industries; considerable scope exists for further integration and it should be remembered that so long as there are markets, there are likely to be demands for barriers and the protection of special interests
- certain issues have polarized opinion in GATT talks: agricultural support, whether of rice growers in Japan or of European farmers was, throughout the 1980s, backed by politically strong sectional interests; another ever-present danger is that anti-dumping action, within frameworks established with the laudable objective of ensuring that trade is both free and fair, might be used to protect domestic producers
- while a supplier to high-tech companies may be able to choose whether to reach all its customers by telephone, fax or electronic mail, a producer of consumer goods may have great difficulty in making contact with customers in certain parts of the world because the 'global village' is far from a reality in much of the developing world where the resources available for investment in telecommunications infrastructure are not sufficient to keep pace with technological developments.

As some barriers are removed, so others are likely to be created. Internationalization is shifting the focus of protection. The manager in an international company should assume that, like the poor, barriers will always be with us. The effective international executive is aware of the more subtle and informal obstacles *and* ways of getting around them.

The challenge for most companies is not whether or not barriers exist, but to understand constraints upon the international mobility of resources and opportunities – which range from language and culture to technical standards – in order that they can be overcome. Each barrier will have been created for a particular purpose and may have a distinct impact upon certain aspects of a company's aspirations and operations. A barrier may be removed overnight, at the stroke of a legislator's pen, but attitudes and behaviour can take longer to adjust. For example, mobility of labour within the EC actually fell over the 1970s and 1980s while an increasing closeness between its constituent nations was being vaunted by politicians.

In the face of the same market environment, some companies are more international than others. An international perspective and a high proportion of non-national employees can reflect the country of incorporation. Only about a fifth of the employees of the Roche Group are employed in Switzerland, for example. The Swiss market accounts for under 4 per cent of Roche sales and this limited domestic market has forced the company to go international.

Global status is not incompatible with national markets. Bengt Eskilson, President and Chief Executive Officer of the Swedish company Esab points out that, 'By tradition, the welding industry is national. This means that Esab is not the market leader in every country. However, Esab is the market leader in the Nordic countries and the UK and is one of the largest companies in most other European countries. Esab is the second largest welding company in the USA and has a dominant market position in Brazil'. Eskilson explains that, as a result of a global vision and its participation in so many national markets, 'Esab is the largest welding company in the world'.

The buying habits of many customers reflect the location of national frontiers. For example, consumer markets in Europe remain highly fragmented and many national factors have retained their influence on buying decisions.[4] Nevertheless companies such as Unilever recognize that Europe may need to be regarded as a regional market within which there are national sub-markets. The heads of Unilever national operating companies in Europe now report to Lever Europe and it has been the intention of the company to reduce the many national market differences in its products in order to achieve greater harmonization of product elements and speed up the introduction of new products across Europe.

Companies like Unilever are having to be pragmatic. They are recognizing that while some responsibilities need to be at local level, others may be better handled on a regional or international basis. Rather than impose a standard solution, some companies are allowing taskforces and other groups to decide themselves the preferred means of achieving their objectives, using whatever form of formal or informal cooperation or coordination is thought to be most appropriate. A spectrum of responses are possible from autonomous or self-contained national units at one end to an integrated global network at the other.

Having a range of resources across the world does not mean that these can necessarily be harnessed in order to provide better services for individual customers. One of the main elements of the business development strategy of Coopers and Lybrand Deloitte, for example, is to 'create a *truly* international business'. According to the Chairman Brandon Gough, 'The trend amongst . . . clients is towards greater internationalism in both ownership and outlook. For us to continue to provide excellent service to clients will therefore require us to operate as an international business. We already have the resources . . . . However, as the trend towards greater internationalism continues, a new commitment is needed to build the strength, cohesion and effectiveness of the international firm'.

1.4 The age of the customer

This is the age of the customer. Yesterday's customer required the protection of consumer lobbies, fighting to keep shoddy goods and exploitation at bay. Many barriers to entry seemed insurmountable, there were larger public sectors and suppliers maintained cosy relationships with relatively undemanding government customers, but today it is different. Consumers not only have, but can – and in some cases must – exercise choice. To become a world-class competitor, a company must everywhere match or improve on the best. For example, the Japanese company Komatsu, taking on Caterpillar in its home US market, had to match the Caterpillar promise of service within 24 hours. Although lacking an extensive distributor network, Komatsu did this by *flying* service engineers to customer locations.

In many markets the legal framework has also become more demanding. Within a regional grouping of states such as the EC, barriers to the free movement of people, money, goods and services are being tackled with commitment and energy. Public procurement is being opened up to competitive tender so that opportunities no longer arise out of nods and winks on the grapevine. Invitations to tender on an electronic database are simultaneously available to thousands of suppliers and this creates new opportunities for many suppliers to go international.

While suppliers seek economies from the organization of production on a regional or international basis, customers are searching for the savings that can stem from purchasing at the regional or international level. For example in order to coordinate purchasing:

- the Netherlands retail chain Royal Ahold joined in 1989 with Argyll of the UK and Casino of Italy to form the European Retailing Alliance
- similarly, another Netherlands store chain Vendex International joined with retailers in Belgium and Germany to form Eurogroupe
- companies such as DAF purchase across Europe from a single point, but Caterpillar has gone a stage further to be among the companies that now purchase on a global basis.

While companies are seeking to enter into longer term arrangements with customers (in part in order to stem the erosion of profit margins), a greater willingness of companies to shop around and buy in the cheapest national market is likely to erode many national price differentials. In some sectors, such as IT and the motor industry, this trend could put further pressure upon profitability.

Companies are under greater pressure to launch products simultaneously in all major markets. Apple has increased its use of sub-contracted and temporary staff in order to speed up the introduction of new products, tailored to local market requirements, from its manufacturing plants in Europe, North America and the Pacific Rim. Apple has also used the production expertise of Sony to supply the volume of 'notebook' computers needed to meet international demand at a more competitive price.

Access to relevant expertise and speed of action are becoming more important. Customers are less tolerant of delays. For them geographic distance is no excuse. Those who are aware of it, and can afford it, want it now. The slow company and the slow society will be beaten to the draw by those that are faster. Speed of response can be critical to competitive success.

1.5 Organizational responses

The diverse range and fundamental nature of the developments occurring in the international business environment are such as to suggest that we are moving into a new era. As the transition from one era to another happens it is apparent that the globalization of business is just one of a number of external demands and pressures facing management:

- emergence of human resources as a critical success factor
- harnessing human potential
- more demanding customers
- exponential increase in the rate of change
- concern for environmental issues
- speed of transfer and processing of information
- markets becoming more open and competitive
- globalization of business
- regional cooperation between states
- application of technology
- demographic trends
- changing expectations
- concern with values
- matching corporate and individual needs
- establishing clear differentiation
- articulating a distinct vision and mission.

Never has there been such a range of services to support a corporate response. International sources of information and professional services are mushrooming. Financial and other centres are increasingly networked. Around the clock trading now occurs as business is handled successively by Tokyo, London, New York and Chicago. International companies need to be able to convert currencies and carry out other financial transactions 24 hours a day. London has emerged as Europe's leading financial services market with a major share of cross-border equity business and the world's largest foreign exchange market.

The circumstances surrounding the collapse of the Bank of Credit and Commerce International (BCCI) suggest that international cooperation between national supervisory and regulatory authorities has not always matched the internationalization of certain sectors. How the global activities of international companies should be monitored and to whom they should be accountable could become a significant issue of the 1990s. For example, how should regulatory authorities in the EC and, say, the USA coordinate anti-trust or market dominance policies?

The UK Minister John Redwood MP has pointed out that 'Sometimes individual subsidiaries in individual countries can look strong, but the group structure reveals cross-holdings and cross-lending which is, in practice, very weak. Any evidence of material assets coming from cross-border, cross-group sources should lead to international discussion'.[5]

Professional firms are themselves internationalizing and their legal and accounting services are available to support internationalization. Coopers and Lybrand, for example, has recognized that clients are increasingly requiring access to dedicated teams with a pan-European sector focus and are able to deliver a service through a single point of contact. Individual assignments had already involved multidisciplinary and multioffice teams, but to ensure closer cooperation between national practices, Coopers and Lybrand Europe was established to encourage pan-European networking across the firm and the establishment of pan-European industry groups. Coopers and Lybrand Europe operates as a European network.

Telecommunications companies are competing aggressively to provide a widening range of international communication services. Cable and Wireless, for example, operates a global network and offers various international network management services. Major airlines also operate globally and around the clock and have entered into various arrangements and alliances to smooth the flow of their passengers around the world – there will be more of this in the near future.

1.6 Coping with uncertainty

Uncertainties and vulnerabilities abound: past performance or track record has become a less reliable guide to future prospects and few, if any, organizations are able to rest upon their laurels. Competitive forces are all-embracing on the global battlefield. Twenty-four hours a day competitors are probing for areas of weakness, market outposts that are asleep or otherwise unready. Sheer scale of operation is no defence if it is not accompanied by vigilance, flexibility and responsiveness.[2]

Many organizations have diversified to spread risks when concentration may be required to achieve a critical mass. A 'swings and roundabouts' philosophy has prevailed. Underperformance in one sector or market has been balanced and compensated for by overperformance in another. In today's global market-place, competitive disadvantage spreads like the plague so that below-average performers are eliminated from competitive markets. One organization can have a portfolio of successful swings; another a bleak playground of empty roundabouts.

More emphasis is being placed upon focus and synergy. Even South Korea's trading conglomerates are having to be selective and identify their core strengths. Achieving a greater capacity to learn and adapt or a swifter response to individual needs can benefit all sectors. Focus, prioritization and segmentation can improve performance in all markets.

ICI has recognized the need to focus on those sectors in which it has the most potential to be a global player. Some businesses have been disposed of and the company is actively seeking to tap relevant ideas and expertise on a global basis. A technical centre has been established in Japan in order to bring research activity closer to Japanese customers. ICI entered the 1990s indicating its willingness to enter into strategic alliances with Japanese companies.

Static, hierarchical, vertical structures and organization charts are being replaced by dynamic flows and processes.[6] Horizontal linkages and cross-unit actions are sought. Understanding is not a stock to be taken out of store and dusted off when needed; it grows out of interactions and relationships. The procedures manual is giving way to participative processes. Movement is international and it is of people, ideas, information, know-how and money.

Whether or not an individual organization opts to go international or not, it may face competitive forces that emanate from many points on the globe. To be in this world is, for many companies, to be a player in an international market-place. Few major organizations, whatever their size, can afford to ignore the international dimension. BMW has largely concentrated its car production in Germany, but Japanese entry into its traditional home market in Europe has forced it to develop more of a global perspective on both production and marketing.

1.7 Implications of the changed market environment

A new market environment (see page 2) has emerged that is very different from that in which many senior managers acquired their early business experience.[2] There are, as we have already seen, a number of changing factors to take into account. The key issues for one multinational company are:

- *easier and more open access:* in spite of the GATT deadlock, international markets are becoming more open as deregulation and privatization establish themselves as key objectives of governments around the globe
- *demanding customers:* more intense competition is strengthening the bargaining position of consumers *vis-à-vis* suppliers and putting pressure upon prices and margins
- *continuing improvements in performance:* in many sectors a steady decline in real cost has been matched by growth in performance and quality
- *rising expectations:* overall, a fundamental shift of attitudes and values is occurring with consumers now expecting reliability and quality
- *the commodity products trap:* to avoid becoming low-margin suppliers of commodity products, companies are having to search for new forms of differentiation
- *a requirement for rapid and flexible response:* these market conditions give an advantage to those companies that can act quickly and operate with slim overheads; size, of itself, and past achievements do not guarantee future success
- *technological innovation and rapid replication continues:* companies are having to work hard to maintain a lead and as they become more conscious of the cost of developing the next generation of technology and related products, so they are becoming more selective and focused
- *the growing importance of relationship management:* customers are increasingly demanding tailored solutions so R&D and other responsibilities are moving closer to, and more products being developed with, the customer
- *a tolerance for diversity:* companies are required to be more aware and tolerant of differences of culture, values, attitudes and expectations; managers need to be sensitive and to empathize
- *it is becoming more difficult to go it alone:* in order to cope with a range of challenges, companies are entering into a range of strategic alliances with even R&D-led companies recognizing the need to buy in ideas and new processes.

1.8 The consequences for people

Individuals are having to cope with a greater variety of requirements and situations and more heterogeneity among those with whom they work:

old	new
– getting ahead	– achieving balance
– the self	– the environment
– individuals	– groups and teams
– personal space and status	– interpersonal relationships
– unsupported	– facilitating and supporting technology
– single discipline	– multidisciplinary
– expertise and knowledge	– personal qualities and competence:
– facts	– values
– security	– challenge
– position	– contribution
– dependent	– inner direction and motivation
– initial qualifications	– continual updating
– lifetime commitment	– mobile careers

Groups and teams are also becoming more diverse. The conscious introduction of complementary skills and the management of diversity can be the key to their creativity and productivity.

Traditionally, many experts have worked as individuals rather than in groups. In the case of professionals, monitoring the quality of practice has sometimes been shared with external professional organizations. As individuals are increasingly required to work together in teams and these teams come to be composed of people from different countries, it becomes more apparent how widely professionals can vary in their experience, competence, attitudes and beliefs.[7] National professional institutions also vary greatly in the extent to which they monitor the activities of their members.

Managerial life is becoming more demanding. Managers are now expected to understand the external business environment.[8] Empathy with values and feelings is also becoming more important as the simple drive for quantity is no longer enough in the world of quality and sensitivity to environmental issues.

Optimal outcomes and solutions that last are becoming more difficult to achieve, success when it occurs is transient and competitive advantage can be fleeting. There are fewer absolutes. Indeed, the right course of action may vary according to time and context.

Trade-offs are often difficult to achieve so that instead of either/or, it may be necessary to do both; give customers some optional features to choose between and they will want them all. An innovation today is commonplace tomorrow.

Differences are sometimes more apparent in an international context.

They can persist and their causes and consequences can be deep-rooted. Achieving a balance between contending forces and influences can require the patience, sensitivity and skills of the diplomat, rather than the activity and drive of the traditional manager.

1.9 Harnessing human potential

The human resource is emerging as a, and in many cases *the*, critical success factor.[6] Goods and services, even a company's underlying technology, can be copied by competitors, windows of opportunity that are the result of innovation quickly open and close and new products are quickly taken apart by competitors and rapidly improved upon, 50 companies are now competing on management processes. It is their flexibility and speed in accessing and utilizing the skills of their people in order to respond speedily to evolving customer requirements that makes the vital difference.

Harnessing human potential has become a critical challenge. For many CEOs interviewed in the surveys undertaken by Adaptation, upon which much of this book is based, it is *the* management challenge.[8] The essence of successful internationalization is being able to secure access to the most relevant skills, irrespective of location and nationality. To do this the twin barriers of distance and culture must be overcome.

In ar era of standard products and substantial barriers to entry, it was possible for a high proportion of significant decisions to be taken by directors and senior managers. These would then be implemented by others. Power was concentrated. Communication, orders and directives, flowed down the bureaucratic hierarchy. Most people did what they were told and, when in doubt, consulted the appropriate page in the operating manual. In many cases individual initiative was actively discouraged.

In today's market conditions there are fewer barriers to competition. With total quality now being a necessary requirement and customers demanding more tailored products and services, there is greater delegation. Communication is two way so the authority to respond is devolved, diffused within networks. All staff in many enterprises are required to assume greater responsibility for their work, to question and to add value.

Development programmes can no longer be concerned largely with high-flyers. A greater contribution needs to be obtained from average or, in many cases, below-average performers. This has to be achieved against the background of more limited numbers of young people in many parts of the developed world so that new sources of skills need to be tapped.

Expectations of employees as well as customers are changing. Where individuals have a choice, either as employees or consumers, organizations must be more responsive to their distinct needs. Companies that do not respond will lose both staff and customers to those organizations that are more flexible. Matching corporate and individual needs is becoming a pre-condition for effective relationships.

1.10 The need for fundamental review

Change in the environment within which business occurs is not a new phenomenon. Throughout history there have been changes, many of which have been sudden and traumatic, such as war, revolution, pestilence and religious crusades. Sequential changes can be coped with one at a time, but when a number of significant changes occur simultaneously and an organization has competitors, the management challenge is of a greater magnitude and the penalties for a slow or inadequate response can be severe.

What is significant is that the findings of a number of the studies upon which this book draws (see Appendix I) suggests that a growing proportion of those responsible for the management of large organizations believe that incremental adjustment to change is no longer enough. The time has come for a fundamental reassessment of the nature of the business organization and, particularly, how it is structured and how it should operate.

The review process

The review that is required is a holistic one (see Figure 1.1). It involves:

- determining a customer-focused vision, mission and strategy in the context of the opportunities and challenges in the external business environment
- securing and developing appropriate people, a flexible and responsive organization and supporting and facilitating technology
- applying management processes that allow these resources to work effectively together and, with the resources of other organizations, in the profitable generation of value for customers.

Importantly, people, organization and technology are interrelated (see Figure 1.1). Not only must the individual elements be right, but their *combination* must be harmonious and productive.

For most companies a fundamental review will involve the international dimension. A reassessment should cover each of the areas that have been identified in Figure 1.1. Challenges, opportunities and resources can all be international. A small selection of possible questions that could be asked is given below.

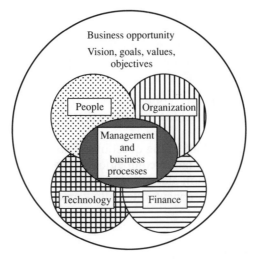

Figure 1.1 Reviewing business structure and operation

- *The business environment:*
  - Are national barriers to international operation being reduced?
  - Are customers demanding an international or a regional service?
  - Who are the key international competitors and what are their competitive strengths?
  - Should we move closer to the international customer?
- *People:*
  - Should the search for relevant skills be extended abroad?
  - Where internationally are the main sources of expertise and experience?
  - Are we too much of a national company in our recruitment and promotion decisions?
- *Organization:*
  - How open and flexible is the use of resources across national borders?
  - Is organization too constrained by geography?
  - Does organization reflect the changing requirements of customers?
- *Technology:*
  - How effectively does information flow across international borders?
  - Can we link up electronically with foreign customers and suppliers?
  - Can our technology support multilocation and multinational team-working?
  - Does systems integration extend across national borders?
- *Management processes:*
  - To what extent are our management processes internationally mobile?

- Can our management processes accommodate significant differences of national culture?
- Do we have the capacity to learn from international experience?
- Are our business functions sufficiently integrated to promote international speed of action?

Rather than mechanically apply a standard check-list, however, each company should pose probing questions that are appropriate to its own situation.

To help formulate challenging questions, teams of managers could be asked to play the roles of major competitors. They could be encouraged to develop and present action plans they would use to wipe out the company in its key markets (such reviews often allow areas of significant vulnerability to be identified).

Review in perspective

Calls for the posing of fundamental questions have long been made by management thinkers, gurus and commentators and, in a typical year, a number of books suggesting a new reality of business will be published. What is of greater significance is that similar sentiments are now being expressed by practising and hard-nosed managers, faced daily in the market-place with the requirements for survival. Fundamental reviews, roles and responsibility exercises, 'capacity to act' taskforces and a host of similar corporate reviews are now occurring as a matter of necessity.

For many organizations there is no comfortable alternative. Those companies that do *not* break out of the endless cycle of headcount reduction programmes, cutting the cost base exercises, squeezed margins and pressures on prices are likely to go under. There is no divine right of existence for the commercial organization; its life has to be continually renewed. The search is on for new games in which it is still possible to be a winner.

Global changes are frequently endemic and the need for change is likely always to be with us. Fundamental changes can take a long time to achieve and so what needs to be done may itself be modified and refined many times during the endless pursuit of the rainbow of its achievement.

Check-list

- Have you prioritized the main challenges and opportunities facing your company?
- Which of the external demands and pressures confronting your company are international?

- How important is internationalization in the context of the various challenges and opportunities, particularly those concerning customers?
- What are the main spurs to internationalization in your company's market-place and how are competitors responding?
- In particular, is your company fully aware of both the direct and indirect impact of the emergence of a single European market upon its business?
- Do your company's board and its management team understand that internationalization is an ongoing process?
- Is your company fully aware of, and does it monitor, the threats and opportunities in the external business environment?
- In the light of the external challenges and opportunities it faces, does your company need to undertake a fundamental review of its people, organization, technology and management processes?

References

1. Coulson-Thomas, Colin J, *Human Resource Development for International Operation*, a survey sponsored by Surrey European Management School, Adaptation, 1990.
2. Coulson-Thomas, Colin, and Richard Brown, *Beyond Quality: Managing the relationship with the customer*, British Institute of Management, 1990.
3. Ohmae, Kenichi, *The Borderless World: Power and Strategy in the Interlinked Economy*, Collins, 1990.
4. Henley Centre and Research International, *Frontiers: Planning for consumer change in Europe*, Henley Centre and Research International, 1991.
5. Redwood, John, speech to 16th Annual Conference of the International Organization of Securities Commissions (IOSCO), 25 September 1991.
6. Coulson-Thomas, Colin, and Richard Brown, *The Responsive Organisation: People Management – the Challenge of the 1990s*, British Institute of Management, 1989.
7. Coulson-Thomas, Colin, *The New Professionals*, British Institute of Management, 1988.
8. Coulson-Thomas, Colin, and Trudy Coe, *The Flat Organisation: Philosophy and Practice*, British Institute of Management, 1991.

Further reading

Bull, H, and A Watson, *The Expansion of International Society*, Oxford University Press, 1984.
Burgenmeier, B, and Jean-Louis Mucchielli, *Multinationals and Europe 1992*, Routledge, 1991.
Burton, John W, *World Society*, Cambridge University Press, 1972.
Casson, Mark (Editor), *Multinational Corporations*, Edward Elgar, 1990.
Dicken, P, *Global Shift*, Harper & Row, 1986.
Eli, Max, *Japan Inc.: Global Strategies of Japanese Trading Companies*, McGraw-Hill, 1990.
Gilpin, Robert, *US Power and the Multinational Corporation*, Macmillan, 1976.

Jacobson, H. K, *Networks of Interdependence* (Second Edition), Knopf, 1984.
Lindblom, Charles E, *Politics and Markets: The World's Political–Economic Systems*, Basic Books, 1977.
Ohmae, Kenichi, *Triad Power*, The Free Press/Collier Macmillan, 1985.
Tuller, Lawrence W, *Going Global – New Opportunities for Growing Companies to Compete in World Markets*, Business One Irwin, 1991.

2
The global business environment

Perspectives

Our assets could not be more localized – they are focused on a hole in the ground. But our perspective is global, as developments all over the world can affect the price of our product. Our profitability is inextricably linked to the health of the global economy.

Deputy Chairman, South African mining company

For us market differences are regional rather than national. In southern Europe the market for diapers has grown more rapidly than that in northern Europe.

Director, Scandinavian hygiene company

In any major city in the world young people know our products. They are symbols of a way of life seen in films and on the televisions. They are cultural icons. Often their allure is more compelling where their world is remote from local experience.

Producer, international record label

Your world is probably different to mine. My globe is covered with lines and dots – a bit like air routes and airports, but they are undersea cables and earth stations. Airlines are concerned with people flows, we concentrate on information flows.

General Manager, international telecoms supplier

Our products sell all over the world, but we try to make everything as Italian as possible. We use Italian names and Italian associations – but the associations likely to be shared by a social group that is very much the same in most continents. These people want to be different from those around them.

Marketing Director, Italian fashion supplier

We have standardized on a common set of tools and techniques. These are used by our consultants worldwide. As a result we offer a consistent and global service.

Partner, international accounting firm

The vehicle or technology of communication is global, but the content has to reflect the local culture. There are also local legal restrictions that vary from country to country.

Director, French media company

2.1 Introduction

What is so special about the international dimension? In Chapter 1 we looked briefly at a range of challenges and opportunities in the external business environment. In this chapter we focus upon the global business environment, examining both internationalization and regionalization.

To encourage an international perspective, a brief overview of international relations and the major actors in international society is also presented. The emphasis is upon certain factors that may not need to be considered in a particular national market, but which can form an important element of the global context within which corporate responses have to be determined.

2.2 Internationalization

Internationalization is a term that is exciting for some and intimidating for others. It can conjure up images of the jet-setting business person, able to slip effortlessly from one language to another at smart receptions, but also those of time away from home and family and lonely stopovers in airport lounges, indistinguishable from each other. In reality, in those organizations in which effective internationalization occurs, it raises neither false expectations nor unreasonable fears. It tends to be regarded as a natural element of a normal job.

Internationalization is more than just a question of learning one or more foreign languages and spending time travelling abroad. In essence it is a frame of mind, an attitude and a perspective. It is a view of the business environment in a company with a vision and mission that extends beyond the territory of a single nation state. It is an approach that recognizes the global nature of business challenges and opportunities.

Without an international perspective, vision and mission, many of the qualities often associated with the international manager are mere trappings. Some business leaders with an international perspective and vision have successfully built global businesses while lacking such personal attributes of internationalization as linguistic skills.

Global ambition or vision can take some time to become a reality. The foundations for the global expansion of the French healthcare company Sanofi were laid in the period 1978–85, particularly with the acquisition of the French pharmaceutical company Clin-Midy in 1980. After a decade of further acquisitions in its chosen business sectors, Sanofi entered the 1990s with a market presence in over 100 countries and considered itself 'a truly international company'. Jean-Francois Dehecq, the Chairman of Sanofi, believes a 'strong presence in all major international markets is required to quickly optimize the results of R&D endeavours under the best possible conditions'.

The customer comes first

An international vision should be firmly rooted in the realistic prospect of being able to understand and respond effectively to customer require-ments. The international market-place can be hard and unforgiving so an understanding of the local culture and an ability to converse in the lan-guage of the customer may do little more than add lines to an overseas expense account if a product does not actually meet the customer's requirements.

A good rule of thumb is to be led by whatever is necessary to add value for customers, and build long-term relationships with them. The product may be good, worthwhile and fun, but what does it do for the customer? The purpose of, and drive for, internationalization must be to benefit the *customer.* This should never be forgotten and is worth repeating when internationalization as an objective develops a life of its own.

In the 1980s, advertising agencies, and public relations and design consultancies engaged in a competitive race to internationalize. The industry took the view that to properly serve multinational corporation clients it was necessary to establish local offices in each of the countries in which they operated. Companies were floated and a spate of acquisitions occurred. Senior partners and directors ceased to work on client accounts in order to supervise the construction and management of global net-works of relationships.

The international agencies that were established proved difficult to staff. Travel and new offices put up both operating and overhead costs and when an economic slowdown occurred in major markets at the end of the decade, some firms realized that they had overextended them-selves as a result of their global ambitions.

In many other companies, internationalization is perceived as a means to an end, defined in terms of customer satisfaction, rather than as an objective in its own right. Hence issues such as customer satisfaction, quality and identifying what constitutes value to the customer emerged in the British Institute of Management (BIM)[1] *Beyond Quality* survey ahead of serving the international customer. The customer issues, ranked in order of 'very important' responses, in the survey were:

- customer satisfaction
- quality
- identifying what constitutes value to the customer
- service and after-sales support
- availability/delivery
- technological change
- serving the international customer
- providing tailored products and services
- corporate image
- global competition
- channels of distribution
- 1992 and the single market
- promotion
- price
- global v local market
- packaging

One must first determine the requirements of customers before considering how best to serve them.

2.3 How much internationalization do we need?

Internationalization costs money. It is also demanding of management time and should not be sought for its own sake. Do we all need to be citizens of the world? It is possible to become carried away with the notion of a global family of managers, all of whom can communicate with each other, allowing human resources to be accessed upon an international basis in order to meet the needs of particular customers.

In reality some quite large organizations operate effectively and profitably with relatively small numbers of international managers. This is particularly true, for example, where standard products are delivered to mass consumer markets. Where these are served by a national operating unit, the linguistic skills of almost all employees need not extend beyond the local language of customers. Only a handful of employees may require a selective knowledge of an international language of business or that of a holding company in order to fulfil a corporate monitoring and reporting requirement.

Internationalization is not easy. It can be a challenge for both large and small companies – while the small company may be lacking in resources, the larger company may find it difficult to change direction.

Honda went through a period of rapid international expansion and, during the 1980s, set up a number of manufacturing units overseas. The pace of expansion put a strain upon management systems and processes that had been designed for home country operations. Managing international operations distracted executives from their focus upon the customer and the added complexity slowed decision making. Honda found it difficult to meet different market requirements with a 'global car'. In response, the company has devolved responsibilities to semi-independent business units and is putting more effort into cultivating its Japanese home market.

Because a company is big does not mean it is automatically international. It is possible to find large national champion companies whose operations are largely concentrated in the home country:

- Siemens employs 350 000 people, almost half of its turnover is accounted for by Germany, its domestic market, and three quarters of its sales are in Western Europe, with only 10 per cent in the US
- BASF considers itself to be an 'international chemical company' that 'contributes to the progress of national economies', but, while it operates in more than 160 countries and has production plants in 35 countries, over two thirds of the company's output still originates in Germany, even though Europe accounts for over two thirds of its sales
- over 50 per cent of the sales of the Italian national champion Fiat occur in its home or domestic market and all its car production plants are in Italy.

The extent to which a national champion company can remain secure in its home base depends both upon the domestic market and the business sector it is in:

- the largest business book publisher in the world is Marosan, its Japanese home market accounts for 90 per cent of its turnover and it is relatively resistant to foreign competition
- Peugeot is the largest private industrial group in France and the leading car manufacturer in France with a 33.1 per cent market share in 1990. But, at the regional level, although it is the third largest European car manufacturer, it had just a 12.9 per cent share of the European market and was cutting costs in the face of weak demand and intense Japanese competition.

In many countries there are still nationalized industries. The newly, or recently, privatized company may find that, while it has the core technology to be a world player, its turnover is almost exclusively accounted for by its home market. The necessity for internationalization can be unrelated to size.

2.4 Local, regional or international?

A relatively limited home market can be a spur to international expansion. Within five years, from 1985–90, Nobel Industries has evolved – according to its President and Chief Executive Officer Anders Carlberg – from being 'largely an ordnance company with its operations concentrated on Sweden' to an international chemicals and electronics company. At the end of its diversification programme, most of its 25 000 employees were based, and some 70 per cent of its turnover arose, outside of Sweden.

Among other Swedish companies:

- SCA, Europe's second largest forest industry company, derives 80 per cent of its sales outside its country of origin, employs some 30 000 people in around 20 countries and the company is listed on stock exchanges in Stockholm, London and Oslo
- the chemical company Perstorp also derives some 80 per cent of its sales from abroad and has manufacturing units in 14 countries in Europe, North and South America and Asia
- Electrolux acquired over 200 companies during the 1980s and, at the end of the decade, some 85 per cent of its sales occurred outside Sweden (according to Anders Scharp, President and CEO, 'without these acquisitions Electrolux would have been a niche-oriented company focused on the Nordic area and would not have been able to compete in an increasingly more global market')
- Esab is the largest welding company in the world and in 1990 95 per cent of its turnover was accounted for by sales outside Sweden and 77 per cent of its staff were employed outside Sweden.

In sectors such as information technology, motor cars and aerospace, the cost of developing new generations of technology exceeds the funding base of single states and Israel, Japan and Sweden have all experienced the pain of trying to go it alone within the aerospace sector. Even with the support of a strong domestic 'buy French' tradition, Snecma is developing future aircraft engines in partnership with General Electric of the US.

An internationalization strategy can be regional rather than global:

- Chairman Pierre Dauzier considers the building of 'a broader international base' to be a prime objective of the French Groupe Havas, but the main focus of expansion in the areas of media, advertising, tourism and publicity has been in Europe: 'An international strategy centred on Europe' is one of the 'five principles' upon which the company's business strategy is based
- the emergence of the single market has had a significant impact on

Scandanavian companies and Swedish packaging and can company PLM AB aims to be a European company – indeed, by 1991, three-quarters of sales were outside Sweden, 60 per cent outside Scandinavia. Food and drink companies were planning to manufacture and market on a pan-European scale so a wave of mergers and acquisitions swept the can and packaging industry as pan-European suppliers of standard packages were sought and, because of the relatively high cost of transporting empty cans and packages, their manufacture is being located closer to the production plants of major customers
– the Swedish company Euroc has progressively specialized in mineral-based building materials, increasing the proportion of its sales in this area from about a half to approaching 100 per cent over a 5-year period, and its dominant market position in the Nordic region has forced it to seek international opportunities elsewhere in Europe in order to expand its business – the European ambitions of the company are explicit in its name.

International rather than regional expansion may be needed to spread some risks. For example, winter storms across Western Europe made 1990 a bad year for many insurance companies.

2.5 Approaches to internationalization

Companies vary in the extent to which they need to be international. They also exhibit a variety of attitudes towards, and approaches to, internationalization:

– dabbler
– wader
– diver
– flocker
– cuckoo.

DABBLERS

A domestic company whose plant and employees are located in a single country might still benefit from a degree of international awareness. For example, the company that is prepared to spend the time building a longer term relationship might become a local supplier of components to an inward investing Japanese company. A local component supplier needs to be technically competent, but it may not become concerned with such questions as international mobility.

Companies that are dabblers dip into markets as opportunities arise.

They are here today and gone tomorrow. They take part in international activities according to circumstances, such as occasional orders from abroad. Dabblers are sometimes not good at providing after-sales service. They travel light, but find it difficult to build longer term relationships with foreign customers and suppliers.

The dabbler needs to be internationally aware and sensitive in order to identify opportunities to dabble. Many dabblers are specialist firms with relatively few competitors and so they can be selective in terms of where they dabble. However, a degree of adaptability may be required as opportunities may differ and the dabbler needs to be mobile in order to move between them.

WADERS

Waders are more involved than dabblers but not too deeply. They spend more time abroad, but operate around the fringes of international operations – perhaps picking up opportunities as a result of the initiatives of others. Waders have a policy of going so far but no further.

Some waders may spend enough time at certain locations to acquire a degree of local knowledge. Movement may then become less frequent and between fewer locations. International understanding, particularly of the whereabouts of the best locations, can be quite important.

DIVERS

In comparison, the diver is prepared to become totally immersed. Such a commitment is selective. The diver is patient. When the right opportunity comes along – one that satisfies its criteria for action – the diver goes straight for it, acting directly and with speed.

The diver needs to be able to draw upon all available resources in order to confront individual opportunities. Over time the diver may put down roots at certain locations and criteria may be established to enable a systematic assessment to be made of whether or not such a commitment is justified.

TNT has sustained an international vision and, at the same time, remained alert to opportunities that are consistent with this vision. Realizing that a number of national post offices had ambitions to enter the competitive express services market, the company moved quickly. In 1991, and in cooperation with the post offices of Canada, France, Germany, the Netherlands and Sweden, TNT set up a new services consortium in which it had a 50 per cent stake. Other post offices were invited to join the new arrangement.

FLOCKERS

The flocker is not as bold or independent as the diver. It avoids risks and operates within a network of supply chain relationships. The flocker internationalizes in cooperation with others, either as a leader or follower. Many professional firms internationalize as a result of working relationships with a portfolio of clients and their advisers.

The flocker needs to be flexible and prepared to be mobile. Flockers have to fit in to a variety of situations and circumstances and so require awareness, empathy and sensitivity. Flockers have to prove their worth and be trusted to remain longer term members of a flock.

Small as well as large companies can enter into cooperative arrangements. The UK company Biotech has linked up with other biotechnology companies in France, Germany and the Netherlands to establish the Combio Group, a European marketing network. There is little that is considered in this book that could not be achieved by a small company that works with compatible and complementary partners.

The capability and security of individual companies can be significantly enhanced through membership of a flock:

- the European Commission actively encourages Community companies to flock together and operates a range of collaborative programmes – the EUREKA programme, for example, has brought together groups of collaborating companies in such fields as high definition television, electronics and traffic control systems
- in the US, local companies responded to the global challenge from Japanese 'chip' producers by forming the US semiconductor consortium, which has had US government support.

CUCKOOS

The strategy of the cuckoo is to internationalize by getting close to and riding on the back of a major international customer or business partner. This can lead to an arrangement to meet a global requirement of a company that already operates internationally. Telecom's suppliers around the world are internationalizing by setting up global networks for multinational corporations and transnational companies.

The point of departure

An approach to internationalization can be constrained by an existing structure and few companies begin with a clean slate:

- a company may feel that it is too small to cope with an international market-place and, indeed, the desire to build a stronger base was a factor behind the takeover of Tootal by Coats Viyella
- the location of responsibilities may encourage introversion – Northern Telecom, for example, has clustered research, engineering and manufacturing in global product groups in order to encourage global thinking
- the existence of a matrix form of organization and dual reporting links may increase the number of managers requiring knowledge of a second language
- the introduction of teamworking, particularly taskforces and project groups drawn from different functions and locations, can increase the need for international managers who can work effectively with those of other nationalities
- the more complex and more tailored a company's products, the more likely it is that a group of people will be involved in a range of marketing, sales, support and service activities, 80 specialist inputs may need to be sought from central units
- many existing employees may be parochial in their outlook, but, as an example of what can be done, although the Rank Xerox service force in Europe was largely composed of mature and settled people with local roots, the company has grasped the nettle and organized service activities on a pan-European basis in order to better meet the needs of its customers.

A company's approach to internationalization will also reflect its business development strategy. When customers seek regional or international solutions to their problems, supplying organizations may need to respond with regional or international account teams. The internationalization of production and distribution can also increase the requirement for international managers, as can arrangements and joint ventures with business partners incorporated in more than one country.

The entry of Japanese companies into the European market-place has been perceived in some countries as a foreign threat. Hence, while internationalizing, Japanese suppliers have bent over backwards to stress their local commitment and credentials:

- Toshiba has emphasized the modest nature of its European sales in relation to total market size and its desire not to create a situation of overcapacity; the company also stresses the strengths it is sharing with local suppliers, its commitment to European R&D through its Cambridge research facility and the efforts it is making to recruit and develop local managers
- Brother puts the emphasis upon good citizenship and its contribution

to training and to local communities: Chairman Akio Morita claims that developments are planned to 'harmonize with the economic and social policies of the host country . . . so that such investments . . . may be integrated with the local society'.

Major US companies have also felt it necessary to become good Euro-citizens and to stress their commitment to Europe:

- Du Pont announced in 1991 that its global agricultural products division was to be headquartered in Geneva, Switzerland and that the company is seeking to increase its R&D commitment to Europe
- in the same year, Rank Xerox announced its intention to significantly increase its R&D commitment to Europe and, at the same time, the company planned to raise the European content of its document management products and announced that it was seeking European partnership arrangements.

The commitment to internationalization will depend upon the significance and likely term of an overseas investment, arrangement or joint venture. The importance of the venture in question will be a determinant of the level of management that may need to be internationalized. The parties to some ventures opt to select a particular language in which they will conduct negotiations and/or operations.

In many cases, full participation in an arrangement or joint venture will require more than internationalization. Indeed, operating within a joint ownership framework can require distinct skills. On occasion ventures that are strong in commercial logic have not progressed because, within the parties involved, it has not been possible to identify managers with experience of running joint ventures.

Within the same business sector firms can adopt differing paths to internationalization. For example, among law firms with international ambitions, Freshfields has adopted a self-development or go-it-alone strategy, opening offices abroad and recruiting local staff, while Allen and Overy have perferred to enter into a network of arrangements with local firms.

A company can pursue a dual-track policy of organic growth and acquisition:

- General Motors has introduced new designs and improved manufacturing in its European operations while also acquiring a 50 per cent stake and management control of Saab, but greater returns have been achieved from the company's own activities than from its investment in Saab so these have been largely the result of product quality rather than management reorganization

– Northern Telecom of Canada has set up operations in the US, established Pacific Rim factories, and in 1991 acquired the UK company STC and responded quickly to the demise of Communist regimes in Eastern Europe by establishing activities in Hungary and Poland.

2.6 The international dimension

Internationalization occurs in the context of an international society. In order to better understand current international issues, it is helpful to examine the major distinguishing features of international society.

International society, like an individual national society, has evolved.[2] Over the centuries there have been mini international systems or regional sub-systems as, for example, in India, and periods of city states – Machiavelli wrote of diplomatic relations between Italian city states all those centuries ago. There have been long periods of war and conquest as well as ages of relative unity and of separate development in the Christendom of the West and the China of the East.

In historical terms, the emergence of nationalism, the nation state and the notion of the balance of power between contending nation states are relatively recent phenomena. The last great age of imperial expansion occurred in the nineteenth century. The twentieth century has witnessed revolution and the challenge of Marxism, which sought, unsuccessfully, to replace the notion of the nation state with the concept of a classless society of equality. Only in the present century has functional integration across national borders and the interdependence of states reached the stage that one can talk of an emerging world society with some conviction. Within this world society there has been a globalization of issues, markets, communication and competition.

The nature of international society

International society is characterized by uncertainty and surprise. When changes occur, they are often dramatic and profound rather than incremental. Indeed, they can involve war and revolution.

The risk of crisis is ever present in international society. Change occurs, generally, by bargaining and negotiation. Revolutions can lead to inconclusive results and issues of recognition. The threatened use of intervention and war is a course of action that few states will rule out when vital national interests are at stake and a dissatisfied or aggrieved state may consider war a legitimate means of achieving change. A resort to military force can be an acceptable course of action in international law in cases of self-defence.

There are trends in international society that can be discerned and monitored. Around the globe national governments are exploring the potential for further liberalization and privatization. Communism appears to be in a phase of decline, the countries of Eastern Europe are seeking to join the world market economy and, elsewhere, regional groupings are becoming more significant as neighbouring states seek to dismantle trade barriers at national borders. International trade negotiations may increasingly involve such groupings rather than the individual member states that compose them.

These are the issues in international society that the company with an international perspective needs to consider. The outcome of an international trade negotiation may be the international equivalent of the results of a vote in the legislature of a nation state.

International agreements

At the level of international society, alliances and agreements between separate legal entities are the norm. There is much that multinational corporations seeking joint venture or arrangement links with other companies can learn from a study of those factors and conditions that lead to success when nation states conclude alliances.

Alliances and agreements between the actors in international society are concluded within an international legal framework.[3] A domestic company experienced at operating in a national framework of municipal law may encounter international law for the first time as a result of an internationalization programme. International law differs from municipal law in its sources, subjects and substances:

– *sources:*
- *international law:*
  international custom and practice; treaties; general principles of law/morality
- *municipal law:*
  custom and legislation; case law

– *subjects:*
- *international law: states*
  organizations endowed with international legal personality
- *municipal law:*
  individuals; corporations endowed with legal personality

– *substance:*
- *international law: agreement*
  between sovereign states.
- *municipal law:*
  sovereignty of state over its subjects.

Influencing the legal framework at the international level may involve representational activity directed at a number of sovereign states that are parties to a particular negotiation.

To have effect, some agreements at the international level may need to be incorporated into national law. This can occur in different forms and according to different timetables in different nation states and can greatly complicate the task of monitoring developments at the international level. An EC Directive with direct human resource consequences may be incorporated into national law in one member state but not in another. Even when incorporated, the extent to which a measure is enforced may vary between states.

2.7 The regional dimension

Within international society there may also be a regional dimension to take into account. A European-based company, for example, will need to distinguish, monitor and understand developments within the EC, in Europe as a whole, in other regions and in international society generally.

Regional groupings of states – such as the members of the EC – are transforming the nature of national borders. Regional cooperation is now a global phenomenon of some significance:

- in South America, where Brazil and Argentina have been working since 1985 to create a common market by January 1995, an economic region is emerging and Argentina, Brazil, Paraguay and Uruguay agreed in March 1991 to create a Southern Cone Common Market, to be known as Mercosul, by the end of 1994
- a North America Free Trade Area (NAFTA) involving the US and Canada is emerging and, at the start of the 1990s, extension of the area to embrace Mexico was under consideration
- in 1991 the Asian nations Brunei, Indonesia, Malaysia, the Philippines, Singapore and Thailand agreed to set up the Asian Free Trade Area (AFTA), the intention being to create a single Asian market within 15 years and, at the time of the agreement, the Asian countries had a combined population of 320 million
- if ratified by the Parliament of the EC and the parliament of each EC member state and each member of EFTA, a European Economic Area of 19 countries will come into existence in 1993.

Whether or not a particular country is included within a regional grouping can have significant consequences for particular industries. For example, in 1991 Meixco's relationship with NAFTA was of some concern to Puerto Rico's tuna industry as suppliers feared Mexican rivals would secure privileged access to the North American market.

A regional framework is likely to be dynamic. The EC in 1991 concluded its negotiations with the seven EFTA countries concerning the question of enlargement and the emergence of a European Economic Area incorporating some or all EFTA members. There were also bilateral negotiations in progress with the countries of Central and Eastern Europe. In some quarters whether the Treaty itself should be revised was a matter of debate.

Certain EFTA countries had already applied to join the EC, while some Eastern European countries had expressed a preference for membership over association. Concluding association agreements with countries such as Poland, Czechoslovakia and Hungary could lead to the emergence of a wider free trade area, followed at a future date by full membership within the community. Eventually at least ten, possibly more, new members could join the EC.

The reduction of internal trade barriers in a regional grouping of states such as the EC will not just benefit Community enterprises. Companies registered outside of the Community will also benefit from a reduction of internal barriers and restrictions when exporting to, and operating within, the Community. Already non-EC companies are responding to the opportunity. US investment in the EC grew by 50 per cent between 1985 and 1988, while the flow of direct investment from Japan increased by over four times during this same period (see Figure 2.1). Over 500 Japanese companies had set up in the Community by the end of 1989. Where external barriers around a common market continue to exist, the desire to take advantage of lower internal barriers is a stimulus to greater inward investment. This encourages internationalization through the establishment of operations and activities abroad. In the case of the EC, an international company operating within the Community should, under Community law, not be discriminated against but treated as a Community firm.

In many parts of the world, an increasing number of enterprises are participating in cross-border operations. Takeovers or mergers by the top 1000 EC companies more than doubled between 1985 and 1989 (see Figure 2.2) in 1989 alone there were 1300 cross-border acquisitions within the EC.

2.8 Fragmentation

Alongside a general trend towards the globalization of markets and the emergence of international and transnational network organizations, has been one towards business, economic, social and political decentralization, delegation, devolution and fragmentation. Regionalism has been

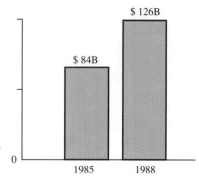

US investment in the EC grew by 50 per cent between 1985 and 1988

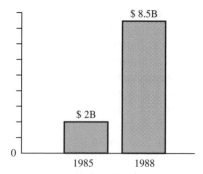

Flow of direct investment from Japan increased by over 4 times between 1985 and 1988

Figure 2.1 The single market and foreign investment
Source: European Commission

accompanied by a resurgence of nationalism as a result of the decline of Communism. New political entities are emerging.

Corporations are having to cope with greater variety in the market-place as well as in the general business environment. Customer segments (as we saw in Chapter 1) are becoming more specific, tastes and require-ments more diverse. Companies are devoting considerable effort to differentiation from competitors, and this activity has encouraged market fragmentation.

Fragmentation, actual or potential, in the international business environ-ment exists at a number of levels. Separatist tendencies exist in various countries around the world. At the European regional level there is likely to be a significant increase in the number of national units a corporation needs to contend with:

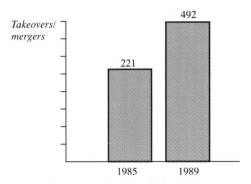

Takeovers/ mergers

492

221

1985   1989

Figure 2.2   The single market and cross-border operations

- within the EC there is a continuing risk of the emergence of a two-speed, or, two-tier membership as a core group of Schengen convention member states abolished border controls ahead of other EC members and the enlargement of the EC could lead to a challenge to the principle that new members should accept the whole of existing policy
- following the unsuccessful August 1991 coup in the Soviet Union, a succession of Soviet republics declared their independence and the three Baltic states of Estonia, Latvia and Lithuania quickly secured wide international recognition, including that of EC and US government, so subsequent negotiations could lead to the emergence of a further group of sovereign states
- within the Balkans, nationalist claims are putting pressure upon federal entities – a process started by the independence claims of Slovenia and Croatia within Yugoslavia (indeed, the crisis in Yugoslavia provided an early opportunity for the EC to play the role of mediator)
- even well-established unions can be put at risk by a change of political circumstances – within the UK, devolution of power to Wales and Scotland has been an issue that has divided the major political parties
- in certain countries, inconclusive elections, the formation of a coalition government or the adoption of a different electoral system (for example, proportional representation in the UK) could lead to political fragmentation.

Fragmentation can be a significant issue for international companies as it can be associated with disruption, turmoil, confusion, economic dislocation and civil unrest. A period of uncertainty and disruption frequently occurs when old political and economic systems break down and new ones take some time to establish themselves. In 1991, companies were faced with the challenge of determining the extent to which they should take a long-term view, and invest in the emerging market economies of Eastern Europe and the countries that made up the Soviet Union (now the 'CIS').

At local, regional and global levels, a company needs to be able to respond organizationally and managerially to both diversity *and* fragmentation. To take a flexible rather than a bureaucratic approach may require adopting a network form of organization that allows responsibilities and relationships to change in step with developments in the external business environment.

2.9 Balancing regional and international opportunities

World trade has been expanding more quickly than has the economic growth of many individual countries. Developments in new technologies – especially information and communications technologies – are increasing the capability of firms to operate internationally. The enterprise culture itself has spread, creating new expectations and a wider desire to participate in international trade. In some parts of the world, for example around the Pacific Rim, highly competitive economies have arisen and the companies there are increasingly active in international markets.

Some companies will need to be careful not to overlook international challenges and opportunities as a result of preoccupation with regional developments. In certain sectors, such as financial services, the trend towards global markets may be more significant than EC developments. Regional rules and regulations should be compatible with emerging world standards if global operation is to be facilitated.

The range of responses needed to cope simultaneously with both regional and international developments is illustrated by the example of Rank Xerox. A selection of the company's recent responses in Europe were:

- *to Global operation:*
  - international accounts have been established with global account managers, supported by an on-line worldwide database
  - global environmental, benchmarking, corporate capacity to act, employee satisfaction and quality programmes have been put in place
- *to strategic commitment to Europe:*
  - Rank Xerox's EuroPARC and Continental Europe research centres, plus European scientific and partnership programmes are evidence of such a commitment
  - there is a programme to increase value added in Europe through manufacturing plants at Coslada in Spain, Lille in France, Mitcheldean in the UK and Venray in the Netherlands

- Rank Xerox's European manufacturing operations source all materials within 24 hours of its plants
- *to managing and communicating across Europe:*
  - Rank Xerox's International Headquarters in Marlow is equipped with state-of-the-art communication networks to cope with both European and global operation
  - multifunction, multilocation and multinational taskforces, have been established
  - a European training network and European-wide concessionaires programme exist
  - a multinational board and senior management team is now in place
  - there is an international focus upon customer satisfaction and linking of remuneration to customer satisfaction
- *to servicing the customer across Europe:*
  - European account management for pan-European customers has been introduced
  - Rank Xerox's European Logistics Centre at Venray provides consolidation of logistic support at a single point to serve a European market
  - Rank Xerox's European Systems Centre has been established to provide products, services and business solutions to the European market
- *to European and international quality:*
  - Rank Xerox has won quality awards in the UK, the Netherlands and France
  - Xerox has also won premier quality awards in Australia, Brazil, Canada, Japan, Mexico and the US.

In deciding whether a responsibility is to be discharged at national, regional or international level, the principle of subsidiarity is increasingly applied. Responsibilities within the EC, for example, are allocated, if possible, at the levels that are most appropriate. The principle of subsidiarity is also relevant to the allocation of responsibilities within an international company. Philips, for example, has responded to the emergence of the EC single market with a consolidation and centralization of production and distribution. The process has continued as the company seeks to reduce its cost base – European strategy having to reflect the broader realities of corporate survival within an intensely competitive international market-place. The organizational approaches of other companies will be examined in Chapter 6.

2.10 Nation states as actors in international society

A company whose operations are limited to a national market will be familiar with individuals and corporate bodies as actors, or, parties to be contracted with. At the level of international society there are other legal entities to contend with. In 1989 there were 215 nation states and a range of international organizations that have been endowed with international legal personality.

Nation states vary enormously in size, population and resources. States are distinguished in varying degrees by:

- territory and borders, which may or may not be in dispute
- a people with a shared history and culture
- recognition by other states
- sovereignty and an ability to conclude binding agreements with other states
- independence from external control in respect of its internal affairs
- rights and obligations under international law.

States use diplomacy and other means to implement foreign policies to pursue their national interests. Pressures that can be applied to further state interests include the diplomatic, the economic, military threat and intervention. In exercising these pressures a state is subject to the constraints of international morality, law and public opinion, plus deterrence – the threat of retaliatory action by other states.

Many states also use their sovereign powers to favour their own domestic companies as much as their international treaty obligations allow. Commercial matters can feature significantly in the relationships between states. The US government has been involved in matters as varied as GATT trade negotiations, anti-dumping actions and specific investigations on behalf of US companies on such matters as whether Japanese suppliers have withheld certain products and technologies from American customers in order to put them at a disadvantage *vis-à-vis* their Japanese competitors.

The affairs of many smaller countries have been significantly influenced by the activities of major multinational corporations.[4] Internationalization and the growing importance of the international investments of multinational corporations and transnational companies pose a severe challenge to the governments of several countries. Interdependence has reached such a degree as to complicate the management of those economies that are open to world trade and reduce the scope for independent action. It is becoming more difficult to sustain national economic strategies that are out of step with those of partners in regional groupings, such as that of the EC.

2.11 International organizations

At the international level, a company with experience of dealing with state or national governmental organizations will encounter new families of organizations.[5] There are international:

- legal organizations, such as the European Court
- functional organizations, such as the World Health Organization
- economic organizations, such as certain institutions of the European Communities
- parliamentary organizations, such as the General Assembly of the UN
- military organizations, such as NATO
- historic organizations, such as the Commonwealth.

In each of these categories there are organizations that have been endowed with international legal personality. Commercial operations in certain areas may be subject to restrictions and conditions established by these international organizations (such as, IATA and air travel). The international, as opposed to a national, company may find it necessary to monitor the activities of these organizations, lobby them and negotiate with them.

International judicial institutions include The Permanent Court of Arbitration, The International Court of Justice, The Court of Justice of the EC and the European Court of Human Rights. International Parliamentary organizations include the Consultative Committee of the Council of Europe, The Nordic Council and the International Labour Organization (ILO).

Governmental organizations include the Security Council of the UN, the Ministerial Committee of the Council of Europe, European Free Trade Association (EFTA), Organization for Economic Cooperation and Development (OECD) and North Atlantic Treaty Organization (NATO). Examples of specialist organizations are United Nations Educational, Scientific and Cultural Organization (Unesco) and the International Red Cross. Some Organizations have a separate status as an administrative secretariat that is distinct from a related parliamentary or governmental organization, for example, the secretariat of the United Nations Organization.

Non-governmental international organizations

There are a range of other international organizations that may or may not be endowed with international legal personality.[5] Examples are major companies with a global reach, trade union organizations and bodies to represent international commercial interests. There is, for example, a European TUC and a European federation of employers' organizations, of which the UK CBI is a member. The Union of Industrial and Employers Confederations of Europe (UNICE) was founded in 1958. It incorporates the industrial and employers confederations of 22 countries, is recognized by the Commission of the European Communities and has links with the Council of Europe.

Churches are among the oldest and longest lived of international organizations. The Scout movement, too, is international. There are international organizations concerned with sports and the arts. Another category of transnational actor includes such non-profit organizations as the Ford, Calouste Gulbenkian, Nuffield, Volkswagen and Krupp Foundations.

There are also international learned, scientific and professional organizations. An example of an international scientific research network is the European Organization for Nuclear Research (CERN). A group such as the PLO can be recognized by some states as the legitimate representative of a people. The Marxists have largely failed to establish classes as actors in international society, although certain revolutionary and terrorist groups have claimed to be operating on behalf of class interests.

Involvement in, and negotiation with, these various actors in international society requires certain skills and attributes. The established multinational corporation will be experienced at monitoring the activities of governments and international organizations that affect their operations and dealing with them. For the growing company, encountering the need for such action for the first time, such expertise will need to be trained or recruited or access to it secured.

2.12 The company as an actor in international society

The major multinational corporation may have physical, human, financial and technological resources that are greater than all but a small minority of nation states. In certain respects it may be in a strong bargaining position *vis-à-vis* the national government. Historically, in certain parts of the world such as Africa and Central or South America, individual multinational corporations have actively involved themselves in the affairs of particular states in order to bring about outcomes favourable to their interests.[4]

Examples of such inward investments that have had a significant impact upon national development include the activities of oil companies in Iraq, of mining companies in Chile and the Belgian Congo, of fruit companies in Central America and of the tourist industry in several Carribean countries. This raises the question of whether, and to what extent, the international multinational corporation is an actor in international society.

An international company may find it a useful exercise to review its own standing as an actor in international society. For example, when in negotiation with an overseas government on a question of inward investment, what are its sources of power, its longer term corporate interests and the pressures and constraints to which it is subject? Under these headings it should ask itself the following:

- *sources of power:*
  - technology?
  - access to finance?
  - customer base?
  - image/reputation?
  - mobile investments?
  - job creation?
  - balance of payments?
- *interests:*
  - open trading system?
  - repatriation of funds?
  - stability of exchange rates?
  - security of investments?
  - access to skills?
- *pressures:*
  - withhold technology/investment?
  - withdrawal of investments/skills?
- *constraints*
  - inflexibility?
  - protectionism?
  - nationalization?

For the international corporation, like the nation state, there are sources of power such as its technology, access to finance, its customer base or its image and reputation. A company's technology may be new to a particular country. The setting up of a new production plant can result in job creation and, when a proportion of the output is exported, can have a favourable impact upon a balance of payments. For example, Japanese motor car plants in the UK are expected to make an increasingly beneficial contribution to the country's balance of trade.

A major corporation may find it easier than many a nation state to raise finance in international markets. Its market image may be more extensive and its customer base broader than that of competing state-run enterprises.

Flexibility, speed and responsiveness can be very important in turning *potential* power into *actual* power. As in the national context, one should not underestimate the importance of the human resource as a source of corporate power. Access to higher level skills is a critical constraint for many countries seeking to develop their economies. A company with such skills will be in a stronger bargaining position than one without them.

Many governments welcome opportunities to enter into various forms of relationship with internationally minded companies. They may be searching for a role in a more interdependent world. Conscious of the practical limitations upon their own freedom of action and short of skills and other resources, they may recognize that they could share common interests with certain companies.

Defining corporate interests

As an actor in international society, a major company should define its corporate interests, its equivalent to the national interests of the state. Defining interests is different from formulating a business strategy and should be undertaken in a distinct but related process. Interests will, of course, be influenced by business strategy. However, whereas business strategy largely concerns what the company itself intends to do, corporate interests will include those things held to be important in the context of international negotiations and the actions of others – states as well as competitors.

The interests of an international company might include the preservation of an open trading system and the ability to repatriate funds from those countries in which it operates. The instability of exchange rates also makes international operation less uncertain. To promote such interests a company may need to support those who stress the benefits in terms of wealth, jobs and lower barriers to trade.

In promoting its interests, a major company is not without pressures it can apply. For example, it could withhold the transfer of technology or incremental investment. Resources can be transferred from one country to another. These courses of action could involve incremental expenditure, the disruption of plans and could lead to a response from the country concerned. A company with significant investments in a country could harm its own local interests through such actions. This is an example of the interdependence that leads many states to exercise caution in their dealings with one another.

Nation states are also not without pressures that they can apply against companies. In some respects, companies, even major international companies, are very vulnerable. Local assets can be seized by nationalization, trade barriers can be erected as a result of a protectionist policy, licenses and various other forms of permission can be refused or legislation could be enacted to favour local enterprises. These are all threats that can damage the commercial interests of an international company, which should be ever-alert to their prospects.

Corporate and state power

The power politics approach to the classification of states[6] offers a framework that could be used to classify companies.

– *nation state*	– *company, particularly multinational corporation*
– *drives:* security/power	market share/profit/customer satisfaction
– *elements of power:* economic, natural resources, military, etc.	people, organization, technology, management processes
– *types of power:* superpowers/great powers medium powers small powers/micro-states land power or sea power, etc.	global companies multinationals domestic companies fast-moving consumer goods (FMCG) or high-tech, etc.
actual power and potential power	market player and potential market entrant
absolute power and relative power	corporate capability and competitive advantage
status quo powers and revisionist powers.	defensive/consolidation and expansion/growth strategies.

The drive of states for security and power could be likened to a corporate drive for market share. In the case of both states and companies there are several elements of power. States, like companies, vary in the extent to which they are able to use the resources at their disposal. One element of national power, say economic strength, may be of considerable weight in one situation, for example an international trade negotiation, while in another context military power might be the decisive factor. In 1990, for example, the oil resources of Kuwait did *not* deter an external invasion.

States can be categorized into superpowers, great powers, medium powers and smaller powers. The position of states in the ranking of power can alter over time as a result of absolute and relative changes. It may make sense to distinguish between land and sea power or between non-aligned states and those belonging to a treaty grouping, such as NATO.

Companies also vary in their capabilities, aspirations and global reach and a few are genuinely global players. Others concentrate on particular markets in which are found concentrations of their target customer segments. Then there are domestic companies that continue to limit their operations to local markets. Companies can also be categorized according to their customers (such as, industrial, consumer or public sector), their products (such as, FMCG or high-tech) or their strategies (for example, organic growth or acquisition).

The competitiveness and capability of companies can reflect similar qualities of their home base country. For example, the competitive conditions of the Japanese market-place provide a hard training ground for Japanese companies.[7] Many emerge as formidable global competitors – corporate power complementing that of the state.

The international manager should reflect upon the reality of corporate power and the relative value of different elements of coporate capability in one context compared with another. Like states, the major multinational corporation needs to be equipped and prepared to deal with a number of eventualities.

In the case of both states and companies there may be a gap between potential and action, between actual and potential power. The threat to enter a market can tie down the corporate resources of a competitor just as the prospect of intervention can force a state to adopt defensive measures. A clear distinction also needs to be drawn between absolute and relative capability. The winner in competitive markets, as in war or diplomatic negotiation, may be the party with the edge, a competitive advantage at the right moment and in the right place.

2.13 International relations: various approaches

The behaviour of, and interrelationships of, the actors in international society is the subject matter of international relations. There are many approaches to the analysis of international relations[8] including:

- the historical, concerned with international history
- the legal, with a focus upon the development of international law and legal disputes
- power politics, emphasizing the pursuit of power by nation states
- the decision making approach, which examines how foreign policy is formulated or conducted and how disputes are handled

- the national attributes approach, which aims to build distinct profiles of states based upon national qualities and characteristics that predispose them to act in certain ways
- strategic studies, with a focus upon the military dimension and such factors as arms and deterrence
- the systemic approach, which views international society as a system
- communications theory, which focuses upon the nature and processes of interstate communication
- integration theory, which focuses upon the extent of common interests and the degree of functional cooperation and integration
- peace and conflict studies, which examines the nature and dynamics of conflict and how conflicts might be settled or resolved
- the revolutionary or Marxist approach, which is concerned with overthrowing the system based upon the sovereign state as a basic entity.

In practice a company could employ any number of these approaches in order to better understand developments in the international system that impact upon its own activities. The same company could find one approach of value in one context and other approaches of more use in understanding a situation in another part of the globe.

Models of international society

Associated with the various approaches to international relations[8] are a number of models of international society (see Figure 2.3).

The billiard ball model considers states as entities with hard shells that collide or bounce off each other.

The cobweb model recognizes that states have interests in common apart from the matters that divide them, resulting in a degree of interdependence and a willingness to trade-off various objectives.

The systems model takes interdependence to such a degree as to stress the extent to which states modify each other's behaviour, the action of one state causing feedback from other states that results in change.

The integration model assumes that the extent of common interests and the positive-sum benefits of cooperation have reached such an extent as to result in an overlapping of interests.

The world society model is one in which the extent of common interests and the benefits of cooperation are such that steps are taken to reduce the impact of national borders as barriers.

Similar models could be used to understand the evolution of relationships between companies. The billiard ball model could be said to characterize the relationship between Coca Cola and Pepsi-Cola. The two

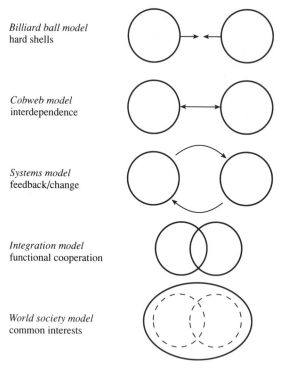

Billiard ball model
hard shells

Cobweb model
interdependence

Systems model
feedback/change

Integration model
functional cooperation

World society model
common interests

Figure 2.3 Models of international society

companies are locked in global combat with Coca Cola's traditional dominance in international markets being challenged by Pepsi-Cola in territories as scattered as South America, Eastern Europe and the Middle East. Only an expected expansion of *overall* consumption of soft drinks will avoid the zero-sum situation where the gain of one company is at the expense of the other.

Alliances between actors, both companies and states, can be informal or formal, short term or long lasting. A relationship could commence as one of competition, followed by some tenuous links and the development of arrangements or joint ventures. This process could lead to some form of strategic alliance or even a merger.

Models, like approaches, represent items in the tool kit, as it were, of the international manager, to be used as appropriate to help explain and understand developments in the international business environment. If their use enables developments to be anticipated or probabilities to be attached to outcomes, the risks of international operation may be significantly reduced.

Certain of the approaches to international relations are of value in understanding the struggle between major companies for market dominance in the international business environment. Many such struggles are similar to the zero-sum games of the power politics approach, as we saw with Coca Cola and Pepsi-Cola.

2.14 The strategies of international actors

There are a number of strategies a nation state can pursue. They range from non-alignment to active involvement. Some states seek isolation, but it is sometimes (as is the case with companies) not easy to be a non-player when other parties take action that threatens important interests. There are fewer protectionist barriers behind which companies can hide in today's more open trading environment.

States rank their interests and will make greater sacrifices to pursue some of them than others. National self-defence and the preservation of sovereignty are key or vital interests for most states. Some companies, similarly, distinguish between vital, important and other corporate interests.

To understand the behaviour of both states and companies, it is important to probe their intentions. There are satisfied, or, status quo states whose priority is the defence of a *current* position, just as there are companies with a policy of protecting or holding market share. At the same time, in the international system, just as in many markets, there will be restive, revisionist powers, eager to expand and grow in diplomatic or market significance. The general behaviour and individual moves of both states and companies can reflect such underlying differences in their strategic view of their own place on the stage on which they are a player.

States and companies can enter into alliances. The treaty commitments of states can be profound and long lasting, as is the case with the Treaty of Rome. Some states have changed alliances in order to preserve what they perceive to be a balance of power. In a system of collective security, states agree to take collective action against an aggressor who breaks certain rules of international conduct. An example of such a collective response is the series of UN resolutions directed at Iraq following its 1990 invasion of Kuwait.

Companies entering into such arrangements as the equivalent of disarmament and arms control negotiations could be accused under national and regional (such as, EC) laws of collusion in restraint of trade. Strategic alliances between companies occur, but they often have to satisfy certain conditions. Whereas many governments give a high priority to increasing collaboration and reducing competition between states, in the business environment the emphasis can shift to the preservation of effective competition.

2.15 International decision making

Economists and MBA students are familiar with rational approaches to decision making. Information is sought, options and outcomes examined and the best course of action adopted. In the subject area of international relations, though, the rational actor model is just one approach to decision making.[9] Other decision making approaches have relevance for understanding the actions of multinational corporations. An example is the bureaucratic model. This examines decisions in the context of processes within foreign policy making bureaucracies. Corporate decisions can, similarly, be strongly influenced by the nature of corporate bureaucracy.

Disjointed incrementalism sees decision outcomes in terms of incremental steps forward from an existing position. Such an approach may be effective when coping with small challenges, but may not facilitate an effective response to dramatic and traumatic change.

In instances where unexpected and major discontinuities occur, crisis decision making may need to be adopted out of necessity rather than choice. A crisis for a nation state, such as a trade embargo or the threat of war, may also put at risk the market revenues and assets of an international company. Such a company needs to understand the pitfalls of crisis decision making and establish contingencies to deal with significant threats to its interests.

Features of crisis decisions

In crisis decisions,[9] certain features are likely to be encountered:

- the span of attention can become more limited, developments occurring elsewhere may be overlooked
- fewer options may be considered because the selection process needs to rapidly assess the most viable options and it may be necessary to work hard to keep certain options open
- behaviour can become inflexible and an awareness that this is happening can help to counteract it
- associated with inflexibility, there may be resistance to new information, so a special effort may be necessary to ensure that key items of relevant information reach decision makers, while the volume of less critical information is reduced
- there may be increased reliance upon an in group as a crisis unfolds and bringing new parties up to date may be perceived as time-consuming and distracting

- longer term considerations may be driven out by an increased focus upon the short term
- within the relatively closed community of key decision makers, personality factors may play a role of greater importance than would normally be the case
- there may be risks of oversimplification and the stereotyping of people and issues.

Some of these features may be the inevitable result of steps that might need to be taken to short-circuit normal procedures in order to speed up the process of decision making. An awareness of what is *likely* to happen can result in the conscious adoption of built in reviews, checks and balances. For example, one or more non-in group members of sound judgement and off whom ideas can be bounced can be of considerable value.

Handling conflicts

The roots of crises generally lie in latent or actual conflict. Corporate monitoring needs to be alert to potential conflicts, as well as those whose symptoms are already apparent. Throughout history, governments have used external conflicts as a means of building national unity when faced with internal problems. On occasions such conflicts may be manufactured or perceived, based upon perceptions rather than fundamental differences of interests.

States and companies sometimes differ in how they handle major and dramatic conflicts. In crisis situations a traditional reaction of nation states has been to reduce interstate communication by cutting off diplomatic relations, but communication in commercial crises tends to be increased. Nations states also tend to resort to strategies of escalation of the stakes involved and the use of propaganda. In contrast, the commercial approach to crisis management tends to stress the need to reduce emotion and uncertainty through open and frank communication.

Effective conflict resolution can involve mediation and an increase in communication. Nation states sometimes exhibit a tendency to think in zero-sum terms in crisis situations, assuming the gain of one party is the loss of the other.

In situations of high tension, particularly when arms are involved, it may be that the efforts of states to achieve individual security will be self-defeating. Conflict resolution could require emphasizing the benefits of joint security, by encouraging the parties to seek positive-sum outcomes that offer benefits to all sides. This approach is frequently adopted by corporate negotiators who recognize the importance of solutions that are acceptable to all the parties involved.

Check-list

– Is your company's approach to internationalization that of the dabbler, wader, diver, flocker or cuckoo?
– Does the board and senior management team of your company understand the distinct features of the regional (for example, European) and international dimensions?
– In the case of your company, what is the relative importance of the regional and international dimensions (for example, the European compared with the global market)?
– Has the impact of the internationalization of business and related employment and population trends, upon your company been fully assessed?
– In particular, how will your company cope with the smaller number of young people coming onto the EC labour market over the next few years?
– Has your company identified the various organizations with which it may need to deal in the regional and international dimensions?
– Is your company prepared and equipped for crisis decision making?
– To what extent is your company an actor in international society?

References

1. Coulson-Thomas, Colin, and Richard Brown, *Beyond Quality: Managing the relationship with the customer*, British Institute of Management, 1990.
2. Bull, H, and A Watson, *The Expansion of International Society*, Oxford University Press, 1984; P Kennedy, *The Rise and Fall of the Great Powers*, Unwin Hyman, 1988; and M Olson, *The Rise and Decline of Nations*, Yale University Press, 1982.
3. Brierly, J L, *The Law of Nations*, (Sixth Edition), Clarendon, 1963; and Jean-Victor Louis, *The Community Legal Order*, (Second completely revised Edition), Commission of the European Communities, 1991.
4. Gilpin, Robert, *US Power and the Multinational Corporation*, Macmillan, 1976; and Robert O Keohane, and Joseph S Nye, *Transnational Relations and World Politics*, Harvard University Press, 1970.
5. Taylor, P, and A J R Groom (Eds), *International Institutions at Work*, Pinter, 1988; and D Mitrany, *The Functional Theory of Politics*, Martin Robertson, 1975.
6. Morgenthan, Hans J, *Politics Among Nations: The Struggle for Power and Peace*, Alfred A Knopt, 1978; John Vasquez, *The Power of Power Politics: A Critique*, Frances Pinter, 1983; and M Wight, *Power Politics*, Penguin, 1977.
7. International Institute for Management Development and World Economic Forum, *World Competitiveness Report 1991*, International Institute of Management Development and World Economic Forum, 1991; and CBI Manufactur-

ing Advisory Group, *Competing with the World's Best*, Confederation of British Industry, 1991.

8. Dougherty, James E, and Robert L Pfaltzgraff, *Contending Theories of International Relations*, Harper & Row, 1971; F Parkinson, *The Philosophy of International Relations: A Study in the History of Thought*, Sage Publications, 1977; and A J R Groom and C R Mitchell, *International Relations Theory: A bibliography*, Frances Pinter, 1978.

9. Allison, Graham T, *Essence of Decision: Explaining the Cuban Missile Crisis*, Little, Brown & Company, 1971; and Morton Halperin, *Bureaucratic Politics and Foreign Policy*, Brookings, 1974.

Further reading

Blau, P M, *Exchange and Power in Social Life*, Wiley, 1964.

Burton, John W, *World Society*, Cambridge University Press, 1972.

Burton, John, *Deviance, Terrorism and War: The Process of Solving Unsolved Social and Political Problems*, Martin Robertson, 1979.

Casson, Mark (Editor), *Multinational Corporations*, Edward Elgar, 1990.

Cox, R, *Production, Power and World Order: Social Forces in the Making of History*, Columbia University Press, 1987.

Deutsch, Karl W, *Analysis of International Relations*, (Second Edition), Prentice-Hall, 1978.

George, S, *Politics and Policy in the European Community*, Oxford, 1985.

Gilpin, Robert, *The Political Economy of International Relations*, Princeton, 1987.

Groom, A J R, and C R Mitchell, *International Relations Theory: A Bibliography*, Frances Pinter, 1978.

Hermann, C F, *International Crises: Insights from Behavioural Research*, New York, Free Press, 1972.

Holsti, K J, *The Dividing Discipline*, Allen & Unwin, 1985.

Krasner, *Structural Conflict*, Berkeley University of California Press, 1985.

Light, M, and A J R Groom (Eds), *International Relations: A Handbook of Current Theory*, Frances Pinter, 1985.

Sullivan, Michael P, *International Relations: Theories and Evidence*, Prentice-Hall, 1976.

Taylor, Trevor (Ed), *Approaches and Theory in International Relations*, Longman, 1978.

3
Operating in the global environment

Perspectives

Corporate nerves have to withstand political revolutions, massive changes in
energy prices, the collapse of currencies and of economies, who knows what is
around the corner. Internationalization is growing up – it's recognizing that
those things on the television screen affect you as well. Your realize how fragile
things are and you start to feel the shocks.

Chief Executive, UK multinational corporation

Globalization is a significant phenomenon for us, but so is political and market
fragmentation. The two trends are sometimes in conflict. We have been trying
to share and consolidate across Europe, but now we have the new Baltic states,
and fragmentation in the Balkans and what was the Soviet Union to contend
with.

Director, German engineering and manufacturing company

The weather doesn't seem to understand our international division of
responsibilities.

Director, UK insurance company

Relationships with government agencies are of crucial importance to us. If a
product does not secure government approval it cannot be sold. Our first contact is with the national regulatory authorities. In Japan the government
imposed price reductions on the whole industry. We operate in both a regulated and at times a very competitive marketplace.

Director, Swiss pharmaceutical company

We operate in shifts to catch markets on the other side of the world. You can
see who is waking up where from watching where the calls are coming from.

Currency trader, international bank

I now have governments to worry about. Nothing that has ever happened to
me in the company has prepared me for this. I discover there are all sorts of
incentives available depending upon where we put our investments. I'm hav-

ing to choose between people who want to give me money for something we
need to do in any case.
Managing Director, European operating company of international industrial group

National borders don't define market sectors. They represent sources of hassle
over standards.
European Managing Director, packaging equipment supplier

At the local level it's tactical pricing decisions and special offers. At the global
level it's war – they are out to kill us. Our local operations need to know to what
extent they are targetted and how much the opposition is likely to spend to buy
market share.
Vice-President, Corporate Strategy, US multinational corporation

3.1 Introduction

To operate effectively in the global business environment, a company
must have the capability to anticipate and cope with external change. To
be aware of longer term trends, likely developments and their consequences, an issue monitoring and management process may be required.
Its scale and complexity will depend upon the significance of a company's international operations. The major company or multinational
may go so far as to behave as an actor in international society, as we have
seen, and develop its own corporate foreign policy.

3.2 Managing external change

The truly international company accepts change in the international system,
including international crises and war, as a norm. It recognizes the need
to act swiftly and decisively in crisis situations. It is aware that even the
foreign office of a superpower, with all the resources and intelligence at
its disposal, can be taken by surprise as developments unfold in particular
parts of the world.[1] In such circumstances a capacity to act and to be flexible
and responsive, distinguishes the global player. Success is generally the
result of quality of advice, sensitivity and sureness of touch, rather than
the quality of information provided.

Sustained success is difficult to achieve. Scandinavian Airlines System
was yesterday's role model, SAS case studies being used on many management courses. Today the turnaround achievements of British Airways
are examined, while customers are deciding whose logo will appear on
tomorrow's discussion group flip charts. Companies with a clear vision
that is rooted in customer requirements and core strengths can find it

easier to maintain a consistent sense of direction in the face of multiple challenges:

- The Norwegian group Orkla Borregaard is focusing upon a limited number of business areas in which it can achieve global competitive advantage and its selective acquisition policy has made it the world's largest producer of lignin, with production plants in Norway, Spain, Sweden, Germany, the UK and the USA, plus, a joint venture with the Italian ENI group, involving new production plants in Norway and Italy, was agreed in 1990 to consolidate the group's position as the world's second largest producer of vanillin
- the Japanese company Yamaha recognizes the need to understand future customer requirements so, within the music business, it is working with experimental musicians in Europe in order to identify likely trends and developments in electronic music.

It is not easy to generalize about the impact of external changes (see Figure 3.1). Some consequences will be a matter of degree, others more substantial. Change itself may be incremental, occurring in predictable stages, or it can be sudden and dramatic.[2] A fundamental reduction in barriers to entry can lead to an influx of new players into a market. In time a shakeout may occur, as was the case in both New York and London when financial markets were deregulated and opened up.

Change may confirm an existing view or shake a whole philosophy to its roots. A change of national government or regime can result in the abandonment of old policies and the introduction of new ones. Specific and advance preparation for some anticipated changes may be possible, but in other cases, maintaining a general openness, flexibility and responsiveness may be the best option. To the extent that changes can enhance relative advantages and vulnerabilities and exacerbate trends, they need to be understood.

A change may stand the test of time or be quickly set aside. A company could find itself having to assess simultaneously such factors as whether:

- Eastern European countries will retain their commitment to open market policies or introduce some form of industrial policy, should the transition from command to market economy prove too painful
- inducements to inward investment are likely to be retained and could become better or worse – this could have a significant impact upon a location decision
- an agreement between the EC and Japan on the voluntary limitation of car imports into the community in the face of overcapacity will be sustained (the timing of any opening of such a market is of considerable

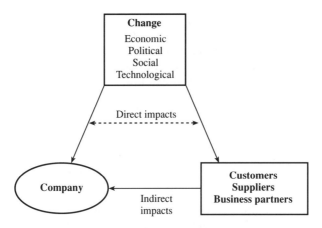

Figure 3.1 The impact of external changes

importance, given the time and cost of establishing dealer networks in the motor industry)
- a locally assembled product will continue to be regarded as either a local or an imported product (this issue affects Japanese cars produced by manufacturers such as Nissan in the UK and, in the US, the question of whether or not anti-dumping duties should be imposed depended upon whether or not Brother should be considered an American manufacturer)
- policies to encourage greater overseas investment in India will be fully implemented by the country's relatively bureaucratic civil service (cautious companies have waited for evidence of practical steps in the everyday lives of the people there to the removal of long standing obstacles to inward investment)
- ownership would remain an emotive issue in national political debate (for the UK, national sensitivities inhibited certain negotiations between IBM and BT in the period 1990–91)
- Japan's trade surplus would increase or decrease and the impact this might have on Japanese investment in the Pacific Rim, trade barriers and international trade negotiations
- a North American free trade area embracing Mexico and with a combined population of 365 million will develop more or less quickly than a European Economic Area comprising the countries of the EC and EFTA and with a combined population of 380 million
- whether or when the European Economic Area agreement between the EC and EFTA will allow a foreign company to acquire a stake in Swedish and Swiss companies that had hitherto been protected.

Direct and indirect effects of change

The impact of particular international developments will vary according to the business sector and location and there may be both direct and indirect impacts (see Figure 3.1). For example:

- financial institutions will be directly affected by the removal of barriers within the EC as there will be cross-border access to banking, insurance and investment services
- an opening up of public procurement might have a significant impact upon national champion companies that transact a substantial volume of business within the public sector.

One major UK manufacturing company considers the harmonization of technical and educational standards and the convergence of manufacturing processes as the keys to effective internationalization. Within its field, regardless of the attitudes, motivation and perspective of its managers, there are substantial technical barriers to the establishment of closer relationships with both customers and suppliers abroad.

Other international developments might have a more indirect effect:

- the reduction of barriers at borders can speed the flow of goods to a range of businesses – the most affected by this being those for whom physical transport represents a relatively large element of the final cost of goods
- indirect effects will also result from the direct impact of certain measures upon customers – for example, the indirect effects of freer cross-border trade can benefit sectors such as defence and oil that are specifically excluded from certain EC direct measures
- the reduction in barriers can lengthen supply chains, enabling more German manufacturers to source components in the UK.

Deregulation across Europe, coupled with home market constraints, has caused a significant increase in cross-border retailing.[3] The internationalization of certain retailing sectors is an example of the impact of indirect rather than direct factors. For example, pan-European markets for some luxury goods have emerged. While not directly affected by many EC Directives, some retailers have internationalized in order to counter the growth in bargaining power of their suppliers. Buying can also become more competitive when it occurs at the regional or international level.

Companies do not need to face challenges alone:

- in Brazil, agricultural cooperatives provide the storage facilities that would be beyond the resources of individual growers of a range of crops

- in Italy, many small- and medium-sized companies join together in cooperatives in order to improve their negotiating power with suppliers and compete with larger companies and Federexport, one such network, or grouping, of over 160 cooperatives representing nearly 7000 businesses, accounts for some 10 per cent of Italian exports
- a number of international federations have been set up by computer dealers to enable them to meet the regional and international purchasing needs of multinational corporations and transnationals and, by 1991, the Swiss-based Allied Computing Services had members in nine European countries; other such federations are COMEC, based in the UK, and the International Computer Group, based in France.

Change and business sectors

In some sectors, such as transportation, pharmaceuticals, telecommunications and financial services, national regulatory barriers have been a significant constraint upon cross-border operations. When these are removed by international agreement, such as that between the member states of the EC, the result may be an increase in cross-border cooperation, mergers and acquisitions. In order to better service the needs of international customers and clients, a scramble for size may result. At the same time, a hiving off of non-core businesses may benefit smaller companies. An opening up of public procurement, such as is occurring within the EC, could also benefit the smaller company.

In the area of professional services, it is sometimes the medium-sized firms that are most at risk. The larger firms are often better placed to supply international services to clients, while smaller firms may be more able to meet a local or niche need cost-effectively. The local firm need not develop the overheads associated with larger scale or international operation. The medium-sized firm may find it is too expensive at the local level while lacking the resources for effective international operation.

When changes in regulations occur, their greatest impact is likely to be upon those sectors in which they have been particularly significant. Some sectors face a higher degree of regulation and more entrenched tariff and non-tariff barriers than others. Hence when the barriers are removed these are the sectors that will be affected the most.

In some sectors, the barriers that companies face are informal rather than formal:

- for example, in Japan it is difficult for foreign suppliers to break into the close supply chain relationships that have been established between Japanese companies – cooperation and collaboration between Japanese companies, even those that are ostensibly competitors, sometimes being encouraged by the Japanese Government in order to confront a foreign challenge

- in certain countries, inadequate protection of intellectual property or non-enforcement can give rise to piracy to such an extent as to create a barrier to trade and in some cases, such informal activity can give rise to requests for formal action, including international negotiations such as those that occurred between the European Commission and the Republic of Korea
- within Europe, many of the calls for tenders that have resulted from the opening up of public procurement give little information and require a very rapid response, but, in practice, only a local firm may be able to obtain the additional information required and meet a tight deadline.

A company may need to be sensitive to issues beyond the confines of its own area of business:

- the interdependence of issues was illustrated during 1990–91 in the Uruguay round of Multilateral Trade Negotiations – a failure to agree in the agricultural sector inhibited progress across the board
- similarly, corporate action in one part of the world can affect operations elsewhere, as we saw during the 1980s when a number of major US multinationals faced a threat to their business in North America as a result of maintaining a local business presence in the Republic of South Africa.

Within sectors, some companies will benefit more than others according to their relative productivity and competitive advantage. The more efficient operators may pull further ahead, while the less effective go to the wall.

Change and the IT sector

The IT industry is a good example of a sector that entered the 1990s facing a combination of significant challenges. At local, regional and global levels:

1. considerable restructuring was occurring – acquisitions included Apollo by Hewlett-Packard and NCR by AT&T; in Europe Zenith was bought by Bull and Nixdorf was purchased by Siemens; ICL of the UK acquired Nokia and was, in turn, acquired by Fujitsu; STC was acquired by Northern Telecom; Philips proposed the sale of the bulk of its computer division to DEC
2. within the new groupings that emerged, the coordination and planning of operations and the allocation of resources was increasingly undertaken at the global level – for example, within a Fujitsu-ICL-Amdahl grouping,

an international product strategy group was formed
3. there was greater commitment to open systems as IBM, IBM and AT&T together, Olivetti, Norsk Data and Data General all announced open systems initiatives; connectivity and open systems became more important issues as bureaucratic corporations strove to make the transition into network organizations
4. companies were finding it more difficult to supply total value to customers by themselves so, within supply chains, they were becoming more interdependent. IBM arrangements included a software alliance with Lotus, marketing and production deals with Apple and an OEM link with Wang; Apple, in turn, formed an arrangement with Sony
5. companies were finding the continuing development costs of core technology an increasing burden, so, to spread the cost of developing future generations of technology, a number of R&D alliances emerged, such as that between AT&T and NEC; Bull, Siemens and ICL in AI; and SGS-Thomson and GEC Plessey, and IBM and Siemens in chip production; within the UK, DEC and Olivetti established a joint research centre at Cambridge
6. companies were having to focus on core activities, so, for example, IBM reassessed its core strengths in order to create strategic units with greater freedom to respond to market-place opportunities.

At just the regional level:

1. European dependence upon Japanese technology was growing: Bull, Siemens and Olivetti were dependent in some areas on Japanese technology, Bull was seeking to deepen its relationship with NEC and growing technological dependence was a factor in the acquisition by Fujitsu of ICL
2. the European Commission was concerned about the capability of European national champions such as Philips, Thomson, Bull and Olivetti to survive as these producers were overdependent on home markets and they lacked the economies of scale available to Japanese and American competitors so initiatives such as the Joint European Submicron Silicon (Jessi) programme were designed to encourage European collaboration
3. public sector business within the EC was dependent upon establishing sufficient community content to be regarded as a European supplier, but Japanese companies were taking steps to increase their European value added content by means of inward investment
4. while community suppliers carried high and 'inherited' overheads, external competitors were preparing themselves for the single market by relatively inexpensive greenfield investments that minimized their cost of doing business within the EC.

The commission has seen little in the way of market-place benefit from its financial support of European R&D and has faced a strong lobby from European producers seeking protection from foreign – particularly Japanese competition. The growing web of international arrangements and joint ventures is making it difficult for suppliers to claim a distinct European identity.

UK Corporate Affairs Minister John Redwood believes that what is needed to compete in the global market-place is 'champion companies in Europe' and not 'Euro champions'. Speaking in June 1991 in Paris to the Franco-British Chamber of Commerce and Industry, Redwood suggested: 'The way to do this is to create open competitive markets within the EC. This means Western European companies challenge each other, developing the new ideas and the new processes that they need to be world competitors. That is the way Japan does it. In motor cars, in electronics, in steel and many other industries the Japanese domestic market thrives on the clash of several major companies. That gives them the edge in world markets. The idea that you can build a single dominant Euro champion in each industry capable of taking on the Japanese is absurd'.

International, regional and local markets

A company needs to understand to what degree it is operating at the international, regional or local level as challenges and changes can occur at all these levels. What happens at one level can also spill over into the others.

Oil, chemicals, raw materials and other commodities are traded internationally. The prices of commodities can change significantly when there are sudden disruptions of supply. There is an international market for many electronic goods and high-tech products such as aircraft and suppliers of textiles and machine tools can also find themselves operating in an international market.

There are regional markets for some universal technologies that are in the process of becoming international. Computers and related products have tended to be priced more expensively in Europe than North America, but the spread of open systems is having the effect of opening up this market and making it more competitive. The globalization of pricing will mean good news for European purchasers, but pressure on cash flows for those suppliers for whom the European price premium has been significant.

There are other markets, such as those for food products, consumer durables and clothing, where a significant volume of international trade occurs, but a high proportion of consumption may be in the hands of domestic suppliers. To become an international supplier, some tailoring may be required to take account of differences between national markets. Within each of these markets changes of taste and fashion occur.

In other sectors, such as personal and professional services, most suppliers will be national businesses. Yet, within the EC more customers may be demanding services at the regional or European level. It may still be possible to operate internationally by establishing operations at local or national level and negotiating corresponding links where required, while some international professional firms are federations or associations of national practices.

In the retail and professional sectors many consumers will expect to buy from a local presence, even though it may be possible to shop or seek advice by telephone or mail and in many countries the sectors are fragmented. International expansion could occur through acquisitions, mergers or some form of joint venture or association.

In other sectors, for example process industries, there may be substantial economies of scale and a high threshold of minimum economic plant size. A search for the low costs associated with long production runs could lead to a high degree of concentration. When artificial barriers to mobility and trade, such as border controls, regulations, standards, safety and testing requirements, are reduced, such a market may become less fragmented and more competitive. National champions can face a severe challenge when artificial barriers are reduced and non-domestic competitors enter their markets.

Positive and negative impacts of change

Managers in organizations that have been shielded by protective barriers will face different problems from those in organizations that have been held back by such obstacles. When looking at companies as a whole in particular sectors, the success of all of them should not be assumed – major change can produce both winners and losers. Many personnel departments, for example, will have to cope with failure; the termination of employment rather than recruitment.

Internationalization could be reactive, that is, in response to external change. For example, global marketing could result from a drive to coordinate a company's relationship with major international corporations. Such corporations may demand a single point of contact with their suppliers so this contact will need to be able to draw upon resources throughout the supplying organization, even when this involves crossing departmental, business unit and geographical boundaries. For example:

– the document company Xerox manages its relationship with corporate

customers through global account managers who are supported by a worldwide, on-line database.
- Citibank has a global vision and its cash machines, in locations as far apart as the US and Japan, are linked by a global network and it aims to produce a range of specialized services for the internationally minded and internationally mobile consumer.

A change will not necessarily be neutral in terms of its relative impact upon customers and suppliers. Where changes, such as those occurring within the EC, give purchasers a wider range of choice, this increases their bargaining power *vis-à-vis* producers and suppliers. Many of the latter will face pressure on profit and contribution margins. More opportunities may be put out to tender. As a result, price could become a more important factor in relation to nationality or country of origin. A renewed focus upon relative prices may occur just when a company may be seeking to stress value beyond price.

3.3 Issue monitoring and management

So how should international changes be identified and their likely impacts assessed? A company that is new to international operations may need to develop processes for identifying significant challenges and opportunities in the business environment and determining appropriate corporate responses. An established international company must ensure that such processes remain relevant and effective. Monitoring and adjustment, therefore, needs to occur on a continuing basis.

A company operating in the international environment faces a much wider range of threats than a domestic company. Instead of the policies of just one government to consider, it may be necessary to monitor the activities of a great many governments. To do this may require an understanding of political forces and issues in unfamiliar political cultures and of political procedures in countries with constitutions quite different from that of home base. For example, a UK manager operating in the US might have to come to terms with a written constitution, a dispersal of powers and pork barrel politics.

Decision making and the external dimension

The international company needs to be able to take the external dimension into account when major decisions are taken. The large company may see parallels in the systemic approach to the decision making of nation states suggested by Karl Deutsch.[4] Company and foreign policy bureaucracies receive inputs from the environment, which are screened prior to presentation to appropriate decision makers (see Figure 3.2). Decisions are made in the context of corporate policy, relevant information and understanding and the attitudes and values of those concerned.

When an organization makes decisions that have a significant impact upon others, it is likely to receive feedback concerning the consequences of its actions. This could come from states, competitors and customers, all of whom could be affected by corporate activity. Depending upon the reactions of others, a company's policy and actions may need modification.

For such a decision making system[4] to operate effectively, the inputs from the environment need to be organized and screened. If this is not done, a company may fail to identify those developments that are significant as a result of being swamped by a great mass of irrelevant information.

Inputs regarding external developments should be collected from those with intimate knowledge of the company and its operations, such as those managing local operating units. They should also be collected from sources that have a degree of independence and objectivity. To achieve this, one major US corporation retains a former senior executive as an external authority to coordinate its issue monitoring process. The individual concerned is intimately involved in the discussion of international issues within the US and is able to contribute a sense of perspective. Some companies have a tendency to screen out information that does not fit in with a prevailing view or current policy so the warning signs may be ignored until it is too late.

Attitudes and values can introduce sources of bias into decision making.[5] They can colour our perceptions of the external world and how, once agreed, policy is implemented. Conscious effort should be devoted to identifying and compensating for sources of bias. Do not forget the customer and customer-related issues. An operating company view may need to be countered by the taking of inputs direct from representative customers.

The impact of selective perception and other sources of bias can be minimized by means of such devices as independent and objective surveys of customer satisfaction. A company needs empathy with, and understanding of, the aspirations and values of its customers in order to understand what represents value to them in *their* terms. If need be, management and business processes should be re-engineered to focus more closely on the vital few activities from the perspective of the customer.

Introducing, and involvement in, the monitoring process

The process of analysing external developments and opportunities and, just as important, responding, needs to occur on a continuing basis. The

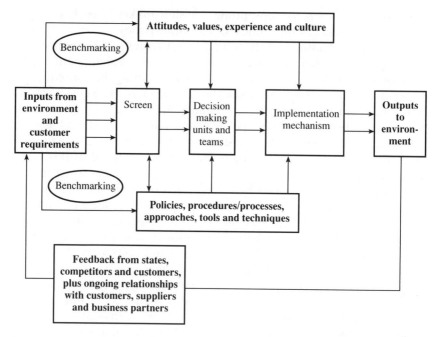

Figure 3.2 A systemic approach to corporate and state decisions
Source: Adapted from Deutsch, 1963

truly international company regards it not as a once a year planning exercise, but as an aspect of normal day-to-day management. The company is in a state of continual dialogue or interaction with particular developments.

In other companies this degree of responsiveness may not naturally occur. It may need to be brought about. A first step towards encouraging management teams to look beyond their immediate concerns may be to introduce an annual issue monitoring and management process. By its nature such a process will need to consider longer term developments and their implications.

WHAT IS HAPPENING NOW

In the case of some companies, issue monitoring and management is carried on quite separately from corporate planning or the development of general business strategy, but, these processes should be integrated. Where possible those directly concerned 'on the ground' should be involved in decisions relating to particular national territories.

The geographic expansion of operations can lead to a concentration of decision making power at a corporate headquarters. In this respect, the analogy with national foreign policy decision making can be dangerous. In the course of the present century the local ambassador has experienced an erosion of freedom to act without reference to the centre. State foreign policy decision making can be highly centralized and heads of state may meet and settle key issues personally.

Such a model may be appropriate for a company marketing a standard product to an undifferentiated global consumer market, but in the case of more tailored products and services in differentiated markets, such a degree of centralization can lead to a lack of responsiveness to local needs.

There is a tendency also for global issue monitoring and management processes to consist largely of vertical flows of information. Down from the apex of the bureaucratic pyramid or out from the core or travel requests for inputs by a certain date – all these are treated as items in the in-tray, to be responded to with varying degrees of interest and commitment. Responses from around the world are collected and considered by the appropriate central decision making body and some time later, local operating units may be informed of outcomes in the form of specific decisions.

EFFECTIVE ISSUE MONITORING AND MANAGEMENT

The ideal issue monitoring and management process involves:

1. *two-way communication* between the corporate centre and local operating units
2. horizontal communication between functional, operating and business units
3. open opportunities for operating and business units to feed their issues and concerns into the system and state their requirements
4. regional discussions and reviews where common interests might exist, for example, bringing together units in the EC
5. prompt and continuous feedback, refinement and review, with opportunities to comment at various stages of the decision-making cycle
6. not just the identification of issues, but what action the corporation should take in response
7. multinational and other project groups and taskforces, where appropriate, to examine particular issues
8. integration into the corporation's business planning and strategy cycle and process.

If a corporation is to respond effectively, issues should be defined in specific terms. Generalizations should be avoided – to simply say that barriers to trade should be removed is not helpful, we should ask which barriers and why? (In fact, barriers to trade at state borders should not be assumed.)

Trade restrictions, as has already been mentioned, often affect some sectors more than others. A company pursuing a strategy of international expansion should examine the relevance of particular national boundaries to its own operations, to flows of:

- people
- information
- technology
- finance
- goods and services.

For example:

- is the company experiencing difficulty in getting work permits for its staff?
- is it able to secure access to the information and technology it needs?
- are there specific restrictions that apply to the raising or movement of money?
- where restrictions occur, what is their impact in terms of cost or service to customers?
- are there voluntary restraint agreements in force, such as that which has applied to machine tool imports into the US from Japan and Taiwan?
- have property rights been satisfactorily defined in countries that are introducing market economies?

There may be obstacles to the free flow of goods and services, but if they can be overcome at a relatively modest cost in terms of money or management time, perhaps they should not feature in the issue monitoring and management process.

Managing the issue monitoring and management process

Those responsible for managing an issue monitoring and management process must make it clear that inputs should be practical and honest. If a problem or barrier exists it should be reported. Trade barriers do exist and a local management should not fear accusations of lack of confidence or motivation merely because they are realistic in assessing likely impacts upon the company. Such barriers include:

- culture
- language

- poor distribution within the country
- technical requirements, such as product safety
- foreign investment control
- import ban
- high customs duty
- quota
- anti-dumping/anti-circumvention.

There will be some issues that, while not of major concern to a corporation as a whole, can be of importance to a particular function. A personnel or human resources function, for example, might wish to operate its own review process in conjunction with a more general corporate process. This could involve regional or international meetings of personnel professionals. Indeed, some personnel departments, for example in those companies within which a growing range of 'personnel' responsibilities are devolved to business and operating units, may find that participation in an issue monitoring and management process is one justification of their continued existence. However such a process should not exist *merely* to improve the employment prospects of staff professionals.

The purpose of an issue monitoring and management process is to improve understanding and enhance the quality of decision making, with an end objective of allowing the corporation to better serve its customers. This should not be forgotten as generating information for its own sake can be harmful where it does not lead to better understanding.

Understanding is needed of issues that are significant and can be managed. Selection and prioritization, therefore, are necessary if a process is to work effectively. It also helps if the information collected from different countries and business units is comparable.

IDENTIFICATION AND PRIORITIZATION OF ISSUES

When monitoring issues, some means may need to be found to ensure that an issue of concern in just one or two countries, for whom it may be very significant, is not screened out just because it is of little or no interest to anyone else. The system must allow a response to the particular as well as to the general.

One way of achieving a balance is to ask general questions of all participants, and to give them an opportunity to state and prioritize *their* issues and what *they* are seeking from the company. Asking the right questions can be the key to securing a relevant response.

A check-list of some possible issues is:

- *economic business/government framework*
  - economic policy

- industrial policy
- trade policy
- policy towards foreign companies
- social policy
- monopoly policy
- public procurement, etc.
- *sector/industry framework*
  - structure
  - competition, etc.
- *political and social trends*
  - stability
  - demography, etc.
- *foreign policy issues* (especially with home country government).

This identifies separately:

- aspects of the regulatory framework that can influence the operations of major companies
- sector-specific issues of direct concern to a particular company
- more general political and social trends that might influence longer term policy.

A special watch should be kept of any discrimination between domestic and foreign companies. Some developing countries operate 'buy national' policies, or exclude foreign companies from certain sectors in which they are seeking to develop a domestic industry and public procurement, even in developed countries, can discriminate against foreign suppliers. Monopoly policy might also inhibit growth of market share or frustrate an acquisition or merger.

An understanding of industrial and trade policies could enable a corporation to identify and prioritize inward investment opportunities. Some governments offer significant incentives to encourage such investments. Changes of economic policy might affect market prospects and a tax change could have a more significant impact upon some products and services than others.

A company might also wish to know of changes in the structure of local competition. The appearance of a particular new entrant may not seem significant at a local level, but at the global level such information, along with that obtained from other markets, could provide important clues to the international strategy of a major competitor. The decision of Japanese companies to manufacture cars within the EC, for example, has changed the prospects for the European market to one of oversupply and intense competition.[6]

Political developments can be particularly significant in countries such as Germany and Japan where there may be close interaction between the worlds of business and politics. Broad political and social trends can span a number of countries. An example would be demographic trends in the EC. There may be common themes in the policies of countries at a similar stage of development. The policies of the UK government in the late 1980s have their parallels elsewhere in the world:

- unemployment reduction
- small business encouragement
- further privatization
- free the market/deregulation
- cover taxation
- greater personal responsibility
- diminished role for the state.

Customer and market opportunities can also be identified through a systematic search process. These can be both strategic and tactical:

- the Japanese company NEC examines strategic opportunities that lie beyond current technology and so the problem of cross-cultural and multilingual communication was identified by the company as an opportunity to investigate the introduction of an automatic translation facility into cross-border telephonic communication
- another Japanese company Seiko monitors tactical opportunities to introduce designs of watches linked to particular themes, crazes or events and the 500th anniversary of the discovery of America by Christopher Columbus in 1992 gave it the idea of introducing an 'Age of Discovery' range of watches.

Particular attention may need to be given to industrial policy at the national and regional levels. A company operating in Europe through national subsidiaries, for example, may need to make special arrangements to monitor EC developments and ensure that these are understood by its national companies.

Each country is likely to have its own industrial policy to promote industrial growth and development, preserve and promote employment and regulate the conduct of businesses in the public interest. This may be pursued by macro-industrial policy, such as demand management, and micro-industrial policies, such as competition policy and selective intervention.

Industrial policies can also exist at the regional level. In the EC there is a framework of competition policy, intervention in sectors with special problems and social and regional programmes. For example:

- a merger or acquisition may need to satisfy both national and EC competition policy
- the EC, rather than individual governments, has negotiated with Japan on the question of the extent of Japanese car exports to the Community.

In some cases a simultaneous watch may need to be kept at the local, regional *and* international levels. The US, for example, sometimes exerts extra-territorial powers:

- exports of the products of US companies, wherever they may be operating, to Eastern Europe have been prevented by the COCOM arrangements, which comprises Australia, all the NATO countries, except Iceland, and Japan (it was established in 1949 to prevent the export of technology with military potential to the then Communist block)
- in 1989 an attempt by a Luxembourg-based company Minorco to take over the UK-based Consolidated Goldfields was prevented as a result of the decision of a US court.

National industrial policies may need to be consistent with a regional or international framework. For example, the state aids to industry of member states of the EC have needed to be compatible with Articles 92–94 of the Treaty of Rome. Aid that 'distorts or threatens to distort competition by favouring certain undertakings' was held to be 'incompatible with the common market'. The European Commission has become more robust in its competition policy, as was evidenced in 1991 when it blocked a proposed Franco-Italian takeover of the Canadian aircraft manufacturer de Havilland.

Monitoring political changes

National industrial policies can and do change. International companies need to be vigilant to identify, and quick moving to respond to, any opportunities that may be created:

- for a number of years, Brazil's IT sector has been highly protected, with foreign participation largely excluded, but in late 1990 the Brazilian government decided to allow joint ventures and, within three months, IBM had negotiated a joint venture with SID, a local company, to produce micro-computers in Brazil
- some companies have viewed developments in Eastern Europe with concern – will Germany become overly preoccupied with its own internal development, will local infrastructures collapse – while other companies see problems as prospects, viewing the inadequate infrastructure as a business opportunity

– the Cerus Group of France established an investment holding company Cohfin in Hungary in late 1989 to coincide with the establishment of a market economy; in June 1990 it signed a joint venture with the Hungarian news agency MTI for the worldwide publication of HR Review, an English-language newsletter covering Hungarian business and financial developments.

Changes of government can have a significant influence upon industrial policy. For example, consider the case of a company monitoring the UK during 1991, when for much of the year the Conservative party of government trailed behind the Labour opposition party in the opinion polls. An issue monitoring report might have examined the likely impact of the return of a Labour government at a general election at local, regional and global levels and come up with the following conclusions:

1. within the UK, a Labour government would be more interventionist and would favour higher social spending:
   (a) a Labour government would be more inclined to be 'protectionist' and to support national champions against foreign competition; expenditure on state aids could increase; there might be less encouragement of inward investment, more resistance to foreign takeovers of UK firms and closer monitoring of the UK activities of multinationals
   (b) the processes of privatization and liberalization could be halted, if not reversed, and there would be less of a concern with an open international trading system
   (c) Government purchasing could be used to further national objectives so that, rather than rely upon market forces, there could be a more proactive industrial and training policy
   (d) employment policies would be more sympathetic to workers and unions and this could reduce the flexibility of the UK labour market
2. at a regional level a Labour government:
   (a) would be more supportive of the EC social dimension and UK opposition to certain elements of the Social Charter could be removed, which could add to a company's cost of doing business in the UK
   (b) would be more sympathetic to an extension of the Treaty in the areas of social policy and 'economic and social cohesion'
   (c) would be more likely to support a 'chauvinist' view and would be more sympathetic to the protectionist claims of European producers
3. at a global level, under a Labour government:
   (a) there would be less emphasis upon the encouragement of a more open trading system and the promotion of liberalization and privatization, instead, the arguments in favour of 'fortress Europe' would be increased

(b) relationships and cooperation between the UK and the US might be less close than they have been in recent years.

Recommendations for action

Participants in an issue monitoring and management process should not only identify issues, but also prioritize them and recommend the action they feel should be taken. There are three stages to be addressed:

1. the nature of each issue should be specified and, where possible, quantified in terms of scale and timing
2. the impact upon the company should next be assessed – this could be in terms of financial cost or relationship to corporate policy
3. finally, next steps or actions that the company might take should be recommended.

Participants throughout a corporate network should be encouraged to feed in their own recommendations for action and suggestions that are important for significant areas of a business will need to be given priority consideration. Where possible, responses should be accompanied by reasons either for or against the adoption of a recommended course of action.

As well as seeking specific recommendations for action based upon a local perspective, a corporation may also seek local information and insight as input into the consideration of global moves. An example might be the decision concerning where to locate a manufacturing or R&D unit or which markets should have priority when new products or services are to be launched.

In some cases joint action with other companies could be considered (arrangements and alliances will be considered later in this chapter). Alternatively, cooperation could take place in the representational area. For example, several companies in Europe's IT sector have jointly lobbied the European Commission.

Local participation and objectivity

Local operating units should be asked to contribute towards the discussion of global issues, especially when they are likely to be affected. Some care may be needed in interpreting their submissions as local units may well play up their own merits in seeking to attract investment. It may be necessary to arrange some independent and objective check of the inputs provided. To use third parties *exclusively* to collect the required information could mean ignoring the advice of those with an unrivalled understanding of the capability of the company and the needs of its customers.

Similar concerns could be applied to information collected by diplomats. Those new to a mission abroad may need a period of induction before they can fully understand the nuances of a local situation. At the same time, too long an assignment can lead to a blurring of objectivity as a result of overimmersion or 'going native'. The remedy tends to be postings of a few years duration.

Companies considering the creation of a cadre of international managers should bear in mind the number of countries that establish a diplomatic service as an entity separate from the rest of a civil service. In the UK such a distinction has traditionally been drawn between the diplomatic service and the home civil service. Whether or not a company adopts such an approach will depend upon how many of its staff need to develop an international perspective.

In the case of an international company a local operating unit may well be largely staffed by nationals. In responding to accusations that they are 'going native' it may be necessary to accept that they probably *are* natives.

A company such as Xerox with a global commitment to benchmarking could ask local operating units to compare notes on local and regional issues with non-competing companies. The following are some shared perspectives of CEOs on the decline of Communism in the Soviet Union and Eastern Europe:

- I've been surprised, and expect I will be surprised again. The reform process will be accompanied by much pain and great uncertainty.
- The risks of operating across an enormous portion of the globe have shot up. But the opportunities for pioneers are also there – it's like a nineteenth century land rush across a continent.
- Will the economies of Eastern Europe be able to absorb investments from the West? Do they have the skills or the infrastructure?
- We need to reassess our approach to marketing. Under Communism they had products rather than brands.
- Before the dramatic changes that have occurred we could generalize. Now we need to take each country separately. Some countries are more likely to succeed than others.
- Market entry is difficult as there are few smaller enterprises to acquire or buy into. Under Communism production was highly concentrated.
- We have to destroy before we can build. Managing the destruction of all that these people have known is not easy.
- Under Communism they waited for orders to come in and administered a waiting list. Now they have competitors and they have to go out and win customers.

Accumulating a number of such views can enable one to build a richer overall picture than might be the case if reliance was placed upon a single source of authority. Even the best informed can have a particular bias.

Country SWOT analysis

However it is collected, data about a country can often be presented in the form of a country SWOT analysis (see Figure 3.3). Such an approach could be adopted in respect of personnel or human resource issues and information in order to allow the situations in different countries to be compared.

A company with a positive policy of international expansion might, when presenting the results of a SWOT analysis, focus first on opportunities and related strengths. Another company with a more defensive strategy could commence with an examination of those threats and weaknesses that might be exploited by competitors.

However the information is presented, management needs to consider the inter-relationships of strengths, weaknesses, opportunities and threats (see Figure 3.4).

Using sheets of acetate, it is possible to overlay one SWOT analysis over another. For example, one could compare a country SWOT analysis with that of the company as a whole. This would enable a management team to identify those countries that complement and best match the company. Alternatively a functional or divisional country or company SWOT analysis can be produced. For example, an analysis could focus particularly upon training or recruitment issues.

3.4 Corporate foreign policy

An international company may need to pursue the corporate equivalent of the foreign policy of a nation state. Positions may need to be prepared and advocated in a number of negotiating situations and representational arenas. Similar arguments may apply in a number of different national contexts.

An international trade example is the issue of whether or not local assembly would circumvent anti-dumping provisions. The issues involved are:

- interests of *producers* v interests of *consumers*
- inward investment: job creation or job destruction; screwdriver assembly v local value added
- protectionism or free and fair trade
- reciprocity v unilateral action.

A company accused of dumping will stress the principle of free trade and the benefits of offering consumers a wider choice at competitive prices. The creation of new jobs, perhaps in an area of local unemployment will

Figure 3.3 Country SWOT analysis

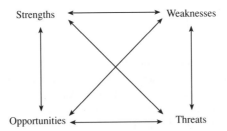

Figure 3.4 The interrelationships of strengths, weaknesses, opportunities and threats

be referred to, along with the prospect of further and future investments. On the other hand, those companies harmed by an alleged circumvention will stress the interests of local producers. They will warn that much inward investment is of the 'screwdriver assembly' variety, with low local value added and that incremental but relatively low-skilled and part-time assembly jobs are no substitute for the loss of local full-time jobs. However, they will also resist accusations of protectionism by claiming that trade must be both free and fair. A domestic company, headquartered and registered in the country concerned, might also argue that any concession on imports from those accused of dumping should be linked to an opening up of the home market of the alleged dumper. This is the principle of reciprocity that has been used by the EC in trade negotiations with both the US and Japan. By supporting or advocating such a linkage, a company might be able to turn a defensive strategy into an opportunity to open up an overseas market.

While attracted and actively sought by some Government agencies, foreign direct investment can cause concerns and resentments in other quarters. Greenfield investments to build upon strengths in areas in which the inward investor already has a competitive advantage can threaten local producers. The sheer scale of foreign investment, such as that from Japan, can lead to fears of dominance. The acquisition of well-known buildings or cultural 'landmarks', such as film companies, has been a particularly sensitive issue in the US.

Alliances and joint ventures can also cause concern. There could be fears that a national champion is being hollowed out, as it were, losing a core capability as a result of a technology agreement with a foreign firm. These worries may need to be countered by reference to the benefits of skill and technology transfer and possible balance of trade advantages when local production comes on stream and a proportion is exported.

Arrangements and alliances

The negotiation and management of arrangements and alliances may require the skills of the diplomat to sustain relationships with both partner companies and host governments.[7] For example, entry to the South Korean market has typically been through a joint venture with a local company. The foreign partner might provide the technology and the local company a site and a labour force. The success of such an arrangement can depend upon the continuing exercise of diplomacy.

The skills of the diplomat may also be needed to end a joint venture. Fujitsu and Hitachi ended a joint venture of some 20 years' standing that had been established to enable the companies to work together to build a capability to compete with IBM. The separation was an amicable one, both parties considering that the arrangement had achieved its original objectives.

An international vision can be a stimulus to the achievement of regional market coverage through arrangement or alliance:

- the Norwegian cement company Aker has established a strategic alliance with the Swedish company Euroc to implement a joint strategy of expansion in selected geographic areas and develop 'a joint sales, purchasing and distribution network'
- the Swedish pharmaceutical company Astra has agreed with Merck & Co. of the USA to form a 50:50 joint venture in the mid 1990s to tackle the competitive US pharmaceutical market, which is the largest in the world
- the French company Sanofi is approaching the US market through an alliance with Sterling Drug Inc. of the USA in the areas of ethical pharmaceuticals and consumer health products.

According to Jean-François Dehecq, Chairman and Chief Executive Officer of Sanofi, the alliance with Sterling is 'perfectly in keeping' with Sanofi's 'strategy for global expansion'. The agreements do not involve any exchange of funds, but bring together complementary 'human, scientific, industrial and marketing resources around the world'. Dehecq has referred to the arrangement as a 'trial marriage' that he believes will be successful because 'the two partners share the same vision of the future'.

Reasons for concluding an alliance, which could be aggressive or defensive, might include:

- the search for critical mass size
- to share development costs, infrastructure and other resources
- to establish a 'toe hold' in a strategically important market
- to exclude a competitor from an area of opportunity
- overcoming internal constraints by linking with complementary skills
- to speed up entry to the market or delivery to customers.

A company may need to cope simultaneously with more than one joint venture:

- during 1990 the international chemical company DSM, which is headquartered in the Netherlands, concluded a European joint venture with Rubbermaid Inc. of the USA, an agreement with Idemitsu Petrochemical Co. to build a plant in Japan, a 50:50 Taiwanese joint venture with the Eternal Chemical Company, agreed acquisitions in the UK and US and planned an expansion of a 50:50 joint venture in China and H B van Liemt, Chairman of the Managing Board of DSM, has announced that the company has 'decided to adopt a strategy of increased focus on areas of activity in which DSM already has or will be able to gain a leading position internationally'
- during 1990 Du Pont, within the European region alone, started a product exchange agreement with Mobil, agreed a North Sea venture with BP and Norsk Hydro, announced a 50:50 joint venture with PowerGen and signed a development agreement with Matsushita, plus a Turkish nylon joint venture came on stream and, among others, international joint ventures were agreed with Merck & Co in the area of research and development and Teijin of Japan to make and sell Mylar polyester film
- the German chemical company Hoechst has formed a number of relationships with Japanese companies, including a dyes joint venture, worldwide cooperation in the polyester films sector and a joint videotape film production plant with Mitsubishi Kasei and, further, a joint company has been established in Japan with Teijin and Hoechst has opened a research centre in Japan.

Some major companies are themselves the product of joint ventures:

- Shell, or, Royal Dutch, depending upon whether one is describing the company from the UK or the Netherlands, retains a relatively complex joint venture form of organization
- Rank Xerox is the product of an original joint venture between the Rank Organization of the UK and Xerox Corporation of the USA
- the Asea Brown Boveri Group – a global company employing 215 000 people operating in the power generation, transmission and distribution and other industrial sectors – is owned equally by ASEA AB of Sweden and the Swiss company BBC Brown Boveri Ltd and the group comprises some 1300 subsidiary companies around the world.

The parties to a joint venture may together negotiate a further joint venture. For example, strategic partners Renault of France and Volvo of Sweden have agreed to contribute to a new partnership relationship involving Mitsubishi of Japan. This Japanese company has acquired a share in Volvo Car, which was itself jointly owned by Volvo and the Netherlands government.

The pursuit of corporate foreign policy

In the case of major investments, direct negotiations may be entered into between inward investor and domestic government. These may extend beyond securing a minister to open a plant to questions of local content and government to government contact on such issues as reciprocal trade. Some discussions may involve both national governments and officials at regional level, for example, appropriate institutions of the EC.

Human resource issues can become an important element of corporate international communications and lobbying. The training and development of local staff and the transfer of skills are actively sought by many developing countries. In Eastern Europe, understanding Western ways of doing business may be the key to the successful transition to a market economy. An opportunity that is offered to local managers for training and development could be highly valued.

Major companies that have formal programmes to promote their interests around the world will need to integrate a number of elements. While tailored to local circumstances, national messages should be consistent with those at regional and international level, which are likely to be encountered by those who travel or who have access to the international media. The number of possible reactions to one international threat, an EC accusation of dumping in this case, illustrates the extent of the coordination problem:

- lobbying
- public protest/PR
- legal challenge
- raise EC prices
- lower export country prices
- 'offload' in other markets
- withdraw from market
- accelerate EC assembly
- seek EC joint venture
- full EC investment/production.

A tradition of British foreign policy is that the UK has no permanent friends or enemies, only permanent interests. The extent to which the UK has friendly relations with other states depends upon whether their actions are perceived as supportive or inimical to British interests. As international developments unfold, often in the nature of surprises, an international company, while determining its responses, should not lose sight of its long-term interests. While these are clearly understood by all key players, local action under delegated powers is more likely to be consistent with global policy.

Long-term interests could be couched in terms of service to customers. In the short term a company might incur considerable costs in supplying a customer when these are such obstacles as trade wars, but it might be worthwhile bearing these in the interests of a long-term relationship or to achieve a general reputation for not letting the customer down.

Human resource considerations could also be an element of longer term interests. A knowledge business could find itself constrained primarily by its ability to recruit those with higher level skills. Securing access to relevant skill could become a vital corporate interest and a primary drive of a strategy of internationalization. The overriding objective in deciding how best to serve customer requirements might be to seek out and obtain a contribution from all those with defined skills, wherever they are located. In the knowledge society, the skill-driven strategy is likely to become more common.

Check-list

- Does your company systematically examine the impact of external changes upon both itself and its customers?
- Does your company understand the major issues and developments affecting each of the markets in which it operates?
- Does your company have an effective issue monitoring and management system?

- What are the main barriers to your company's effective regional (for example, pan-European operation) and how might these be overcome?
- How relevant are national boundaries and other barriers to the further internationalization of the operations of your company?
- Should your company formulate regional (for example, European or Pacific Rim) strategies within the context of its global or international strategy?
- Who within your company should be responsible for regional (for example, EC or Pacific Rim) affairs?
- How effective is your company's monitoring in relation to regional common markets and the possible effects of proposed (for example, EC) measures?
- Does your company make, or participate in networks that are able to make, appropriate representations at national, regional and international levels?
- Does your company have effective processes for involving all those concerned in determining and implementing what needs to be done to respond to international developments?
- Does your company utilize international or Euro-benchmarking in order to learn from others, including customers and suppliers, concerning aspects of internationalization?
- Does your company need a corporate foreign policy and, if so, what should its main elements be?

References

1. Halperin, Morton, *Bureaucratic Politics and Foreign Policy*, Brookings, 1974.
2. Johnson, Chalmers, *Revolutionary Change*, Little, Brown & Company, 1966.
3. Corporate Intelligence Group, *Cross-border Retailing in Europe*, Corporate Intelligence Research Publications, 1991.
4. Deutsch, Karl W, *The Nerves of Government*, Free Press, 1963.
5. Jervis, Robert, *Perception and Misperception in International Politics*, Princeton University Press, 1976; and R Little and S Smith, *Belief Systems and International Relations*, Basil Blackwell, 1988.
6. Ludvigsen Associates, *Year 2000 and Beyond: The Car Marketing Challenge in Europe*, Euromonitor Reports, 1991.
7. Barston, R, *Modern Diplomacy*, Longman, 1988; and H Raffia, *The Art and Science of Negotiation*, Harvard University Press, 1982.

Further reading

Baldwin, D, *Economic Statecraft*, Princeton University Press, 1985.
Bovard, James, *The Fair Trade Fraud: How Congress Pillages the Consumer and Decimates American Competitiveness*, St Martin's Press, 1991.

Burstein, Daniel, *Euroquake – Europe's Explosive Economic Challenge Will Change the World*, Simon & Schuster, 1991.

Burton, John, *Deviance, Terrorism and War: The Process of Solving Unsolved Social and Political Problems*, Martin Robertson, 1979.

Cavusgil, S T and P N Ghauri, *Doing Business in Developing Countries: Entry and Negotiation Strategies*, Routledge, 1990.

Dicken, P, *Global Shift*, Harper & Row, 1986.

George, S, *Politics and Policy in the European Community*, Oxford, 1985.

Gilpin, Robert, *The Political Economy of International Relations*, Princeton, 1987.

Harris, N, *Of Bread and Guns: The World Economy in Crisis*, Penguin, 1983.

Keohane, R, *After Hegemony*, Princeton University Press, 1984.

Keohane, Robert O and Joseph S Nye, *Transnational Relations and World Politics*, Harvard University Press, 1970.

Krasner, *Structural Conflict*, Berkeley University of California Press, 1985.

Lindblom, Charles E, *Politics and Markets: The World's Political-Economic Systems*, Basic Books, 1977.

Lodge, J, *The European Community and the Challenge of the Future*, Pinter, 1989.

Rugman, Alan M, and Alain Verbeke, *Global Corporate Strategy and Trade Policy*, Pinter, 1990.

Strange, Susan, *States and Markets: An Introduction to International Political Economy*, Pinter, 1988.

Wallerstein, I, *The Politics of the World Economy*, Cambridge University Press, 1984.

4

Global operation and human resource development strategy

Perspectives

Total quality is a universal business principle for us, it knows no boundaries. Our HRD strategy is derived from our global quality strategy.

Managing Director, Japanese plant in the Republic of Ireland

Our whole international strategy is based upon the acquisition of good local companies. We buy our people from those likely to have recruited the best. Global coordination is by a small group who apply strict business criteria. We let the professionals on the ground network with other offices to the extent that they need to.

Director, international business services company

We just have an HRD strategy – we follow it all over the world. It complements our technology and our products are universal. Does that make it a 'global HRD strategy'?

Personnel Director, Japanese manufacturer of consumer products

Opportunities are opportunities, not finance opportunities or production opportunities or personnel opportunities. I want business plans, not finance plans or production plans or personnel plans.

Chief Executive, UK financial institution

I want our people to be international from a business perspective, not a functional perspective. They need an understanding of international business issues, and too much experience in a particular location can distort this international perspective.

Chairman, international trading company

Our global vision is all about us and 'on the ground' many of our own people see us as foreigners. The vision ought to be about our customers, then it would

84

be about their friends and their families. The emphasis would shift from what we are taking out to what we are putting in.

Distributor of overseas products in Central America

4.1 Introduction

A company could have a variety of reasons for seeking to expand its international operations. Some possible corporate objectives could be:

- *build on market strengths*
  - geographic expansion/extend network
  - repeat successful pattern
  - Europe as home market
  - prioritization and focus/differentiation
- *build image*
  - Euro-brand?
  - global-brand?
  - articulate vision/distinct values
- *build volume*
  - economies of scale/partnership arrangements
  - vertical or horizontal integration
- *build added value*
  - leverage from technology, people skills, management, etc.
- *build closer relationships with customers*
  - local representation/production
  - tailoring to requirements
  - organizational links/value chain collaboration
  - increase speed of response
- *build defences*
  - reduce risks
  - defence against takeovers.

Before it can establish a strategy for international operation, a company must first clarify its purpose, or, reason for existence. A company should not assume it will continue to be a player in competitive markets. It must be able to make a distinct contribution and to add value beyond what would otherwise be the case. If it is to attract and retain the interest and commitment of customers and suppliers and human, financial and other resources, it must develop and articulate a corporate vision and mission.

Many companies do not have a unique reason for existence. If they were to fail and be wound up, what would be the consequences? Would anyone notice, apart from some consumers who could simply buy a virtually identical commodity good or service from another supplier? Such management teams need to look in the mirror and ask the question, 'What is so special about us?' *Being* special, and *staying* special, in the international market-place is a formidable challenge.

In this chapter, the value of a clear vision and mission is examined. Then the formulation of human resource development (HRD) strategy and the importance of HRD issues in international business development strategy are looked at.

4.2 Vision and mission

Great universities breed a lifetime of devotion that is sometimes fanatical in many of their alumni spread across the continents of the world. So should the great company, but only too often a previous company is forgotten within weeks of a person joining a new employer. The university is remembered because, whatever the reality, its purpose seems noble and worthy of undying support.

Many Japanese companies stress the contribution that a philosophy of business can make to securing the lifelong commitment of employees. Kiyoshi Ichimura, the founder in 1936 of Ricoh, a Japanese producer of office automation products, established as a basic business philosophy for the company: 'Love your neighbour, Love your country, Love your work'. Hiroshi Hamada, President of Ricoh clarifies what is meant by 'Love your work': 'Throughout a person's life he or she must work, and if it is to be useful work, then it must provide a service to others in society'. Hamada sums up the Ricoh business philosophy as: 'Provide genuine service to others'.

A vision represents a better future, one that 'grabs' and 'turns on'. It is a dream of where the company would like to be. It should be compelling, challenging and shared. It should be acceptable to all the stakeholders in a business, but if it does not benefit customers it will fail all of them. The vision of Matsushita is to contribute to human happiness by means of material affluence afforded by quality and inexpensive products.

The vision need not be long and everyone in the organization ought to be able to understand how they can contribute to its achievement. It should be ambitious and a catalyst of action, capable of motivating people 'at home and abroad':

- the internationalization of TNT was sustained by a simple but ambitious vision of a global physical distribution network – a global telecommunications network could be the vision of a telecoms supplier, and a global trading market that of a commodity broker

- the vision of one US pizza house was to deliver a pizza anywhere in the centre of a town within 15 minutes and a delivery person, peddling up a hill at night in the pouring rain, knew what needed to be done to meet this commitment.

The mission statement may be longer and more precise, but not so detailed as to constrain and inhibit. Equally, bland statements fail to inspire – the dull mission document just gets filed away whereas the vision that reaches the heart lives and spreads by word of mouth.

A company's values may be explicit in its mission statement:

- Japanese companies stress the importance of realizing the potential of the individual through relationships with others – Ricoh stresses the value of 'putting oneself in the other person's place', but at the same time, Hiroshi Hamada, President of Ricoh, believes that people need to find 'personal value' in their work: 'only when someone finds personal value in what they are doing, can they be of service to others. Just to improve one's ability is not work – that is study'
- satisfied customers have been at the heart of the values of the Xerox Corporation for many years, indeed, the company's first chief executive officer, Joseph Wilson, recognized that: 'It is the customer and the customer alone who will ultimately determine whether we succeed or fail as a company. Serving the customer is the responsibility of every Xerox employee'
- integrity is a feature of the Sainsbury mission statement, but such a statement is of little value if it does not influence behaviour; one international pharmaceutical company operates an internal course on the ethics of medical practitioners and competitors in particular markets and unethical conduct in prescribing practices and in pirating medicines have been factors in the decision not to enter certain markets.

The more diverse an organization in terms of its activities and culture, the greater the value of a clear vision and mission in achieving international understanding and securing a sense of unity and purpose. It is a shared vision and mission that can act as a unifying force and hold an international network together. Without it a network can fragment.

The vision, mission, ideology and culture of a company can all be shaped by its international history and development. The more international and cultural variety there is and the more diversified an organization, the more difficult they may be to formulate.

The importance of vision

In a survey for the 1991 BIM report *The Flat Organisation: Philosophy and Practice*[1], 'clear vision and mission' came top of a list of factors thought to be important in the creation of a new philosophy of management (see Table 4.1). Every respondent considered clear vision and mission to be either 'important' or 'very important', with about three quarters of them considering it 'very important'.

In another survey, *Quality: The Next Steps*,[2] interviewees stressed the importance of a compelling quality vision. The survey reveals that:

- many organizations do not have a 'quality vision', there is a lack of top management commitment to quality and of both a common understanding of what quality is and a shared 'quality vision' of what it ought to be (see Table 4.2)
- in general, the 'quality message' is not being effectively communicated, with approaching three quarters of respondents agreeing that 'quality too often consists of "motherhood" statements'

A further survey, *Communicating for Change*[3] also confirms the importance of articulating and communicating a clear vision:

- clear vision and strategy and top management commitment are jointly ranked as the most important requirements for the successful management of change (see Table 4.3) – approaching nine out of ten of the respondents ranked these as 'very important'
- sharing the vision is considered 'very important' by seven out of ten of the respondents, followed by communicating the purpose of change and employee involvement and commitment – both considered 'very important' by two thirds of the respondents
- every respondent considers clear vision and strategy, sharing the vision, top management commitment, communicating the purpose of change and employee involvement and commitment to be either 'very important' or 'important' in the management of change.

The effective vision

The organization of a successful company will reflect its vision and mission. The more shared the vision and mission of an organization are, and the more homogenous and understood are the beliefs and values of its people, the greater the delegation of authority that may be allowed. However, too tight a definition of mission can result in it becoming the 'word'. The consequence could be a centralization of authority and a reluctance to change. In a dynamic business environment, the mission itself may need to be periodically discussed and refined.

As an organization strives to become more flexible in responding incrementally to changing circumstances, there can be an increasing risk of a drift in the wrong direction or a failure to see the wood for the trees. A clear and long-term vision beyond the sanitized wording of the formal

Table 4.1   Factors for creating a new philosophy of management in order of 'very important' replies

Replies	Percentage
Clear vision and mission	74
Customer focus	66
Harnessing human potential	66
Attitudes, values and behaviour	52
Personal integrity and ethics	40
Individual learning and development	29
Processes for ongoing adaptation and change	29
Turbulence and uncertainty	19
Organizational learning	14
Management techniques	5
Others	3

Source: Colin Coulson-Thomas and Trudy Coe, *The Flat Organisation: Philosophy and Practice*, British Institute of Management, 1991.

Table 4.2   Barriers to quality ranked in order of 'very significant' replies

Replies	Percentage
Lack of top management commitment	92
Too narrow an understanding of quality	38
Horizontal boundaries between functions and specialisms	31
Vested interests	29
Organizational politics	28
Cynicism	28
Organizational structure	27
Customer expectations	26
Speed of corporate action	24
Too general an approach	18
Loss of momentum	17
Boredom	15
Gap between management expectation and process achievement	15
Vendors'/suppliers' capabilities	15
Subsidiary/parent relationships	9
Cost	6

Source: Colin Coulson-Thomas and Susan Coulson-Thomas, *Quality: The Next Steps*, Adaptation and ODI, 1991.

mission statement can help ensure that small steps are consistent with strategic objectives. A longer term perspective is particularly important in the international context. The penetration of certain markets, such as Japan, can require persistence and consistency of purpose.

Table 4.3 Requirements for change in order of 'very important' replies

Replies	Percentage
Clear vision and strategy	86
Top management commitment	86
Sharing the vision	71
Employee involvement and commitment	65
Communicating the purpose of change	65
An effective communications network	54
Communicating the expected results of change	44
Understanding the contributions required for the achievement of change	42
Communicating the timing of change	38
Linking a company's systems strategy with its management of change	38
Project management of change	27
Ongoing management education and development programmes	23
One-off management education and development programmes	8

Source: Colin Coulson-Thomas and Susan Coulson-Thomas, *Communicating for Change*, Adaptation, 1991.

For it to be an effective guide to action, a vision and mission should be rooted in opportunities to create value for customers. The TNT vision of becoming a global service company, for example, matched the emerging needs of its customers for international distribution.

To ensure that a vision is customer focused, fundamental questions should be asked, such as:

- 'What is special or distinctive about the company?'; 'Why should it continue to exist?'; 'What would the world lose if the company ceased to exist?'
- 'Who is the customer?'; 'Why should a customer be interested in the company?'; 'What value does or could the company add for its customers?'

Care needs to be taken not to elevate the vision and mission of an organization to the level of dogma. When this occurs and it is not shared by those outside, a company, having failed to 'convert' others, can fall back upon itself and become introverted. A strong corporate culture can also isolate a company from its market-place, perhaps at a time when it needs to develop closer relationships with customers and suppliers.

Sharing the vision

Why is so much emphasis being placed upon articulating and communicating a compelling vision? The BIM *Flat Organisation* report[1] reveals the relatively common phenomenon of a credibility gap:

- while clear vision and mission are thought to be essential, in many companies both are regarded as just words on paper and they do not serve as a guide to action
- the short-term actions of many boards in response to economic recession are not always consistent with either a company's vision or the building of long-term relationships with its customers.

The *Communicating for Change* survey[3] reveals that many managers are failing to share the vision. Communication skills emerge as a significant barrier:

- most participants believe that the communication and sharing of vision and strategy throughout their organization could be much improved, many directors acknowledging that their middle and line managers are not able to communicate effectively, but there is limited awareness of how to remedy the situation
- communication skills are felt by respondents to be the top barrier to both internal and external communication – not a single respondent considered communication skills to be insignificant as a communication barrier
- communications technology is not perceived as a significant barrier to communication, but rather the problem is one of attitudes, perspective and how the technology is used.

Participants in the BIM *Flat Organisation* survey[1] were asked to rank in importance the management qualities that will enable organizations to implement the changes that are desired in order to respond more effectively to challenges and opportunities within the business environment. When these are ranked in order of 'very important' replies, the ability to communicate comes top. Two thirds of the respondents considered it to be 'very important'.

When setting up new operations overseas and appointing staff to run existing overseas activities, care should be taken to select those who share, and can share with others, the vision and mission of the organization. When this occurs, there may be less of a need to establish local bureaucracies, with their functional groups and built in checks and balances, to ensure that corporate policy is followed. Smaller teams may be possible, subject to fewer controls from the centre.

International vision and the board

The formulation and articulation of an agreed international vision must begin in the boardroom. An Institute of Directors discussion document

The Effective Board[4] suggests that the board itself may be partly to blame for the disillusionment found in many companies:

- under pressure to perform and survive, the focus of many boards has become visibly internal and short term, while the messages being communicated to managers encourage them to develop longer term relationships with external customers – this is the source of misunderstanding and distrust in many companies when actions do not match words
- there is little satisfaction with the performance of boards, three-quarters of chairmen believing that the effectiveness of their companies' boards could be improved
- poor teamwork is frequently given as a factor that is limiting the effectiveness of boards and so improved communication, open discussion, regular meetings and a shared or common purpose are all given as ways of ensuring that a board works effectively as a team.

The effective board is composed of a united team of competent directors who share and can communicate a common vision. The first step in formulating and communicating an international vision and strategy is for the chairman to ask the following questions.[5]

- *'Do the members of the board share a common international vision?'*
  If fundamental change is to occur, there must be an agreed vision of a better future.
- *'Are they committed to an agreed strategy?'*
  The directors should be committed to both a clear and compelling international vision and a common and realistic strategy for its achievement.
- *'How effective are they at communicating with customers, employees and business partners?'*
  A clear and compelling vision has to be communicated and understood if it is to be shared and if it is to motivate. In the global market-place the international vision has to transcend barriers of nationality and culture.

Akio Morita, Chairman of Sony, has had both *product* visions, such as 'mobile music', and an *international* vision of 'global localization'. The global localization vision has resulted in the sustained movement of resources and responsibilities closer to customers. Sony is committed to achieving a more comprehensive relationship with local customers and, in recognizing the strengths and potential contributions of cultures other than Japan, is further along the path from multinational corporation to transnational than many other Japanese companies.

A CEO must make sure that their management team not only agree the wording of a mission statement, but also share an understanding of its meaning. The clearer a vision and mission, the less likely it is that questions concerning interpretation and implementation will give rise to internal politics. When expressed in overly general terms, a mission statement might be used by two sides in an argument to support what *each* of them would like to do.

Some differences of viewpoint, however, can be helpful in ensuring that there is proper consideration of a range of issues. To achieve change there needs to be some dissatisfaction with the present and revisionist views may need to confront those of the status quo. Participation in debate can help those involved to more fully understand the issues at stake. The view of a minority within the company could eventually triumph and might be vindicated by market experience and performance.

4.3 International HRD strategy

The review of HRD strategy must begin with the vision and mission of a company – the basic essence of the reasons for its existence. HRD strategy – like vision and mission – should be formulated in the context of discussion of the requirements of customers, while general business strategy should identify the major areas in which the company believes it can add value for customers.

In many companies the formulation of HRD strategy begins with the organization's own requirements for continuing operation. Corporate bureaucracies can develop a life of their own, activities and departments can continue and grow quite independently of customer requirements.

Business development and HRD strategy need to be continually reviewed and refined and each is dependent upon the other. The extent of HRD involvement in the formulation of business strategy can vary between countries. For example, the HRD functions in many Swedish companies appear more involved in strategy formulation than their colleagues in equivalent German companies. In comparison, senior German personnel professionals can appear more preoccupied with satisfying legal requirements.

The availability and quality of an organization's people will reflect past decisions and policies. To determine a strategy and direction, a company requires a realistic and objective understanding of where it *is* and a clear vision of where it is seeking to *go*. In a turbulent and demanding environment, progress is likely to be achieved by a continuing series of steps of various sizes.

By using communications technology to link up those with a strong sense of shared vision and mission, a network organization consisting of active participants and partners can grow organically. Decisions relating to people, their recruitment, retention and remuneration, their training and development and their support, should be based upon maintaining or enhancing a capability to add value for customers.

In a growing number of companies HRD is a critical success factor, perhaps the only source of sustainable competitive advantage over the longer term.[6]

According to Paul Allaire, President of the Xerox Corporation: 'Our people provide us with a competitive edge in the global marketplace. They are among the brightest. They understand that their personal success as individuals and the success of Xerox as a business enterprise are comingled'. Employee motivation/satisfaction has become the second priority of the Corporation, *behind* customer satisfaction and *ahead* of return on assets and market share.

In companies such as Xerox, people issues lie at the heart of business strategy: how will the company be able to attract, retain, motivate, develop, support and facilitate the contribution of those with the skills it will need to satisfy customer requirements, how might it better harness human potential?

Successful internationalization generally requires a global search for relevant expertise. In 1990 Roche, recognizing the existence of non-Swiss centres of excellence in research, acquired 60 per cent of the San Francisco-based Genentech Inc., the leading US genetic engineering company. In the same year, Roche also acquired companies in Belgium, France, Switzerland and the US and entered into research alliances with British, Japanese and US companies. Roche positioned itself for the 1990s with 15 R&D centres spread across eight countries.

HRD strategy formulation

A holistic view needs to be taken of strategy. There is a tendency in many companies to think in terms of dichotomies – perhaps the need to reconcile European and international strategy or to achieve consistency between international and local requirements. Where inconsistencies arise, as they frequently do, this is prima-facie evidence of the existence of a compartmentalized bureaucracy.

Where an international network develops organically, there is open and all-channel communication between its elements and its people are motivated by the desire to better serve the evolving needs of customers, so inconsistencies need not persist. Reconciliation should be based upon customer requirements, rather than the status of internal protagonists or their seniority within a bureaucratic hierarchy.

The strategy formulation process will reflect whether a company is an experienced or relatively new international operator:

- for a company that is already operating internationally, determining the HRD and other requirements for effective international operation is likely to be an integral part of the normal operations and existing management processes
- where an international development is either new or of some significance, a special process might need to be developed and adopted, its form depending upon the particular circumstances of the situation.

Whatever the position the company is in, care should be taken to involve all relevant interests in strategy formulation. In many cases it is preferable for a review process to be cascaded through a management and value added chain so that each function and operating unit can itself examine what is required and determine the nature of its own response.

Wherever possible, use should be made of existing processes and established activities. For example, a year-start meeting or a regular management forum or periodic conference could be used to discuss the HRD implications of an international development. As would normally be the case, any information that is given and the resulting understanding that is secured, may need to be shared with other staff who were not invited to, or able to attend, the event in question.

4.4 Business development strategy and skill requirements

A human resource element should be incorporated at each stage of formulating a business development strategy. Each organization should develop a business planning process that suits its own requirements. Figure 4.1 sets out an example of such a process. Let us analyse the individual elements given in the example.

VISION AND MISSION

The formulation of business development strategy must begin with some distinctive vision of what the organization's contribution to the world is to be. Why should it operate or continue to trade? The latter, as has been pointed out, should not be assumed in the case of an organization that does not have a purpose in terms of adding value for customers. The mission of an organization should be compelling if it is to attract the interest and commitment of both customers and suppliers of skill.

A vision and mission needs to be rooted in a customer requirement. If this is not the case, then all else will be built upon a foundation of sand.

Input considerations   *Element*   *HRD considerations*

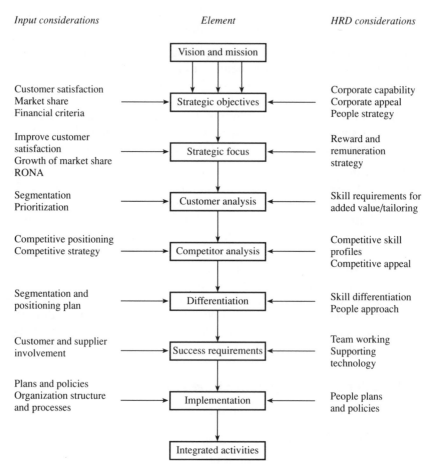

Figure 4.1   Business development strategy process

STRATEGIC OBJECTIVES

These could be set in terms of customer satisfaction, market share targets or financial criteria, such as return on net assets (RONA). When multiple objectives are set they should be compatible. For example, a RONA objective may be quite specific and perceived as achievable, while a customer satisfaction target is seen as a 'motherhood' generalization. In such circumstances RONA could be pursued at the expense of customer satisfaction.

The strategic objectives selected by a company may reflect its country of 'origin'. Thus, when compared, a US company may place a higher priority upon medium-term return on capital employed, while a Japanese competitor may be more concerned with achieving growth in market share. The Japanese company might be more willing to buy market share at a price for some years of lower rates of return that would not be regarded as adequate by the board of a US or UK company.

There are many forms of strategy that could be adopted. For example:

- a strategy could be 'offensive', designed to increase market share at the expense of a competitor
- a strategy could be opportunistic, for example, to take advantage of '1992'
- another company might have a defensive strategy of seeking to hold market share and preserve margins through cost reduction or, more positively, by quality improvement
- a survival strategy could involve significant reorganization and rationalization
- a compensating or balance strategy could encourage a company subject to short-term pressures to put a new activity into an arrangement or joint venture with another company that is able to take a longer term perspective.

Each of the above strategies will have its own human resource consequences.

People can be an important consideration when strategic objectives are set. An important objective for the Japanese company Brother is localization, recognizing and drawing upon the skills and strengths of the labour force at each corporate site. The aim is to bring out the best at each and every location.

People can be the key element of corporate capability. The ability to act quickly and to continually learn and refine, add value to and interact with customers can all depend critically upon people. People may be so important in many sectors, that competitive appeal to attract and retain staff, or a staff development strategy, could become an important consideration when strategic objectives are set.

STRATEGIC FOCUS

Examples of the strategic focus of an organization include: to improve customer satisfaction and to achieve a certain market share or reach a target level of RONA, in all cases within a given timescale. At this level, HRD considerations should also apply. For example, a reward and remuneration strategy should relate to the focus that is established.

In some companies, a remuneration and reward strategy is established quite separately from the business development strategy. When asked to give a rationalization for a particular strategy, many personnel practitioners refer to such factors as 'securing commitment'. What is really important is commitment to what?

In many companies few, if any, people are encouraged by a remuneration and reward strategy to satisfy the customer. Measures used may be internal and concerned with the company's own requirements for financial performance. A concentration upon purely financial measures can encourage managers to take action that is at the expense of the customer.

CUSTOMER ANALYSIS

An understanding of customer requirements should underlie the company's original mission, its objectives and its focus.[7] At this stage of the process the emphasis is upon the segmentation and prioritization of customer opportunities.

The nature of chosen segments will depend upon the company and the business it is in. For one company a segment may consist of millions of consumers, while, for another, a segment could consist of just one customer.

When prioritizing segments, or even individual customers, one should begin with the extent to which the company is able to add value. There may be a relatively small number of customers for whom the company could do a lot to add value and a larger number of customers for whom it could offer less added value. The contribution of people and their skills may be higher in the case of those customers where there is the greatest potential to add value. In many business sectors this high added value may come from the provision of people-intensive personal service or individual tailoring.

A company that selects a strategy of volume (see Figure 4.2) might produce relatively undifferentiated products in order to reach a large volume of customers ('a' on the chart). This might mean losing the opportunity to supply the added value above level 'b' to those customers between O and 'a'.

Another company might pursue a strategy of meeting the added value requirements of individual customers. While supplying a lower number of customers ('c' on the chart) it might, overall, supply greater added value. Which course of action makes the most sense depends upon the relative costs and profitability of tailoring versus volume production.

The human resource contribution will vary according to which strategy is selected. Whether or not value can be added for particular categories of customer will depend critically upon the availability of relevant skills and expertise.

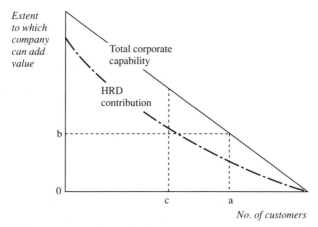

Figure 4.2   Volume versus value added strategy

COMPETITOR ANALYSIS

Traditional competitor analysis has concentrated upon competitive positioning and competitive strategy in the market-place of customers. In the emerging knowledge society, there is also a competitive market-place for the skills that are most in demand.

Whether or not a company will succeed with its chosen customer segments may be strongly influenced by the skill profiles of competitors:

– will the people of competitors be better able to supply the value sought by customers?
– are they more or less flexible, responsive and receptive to changing customer requirements or more willing to learn?
– are competitors better able to harness the talents and potential of their people?

A large UK retail chain whose existing operations are almost entirely in the UK sends selected staff on an international programme to encourage them to monitor international developments in retailing. A particular watch is kept upon potential entrants to the UK market. Staff are also asked to identify innovations and practices of competitors and overseas retailers that might be implemented in the UK. A UK utility operates an exchange programme, the main purpose of which is to learn how Continental utilities operate and tackle common problems.

Where skill shortages exist, one needs also to consider the competitive appeal of other companies to those with scarce skills. Will the company's key employees defect to a competitor that is better able to meet their needs? Will difficulties be encountered in recruiting or training the skills needed to meet the needs of the chosen customer segments?

DIFFERENTIATION

It is not easy to exaggerate the importance of differentiation. Why should customers want to buy from, and why should people wish to work for, a particular company? People around the world, both as customers and as potential employees, have a widening range of choice. Most of them have more of a choice than any generation in history. Companies and individuals need to distinguish themselves from the alternatives available. The basis of their differentiation must relate to the priority requirements of customers and suppliers of skill.

Hewlett-Packard has differentiated itself by its way of working – the loose, informal and relatively open culture appearing to encourage creativity among its highly skilled knowledge workers. The corporate culture is regarded by 'HP' managers as sufficiently strong and distinct to act as a significant retention factor. Some HP managers are sufficiently relaxed to talk of working as fun.

The skills and attitudes of an organization's people could become a key source of differentiation. In service sectors great stress is laid upon the 'people factor'. Airline advertisements, for example, feature cabin service staff. When all competitors on a route fly the same aeroplanes within a single regulatory framework, cabin service becomes an important arena of differentiation.

An organization's approach to people needs to be distinctive and it helps if the basis of differentiation can be sustained. This is more likely if a company's appeal to actual and potential suppliers of skill is based upon a number of factors, both tangible and intangible, rather than the gimmicky innovation that can be copied.

SUCCESS REQUIREMENTS

Prior to carrying out specific policies and undertaking related activities, it is important to understand the key success requirements. These may vary by customer segment and will reflect competitor activities and the chosen area of differentiation.

For many companies, success in delivering value to customers depends upon relationships with both customers and suppliers. They should be regarded as a part of the organization and it may be necessary to involve them in training and development activity. Perhaps joint and collaborative training could be undertaken:

- Rank Xerox offers a range of customer training services – Rank Xerox (UK) has opened its national training centre to customer participation and joint or collaborative training, a more capable customer being able

to better tap the potential of the goods and services that are supplied and, hence, tending to be a more satisfied customer
- a Scandinavian high-tech company secures an overview understanding of international developments within its field by asking all its suppliers, and some of its major customers, if certain of its staff could participate in their internal training programmes, which means that, not only does the company save on the cost of developing its own courses, but relationships are forged and commitment is demonstrated to both customers and suppliers.

There will be other human resource issues to consider. For example, effective teamworking may be the key to operating a new approach to account management that meets the desire of customers for fewer points of contact with a supplying company. In order to harness the full potential of both individuals and groups, more thought may need to be given to supporting technology and facilitating processes.

IMPLEMENTATION

Implementation is itself a process and should be flexible and responsive rather than mechanical.[1] Changes may be needed to organization structure, management processes and to people plans and policies in the interests of successful implementation. If modifications are not made to meet the changing requirements of customers, these may go elsewhere.

INTEGRATED ACTIVITIES

The activities that result from implementation should be integrated. There should be a common and unifying focus, namely meeting customer requirements. There is little point in commercial work for its own sake. The results of activity should be measured in terms of impact upon customer satisfaction and changes made as appropriate.

Strategy formulation and implementation needs to be thought of as a dynamic and interactive process rather than as a sequential procedure. In essence what is required is a continuous cycle of refinement and review (see Figure 4.3). The cycle will go on so long as company responses meet the needs of its customers.

Skill requirements and business development

In order to estimate the future demand for international skills, an examination should be made during the review cycle of the product profile of a company (see Figure 4.4).

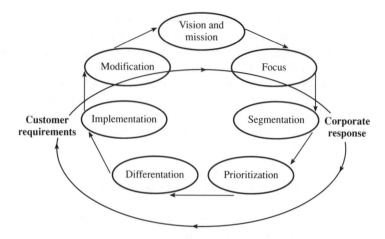

Figure 4.3 A continuous cycle of refinement and review

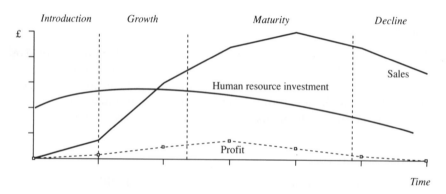

Figure 4.4 Product life cycle and HRD investment

A company introducing a product for the first time may manufacture at home for the global market. In due course the company may start to manufacture abroad, while rivals may commence the manufacture of competitive products at home and abroad. The international skills required may, therefore, shift over time from export skills to local manufacturing and selling skills.

Investment in developing relevant skills may need to precede other expenditures. Shortening skill development lead times can bring forward market revenues and profits.

Where an opportunity lies on the 'product/market expansion grid'[8] can also influence HRD strategy. For example, the requirements for skill and training will depend upon whether existing products with little or no modification are to be supplied to new overseas markets or whether new or significantly modified products are to be launched (see Figure 4.5). In the case of a new product in a new market, the training and development challenge is likely to be the greatest. Where a large investment in training is required this will need to be funded from the cash generated by more mature products.

In the case of a knowledge or service business, the *person* may well be the product. In this case new staff may need to be recruited in the local market and trading can commence as soon as they have been equipped to provide an acceptable service.

The quality of an organization's human resources can be the key to exploiting greater added value opportunities (see Figure 4.6). For example, many producers compete primarily on product quality, one of the arenas in which international competition may be the greatest and the margins the slimmest. Often there are other opportunities, such as an initial investigation of the need for the product in question or whether it might be tailored to an individual requirement. There may be post-purchase opportunities for the provision of services and various forms of support such as training and updating. This may be needed if a customer is to obtain full value from the equipment that has been purchased.

These new value added opportunities generally require people. They involve meetings with customers and building relationships with them. Value results from the interaction of individuals and team rather than the operation of the production line robot. A supplier with people 'on the ground' has a competitive advantage over another company that just ships products there from a remote location.

Internationalization of ownership

Not all internationalization strategies need be demanding of HRD input. There are routes to, and aspects of, internationalization quite apart from those involving customers or employees. Some companies are seeking to internationalize their ownership through regional or international investment in their shares:

- the Norwegian industrial group Kvaerner is listed on both the Oslo and Stockholm Stock Exchanges and on the International Stock Exchange in London; acquisitions in Finland (shipbuilding) and Sweden (energy) have consolidated its Scandinavian base; by 1991 over a quarter of total shares, but less than 14 per cent of voting shares, were held by non-Norwegians.

Market

	Present	*New*
Present	*Market penetration* Update, added value opportunities	*Market development* Mobility, skill transference
New	*Product development* Retrain, induction	*Diversification* Mobility, selection, recruitment, induction

Product

Figure 4.5 Product/market strategy and skill requirements

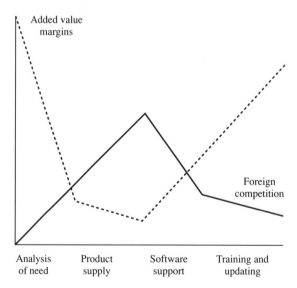

Figure 4.6 The added value chain

– the Skandia Group considers itself 'an international corporation engaged in insurance and related financial services with a home market in the Nordic countries' and its shares have been listed on the Stockholm Stock Exchange since 1863, but in 1989, they were listed on the Oslo

Stock Exchange and, during 1990, were listed on both the Copenhagen Stock Exchange and the International Stock Exchange in London – this was the first time EC rules were used to allow simultaneous introductions on more than one stock exchange through a single prospectus – outside of Germany, VEBA shares are quoted on the stock exchanges in Amsterdam, Basel, Geneva and Zurich and a survey undertaken in February 1990 found that 42.6 per cent of its share capital was held by foreign investors, but its ownership is more international than its sales, some 70 per cent of which in 1990 was still accounted for by Germany.

Many companies recognize that there is an international market for information concerning corporate performance. For example, the Swiss company Ciba-Geigy has held the press conference to announce its annual performance in London rather than Zurich in order to emphasize its international credentials.

The need for global flexibility

The international market-place, as we saw in Chapters 2 and 3, is one of considerable uncertainty and challenge. Consider some CEO's views on the prospects for South America or the Pacific Rim in the 1990s:

– *South America:*

The bureaucracy still stifles, and cutting through the red tape depends upon who you know.

Democracy is a tender plant and it could all go wrong. Dictators have traditionally waited in the wings for economic collapse and opportunities to restore order.

The region is short of investment, finance, skills and infrastructure. Freer and more open markets are an aspiration, but they have yet to be achieved.

– *the Pacific Rim:*

The introduction of greater political pluralism could be a source of uncertainty, but it's increasingly a place to go to for software skills or to get things made.

Japan's growing economic investment in 'offshore" production could give it greater political leverage.

One by one the high-tech sectors, with their associated skills, will fall to Japan's relentless drive for competitiveness. They will go after higher added value opportunities.

Global HRD strategy needs to be able to cope with major, even revolutionary, changes in the business environment. The dramatic developments in Eastern Europe and the former Soviet Union that occurred over the period 1989–90 have had a very significant impact upon many companies and taking advantage of emerging opportunities has tested the flexibility of their personnel practitioners.

For many companies, the former 'iron curtain' between Eastern and Western Europe represented a business as well as political barrier:

- three quarters of the business of the Brussels-based Solvay Group had derived from Western Europe prior to 1990 and, only following political changes in the East, did the company make its first significant investment in Central Europe by taking a stake in a Hungarian company; discussions were also initiated in Poland, Czechoslovakia and Yugoslavia
- Sweden's Electrolux has also been prepared to take the plunge: Electrolux acquired Lehel, the largest white-goods company in Hungary in March of 1991 as 'part of efforts to create a base for expansion in Eastern Europe'.

Problems create opportunities. The infrastructure needs of Eastern Germany have had a major impact upon German companies:

- the investment strategy of the German industrial group VIAG has been significantly affected by the reunification of Germany and, for example, its energy division is helping to establish an electricity and gas supply system in the post-unification Lander of Eastern Germany.
- by 1991 over a quarter of the DM 30 billion medium-term capital spending programme of VEBA was to be invested in Eastern Germany and during 1990, all divisions of the VEBA group became active in the five new Lander – VEBA has become particularly active in the area of power supply.

HRD requirements must reflect changing international business priorities. Asea Brown Boveri has recognized the special development needs of those in Eastern Europe. Within months of the political changes that had occurred, several hundred managers and engineers from Eastern Europe had participated in various ABB seminars.

The opportunities that exist in Eastern Europe are accompanied by great uncertainties. Within a year of the demise of Communist regimes, Marc Moret, Chairman and Chief Executive Officer of the Swiss company Sandoz, could refer to, 'the frustration of hopes for economic renewal in the countries of Eastern Europe, where much of the euphoria has vanished as implementation of the necessary reforms has proved to be considerably more difficult than expected'.

Some companies that had established business operations in Eastern Europe suffered a loss of sales as a result of the upheaval that occurred. For example, the lack of currency for imports had an adverse effect upon the 1990 sales of the welding company Esab. Not all international events are beneficial.

Rapid accommodation to changing circumstances is the hallmark of the international company. The German pharmaceutical and chemical company Schering quickly opened new technical information offices in most Central and Eastern European countries during 1990. Forseeing the possibility of political fragmentation in the Soviet Union, Schering 'established new business ties with the individual republics within the USSR'.

Check-list

- Does your company have a clear and shared vision and, if so, does it need to be refined in the light of the international dimension?
- In particular, to what extent is human resources a limiting factor and a critical success factor for your company?
- Does your company have an international HRD strategy and, if so, is this integrated with its international business development strategy?
- Does it also reflect the requirements of major customers and groups of customers?
- Has the personnel function in your company participated in roles and responsibilities exercises to ensure that all significant human resource issues are taken into account and the potential contribution of the function is understood?
- Should your company introduce new patterns of work in order to secure more flexible access to international skills?
- What should your company do to ensure more effective employee involvement in the light of the differences of approach and practice between national labour markets?
- Who are the key players and opinion formers at each level in your company and do they understand the critical importance of human resources in the context of internationalization?

References

1. Coulson-Thomas, Colin, and Trudy Coe, *The Flat Organisation: Philosophy and Practice*, British Institute of Management, 1991.
2. Coulson-Thomas, Colin, and Susan Coulson-Thomas, *Quality: The Next Steps*, an Adaptation survey sponsored by ODI International, Adaptation and ODI International, 1991.
3. Coulson-Thomas, Colin, and Susan Coulson-Thomas, *Communicating for Change*, an Adaptation survey sponsored by Granada Business Services, Adaptation, 1991.
4. Coulson-Thomas, Colin, and Alan Wakelam, *The Effective Board: Current Practice, Myths and Realities*, an Institute of Directors discussion document, Institute of Directors, 1991.
5. Coulson-Thomas, Colin, *Creating Excellence in the Boardroom*, McGraw-Hill, 1992.

6. Coulson-Thomas, Colin and Richard Brown, *The Responsive Organisation: People Management – the Challenge of the 1990s*, British Institute of Management, 1989.
7. Coulson-Thomas, Colin, 'Customers': Marketing and the Network Organisation, *Journal of Marketing Management*, pp 237–55, Vol. 7, 1991.
8. Ansoff, H Igor, 'Strategies for Diversification', *Harvard Business Review*, pp 113–24, September–October, 1957.

Further reading

Bartram, Peter, and Colin Coulson-Thomas, *The Complete Spokesperson: A workbook for managers who meet the media*, Kogan Page, 1991.

Bartlett, Christopher A, Yves Doz and Gunnar Hedlund, *Managing the Global Firm*, Routledge, 1990.

Burgenmeier, B, and Jean-Louis Mucchielli, *Multinationals and Europe 1992*, Routledge, 1991.

Connock, Stephen, *HR Vision: Managing a Quality Workforce*, Institute of Personnel Management, 1991.

Coulson-Thomas, Colin J, *The Change Makers: Vision and Communication*, Booklet to accompany Sir John Harvey-Jones, *et al.*, *The Change Makers*, Didacticus Video Productions/Video Arts, 1991.

Dudley, J W, *1992 – Strategies for the Single Market*, Kogan Page in association with the Chartered Institute of Management Accountants, 1989.

Eli, Max, *Japan Inc.: Global Strategies of Japanese Trading Companies*, McGraw-Hill, 1990.

Evans, Paul, Yves Doz, and André Laurent (Eds), *Human Resource Management in International Firms: Change, Globalization, Innovation*, Macmillan, 1989.

Johnson, Chalmers, *Revolutionary Change*, Little, Brown & Company, 1966.

Lynch, Richard, *European Business Strategies*, Kogan Page, 1991.

Manpower PLC., *Employment and Training*, Mercury Books/CBI Initiative 1992, 1990.

5
Evaluating international opportunities

Perspectives

We evaluate international opportunities with our customers. They come out of account teams and good account management. You don't need to invent them – just talk to your customers.

Vice-President, US office products, multinational corporation

They come to me when they have problems. Generally, it is then too late. Arabic law applies, which they don't understand. If they came to me first, we could prepare the ground for any problems that are likely to arise.

Saudi Arabian lawyer

Although separated by the Atlantic our industrial bases used to compete. Both of our industries have gone under and we are now competing for Japanese inward investment.

Director, industrial development corporation

In our industry and others we draw up our criteria, apply them and come to our decisions. Then the US reaches a new 'understanding' with Japan on imports and all of a sudden the numbers are different. Our target market can go up or down overnight without any reference to anything we can do.

Owner director, US vehicle distributor

By the time a full 'country analysis' has been undertaken, we have looked at all the incentives and our professional advisers have made all the money they can from us, the business opportunity is sometimes forgotten. I usually ask: 'is anyone going to buy it?' I once got a 'probably not' from one group that had satisfied every corporate guideline in sight.

Director, international publishing company

You can put in your investment, but that doesn't give you the close network of supply chain relationships your Japanese competitors will have built up over many years.

Japanese representative of UK company

Going and talking to customers is better than research reports. We send people to live in local markets. Their task is to find out about life-style aspirations. The strength of the drive of people to consume and feel good is important to us, not a mass of data on what they have done in the past.

Marketing Director, Japanese manufacturer of consumer products

5.1 Introduction

Senior personnel staff and human resource professionals should be involved in the analysis of international opportunities. This requires an understanding of the context within which such opportunities occur. There are a number of models and approaches that can help to clarify the general business and people issues involved.

In this chapter we will examine some strategic HRD and financial considerations that apply when evaluating international opportunities. It is important that personnel practitioners understand the risks involved in international operations and these will also be explored.

5.2 Involving a people perspective

In some companies the evaluation of international opportunities is largely a matter for marketing and business development teams. On occasion the personnel specialist is brought in after the lawyers have finished their work, only to discover a host of human resource problems in the implementation of what is sought. It may then be too late to avoid some of these problems.

Rather than being left to pick up the pieces, personnel staff should be included in the review team whenever significant international developments are considered. This can enable an early identification of likely people problems. With human skill increasingly emerging as a key success factor, the personnel function, or a personnel perspective, should be involved at the outset.

Such an involvement should begin with the strategy considerations underlying an internationalization policy, the:

- vision and mission
- strengths and weaknesses
- opportunities and threats
- critical success factors
- limiting constraints
- maximizing added value
- value chain relationships.

A limiting constraint could be a strategy consideration. For example:

- a company with a high share of a domestic market may find it more difficult to achieve incremental gains at home than in a foreign market, while, on the other hand, it is the constraints of a limited home market that have caused several Scandinavian companies to seek opportunities abroad
- in some cases the investigations of national anti-trust authorities, such as the UK Monopolies and Mergers Commission, may inhibit the creation or extension of what is considered to be 'market dominance', while the opportunities for market share growth may be greater in those markets that are fragmented and those within which there are few major players.

We considered the importance of a clear vision and mission in the last chapter and, from this, we can see how corporate values can be strongly influenced by vision and how core values can become a significant element of a philosophy of business. An international business can be faced with the challenge of maintaining and sharing company values across national borders and reconciling them with a diversity of local cultures. People in all these locations may need to be actively involved in sharing the vision as it is generally preferable for an international perspective to evolve. Attempts to *impose* an international vision, and a perspective derived from it, can cause resentment.

General Electric of the US uses work-out sessions to spread understanding and encourage involvement. All managers are required to share their visions with their teams. Members of the group are then given an opportunity to reflect and comment. By such means a vision can be cascaded through an organization, with each unit or team ensuring that its own vision is compatible with a wider corporate vision.

The strengths and weaknesses of a company could include the availability of, or a shortage of, skills. BT, for example, emerged, post-privatization, as a commercial giant, but with many of its managers lacking any experience of competitive markets. It took some time to assemble a team able to formulate and implement an international strategy.

Similarly, access to needed skills could be an important element of an opportunity, while the possible loss of skills to a poaching competitor could represent a significant threat. In the IT industry, technology and capital move increasingly freely across national borders. The acquisition in 1990 by Fujitsu of Japan of an 80 per cent shareholding in the UK national champion ICL appears in large part to have been motivated by Fujitsu's desire to secure access to European software development skills.

For many knowledge-based companies, human skill and experience will be a critical success factor.[1] For some it will be a limiting constraint, growth being held back by a lack of skills. People considerations in such a case will be paramount.

The internationalization of some Japanese companies is being frustrated by a shortage of Japanese managers with experience of setting up operations abroad. A company that has hitherto supplied all its customers from a manufacturing base in Japan may find that it has few non-Japanese employees. Many Japanese managers are reluctant to move abroad and the track record of the management of foreign acquisitions by Japanese companies is not good.

Whether or not a proposed venture will succeed can largely depend upon selecting the right people to run it. This is particularly true of establishing business units abroad. In the case of a joint venture between the US component supplier Elco and Nagoya Screw Manufacturing of Japan, some time has been required for a degree of mutual understanding of quite distinct US and Japanese attitudes and approaches to emerge. It can take years to recover from an initial adverse reputation that results from putting the wrong people in charge of a programme to open up a particular market.

We will see in Chapter 7 that particular skills and competencies are required for successful international operation. These are largely a question of attitude, approach and perspective. An international outlook or perspective may be a requirement for success in certain sectors and can, of itself, lead to opportunities to add value for customers.

A company that focuses upon the customer is likely to be driven by *their* requirements rather than its *own* desire for expansion.[2] This approach could lead to incremental business opportunities:

– the 1990s is likely to see a significant increase in competition in the global telecommunications market-place because liberalization is being accompanied by developments in optical fiber, satellites and radio links that have reduced the time and cost of developing alternatives to public telecom networks: Swedish Telecom entered the 1990s with a quarter of its traffic revenues deriving from international calls, the company's customers including some of the world's most international companies – ABB, Electrolux, Saab-Scania, SKF and Volvo – and its international strategy is to 'accompany' these customers outside of Sweden by providing 'total solutions for data, text, voice and image communication', which requires close collaboration with the customers themselves and foreign telecom companies and participation in international cable and satellite projects
– Du Pont has recognized the opportunity created by accelerated Japanese investment in European manufacturing that has enabled them to par-

ticipate in the single market and Du Pont's approach to this opportunity is global: 'The company is working in Japan to be specified as a supplier, so that Du Pont's European subsidiaries are seen as business partners as Japanese automobile production expands in Europe. Du Pont employs Japanese marketers in Europe to work with Japanese company managers relocated there'.

In many incremental market opportunities, a production and distribution base for the supply of high-quality products may already exist. The key to adding further value for customers may lie in local service and support or tailoring to their local requirements.[2] To do this may be largely a matter of identifying and developing those with relevant skills and experience. Human resource should be an integral part of this and other aspects of strategy consideration.

Japanese companies appear to pay particular attention to people considerations.[3] The shift of Japanese production to Asia has been the result of labour shortages at home and lower labour costs abroad. Japanese investment abroad is also motivated by a desire to outflank trade barriers.

5.3 International opportunity analysis

An international opportunity could be investigated from the perspective of an individual product, a function, a division or strategic business (SBU) or of a company as a whole. In Chapter 4 we saw how a total business could have a variety of reasons for seeking to internationalize and so it is with product and SBU teams. Some possible SBU objectives in respect of a particular market are:

- market entry
- market penetration
- market maintenance
- vertical integration
- partnerships
- harvest/milk
- build added value
- to improve quality
- speed of response
- rationalization
- market exit.

The people consequences of each objective could be very different.

The most exhaustive techniques for evaluating international opportunities are those that pass the total population of possible international sectors or national markets through a series of filters. At each stage those international sectors or countries that do not satisfy the criteria of the filter in question are eliminated:

- a first filter could consist of macro-level criteria, such as economic potential and the prospects for economic growth or the stability of the political environment
- a second filter could be the general market situation relating to similar products, e.g., consumption trends, market size, cultural acceptance, etc.
- a third filter could consist of factors that relate specifically to the product in question, such as the nature of competition and any specific barriers to entry, such as standards and technical requirements
- the final filter could consist of factors that relate to the individual company, for example, its treasury requirements relating to access to funds or whether its ownership or domicile might be an impediment to business.

At the end of this process of sequential elimination, relatively few sectors or countries may remain and these can be subjected to more extensive analysis. At least the number of options will have been reduced to manageable proportions.

Final selection decisions can sometimes be finely balanced – should a European leisure park be built outside London or Paris, should a European research centre be located at Cambridge, in the south of France or at Munich? As more companies become aware of the importance of supply chain relationships,[2] factors of particular importance are:

- proximity to customers and suppliers – physical proximity may be a necessary, but not a sufficient, condition for success as it may need to be matched by action to overcome 'attitudinal distance'
- the availability of communications, telecommunications and other business services as these form the corporate 'life support' system.

Similar selection criteria can result in widely separated location options. A search for a significant development site that is close to air and other links, with a supply of labour with heavy industry skills and supported by new infrastructure investments, could throw up both Pittsburg in the USA *and* Sheffield in the UK. In each case, urban redevelopment agencies have been 'reclaiming' large sites and actively encouraging inward investments.

Market entry options

An organization may have a preferred market entry strategy. Some possible strategies are:

– greenfield start-up
– licence/agency arrangements
– strategic alliances
– joint ventures
– acquisition and merger
– trading relationships.

These may have already proved their worth in the company's product-market context, in which case, existing preferences will colour the filtering of new information. The more flexible the company, the more willing it will be to tailor a market entry strategy to the requirements of each distinct market.

There is some evidence of distinct national approaches to overseas market entry.[3] For example, whereas a UK company might acquire a local company in order to enter the US market, a Japanese supplier might conclude a joint venture, while a German competitor might explore the possibilities for start-up and organic growth. Once a local base has been established, *all* the growth options can be explored according to circumstances and opportunities.

Each company may have its own reasons for adopting a particular strategy, for example:

– Hanson has built up a significant business empire in the US as a result of an acquisition strategy and, in doing this, it has followed the pattern of its operations in the UK
– the French company Alcatel acquired the transmission equipment division of Rockwell International not because of a past pattern of operation, but because, within the context of a global market-place, it wished to increase its presence in the US quickly.

Information and opportunity

The organization with an international network is able to quickly access information about market opportunities and communicate this to the individuals and groups best able to respond.[4] At the international level, there are many hundreds of databases in various countries of the world that can be accessed through a compatible terminal.

At the national level there are relevant services. For example, in the UK:

– there is the DTI's SPEARHEAD 1992 and BOTIS database or the computerized 'export intelligence service'
– updating information on 1992 can also be obtained by fax from HMSO's DOCUFAX service.

At the regional level, there are a growing number of relevant services. For example, in the case of Europe:

- a company could subscribe to the Tenders Electronic Daily (TED) database and receive each day details of public tenders, in specified industry sectors, that are issued in the EC
- a company could obtain contact details of potential business partners through the Business Cooperation Network, or, BC-NET
- a wealth of statistical information covering a variety of economic, trade and social indicators can be obtained from Eurostat, as can sector and country data, covering Central and Eastern Europe.

As well as BC-NET, there are other routes within the EC to the identification of possible business partners:

- the small- or medium-sized enterprise (SME) could make use of the Bureau De Rapprochement Des Entreprises (BRE) network of correspondents to search for business partners
- there are also more specific EC initiatives such as the Europartenariat, which has an objective of encouraging partnerships between firms in less developed regions and those in other member states and outside the community
- the INTERPRISE programme is designed to encourage business cooperation, particularly of SMEs, within countries or an area of a particular country.

So *much* data may be available that there could be a danger of information overload. The response that goes out is more important than the information that comes in. Not all of it will be of a consistent quality so it is important to be selective. Indeed, access to relevant experience and judgement may be more important than information *per se*. A small group at the top of a bureaucratic organization that makes flexible use, as individual issues emerge, of inputs from those of external peer groups with more relevant understanding might increase the intelligence available to their company at the level concerned manyfold.

Acquisitions

PEOPLE AND ACQUISITIONS

Where skill and knowledge are important ingredients of competitive advantage, human resource questions should be considered when a diversification or acquisition option is being evaluated. To help distinguish between alternatives, one could map out or compare their characteristics by means of a series of matrices.

In Figure 5.1, the two aspects being considered are whether an acquisition or diversification target can be achieved by looking at whether the company has the key skills needed for market success and whether it has compatible personnel 'arrangements' where an 'arrangement' means, for example remuneration policy or a career planning system. The most attractive option is clearly one for which relevant skills are present *and* there is compatibility of personnel arrangements. The least attractive option is where neither of these conditions are present, however attractive it is in principle.

As well as considering the availability of people skills, it is also important to consider its cost. Germany has become less attractive as a location and source of acquisition targets as a result of relatively high employment and social costs. A US company that has traditionally reorganized at will may not relish the thought of long discussions with 'the social partner' following an acquisition in Germany.

Where personnel arrangements appear to be incompatible, an investigation could be undertaken into whether or not, and at what cost, compatibility might be achieved. Similarly, if key skills for market success are *not* present, one could examine the extent to which they could be developed or transferred. It may be that any gaps which emerge could be bridged in the case of one prospect, but not in the case of another.

Key questions to be asked when assessing a prospect prior to an acquisition will be those concerning the quality of the organization and human resources. The potential acquirer should explore the extent to which the target's people complement its own, are relevant to its customer needs and are likely to be retained following an acquisition. The cooperation of the target acquisition may not be achieved and the investigation may need to be undertaken on an external basis.

The experience of the UK's Midland Bank with Crocker Bank in the US illustrates the need for careful investigation and relevant skills. Some international moves *will* result in failure and, in these situations, the focus of further evaluation should be to learn from mistakes. In the Midland-Crocker case, the failure was such as to pose some threat to the competitive position of the group as a whole.

As acquisitions have become more common in competitive markets, so senior executives of many companies have concluded new contracts of employment to protect their interests in the event of a takeover. Some of these may be so favourable to those involved as to constitute a poison pill deterrent to an acquisition. It is important that such arrangements, which

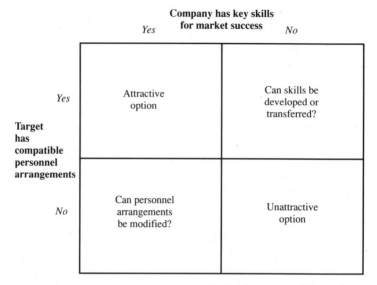

Figure 5.1 Weighing up whether a diversification or acquisition target can be achieved given the company's skills

may involve substantial termination payments, are understood, particularly when they relate to directors and key staff.

Great flexibility may be required in acquisition and arrangement situations as the involvement of national and regional regulatory authorities can delay the implementation of a proposed joint venture. As a consequence of such involvement, and of other foreseen and unforeseen factors, what emerges can be far removed from the original plans. It took GEC and Siemens about a year to acquire Plessey and the two companies ended up running only *one* of Plessey's businesses as a joint venture, rather than the *nine* that had been intended.

ACQUISITION MANAGEMENT

So what has been acquired? Reality may differ from expectation. It is sometimes easy to confuse form and substance. Providing customers with reassurance concerning a continuation and enhancement of service may be the priority, not imposing the trappings of new corporate ownership.

It may be possible to impose a superficial degree of homogeneity upon an international organization by adopting a standard logo and a corporate-wide set of operating procedures, which masks fundamental disagreement on key matters of strategy. Following an acquisition it may be particularly important to ensure that all the parties involved are in full agreement as to how a local market opportunity should best be developed. Where the acquired organization is to be given considerable discretion, it is important that its management fully understand the vision and mission of the international network it has joined.

While not wishing to disrupt ongoing activities or to imply a lack of trust, it may be necessary to closely monitor the performance of the acquired company's management for a period following an acquisition. If this is not done, hoped for benefits may not materialize. Where an acquired company has satisfactory relationships with its customers, there may be much that an acquiring organization can learn. If changes need to be introduced, it may be sensible to make them relatively soon after an acquisition has been concluded.

The acquisition by Whirlpool of the 'white goods' business of Philips was accomplished in stages. From the outset both groups exhibited a commitment to learn from each other. Identifying early opportunities for two-way skill and technology transfer can smooth post-acquisition integration. Following an acquisition, human resource professionals may need to be closely involved in the integration of a new unit into the rest of the organization. The company's management style, culture and organization might suggest some danger areas. For example:

– a bureacratic company may impose a range of changes upon a new acquisition in order to achieve consistency with its own systems and procedures
– in a more flexible network organization, there may be greater tolerance of the continuation of processes and practices with which local staff are familiar.

Consistency and compatibility should not be sought for their own sakes. Care should be taken not to disrupt ongoing and satisfactory relationships. The acid test should be the extent to which proposed changes are beneficial to *customers*.

Another consideration will be the extent to which change can be introduced within the framework of the local labour law that is applicable. Local labour law and practice (as we will see in Chapter 9) may act as a constraint upon the achievement of a preferred post-acquisition course of action. An organization that wishes to operate effectively across national borders must accept the need for flexibility in response to local circumstances.

Arrangements and joint ventures

An acquisition may not be the only option or even the preferred choice. When objectives are shared and complementary resources can work together for the benefit of customers, some form of arrangement or joint venture between companies may be possible. An example of a relationship that has evolved is that between ICI and EniChem of Italy. Following a period of commercial and marketing cooperation, the two companies each transferred assets and resources to a joint venture plastics company, European Vinyls Corporation. This subsequently became Europe's largest PVC manufacturer.

How such an arrangement might best be managed will depend upon the circumstances. The more self-contained a joint venture is and the better able it is to operate independently in the market-place, the greater the responsibility that may be given to its management. These factors need to be borne in mind when opportunities are evaluated.

The amount and quality of information about prospective arrangement or joint venture partners can vary greatly across countries. Elsewhere in the EC, corporate information is often less accessible than is the case in the UK. Available databases are sometimes limited and, in certain sectors, a significantly higher proportion of companies may be in private hands.

Effective ventures are those that bring together complementary skills. The parties should focus and build upon what they have in common:

- a long-running and successful joint venture is Fuji–Xerox, a 50:50 joint venture between Rank Xerox, itself having a UK–US joint venture parentage, and Fuji Film company of Japan – drawing upon the complementary strengths of its constituent elements, Xerox has successfully fought off formidable market-place challenges.[5]
- a more recent and hitherto successful US–Japanese joint venture is that between Caterpillar Tractor and Mitsubishi Heavy Industries in the hydraulic excavator field
- Scandinavian Airlines System (SAS) is a good example of an enterprise that resulted from international negotiation between both governmental and private interests.

However, many latent international joint venture possibilities founder during the course of detailed negotiations:

- early in 1991 British Aerospace and Thomson-CSF announced the adjournment of their plans to merge some areas of their businesses in the light of changes of circumstances that had occurred during the course of their negotiations
- an arrangement in the publishing industry between Pearson of the UK and Elsevier of the Netherlands that began in 1988 with a cross-shareholding agreement also subsequently failed to meet the original aspirations of the parties.

Further organizational and management considerations relating to joint ventures are considered in Chapter 6.

5.4 Location decisions

The key factors influencing those interviewed when they choose locations for inward investments are set out below.

The *decisive factors* are:

- customer requirements
- access to skills, especially higher level skills
- likely future availability of skills
- immediate skill environment (e.g., local technological university?)
- state of labour relations.

The *cost factors* are:

- local employment costs
- specific financial incentives
- congestion costs
- value chain costs.

The *pragmatic factors* are:

- component supply and sub-contractors
- availability of a suitable site
- transport and relevant infrastructure (e.g., telecommunications).

The *general factors* are:

- general economic, social and business/legal environment
- proximity to markets
- opportunity for creating a shareholder base.

The *quality of life factors* are:

- housing, education, crime, etc.
- sun, sea and sand.

In many cases, especially with high-tech, R&D and high value-added investments, the most decisive factors involve the availability of skills. Without suitable people *any* proposal is a non-starter.

The factors that followed in priority were financial considerations, such as the cost of the skills that were sought and whether special financial incentives were available for inward investors, plus pragmatic considerations, such as the availability of a site. Infrastructure considerations, such as the availability of telecommunications and transportation services, were also important. Compared with a few years ago, it appears that less weight is now attached to 'quantitative analysis' and more importance is, instead, attached to qualitative factors, such as the quality of skills and skill potential.

Many other general and 'quality of life' factors were mentioned, but these tend to be considered once a prima-facie case for a possible investment has been made on the basis of skill and site quality. Quality of life considerations appear most important in the case of think tanks, R&D teams and other specialist groups.

The relative importance of individual factors will vary between companies. Transportation and proximity to markets will increase in importance in proportion to the bulk and weight of a product in relation to its value and to whether any special transportation and storage arrangements need to be made. Not surprisingly, a number of companies may take a similar view of the merits of some locations over others. Apple, Compaq and Rank Xerox are among high-tech companies that have established European distribution centres in the Netherlands. The Wincanton Group, a transportation specialist, has done likewise.

Within the EC, many companies seeking to be closer to their markets appear attracted to the golden triangle economic heartland of the Community (see Figure 5.2). This is also an area of skill shortages in many business sectors. When the availability of labour is the decisive factor, the peripheral regions of the EC, such as Spain and Portugal or the Republic of Ireland, become more attractive. Labour cost was a significant factor in the decision of Ford and Volkswagen to locate their multipurpose vehicle project in Portugal.

The investigation of short list options should involve a search for key differentiators. For example:

- a local community and local institutions can have visions that may or may not be compatible with that of a company, for example, a company intent on becoming a learning network might be attracted to Birkenhead in the UK where Wirral Metropolitan College has made significant investments in learning technology
- national practices, such as centralized bargaining, may distort local labour markets – a company examining options in Italy might find that although wage levels in the South have been catching up those in the North, productivity may have lagged some way behind
- local planning restrictions sometimes prevent a move to what would otherwise be an attractive location, for example, a retailer might find Italian planning restrictions particularly difficult to penetrate

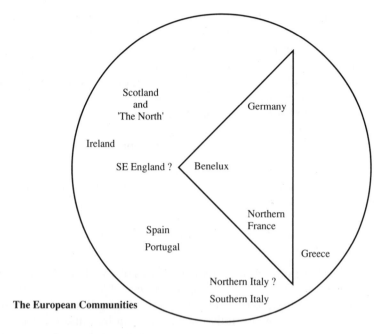

Figure 5.2   The 'golden triangle'

– in another market, there could be historic or regulatory factors that are particularly significant for a particular sector – in Denmark, for example, a significant volume of trade may be in the hands of the cooperative movement – while there could be other restrictions, such as licensing laws, health and safety requirements or other limits on hours of opening.

Relocation, like politics, is 'the art of the possible'.

Centres of excellence

Units that can learn from each other could be placed together, while there are often advantages in locating staff functions as close to customers as possible. Nestlé has relocated its product managers, who used to be based at its corporate headquarters, to individual business units at various points around the world. The locations chosen are those thought to be most appropriate for the activity in question. Clustered activities form international centres of excellence.

Price Waterhouse selected Menlo Park in California as the location for its international Technology Centre. The Centre is the focus of the firm's global technology assessment and development activities. The library and information services at Menlo Park are linked to those of a cluster of local research establishments, including the centres of Apple, Hewlett-Packard and Xerox Corporation, and several units of Stanford University.

To avoid particular locations becoming part of the 'periphery' of a network, as many significant centres as possible could be encouraged to become the global focal point of some activity or responsibility. Each major operating unit could be encouraged to act as a home base, core or centre of excellence. IBM has adopted this approach in Europe. There are dangers:

- too many centres with regional or global responsibilities could lead to a loss of the synergistic and 'interaction' advantages of co-locating activities
- too few could lead those centres not chosen to act as the hub of sub-networks within a network to feel excluded.

Coopers and Lybrand has established Centres of Excellence at particular offices around the world to act as an international focus of expertise and best practice methodologies. The Centres of Excellence can provide national practices with specialist backup as required and offer international training, as well as facilitating the transfer of knowledge between practices that increasingly understand the extent to which they are interdependent and need to match the world-wide requirements of clients. Daimler-Benz has reorganized its research activities into 'centres of competence', each of which has a particular area of focus.

5.5 Economic and financial considerations

International expansion can result in economies of scale, an increased utilization of capacity and can assist further movement along a learning curve. For a business as a whole, the possibility of such outcomes can itself act as a spur to international expansion.

The activities of a personnel function can similarly be affected by an increased scale of operation. The fixed cost of a central personnel function might be spread across a larger number of operating units. The capacity utilization of an international training centre might be increased.

Likely outcomes should be assessed not assumed. Economies of scale will not necessarily be the result of an international expansion. For example, a central facility might already be fully utilized and so a further increase in capacity may prove expensive. Having to accommodate additional differences of culture might also raise average costs.

Establishing operations abroad could secure access to cheaper resources or enable an activity to be established at a more favourable location. Alternatively, the cost of employing an incremental trainer or of buying in development services may rise when a new operation is established in a high wage economy.

Whether or not to establish one's own operation or continue to buy in an external service from an agency will depend upon a number of factors. These include quality, relevance, availability, flexibility and cost. At low levels of activity or throughput or in the case of a one off requirement, it might be cheaper to buy in (see Figure 5.3). At higher levels of activity, even with fixed and setting up costs, it may be cheaper to establish one's own operation. When assessing local start-up costs it should be borne in mind that these will not necessarily reflect equivalent domestic costs.

Incremental international developments will not necessarily involve more of the same. The opportunity should be taken to examine the scope for achieving improvements in operating efficiency as a result of a changed international division of labour.

Evaluating the financial aspects

Jimmy Cliff
" I can see clearly now "

When deciding on a course of action, it may be important to distinguish between marginal and average costs. While there may be budgets to cover the marginal costs and revenues of a new activity, what will the impact of it be upon existing operations and average costs? Will these rise or fall and how will this affect contribution and profit margins?

One should also be aware of the differences between incremental and sunk costs. Sunk costs have already been spent and will not be affected by new activities. When deciding whether or not to proceed, it is the incremental costs and incremental revenues that should be considered. A preoccupation with recovering sunk costs or past investments, can result in an organization failing to grasp opportunities whose incremental revenues may exceed their incremental costs. Such projects can yield a contribution to current overheads.

In some instances an international expansion may allow a central personnel department to derive an income from the supply of a service abroad. Where the manpower does not exist to provide a service directly, it may still be possible to secure a return from one's know-how. For example, a licence might be granted to an overseas operation or organization to use training materials that have been developed.

A caution is needed here. A number of the companies that stress the need to focus upon core activities are, at the same time, tenaciously holding on to specialist and staff functions that could be considered *not* to form part of the core. In some cases, considerable effort is being devoted

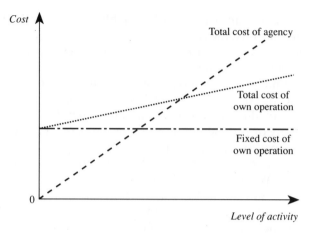

Figure 5.3   Agency versus own operation

to recouping a proportion of what are seen as overhead costs by charging for services provided to other organizations. Much less effort appears to be devoted to questioning whether the activity should be done at all, or done differently, from the perspective of the extent to which it benefits customers.

Overhead justification

A new activity abroad can provide a central group with a fresh opportunity to reassess the service that it provides and the extent to which this could be tailored. A service function that is responsive to the requirements of its users or customers needs to be aware of, and prepared to negotiate, a trade-off between quality, cost and time (see Figure 5.4). Where speed of reaction is of critical importance, it may be worth a cost premium, but, on the other hand, bureaucratic delay can itself lead to higher costs.

Central and head office functions are facing greater pressure to justify their levels of staffing and the overhead costs their existence imposes upon operating units.[6] Such functions should be required to demonstrate the value they are adding to a business in comparison with the costs.

In some companies, the emphasis is shifting from cost-cutting and delayering, which can result in negative and defensive attitudes, to assessing customer requirements and positive opportunities to contribute, which can lead to a more open and balanced evaluation.

When delayering and reorganization occurs, it is important that the staff who remain are properly equipped to handle their new responsibilities. There is evidence to suggest that often this has not been the case.[7]

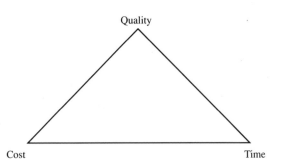

Figure 5.4   Trade-offs

On occasion, experts will provide more detail than is required so that, in effect, the quality of output may be too high. Relevant information and understanding is rarely cost free; less relevant information may be in abundance and relatively cheap. Working with information to improve its quality and relevance, especially when a number of people are involved, can be relatively expensive. (See Figure 5.5).

In addition, there is also the opportunity cost of the time spent on one activity rather than another. The service may be desired and worthwhile, but could the resources be used to better effect elsewhere?

5.6 International risk

International expansion can result in new exposures to sources of risk that may be different in kind from those experienced in the domestic market-place:

- overseas customers may have quite different attitudes towards obligations and commitments as expectations and levels of understanding among equivalent customers, staff and among users of products and services can vary greatly between countries
- there may be unique risk factors relating to operations in a particular country – for example, those of a certain religious or ethnic background might be discriminated against, sudden restrictions might be imposed upon the flow of goods, services, people, money, information or technology or measures could be introduced that discriminate against foreign company operations
- there may be international risks associated with international trade negotiations, embargoes or conflict, such as trade with a whole region being affected by a dispute between two or more neighbouring states and the employees becoming pawns in such disputes

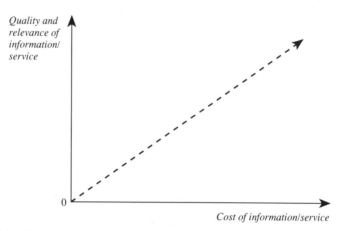

Figure 5.5 The cost and quality graph for information or service

- one should not forget the risks associated with a dependence upon suppliers – an existing supplier may not be able to support activities in a certain country or region and, while no restrictions may apply to a company's products and staff, they might apply to those of a supplier.
- personnel professionals should be aware of the major risks that apply to securing and providing needed skills, so it may be advisable to undertake some form of formal assessment of the risks involved (see Figure 5.6) – where the risks associated with a customer or supplier are low, but those of operating in a country are high, a company could aim to maximize home-based value added and, when the reverse is the case, that is the country risk is low but the customer or supplier risk is high, then arrangements concerning people should be contracted with care and steps taken to minimize the risk of financial loss
- finally, there are financial risks to be managed, such as currency risks and exchange control risks. Relative currency movements can affect both costs and revenues.

There may also be further risks that reflect the business sector a company is in. For Swedish can and packaging company PLM AB, international trade restrictions on flows of agricultural products affect the demand for its products. Changes in the weather also often affect consumption more than do the general states of national economies. A warm dry summer means high sales of cans of drink and demand for tinned vegetables depends on whether or not harvests are bountiful. PLM's internationalization programme, by widening its geographic coverage has reduced its susceptability to climatic variables.

Country and/or international

Low risk   *High risk*

	Country and/or international Low risk	Country and/or international High risk
Low risk	Priority, relatively free people access/supply	Can services/ value added by people be supplied from UK ?
High risk	Negotiate individual arrangements at relatively high prices	Avoid restrictions/barriers to people access/supply

Customer and/or supplier

Figure 5.6   Risk assessment

For many companies, employment costs can represent a substantial proportion of total operating costs. Developments within the EC add to the risks associated with the cost of employing people in Europe. The UK government calculated that the five draft EC employment Directives produced in 1990 would add some £3 billion to the costs of UK employers. It expressed concern that Europe's employers should not be put at a competitive disadvantage as a result of bearing higher social costs than those of companies overseas.

At a number of points this book stresses the advantages of the more flexible use of skills. The EC proposals would make part-time and temporary work more expensive for employers and more difficult to introduce. The UK government has estimated that the direct costs of these proposals to UK employers would be about £1 billion. This possible prospect increases the risks associated with new patterns of work.

The significance of international risks

The people and other risks involved in an international development should be lower the greater the experience a company has of the products and services in question and of similar market situations (see Figure 5.7). Some caution however may be necessary as not all skills and not all understanding are easily transferable.

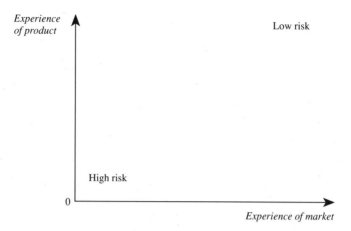

Figure 5.7   People risks in international development

A number of US multinational corporations have traditionally operated on a pan-European basis. Du Pont 'has been thinking, planning and
working on a pan-European basis ever since it began manufacturing
operations in the region in the late 1950s. The company's plants were
built to serve European, and in some cases global, markets; its organization has always approached the region as a single market'.

Success in one situation can lead to overconfidence, if not arrogance,
and a reduced sensitivity to the need to tailor or modify to meet the
demands of different circumstances. Experience without flexibility can
blind a company to the need for product modification or lead it to overlook certain unique features of a market.

Past experience may not be an appropriate guide for the future. For
example, there are many uncertainties concerning the prospects for the
international trading superstar, Hong Kong. A company with significant
interests in Hong Kong will have needed to monitor very closely negotiations between the UK and Chinese governments and, perhaps even more
importantly, the reactions of the people with the key skills upon which
the colony depends.

So far as internationalization budgets and investments are concerned,
it should be remembered that, quite apart from the uncertainties associated
with revenues and costs, there may be currency risks. The value of a currency fluctuates up or down according to the supply of, and demand for,
the currency concerned. An appreciation or depreciation of a currency
vis-à-vis the home, or, domestic currency can affect both revenues and
costs.

Most senior managers are likely to be familiar with various techniques
of investment appraisal that take account of the timing of cash flows. In

the case of international investments, one also needs to take account of the location of cash flows: can funds be easily repatriated, to what extent will revenues be subject to local taxation and what are the prospects of significant exchange rate movements?

Public as well as private corporations are internationalizing and examining international opportunities. They may or may not have a different attitude towards risk than companies that are privately owned. Statoil is wholly owned by the Norwegian state, yet, in 1990 alone, the company brought on stream a joint venture polypropylene plant in the Netherlands, acquired a Swedish plastics company, established an office in Thailand, agreed to enter into a strategic alliance with BP Exploration Company Ltd and to build a methanol plant with Conoco.

The management of international risks

Financial risk can, of course, be managed by selecting appropriate payment arrangements and securing export credit insurance. While these steps can, to some extent, protect the outcomes of transactions with third parties, they may not cover a company's own direct expenditure abroad at an acceptable cost.

The financial risk associated with international operations will depend upon such factors as the proportion of total value added that occurs in higher risk environments, such as those found in certain overseas markets:

Low risk
- *home-based manufacture:*
  - home sale to export houses/buyers
  - home sale to home-based subsidiaries of customers
  - operation abroad through a local agent
  - operation abroad through a local distributor
  - direct sale to overseas customers
- *operations abroad in a local market:*
  - local warehousing
  - local sales and marketing operations
  - local assembly
  - local manufacture
  - local R&D
  - integrated and semi-autonomous local manufacturing and marketing unit.
High risk

Where goods are produced in the home market and sold to home-based export houses or buyers, the risk involved may be relatively low. At the other end of the scale, is the establishment of an integrated overseas operation, involving manufacturing and perhaps R&D abroad.

Certain options could move a risk up or down the risk 'league table' according to whether or not risks are shared with local partners. The ranking of individual options may also vary by company, product and market and the volume of business transacted.

In view of the greater uncertainties that may be involved in international operation, it is often prudent to think in terms of probabilities or a range of possible outcomes. Risk and return tend to be related. While the risk of international operation may be relatively high, so too can be the rewards of success.

In general, international operations will involve higher returns and correspondingly higher levels of risk. This, however, need not always be the case. International collaboration can reduce risk and raise returns as below-budget performance in one country might be balanced by exceeded expectations in another.

Whatever the relationship between risk and return, a management should be conscious of it and seek to manage it. This could involve the establishment of a minimum level of return, perhaps related to the cost of finance and a maximum level of risk (see Figure 5.8). Activities around the world could be managed to secure balance in an overall international risk-return portfolio.

Check-list

- To what extent is your company's assessment of particular international opportunities led by customer requirements rather than its own internal needs?
- In particular, is your company's international strategy consistent with, and complementary to, those of its major customers?
- When your company evaluates international opportunities, are the personnel aspects taken fully into account?
- In particular, in the case of mergers and acquisitions, or arrangements and joint ventures, are the personnel issues fully explored at the exploratory, negotiation and implementation stages?
- Is your company aware of, and its plans consistent with, local legal requirements relating to such matters as reorganization and redundancy?
- Has your company given sufficient attention to the people problems and consequences of internationalization?
- Is there an adequate personnel input into your company's market entry, acquisition, arrangement, location and other important decisions?

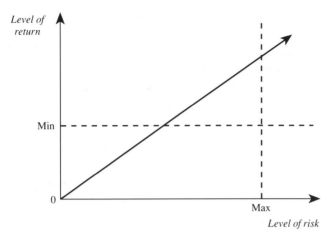

Figure 5.8   Risk and return

- Does the personnel community in your company fully understand the financial considerations and risks involved in international operations, both generally and in so far as they relate to its own activities?
- Does your company's international strategy take sufficient account of the differential sector and market impacts of EC and international developments?

References

1. Coulson-Thomas, Colin, and Richard Brown, *The Responsive Organisation: People Management – the Challenge of the 1990s*, British Institute of Management, 1989.
2. Coulson-Thomas, Colin, and Richard Brown, *Beyond Quality: Managing the relationship with the customer*, British Institute of Management, 1990.
3. Lamoriello, Francine, *European Investment in the United States*, KPMG Peat Marwick International Practice, 1991.
4. Coulson-Thomas, Colin, 'IT and New Forms of Organisation for Knowledge Workers: Opportunity and Implementation', *Employee Relations*, pp 22–32, Vol. 13, No. 4, 1991.
5. Jacobson, Gary, and John Hillkirk, *Xerox: American Samurai*, Macmillan, 1986.
6. BIM/CRESAP, *The Effective Head Office*, British Institute of Management/ CRESAP, 1988.
7. Coulson-Thomas, Colin, and Trudy Coe, *The Flat Organization: Philosophy and Practice*, British Institute of Management, 1991.

Further reading

Benson, Vince, and David Stoker, *1992: The Single European Market and The Business Start-up*, Trainer Resource Pack, Training Agency, 1990.

Burgenmeier, B, and Jean-Louis Mucchielli, *Multinationals and Europe 1992*, Routledge, 1991.

Burstein, Daniel, *Euroquake – Europe's Explosive Economic Challenge Will Change the World*, Simon & Schuster, 1991.

Business International, *Business Europe Annual Survey of Comparative Labour Costs in Europe*, Business International, 1991.

Cavusgil, S T, and P N Ghauri, *Doing Business in Developing Countries: Entry and Negotiation Strategies*, Routledge, 1990.

Citron, Richard, *The Stoy Hayward Guide to Getting into Europe*, Kogan Page, 1991.

Dudley, J W, *1992 – Strategies for the Single Market*, Kogan Page in association with The Chartered Institute of Management Accountants, 1989.

Eli, Max, *Japan Inc.: Global Strategies of Japanese Trading Companies*, McGraw-Hill, 1990.

Lynch, Richard, *European Business Strategies*, Kogan Page, 1991.

Manpower PLC, *Employment and Training*, Mercury Books/CBI Initiative 1992, 1990.

McDonald, Malcolm H B, and S Tamer Cavusgil (Eds), *The International Marketing Digest*, Heinemann Professional Publishing, 1990.

6
International organization

Perspectives

You can spend hours redrawing organization charts and change nothing. At the end of the day we are competing all over the world on our processes for motivating and managing people and delivering quality to our customers. The key thing is to get them right and prevent organization from getting in the way.

Chief Executive, UK office equipment supplier

The only organizing principal we have is account management. We aim to determine whether our customers want to be serviced at the local, regional or international levels. This tells us what we need to support. If people do a good job and can support the customer from where they are, why move them?

Deputy Chairman, UK industrial company

I regularly get together with the managing directors of the other European subsidiaries. We attempt to anticipate head office initiatives on pan-European organization in order to prepare the arguments against. In the meantime we cooperate among ourselves to cope with an evolving marketplace.

Managing Director, German subsidiary of a US multinational corporation

Something has to be changed because that is what they expect at global HQ. We are competing with consultants who have never met a customer, but who tell HQ about the need to change. The problem is finding changes that look good, but which are not too disruptive to our customers.

General Manager, Hong Kong, international group

Within the EC we need to reduce our costs of operation in order to remain competitive. Yet the organizational bureaucrats have seized upon '1992' as an excuse to build up a European HQ. Instead of lower costs we get a new regional level of overhead.

Managing Director of a European subsidiary of a US multinational corporation

We are dead within five years if we cannot change our matrix form of organization. It takes too long to get decisions through – our Japanese competitors usually beat us to the punch.

European Regional Director, US multinational corporation

6.1 Introduction

This chapter examines organization for effective international operation. Many companies are in a state of transition to more flexible forms in order to cope with a variety of challenges and opportunities. Fundamental changes are occurring quite independently of internationalization. In general, developments that encourage flexibility, greater responsiveness and speed of action are likely to be conducive to international operation.

The traditional multinational operates through national companies that are monitored and controlled by a global headquarters. The transnational company no longer concentrates all its headquarter's functions and responsibilities at a single point. Such companies as Ericsson, NCR, Philips, Procter and Gamble and Unilever have, for some years, operated as transnationals. The global headquarters of significant areas of these corporations' businesses have been located outside of the country in which the ultimate holding company is registered.

The international network company advocated in this book operates as a flexible and global network. Power and responsibilities are dispersed and shared so that they, and relevant resources, can be accessed and harnessed at locations, and in ways, most appropriate to the responses that are required to particular challenges and opportunities.

6.2 Marketing organization

The evolution of international marketing organization

The marketing organization of a company that is expanding its international business will, typically, pass through a series of stages. The evolution of the approach of one high-tech company followed this pattern:

export department

international division

multinational matrix

international network

Initially, overseas sales were treated as exceptions. Subsequently, their growing volume justified the establishment of a separate export department.

Then, as the volume of overseas business steadily increased, the company began to distinguish between individual overseas markets and different international business sectors.

Local agents and distributors were appointed and, as the company itself established direct operations in certain territories, the export department evolved into an international division. Compensation emerged as a more significant 'international' issue as particular arrangements began to apply to overseas sales and overseas service.

In time, the growing attention given to certain foreign markets resulted in sufficient business to justify the establishment of local operating companies. In the former Communist block, the company went through an intermediate stage of establishing technical representation offices. At this stage in the company's evolution, mobility, overseas, or, foreign employment and specific development for international operation assumed greater importance. Efforts were made to 'internationalize' the management team through international recruitment and the use of international assignments, taskforces and teams. A multinational company began to emerge, along with a matrix of internal functional and geographical reporting relationships. Honeywell Europe, for example, has operated through a matrix form of organization, with both business units and national operating companies having profit responsibilities.

The multinational had now become a significant global player. Competitive challenges became more intense and customers more demanding. Greater cross-cultural awareness was required and the international cadre of managers that had been established began to expand. A conscious attempt was made to mix nationalities and cultures within teams and on training courses. Multinational taskforces became a part of normal operations.

The company now wished to enter into a variety of external relationships with customers, suppliers and business partners. To achieve a more effective response to changing circumstances and to better access and deploy its available resources, a higher degree of integration was required. As a consequence, the company has evolved into an international network organization. BP is an example of a company that is encouraging networking across national borders to bring together groups and teams for specific tasks.

A global rather than multinational perspective is now required. More people are mobile and international opportunities are for 'the many', not just the preserve of 'the few'. It is recognized that across the world different management styles can contribute to the achievement of a shared vision. Sensitivity to, and awareness of, differences becomes very important as integration is encouraged in order that people in various locations can learn from each other and share best practice.

Marketing organization and the allocation of responsibility

The organization of the domestic company tends to be concentrated almost exclusively in one country within which most of its staff are recruited. The multinational will have units of organization in more than one country. Whether the result of start-up operations or of acquisitions, these will tend to be relatively autonomous, developing a range of staff and support functions as they grow. The multinational may recruit from all those countries in which it has units of organization, but the career prospects of those recruited are likely to be limited to their country of origin or residence.

The transnational or global company, such as IBM or Sony, while not necessarily a fully developed network organization, attempts a greater degree of integration of its dispersed organization into a unified whole. A higher proportion of those recruited in such a company may have career prospects in other countries. Senior managers in particular are likely to share a common vision and strategy and may be mobile between a succession of positions in various countries.

Companies such as Unilever and Procter and Gamble operate as transnationals, with global responsibilities spread between a number of locations in different countries, rather than concentrated at a single point. Responsibilities are allocated to those locations at which a core of common interests and a pool of resources exist.

Over time, to ensure communication, coordination and control, the transnational is likely to put more emphasis upon establishing an integrated telecommunications and computing network. As the amount of networking and interaction across national borders increases and this can be supported and facilitated by appropriate attitudes, competences, processes and technologies, the transnational organization comes to resemble the international network that is advocated in this book. The people of the international network share a common vision, can communicate freely with each other and the most relevant resources of the network can be accessed and applied as required to respond to customer opportunities.

6.4 Prioritizing people issues and challenges

So how important is internationalization in relation to other issues? In the SEMS internationalization survey[1] questionnaire, recipients were asked to rank in importance 12 human resource issues (see Appendix 1 for details of this and other surveys cited). The results in terms of both 'very important' and when 'very important' and 'important' replies are added together are set out in Table 6.1.

Table 6.1 The importance of creating a more flexible and responsive organization

Human resource issues in order of 'very important' replies	Percentages
Creating a more flexible and responsive organization	77
Quality and teamwork	58
Continuing updating and development of knowledge and skills	40
Succession	32
Building broader and more mobile managers	30
Internationalization (preparation for the globalization of business)	28
Changing the corporate culture	28
Individual assessment replacing standard terms and conditions	27
Remuneration	21
Europeanization (preparation for 1992)	17
Preparation for appointment to the board	15
Alternative patterns of work (e.g. teleworking)	1

Human resource issues in order of importance when adding together 'very important' and 'important' replies	Percentages
Creating a more flexible and responsive organization	100
Continuing updating and development of knowledge and skills	97
Remuneration	95
Building broader and more mobile managers	93
Succession	92
Quality and teamwork	88
Changing the corporate culture	80
Europeanization (preparation for 1992)	77
Individual assessment replacing standard terms and conditions	72
Internationalization (preparation for the globalization of business)	70
Preparation for appointment to the board	58
Alternative patterns of work (e.g. teleworking)	41

Source: Colin J Coulson-Thomas, *Human Resource Development for International Operation*, a survey sponsored by Surrey European Management School. Adaptation, 1990

'Creating a more flexible and responsive organization' emerges as the *top* human resource issue in terms of both 'very important' replies and when 'very important' and 'important' replies are added together. In the latter case *every* respondent considered it to be important.

Creating a more flexible and responsive organization, therefore, is the top issue for the UK companies and the UK professional firms and associations participating in the survey. It is also the most important issue for the European and international companies. (Significantly, for the European and international companies, the second most important human resource issue is 'Internationalization (preparation for the globalization of business)'.)

140 CREATING THE GLOBAL COMPANY

Discussions with respondents suggest that creating a more flexible and responsive organization is perceived as providing a basis for tackling a whole range of challenges and opportunities, including internationalization. A number of the other human resource issues were weighted in importance according to the extent to which they would facilitate the creation of a more flexible and responsive organization. 'Quality and teamwork', which ranked second in terms of 'very important' replies, is thought to facilitate flexibility. 'Continuing updating and development of knowledge and skills' is ranked third in terms of 'very important' replies, closely followed by 'Succession'.

The importance of a flexible and responsive organization is confirmed by other surveys. For example, 'making the organization structure more flexible' came top in terms of 'very important' replies to 14 human resource challenges in a survey of 100 organizations undertaken for the BIM *The Responsive Organisation*[2] report in 1989. There is some consensus among survey respondents concerning change requirements:

- customers are becoming more demanding – delivery of quality products and services is of prime importance, which requires an understanding of what constitutes value in the eyes of the individual customer
- the customer should be regarded as part of the organization – a business partner – so delivering value to customers requires the effective management of value chain relationships and, to survive in today's turbulent business environment, organizations need to be flexible; there should be clear identification of responsibilities and tasks concerned with the facilitation of flexibility, adaptation and learning
- processes for the achievement of change should replace rules and procedures and the use of teamworking should be encouraged
- priorities concerning human resources as a critical success factor should be pushed right to the top so senior managers must retain responsibility and ensure proper management processes are in place
- continuing management education and development is crucial and should be seen as the responsibility of all managers
- staff career development needs to be continous, with remuneration reflecting value to the company rather than position within it
- an organization needs to understand and accommodate the individual interests and motivation of employees, external suppliers of services and of potential recruits and those in the organization should be regarded as members rather than as employees
- human resources activity should be pro-active, developing an ability to anticipate and cope with change, and this approach will require personnel practitioners of the highest quality with a broad outlook and remit

- IT should be applied to secure rapid access to relevant skills, support professionals and knowledge workers, facilitate group and team working and enable tasks to be undertaken on a flexible basis.

More recently, a survey of senior personnel practitioners[3] has confirmed the continuing ranking of 'Creating a more flexible and responsive organization' as the number one personnel issue. It is considered to be 'very important' by eight out of ten respondents. 'Creating a more flexible and responsive organization' is regarded as particularly important by main board directors.

The search for flexibility and slimmer, flatter organizations, derives from the sheer scale and range of changes that are occurring in the business environment[4] and which were examined in Chapter 1 (see page 2). The changed market environment has had a significant impact – at local, regional and global level – upon suppliers. For example, at the start of the 1990s within the IT sector:

- levels of profitability were falling – Wang, Unisys, Bull and the computer division of Philips all reported losses, while, in a fragmented European industry, national champion companies such as Philips, Thomson and Olivetti were experiencing financial problems
- companies were having to slim down, become more flexible and responsive in order to survive: IBM, DEC Unisys, and BT were among the suppliers that announced major manpower reduction programmes.

A 1991 BIM survey *The Flat Organisation: Philosophy and Practice*[5] reveals that:

- approaching nine out of ten of the participating organizations are in the process of becoming slimmer and flatter as the 'recessionomics' of the period 1990–1 has put further pressure upon the costs of 'corporate overheads'. while more competitive market conditions have increased the requirement for flexibility
- in some eight out of ten of the participants, a more responsive network organization is being created and more work is being undertaken in teams
- over two thirds of the participants acknowledge that functions are becoming more interdependent and that permanency is giving way to flexibility and temporary arrangements
- when asked what their organizations ought to be doing in order to better respond to challenges and opportunities in the business environment, over two thirds of the respondents thought that 'organizations should become more interdependent'.

It[5] also suggests that many organizations are experiencing some difficulty in achieving corporate transformation (the barriers and priorities will be examined in Chapter 14).

6.5 Customers and the organizational response to internationalization

Creating an international network organization takes time. There is a danger that some companies may believe that changing an organization is itself a sufficient response to a drive for international development. A company may feel that it has responded to the emergence of a single European market just because it has established a European regional headquarters. Many Japanese companies understand the need for greater local commitment. For example:

- global players, such as Sony, operate a 'localization' policy of understanding, adapting to and learning from local circumstances
- Matsushita has sought to achieve a greater appreciation of the actual and potential roles of its products in the lives of its customers by establishing 'life-style centres' in major cities.

Realtionships with customers are ongoing, they do not await corporate reorganization. A successful response to the requirements of an international customer can require the cooperation of many elements of an organization, each of which is likely to have its own priorities and goals. The benefit to each of these units of a successful international relationship may be small, while for a supplying corporation as a whole it could be of strategic significance.

To effectively service international accounts, relationships must transcend the shifting boundaries of corporate organization. The Xerox Corporation has created a category of international accounts, while retaining existing reporting relationships and without creating a new organization. Operating companies continue to provide sales and service within their national boundaries, although sales, service and administrative staff now work together in teams on a partnership basis. What the international account managers provide is coordination and focus. What is new is awareness of, and commitment to, the solution of international customer requirements. These requirements exist and must be met independently of a supplier's current form of organization.

In the case of Xerox, as well as more satisfied customers, there has been a significant increase in learning from best practice across national borders. What is learned from servicing international accounts spills over to the benefit of national accounts.

General Electric of the US disposed of activities accounting for a quarter of its turnover and made various acquisitions in order to assemble a portfolio of global business, each of which has the potential to be number one or two in the world. The company has actively encouraged cross-border cooperation and integration. Without the flows of ideas and people across national borders that have resulted, General Electric believes it could not have remained world class in some sectors.

6.6 The bureaucratic organization

The flexible global network represents an aspiration for many companies. The bureaucratic organization, though, is more often the reality, but is a useful point of departure because, in its varying forms, while much maligned, it is so widespread.

The harmful symptoms of bureaucracy appear to be widely recognized, along with the importance of learning, adaptation and change.[5] Bureaucracy may have some advantages in certain contexts, but today it has few friends. Corporate transformation has become an international preoccupation:

- ICI is an example of a major British company that, in 1990 initiated a process of fundamental restructuring in order to become less bureaucratic and more flexible
- the US IT supplier Hewlett-Packard is restructuring to break away from the constraints of its matrix form of organization
- the restructuring of the US computer company Data General was necessary for it to survive and dramatic, resulting in the loss of over a half of the company's employees
- another US company Alcoa has inverted the traditional organizational pyramid in order to put the various business units that are serving customers 'on top'
- in France, Groupe Bull is restructuring in order to become a global organization
- in the Netherlands, Philips is restructuring in order to survive.

In the BIM *The Flat Organisation: Philosophy and Practice* survey,[5] 95 per cent of respondents considered 'Processes for ongoing adaptation and change' and 'Individual learning and development' to be either 'important' or 'very important'. Interviews for a parallel survey undertaken in 1990 for SEMS on HRD for international operation[1] suggest that, while its critical importance is recognized, continuing education and developments is, for many organizations, an aspiration rather than a reality.

In a more stable environment, the centralization of authority, the extensive division of labour and the vertical command system of the bureaucratic organization can allow measured and predictable responses to occur. The bureaucratic organization appears relatively easy to direct and understand. However, it can encourage a narrowness of views and skills and conflicts between functions. While vertical communication down the management hierarchy can be rapid and controlled, departmental barriers can inhibit cross-functional working. There is little two-way communication.

In the dynamic and demanding global business environment profiled in Chapter 2, the bureaucratic organization becomes a problem in itself (see Figure 6.1). The lack of delegation and horizontal communication between functions and divisions inhibit speed of action and a flexible response. Edzard Reuter, the Chief Executive of the German industrial company Daimler-Benz, quotes the caption of a cartoon on his desk: 'History is full of giants who couldn't adapt'.

The bureaucratic organization that is the source of such anguish in a domestic context can significantly increase the complexity of international expansion when all the key elements of a bureaucracy have to be replicated in each new location. Establishing national operating companies as local bureacracies with a range of staff functions can significantly raise the cost of entry to new overseas markets.

6.7 Organizing for international expansion

In contrast with the bureaucracy, the more flexible network organization finds it easier to spread around the globe. It can expand wherever a vision is shared and a telephone or fax machine is to be found. It can link up those with compatible values and compatible terminals.

Activities do not always need to be located together for interaction to occur. In the network organization, communications technology can allow people to work together across the barriers of geographic distance. Electrolux has adopted this approach for certain activities, and groups within Hewlett-Packard operate from split locations.

The most geographically remote units of the network organization may have almost instantaneous access to the full range of corporate services that can add value for their customers. These customers themselves can be added to the network without waiting for the establishment of a local office. Once set up, a local presence can be free to grow organically according to local requirements and circumstances.

Established international companies are not immune from the need for organizational change. Multinational corporations, like people, can be constrained by their past. Many will have established their operations

Figure 6.1   The problem with a bureaucratic organization structure
Source: Coulson-Thomas and Brown, 1990

in various nation states prior to the emergence of a new determination within regional groupings to reduce the impact of national borders. Redeploying the resources of an existing operation may involve significant relocation and termination costs and other penalties. A new entrant may have the luxury of a blank canvas on which to sketch whatever is appropriate in the face of a new reality.

BT is an example of an organization that has needed to undergo a fundamental restructuring while at the same time seeking to become an international player. It's Operation Sovereign was designed to create a flatter and less bureaucratic organization. In the process, the work-force was to be reduced by one third. A higher degree of flexibility and responsiveness is essential if BT is to work effectively with major companies to develop and manage their global networks.

Attitudes and behaviour may need to change as well as the structure of an organization. BP's Project 1990 is another corporate change programme. BP recognized the importance of the management of performance, assessment and remuneration and of training and development in the achievement of cultural change. Remuneration and other policies and practices for successful internationalization should be consistent with those needed to create a more flexible and responsive organization.

One could give further examples of corporate reorganization for the international market-place. The important point is that what is right for one company may be inappropriate for another. Each management team should set out the options that have been identified and assess their advantages and disadvantages in the context of customer requirements.

The related advantages and disadvantages, identified by one management team, of certain international organization options are set out in Table 6.2, (note that these are not exhaustive and are set out for the purposes of illustration only).

Table 6.2 International organization options

Options	Advantages	Disadvantages
National operating companies	Close to customers Local service support Flexibility/autonomy Know your culture Local industries known Local representation and investment Instant response Good distribution Potential IT use	Fragmented reaction to customers and competitors Geographical constraints v customer constraints Political organization Redundant structures No company culture Communication No whole market view Costly Difficult to exit and grow Empire building Thinly spread corporate resource Poor central coordination
European market sectors	Transcend national boundaries Tight focus on customer needs Establish close customer partnerships 1992 makes Europe single biggest market Represents the market Effective selling general to market Consultative selling Pan-European selling and support Major account sales and marketing	Limited to regional boundaries Not able to respond to cultural differences Might miss target segments Demarcation between segments – lateral communication Miss stars – concentrate on cows
International unit	Global perspective (customer and company) Economics of scale Consistency of approach Long lifetimes of products	Loose focus, too general Motivation Become dinosaur Product sold to exclusion of customer need

Options	Advantages	Disadvantages
	Clean financial reporting	Redundant selling
	Easy to track profits	Out of touch with markets
	Central R&D and management direction	Needs thorough global market research
	General products	Resources
	Separate organization decisions – e.g., management R&D, etc.	
Arrangements/ joint venture(s)	Shared risk	Split loyalties
	Combined resources	Short term
	Gain company advantage	Shared profits
	Strengthens global business	Mistrust 72/7.5/10
	Critical mass	Lost autonomy
	Turn competitor into partner	Tied to development of partner
	Allows attack of remote markets	Inertia
	New ideas	Two cultures
	Technology transfer	Merged sales and marketing
		Channel conflicts
		Prevent other alliances
		Corporate ID or shared vision
Strategic alliance(s)	Complementary fit	Low commitment
	Flexible	Implementation inertia
	Maximize opportunity	Who leads?
	Reach critical mass	Communication
	Gain competitive advantage	Organization cultures
	Win target	Different visions
	Together 'strength through unity'	Only effective for specific target
	Technology transfer	Continuity
	Effective use of technology/ resource	Competitive
	Maximizes win	
	Exposure to mixed industries	

Variations in international organization

The same form of organization may not be appropriate for all business sectors. According to Professor Dr Wolfgang Hilger, Chairman of the Board of Management of Hoechst, many of the company's division came to 'resemble large companies in their own right'. 'In order to react fast and flexibly to . . . customers' wishes', Hoechst formed 'business units that run their operational business autonomously'. Hilger explains: 'Each looks after a particular product range in a specified region. Some of the units are responsible for their business on a European or even world-wide basis, whereas others concentrate on a specific national market. Our organization is as adaptable and varied in structure as the products we sell and the markets we serve'.

The same form of organization may also not be appropriate for all business functions. For example, a number of companies with international ambitions have examined R&D in a global context:

- one in five employees of the Swedish pharmaceutical company Astra are engaged in R&D as Hakan Mogren, President and Chief Executive Officer of Astra, recognizes that 'the bureaucracy of large companies is not compatible with innovative research, and the corporation's research programme is based upon a network of independent units linked to university research centres
- Du Pont takes the view that R&D, the key to many higher value added opportunities, should be located as close to the customer as possible: 'the company is working to bring innovation and the ability to tailor-make products closer to the European customer through the build-up of local technical and research facilities' so, as part of this process, in 1990 Du Pont opened a new European Technical Centre in Geneva and plans to double the number of European-based employees working in research and development during the 1990s.

The decentralization drive

Decentralization, examined earlier in this chapter, and an associated delayering of organizations is one of a number of interrelated trends that are occurring. The trends identified by interviewees and participants in the BIM *The Flat Organisation* report[5] are:

- primacy of quality and customer satisfaction
- slimmer and flatter organizations
- delegation of responsibility
- flexibility: multifunctional teams
- internationalization: multilocation teams
- interdependence of functions and organizations
- technology that can facilitate group and teamworking
- greater responsiveness and flexibility
- demography: making maximum use of scarce skills
- roles and responsibilities: specific tasks
- prioritization and focus
- shift of emphasis from input to output
- access to skills more important than ownership

- temporary arrangements in place of permanency
- change as normal activity

Table 6.3 shows how respondents' organizations are responding to the challenges and opportunities in the changing business environment and what they thought they should be doing to improve on this.

Table 6.3   What organizations are and should be doing to be able to respond to the business environment

What respondents' organizations are doing to better respond to challenges and opportunities within the business environment	Percentages
Creating a slimmer and flatter organization	88
More work is being undertaken in teams	79
Creating a more responsive network organization	78
Functions are becoming more interdependent	71
Procedures and permanency are giving way to flexibility and temporary arrangements	67
Organizations are becoming more interdependent	55

What respondents' believe their organizations should be doing to better respond to challenges and opportunities within the business environment	Percentages
More work should be undertaken in teams	86
Creating a slimmer and flatter organization	81
Creating a more responsive network organization	79
Procedures and permanency should give way to flexibility and temporary arrangements	79
Functions should become more interdependent	76
Organizations should become more interdependent	67

Source: Colin Coulson-Thomas and Trudy Coe, *The Flat Organisation: Philosophy and Practice,* British Institute of Management 1991

Decentralization is frequently sought as a means to an end rather than as an end in itself. For example, delegation can assist the achievement of flexibility *or* it can be the consequence of a desire to shift the focus of motivation and assessment to the generation of tangible outputs.

In general terms, older and larger organizations in established business sectors are likely to be more bureaucratic than new businesses in emergent industries. Complexity sometimes causes bureaucratization when its effective management demands flexibility. The more rapidly changing the external business environment, the stronger the arguments for decentralization and flexibility, although, when faced with a sudden and traumatic challenge, it may be necessary to temporarily centralize authority. The extent of delegated authority a board will allow often depends upon how strong and confident it feels in respect of challenges in the external environment.

Along with delegation and local discretion comes greater responsibility for local performance. Fred Sier, CEO of Brother International Nederland, points out: 'We have no Japanese staff members, but of course it's important to remember that our shareholders and board members are Japanese. They give us the freedom to run the company as we judge best, but in return for that freedom we carry the responsibility for success or failure'.

In the case of a diversified company operating in a number of quite different business areas, there may be a need for the decentralization of implementation and the centralization of portfolio management. In order to successfully manage internationalization, both these trends may have to be reconciled.

Lengthening production runs in order to reduce the cost of commodity products is an argument for centralization. However, as companies seek to tap higher value added opportunities, for example, by offering tailored services, local and culture-specific factors become more important. This latter trend increases the attractiveness of decentralization. It also strengthens the case for cooperation and collaboration, which is considered in a later section of this chapter.

Flexibility, devolution and delegation

Among companies with international ambitions, a visible sign of the search for responsiveness is the emphasis that has been given to devolution and delegation:

- 'In just four years' the French Groupe Havas has, according to its Chairman Pierre Dauzier, 'been transformed from a primarily domestic concern into an international frontrunner in communications and media' – the company has created a decentralized framework in order to allow each of its subsidiaries the maximum of discretion in responding to local customer requirements, indeed, a 'flexible and dynamic organisation' is one of 'five principles' upon which the company's business strategy is based
- the Swiss company Sandoz introduced a new divisional group structure on 1 January, 1990, which has 'strengthened the entrepreneurial element in Sandoz and further increased its effectiveness and flexibility by placing

full responsibility for the creation and expansion of markets in the hands of the divisions, within the framework provided by the Group's overall objectives' and, in countries where Sandoz has a wide range of activities, Group functions are the responsibility of a local President of a national supradivisional organization so certain former parent company functions have been transferred to the new operating subsidiaries
- Sweden's SKF Bearing Industries also introduced a new and decentralized form of organization on 1 January, 1990 so that now its companies are organized into a number of product divisions that are responsible for both production and marketing, in contrast to before when the organization was 'strictly functional . . ., consisting of a national company in each country, with separate functions for manufacturing, domestic sales and international marketing'
- another Swedish company Perstorp aims to position its manufacturing units and operating companies 'close to their customers' and seems to have achieved this as according to Karl-Erik Sahlberg, the President, 'in our key markets we are considered a domestic supplier'
- Asea Brown Boveri is implementing a reorganization programme to devolve responsibilities to profit centres, reduce headquarters staff, encourage local entrepreneurship and achieve a flatter organization and has described its international organization as 'multi-domestic', which, according to Percy Barnevik, President and Chief Executive Officer of ABB, 'means we strive to be a local company everywhere and that we have many "home countries". Our decentralised structure with 1300 legal entities and some 5000 profit centres reduces bureaucracy and brings the entire organisation closer to the customer'.

Decentralization and the international customer

Decentralization should not be seen as inevitable and it may have been taken too far. For example, some concern has been expressed that the widespread delegation of personnel responsibilities to line managers and operating units has made it more difficult to identify and manage the careers of high-flyers.[2]

There could be a good case for re-assigning some responsibilities to a regional or international level. Some customers will require local tailoring while others may request an international point of contact. Certain customers may demand both.

There may be arguments for and against devolution of responsibilities to national operating units as opposed to consolidating accountabilities at the regional level. The approach adopted should reflect customer requirements:

- ICI is an example of a company that has reorganized in order to get closer to its international customers, with responsibilities having been shifted from geographic to international business units and, within Europe, from national subsidiaries to ICI Europe.
- Honeywell is another company that has moved responsibilities from the national to regional level
- BP, while implementing its extensive programme to cut layers of bureaucracy from its organization, is establishing a European regional headquarters in Brussels
- the pharmaceutical division of the German company Schering has adopted a regional form of organization and four Strategic Business Units have also been created, each with responsibility for product development and marketing strategy, and supported by global R&D units
- the US company Alcoa has introduced a more customer focused organization, with delegation of responsibilities having been pushed to such a point that the Chairman and Chief Executive Paul O'Neill now has direct reporting links with the heads of over two dozen operating units and so, in coordinating the activities of these units and reviewing the strategic framework within which they operate, O'Neill is assisted by a Chairman's Advisory Council of three people.

The point has already been made that where decentralization occurs it tends not to be sought for its own sake but in order to achieve an end goal of creating a more flexible and responsive organization that might better serve customers. The broad parameters of what is sought are:

- slimmer, flatter and tighter structure
- processes for learning and adaptation are put in place
- non-core activities are hived off
- delegation and devolution are put into practice
- there is a sensitivity to local cultures and requirements
- output is assessed
- human skills are perceived and valued as a critical success factor
- access to skills becomes more important than 'ownership'.

Managing the devolution of responsibilities in an international context

When decentralizing, an organization has to decide 'what and how' to devolve responsibilities. Some preparation may be required. Should responsibilities be devolved on a customer, market sector, business unit, product, function or geographic basis? What will the workload implications be for those concerned? What new forms of liaison and coordination will be required? Delegation could occur down a hierarchy, along value chains, out from the core towards the periphery or initially to those most likely to be receptive.

It is not easy to generalize about how much responsibility is likely in practice to be developed when certain conditions are met. Some entrepreneurial leaders, for example, like to retain strong central control, while others may appoint local entrepreneurs in each local market. Also, the logic of what *ought* to happen, taking into account such factors as customer requirements, production technology or available skills, may be undercut by bureaucratic politics.

A variety of ploys may be used to resist change and put the case for overhead units, staff groups and centres of specialist expertise. A number of those interviewed stressed the importance of creating an affordable organization. One US company has told certain staff functions that their services would continue to be 'bought' to the extent they can continue to 'get their price down'.

Speed of response can be a significant factor in deciding the nature and extent of delegation:

– DSM, an international chemical company headquartered in the Netherlands, is seeking to create 'a flexible internal organization' that allows 'quick adaptation of activities to changes in its markets' and it recognizes the need to 'take account of the continuing process of individualisation in Society, which calls for an increasingly flexible social policy'.
– the US construction equipment company Deere and Co. adopted 'integrated engineering' and a product line rather than functional form of organization in order to accelerate the product delivery process and greater responsibilities have been delegated to cross-functional product teams.

On occasion, a delegation of responsibilities to cross-functional teams can appear to slow down decision making as it may take time to achieve a consensus when a number of distinct functional or sectoral interests have to be reconciled. Also, staff may need to be trained and developed to encourage them to work effectively in cross-functional teams. However, the result can be greater understanding and more rapid, integrated and consistent implementation. A certain amount of overlapping and duplication within various functions can also be eliminated.

A dispersal of responsibilities can be achieved in various ways, for example, by setting up new head office units or asking a national operating company to take global responsibility for a particular activity. Electrolux has become a transnational in part as a result of its acquisition strategy. Procter and Gamble, Unilever and L'Oreal are continuing their internationalization as it is cheaper to acquire existing brands than establish new ones. Hewlett-Packard, as an element of its organic growth strategy, has moved the global headquarters of its PC operation from the US to France. The challenge for leading edge companies is how to make the transition from transnational to an international network organization.

6.8 The network organization

What are the distinguishing characteristics of the international network organization? Some consensus emerged in interviews[2-5] concerning the form of responsive network organization that is sought (see Figure 6.2). Its main elements are:

- electronic links along supply chains forward to customers, backwards to suppliers and sideways to business partners, which results in
- a more blurred or less clear cut boundary between the organization and the external world
- the importance attached to the management of relationships between organizations, harnessing human talent, supporting technology, facilitating processes and the integration of learning and working
- work undertaken by a community of people organized into multifunctional, multilocation and multinational project groups, taskforces and teams that are
- coordinated by a core group that focuses upon refining the vision and mission of the network and ensuring that it is able to learn and adapt in order to maintain responsiveness and flexibility.

By its nature, in that it might embrace a number of companies, the network is negotiated and capable of organic expansion abroad. A Euro-network or sub-network could be established in response to the emergence of a single market. As it becomes international, more work within the network is undertaken by multinational teams.

To the network organization, the business environment is rich in potential people and other resources that can be tapped on an *ad hoc* basis or by means of more permanent arrangements and ventures. Lewis Galoob Toys of the US retains a small core team who coordinate a network of sub-contracted activities. These range from design, manufacturing and distribution to account collection.

In many cases the cooperation and involvement of external parties within an international network will stem from the fact that the vision of the network has inspired them. Indeed, a desire to contribute to the achievement of the vision may be a more significant motivator of participation than the prospect of financial rewards.

The quality of the network's facilitating processes and supporting tech-

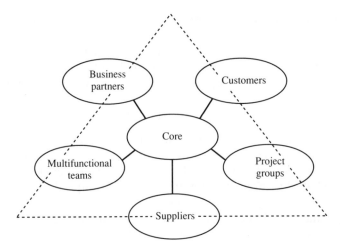

Figure 6.2   The responsive network organization
Source: Coulson-Thomas and Brown, 1990

nology becomes an important source of differentiation from other net-works.[6] By and large people work for and within the network because they share its values and empathize with its mission. Many will consider themselves to have joined a community of knowledge workers with a common purpose. Members of the core team are seeking participants, colleagues and partners rather than employees.

In the network organization, senior managers act as counsellors, facilitators and guides. Their advice and participation will be sought to the extent that they are able to add value, rather than because of their position in a management hierarchy. The transition may not come so easily to some who have experienced a more authoritarian framework. Success will require the ability to understand how local, regional and global perspectives may differ and build relationships based upon mutual respect, reciprocity and trust at each of these levels.

6.9 Network partnerships

The various organizational members of a supply chain network can adopt a variety of relationships and each can give rise to particular organizational and management problems. Alliances and other forms of relationship need full investigation ahead of commitment. Partners need to be selected with care and each case should be considered on its own merits.

Relationships can enable companies to share resources and risks, achieve critical mass and consolidate or supplement core strengths. They can also be unstable and making them work can impose heavy demands upon managers. Success requires compatibility of vision and culture and sustained commitment to implementation. Even completed mergers, such as those between the UK tyre company Dunlop and Italy's Pirelli, or the German aerospace company Fokker and VFW of the Netherlands, can fall apart.

The motivations of network partners need to be understood:

– the Japanese have used alliance relationships to penetrate trade barriers and become 'insiders', an example of this type of relationship being that between Rover and Honda and another being the Japanese company NEC, which has used its relationship with Groupe Bull of France to secure access to the European market
– airlines have used networks of relationships to develop travel products and coordinate procedures, systems and sales activities, such as the European Quality Alliance, a partnership of Austrian Airlines, SAS and Swissair
– the blurring of borders between business sectors, such as between computing and telecommunications, can encourage mergers, acquisitions and joint ventures, such as the acquisition by AT&T of NCR, and a common approach to open systems is bringing together networks of IT suppliers
– within the UK, the DTI has acted as a catalyst in bringing together collaborative networks of companies who, regardless of business sector, have a common interest in exporting to a particular country (the first network was formed in 1991 to tackle the Venezuelan market).

A company may have a choice of alliance partners and lean first one way and then another. The decade of the 1990s opened with a scramble among such telecommunications companies as AT&T, BT, Deutsche Telecom, MCI, Northern Telecom and Japan's NTT for alliance and arrangement partners. With overlapping and parallel negotiations underway, a number of different groupings could have emerged. Holding a course in such circumstances requires both vision and pragmatism.

6.10 The global network

Many opportunities and resources are more likely to be found in some locations than others. Rarely, however, will they be concentrated at a single point. The Ford global network links designers in the US and engineers in Belgium with its manufacturing plant in Spain. All can work together and with colleagues throughout the world by means of an international corporate network.

The truly global network is, by its nature, decentralized. Its purpose is to respond to customer opportunities and access relevant resources wherever these might be.[7] Information technology provides a variety of means of securing access to relevant skills:

- telephone
- fax
- telex
- word processor
- computer
- typewriter
- photocopier
- laser printer
- calculator
- answerphone
- mobile phone
- paging system
- modem link to organization's network
- various on-line services
- satellite dish.

Given that human talent is spread around the world and many centres of excellence may exist, global companies are finding it almost impossible to support and staff a comprehensive corporate headquarters at a single point. Staff functions can themselves become international networks, linking professionals who may work together on projects, sharing understanding and insights independently of their geographic locations.

The cost of prime real estate in city-centre locations and tight local labour markets may mitigate against establishing all head office functions at a single site. A corporation may find it easier to tap a wider range of talent by spreading functions between a number of locations.

Within the international network business, units with particular needs can form direct linkages with other units and groups that may be able to help them. In the bureaucratic organization such units may have been tucked under a layer of management that was not sympathetic to their requirements or into a part of the organization that they did not really fit. In the network organization there is greater freedom and the opportunity to seek out relationships based upon mutual interests and needs.

Subsidiarity

On the principle of subsidiarity, a company should periodically reassess its international division of responsibilities and re-assign duties to those levels and locations that are most appropriate. While some responsibilities are delegated, others could be centralized.

What is important is a continuous dialogue between those units with local, regional and central responsibilites. Too little local involvement, as a result of overcentralization, could lead to a failure to understand the distinctive features of a national market. Too much decentralization could make it more difficult to negotiate and implement a satisfactory arrangement strategy. Where the power really lies may well need to shift from issue to issue, the key decisions being taken at the level that is most relevant, following discussion with the others as appropriate. Elements of the network will participate to the extent that mutual benefits are achieved.

Moving closer to customers can lead to greater responsibilities being devolved to locally based units. IBM, for example, has moved some marketing responsibilities from regional to national operating units. At the same time, the company is encouraging greater regional cooperation among the heads and management teams of national companies, while product development decisions are taken on a global basis.

IBM is in the process of becoming a transnational in that all significant global decisions are no longer to be taken at a single headquarters location. During 1991, for example, the headquarters of the company's communications systems business moved from New York to the UK.

Organizational overheads tend to be invisible to customers as, in general, their perceptions are formed in response to the speed and relevance of service in relation to their requirements rather than the office furnishings or staff functions. Given that these customers may be distributed around the world, professional and technical issues relating to a supplier's relationship with them may also arise from any number of points. An organization able to access relevant expertise around the globe is more likely to understand these issues.

Working within the global network

Geographic dispersal need not result in a loss of core bonding. Unilever is an example of a relatively successful global company that considers geographic diversity to be a source of strength. Physical proximity can encourage managers to put up barriers to safeguard their sense of identity and establish psychological space. These same individuals may be quite open to, and may feel less threatened by, periodic exchanges by electronic mail or telephone conferencing.

Geographic proximity is as arbitrary a way of selecting professional colleagues as limiting one's choice of spouse to those who happen to have been born in the same village. The centralized bureaucracy or company town can appear closed and cliquish and lead to those at other locations feeling that they are outsiders. It can also lead to introversion and the narrow, parochial view of the world that is demonstrated by some US multinational corporations. The UK trading company Inchcape sought over the years to reduce the impact of a provincial head office view upon its overseas operations by paring its headcount to the bare minimum needed to coordinate and account for its international activities.

In contrast, in the case of the global network, there are fewer permanent insiders. The extent to which an individual is accessed and involved tends to depend upon the quality of their contributions. The cement that bonds is not geographic proximity, a common status or facial familiarity but a shared vision and mission, as well as an understanding of each other's values and positions on issues.

The concentration of power can also lead to power politics at the centre.[8] In the rarified atmosphere of the corporate head office, the key players can circle each other, playing internal games and ignoring external reality – promotion decisions and perceptions reflecting *style* rather than *substance*. The superstars may be picked because they look the part, they flatter or are felt to be of 'the right stuff'.

The introduction of geographic distance as a result of a dispersion of expertise and power can result in less importance being attached to presence, and more weight being given to business performance. Results are relatively easy to transmit around the corporate network.

Balances of power can emerge and, as a result, the domination of particular interests can be less likely in the dispersed network organization. When all the key players are accessible to each other, those with similar views and interests can get together. Across the global network each person may be no more or less isolated or accessible than any other. The clues to the location of contemporary power lies in the usage of, and traffic on, the network.

Communication costs

Geographic dispersion can increase operating costs. For example, as the volume of communication increases between individuals across functions and between locations, a significant increase in telecommunications costs can occur. The rise may be even more pronounced when international communication is involved.

Making people aware of the time taken to transmit fax messages and documents by electronic mail may help them to understand the true cost of information. This awareness may enable them to assess the value of information received, and of time saved, in relation to the costs involved.

Global and other companies are forming long-term relationships with suppliers of telecommunications services. Mercury Communications, for example, offers a range of all-digital international services that can cover data, voice, image or text applications. Routes are available by satellite and fibre to Europe, North America and the Far East. Private international circuits are available that can offer full-colour video conferencing to reduce international meeting costs, support multilocation teamwork and allow interactive processing of information 24 hours a day. If required, a telecommunications supplier, such as Mercury, will develop and manage a company's international network.

6.11 Regional organization

Around the world, regional groupings of states and common markets, such as that of the EC, are emerging. An organization could respond to the changing nature of the European market-place in a number of ways:

- each function could be allowed to determine its own response
- a new geographical area of operation could be created to which regional responsibilities could be allocated
- assessments could be made of whether particular brands should be promoted as Euro-brands or European partnerships forged
- the existing vertical reporting relationship could be retained, but new horizontal links established to achieve better European coordination, resulting in a matrix form of organization, but
- the most flexible pattern of relationships is the integrated network that allows European teams to be brought together as appropriate.

Customer requirements can demand a regional level of organization. ICI has recently significantly strengthened its European level of operation. Its customers have been seeking to purchase at the European level, in part in response to the emergence of the single European market.

All ICI European sales staff are to report to European-level business units rather than to national companies. Within the European framework, geographic units will transcend national borders. For example, the 'Mid-Europe' area organization will cover Germany, Austria and Switzerland, while Spain and Portugal together form an 'Iberia' area. Although this approach will increase staffing at the European level, substantial savings are expected to result from the elimination of a duplication of staff, facilities and other resources at the national level.

Regional headquarters

Corporate head office organization also has to cope with the emergence of regional trade blocks and common markets. In certain parts of the world, for example, Europe, North America and the Pacific Rim, some companies have established regional headquarters to coordinate their activities.

In 1991, the UK company Pilkington announced its intention to move the headquarters of its flat and safety glass business from its traditional base at St Helens to Brussels. The Brussels base would coordinate glass making activities in Germany, Scandinavia and the UK. The move follows other efforts of Pilkington to become more European, such as the formation of a European board in 1990. Only a modest head office with the responsibility for global strategy would remain in Merseyside.

Some US multinationals appear to feel that their commitment to Europe will be challenged if they do not establish a European tier of organization. However, whatever benefits are achieved may be secured at the cost of a new slug of overheads, the recovery of which can be a further burden upon operating units.

The creation of regional headquarters can create additional layers in an organization, extend reporting chains and create bottlenecks that can inhibit direct communication between the various parts of a network. For example, marketing and production may need to work more closely together in order to deliver value to customers. Given agreement on vision, mission and strategic objectives, a greater degree of all-channel communication may be preferable to the establishment of particular multipurpose reporting relationships.

A regional headquarters can create a further opportunity for a group or bureaucratic view to emerge that may be in conflict with those at local operating unit or central headquarters levels. Operating units may feel that their views are being passed through a selective filter *en route* to central headquarters and vice versa. In some companies, intense rivalry can break out at the level of a regional headquarters as different nationalities vie with each other for control of senior management positions.

National sensitivities among employees can also be brought to the surface when selecting the site of a regional headquarters. Nationals in other locations may feel that they have lost ground in some way. They may feel further removed from the real centre of power.

National governments and customers may both believe that the creation of a regional headquarters has reduced the authority and standing of their local national operating company. The opposite side of the coin to securing a visibly increased commitment to Europe may be a perceived lowering of commitment to individual national states.

As an alternative to the creation of a regional level of organization, regional product or sector responsibilities could be given to the head of a particular national operating unit. For example, IBM UK has been given responsibility for European personal computer strategy and the banking financial services sector, while IBM Germany is responsible for European mainframe computer strategy and the manufacturing sector. IBM Italy's European responsibilities cover mid-range and scientific machines and the government sector. The European responsibilities of IBM France include telecommunications. As a result of this re-allocation of responsibilities there is expected to be a significant reduction in IBM Europe staff.

Within the network organization it may be necessary to retain a national presence in order to mount local representations when dealing with government customers and issues. ICI Pharmaceuticals for example is an exception to the company's new regional structure. ICI needs to maintain a national unit when dealing with a national health service in a country whose regulations concerning pharmaceutical products may be distinct from those of other states.

6.12 International joint ventures

Many companies, as we have already seen, both here and in Chapter 5, internationalize through a network of arrangements and joint ventures. A company could, of course, conclude an arrangement or joint venture for reasons quite unconnected with international expansion:

- a hardware company such as Fujitsu might seek software skills or access to a library of films, as was the case with Sony or Toshiba
- a joint venture could be entered into to share research and development costs or in order to assemble a consortium to bid for a public contract: the US company AT&T has worked with NEC of Japan to develop new generations of semiconductors, while Thomson-CSF of France and Pilkington of the UK used the framework of a joint venture to develop optronics technology.

The joint venture is not a phenomenon that is particular to international operation. In many countries joint ventures between domestic companies are growing at a similar rate as those involving both domestic and foreign companies. Within the EC, however, joint ventures across borders within the Community appear to have increased in number more rapidly than those occurring within member states.

At the global level, joint ventures are also becoming more common, due to the cost and complexity of achieving global coverage and competitiveness. For example:

- Swedish Telecom and Telecom Netherlands have formed a 50:50 joint venture, Unicom, to provide international services to business customers;

France Telecom has formed a joint venture with US West to offer electronic information services in the US
- Japan's Toshiba has established both marketing and product development joint ventures with the General Electric Company of the US, the marketing joint venture covering the Japanese market-place
- developing new generations of cars, computers and aeroplanes requires such high levels of investment that joint ventures are becoming the norm, an example of this is a set of joint venture and other links between the US car maker Chrysler and Mitsubishi Motors Corporation of Japan, while another is Thomson-CSF of France and GEC-Marconi of the UK, which are jointly developing radar technology
- a joint venture could 'share' the cost of a major new production investment: Ford and Volkswagen have established a jointly managed 50:50 joint venture to build a new vehicle plant in Portugal and the venture represented the biggest foreign investment that has ever been made in the country
- ICI of the UK and Huntsman Chemical of the US are among industrial companies that have established joint ventures as a route into the republics that constituted the Soviet Union; British Airways has formed an international joint venture airline, Air Russia, with Aeroflot; the UK-based ICL has formed a computer joint venture with the Kazan Manufacturing Enterprise of Computer Systems.

Across companies there are many different criteria for determining when an agreement or relationship constitutes an international joint venture. In some companies the definition is as loose as organizations in more than one country coming together in a relationship that involves more than just the sale of a product or service. A form of continuing relationship, with contact points and an allocation of roles and responsibilities leading to some agreed outcomes, is usually implied.

Joint venture strategies

There could be many reasons for concluding a joint venture. Some joint ventures are defensive – for example, to avoid a takeover – while others are aggressive in intent – such as to secure a distribution channel.

A joint venture may be a legal or *de facto* requirement for successful entry to certain markets:

- Rank Xerox chose a joint venture with the Modi company of India as its route into the Indian market and Hewlett-Packard has, similarly, formed a joint venture with India's Hindustan Computers, but IBM withdrew from India as a result of its reluctance to form local joint ven-

tures (from 1991 the Indian government has been willing to allow foreign companies to set up wholly owned subsidiaries in the country)
– some companies have found it difficult to penetrate the Japanese market other than through a link with a local company – the Toshiba-General Electric marketing joint venture in Japan having already been mentioned, while the Swiss company Ciba-Geigy acquired an interest in the Japanese company Tomono Nohyaku in order to improve its access to the Japanese market.

Governments can establish a framework covering the terms of such arrangements. The Chinese government's approval of joint ventures depends very much on the extent to which technology is transferred. The joint venture partners of major IT suppliers in China include computer and steel companies, a government department and a university. International players such as IBM, Digital Equipment and Hewlett-Packard are now competing through their joint ventures in the Chinese market.

The desire of major companies to focus upon particular core strengths and competencies has led in some sectors (such as chemicals) to a re-allocation of business units between companies. In other cases, suppliers have sought to get closer to their customers or to achieve a new division of labour between business partners. Being close to customers may be the key to tapping such higher value added opportunities as providing a local service beyond the delivery of a commodity product.

More international joint ventures are occurring in some sectors than in others. Joint ventures are particularly found in production or process businesses in which relatively high investment costs may be involved in developing new products or the core technology as it is possible to share these costs between the parties. In some high technology sectors, an increasing proportion of the value of the final output is contributed by sub-contractors. Care may need to be exercised so that a key skill or competence is retained that, once lost, may be difficult to regain.

A joint venture tends to have a specific purpose and to be less of a general and long-lasting relationship than a strategic alliance or full merger. Those offering professional services may find it necessary to form arrangements to serve the regional or international needs of their customers. These, however, may take the form of a merger or strategic alliance rather than a joint venture.

An international joint venture could be used as part of a 'down-sizing' or 'core focus' strategy. Core businesses could be retained as wholly owned operations, while less central but related businesses could be put into joint ventures with other companies for whom they represent core activities. Peripheral activities could be disposed of.

Some joint ventures are entered into in order to reduce the perceived risks of operation in an uncertain and demanding international market-place. For example, given political instability and uncertainties concerning economic prospects and infrastructure support, the joint venture could be the preferred route into the territory of the former Soviet Union. While certain financial risks may be reduced, the probability that management problems will occur may significantly increase as a result of concluding an international joint venture.

Joint venture and arrangement management

Arrangements, alliances, mergers and acquisitions all present management problems. For example, Rover struggled for many years to achieve a significant financial benefit from its relationship with Honda and the performance of Siemens has been depressed by the consequences of its acquisition of Nixdorf. Japanese companies often enter into alliances expecting them to last no more than a decade. However, some arrangements do stand the test of time, such as the unusual merger framework that brought together Shell Transport and the Royal Dutch/Shell Group in 1907.

Alliances involve the reconciliation of the objectives of more than one party. Whatever the reasons for an arrangement or joint venture, a number of management issues frequently arise when they occur that need to be addressed both prior to, and subsequent to, an agreement:

- compatibility of objectives
- potential for synergy
- capacity to add value
- compatibility of technology and systems
- ability to manage relationships.

Many companies enter into joint ventures even though they may be aware of the failures of those organized by their competitors. Failure rates of between a third and a half of all joint ventures that are cited by some companies should be seen in context. Many joint ventures are concerned with developing new products or advancing technology, areas in which the risk of failure is relatively high anyway, hence a proportion of the failures are the result of the subject matter of the joint venture rather than its management.

The extent to which a merger, acquisition or joint venture across national borders will succeed depends upon a number of factors. For example:

- whether or not the arrangement makes business sense, is understood by customers and is acceptable to them are clearly important – successful

arrangements often being those that involve complementary organizations, while overlaps of activities, skills, technology and geographic coverage can all cause boundary problems
- where the relative contributions of each of the parties are clearly defined, an arrangement may succeed with less international contact than might otherwise be the case as the need for it is likely to increase proportionally with the extent of interdependence
- the impact of differences of opinion may depend upon how they are handled and, clearly, the framework that is established should make provision for handling the disputes and differences of opinion that are likely to arise, especially within the first couple of years
- effective relationships between those from different organizations and of various nationalities are more likely where there is a shared vision and mission, common values, mutually acceptable behaviour and agreed objectives
- the pattern or structure of ownership can be important for management as well as financial and tax reasons, an equal degree of ownership of a joint venture, for example, *can* result in two committed parties, *but* it is often advisable for one partner to take a management lead or management responsibility in order to avoid management paralysis.

The organization and management of different joint ventures vary. Their success demands attitudes and skills that are more likely to be found in an international company than a multinational where operations abroad have been managed through wholly owned subsidiaries. International project management skills become relevant for the joint ventures that are in the nature of projects.

There may also be relationships with governments and other parties and anti-trust and other regulations to negotiate and manage. Handling these can require some sensitivity. The French Government, for example, reacted strongly to the prospect of NEC taking a stake in the national champion Groupe Bull.

Within Europe, an EC regulation of mergers framework; which is much more rigorous than that provided by Article 86 of the Treaty of Rome, has been in force since 21 September 1990.[9] This is directly applicable in all member states and applies to all 'concentrations' that have a 'community dimension'.

People and joint ventures

Individual employees are stengthened in their ability to respond and perform the more open the access they have to the wider resources of the organization. This can be a major rationale of the transition from a multinational to an international network form of organization. This open access to wider resources may be more difficult to achieve in a joint venture context. A new 'arms length' form of organization may have been created for the venture and there are likely to be many other areas in which the parties are not in cooperation. Indeed, elsewhere they may be in active competition.

Boundaries between the units or elements of an organization should be made more 'porous' to allow a wider range of groupings to occur within it. Many of the relationships that are necessary may occur spontaneously when the barriers to their formation are reduced.

Joint venture management skills should not be assumed. Some familiarity with internal ventures across national borders may prepare staff for external joint ventures. A compatibility of interests and commitment among the parties to a joint venture is of central importance. Less friction may occur if the parties allow the joint venture management team some freedom to operate within agreed guidelines than if they seek to continually interfere about mere details.

In the case of joint ventures involving significant numbers of employees, a choice may need to be made between alternative approaches to employee involvement and participation. Much will depend upon the form and place of incorporation and the number of joint venture employees at different locations.

As in the case of internal joint ventures, the individuals involved may have become used to different approaches to remuneration, working practices and management style, while their employment may have occurred within the framework of the employment law of more than one state. Where units need to work together across national boundaries, it should be remembered that the consequences of these differences will need to be managed *whether or not* a joint venture is formed.

In the early stages of a relationship there may be a tendency to conceal differences of opinion, attitudes and approach in order not to rock the boat. It is often better, though, for such differences to be brought into the open so that they can be addressed. The general climate of a corporate culture should encourage this.

Why do we assume and expect that corporate alliances should be relatively long lasting? People come together for an agreed period to work on projects and tasks. So can companies. Much anguish tends to accompany the break up of corporate alliances, but, in some cases, the arrangements, such as that in the computer field between Fujitsu and Hitachi, may have come to the end of their useful life. Conditions may have changed. Termination of an alliance or joint venture could, therefore, be a sign of flexibility rather than of failure.

Check-list

- How appropriate is your company's organization for its vision and international strategy?
- Does it reflect the requirements of major customers and groups of customers?
- Is your company's organization sufficiently flexible, adaptable and responsive to cope effectively with the challenges and opportunities of international operation?
- In particular, is your company's form of organization, its patterns of work and its access to skills conducive of successful pan-regional (such as EC) operation?
- On the principle of subsidiarity, how appropriate is the allocation of responsibilities in your company to the local, regional and international levels of organization?
- Is the value added by any regional or international levels of organization in your company in proportion to their overhead costs?
- How well equipped is your company to manage international joint ventures effectively?
- To what extent could internationalization be used as a catalyst to facilitate the creation of a more flexible and responsive network organization?
- In particular, has your company the people competences, the facilitating management processes and the supporting technology for the integration of working and learning and continuing adaptation and change?

References

1. Coulson-Thomas, Colin J, *Human Resource Development for International Operation*, a survey sponsored by Surrey European Management School, Adaptation, 1990.
2. Coulson-Thomas, Colin, and Richard Brown, *The Responsive Organisation: People Management – the Challenge of the 1990s*, British Institute of Management, 1989.
3. Coulson-Thomas, Colin J, *The Role and Development of the Personnel Director*, an Adaptation survey conducted in association with the Institute of Personnel Management, Institute of Personnel Management, 1991.
4. Coulson-Thomas, Colin, and Richard Brown, *Beyond Quality: Managing the relationship with the customer*, British Institute of Management, 1990.
5. Coulson-Thomas, Colin, and Trudy Coe, *The Flat Organisation: Philosophy and Practice*, British Instiute of Management, 1991.
6. Coulson-Thomas, C, 'Directors and IT, and IT directors', *European Journal of Information Systems*, pp 45–53, Vol. 1, No. 1, 1991.
7. Coulson-Thomas, Colin, and Susan Coulson-Thomas, *Implementing a Telecommuting Programme: A Rank Xerox guide for those considering the implementation of a telecommuting programme*, Adaptation, 1990.

8. Allison, Graham T, *Essence of Decision: Explaining the Cuban Missile Crisis*, Little, Brown & Company, 1971.
9. Commission of the European Communities, *Merger Control Regulation*, 4064/89, ('MCR'), 1989.

Further reading

Bartlett, Christopher A, Yves Doz and Gunnar Hedlund, *Managing the Global Firm*, Routledge, 1990.

Burgenmeier, B, and Jean-Louis Mucchielli, *Multinationals and Europe 1992*, Routledge, 1991.

Casson, Mark (Ed), *Multinational Corporations*, Edward Elgar, 1990.

Evans, Paul, Yves Doz and André Laurent, (Eds), *Human Resource Management in International Firms: Change, Globalization, Innovation*, Macmillan, 1989.

Halperin, Morton, *Bureaucratic Politics and Foreign Policy*, Brookings, 1974.

Jacobson, Gary, and John Hillkirk, *Xerox: American Samurai*, Macmillan 1986.

Jacobson, HK, *Networks of Interdependence* (Second Edition), Knopf, 1984.

Ohmae, Kenichi, *The Borderless World: Power and Strategy in the Interlinked Economy*, Collins, 1990.

Pascale, Richard, *Managing on the Edge*, Viking Penguin, 1990.

Plenert, Gerhard Johannes, *International Management and Production: Survival Techniques for Corporate America*, Tab Books, 1990.

Tuller, Lawrence W, *Going Global – New Opportunities for Growing Companies to Compete in World Markets*, Business One Irwin, 1991.

Yergin, Daniel, *The Prize – The Epic Quest for Oil, Money and Power*, Simon & Schuster, 1991.

7
Skills and competences for international operation

Perspectives

The skills have become more subtle. Empathy and listening have become more important. Local teams need to feel understood. We invite them to as many international events as possible.

International Personnel Director, Canadian consumer products company

Those who were there before the elections are our biggest problem. They stay together and spend the evenings talking about how things used to be. It's the newcomers who are keen to make a mark and to understand what is happening now.

UK-based Director responsible for African operating companies

We encourage our people to be Scottish, to stand out rather than fit in. The more they wear kilts the better.

Personnel Director, Scotch Whisky manufacturer, on the Japanese market

Very often I don't know what local skills we will need. Neither do the people on the ground at first. What other people tell us may be fine for their marketplace, but not necessarily for ours. By the time we learn it is sometimes too late.

Operations Director, with personnel responsibilities for Pacific Rim countries

Very often experience of international operation just means they are 'street wise' and know how to get hold of cheaper whisky and all the other local perks. They may also accumulate unreasonable expectations regarding domestic staff and other benefits.

US General Manager, South American operations

Consultants are the bane of my life. They offer standard and simplistic solutions. We are putting enormous effort into differentiating our culture and our processes. We need solutions that are tailored to our particular requirements. Increasingly we are relying upon ourselves.

Chairman of a UK company

7.1 Introduction

In Chapter 6 we saw how the organization of a company tends to evolve to match the growing internationalization of its business. The awareness and perspective of a company's staff may need to broaden as their focus shifts from domestic to international operation:

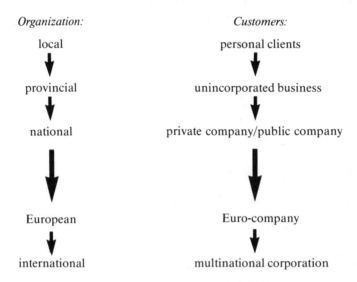

This chapter examines the skills and competences that are relevant to effective international operation. Some of these are related to those needed for survival in competitive national markets. However, international operation can also require an awareness of a wider range of cultural factors than are normally found in a national context. Cultural factors and cross-cultural communication will be considered in the next chapter.

Reference has already been made in Chapter 6 to the role of international project groups, taskforces and teams in internationalization. There is a growing requirement for experience and competence in the management of international projects.

7.2 International skills and competences

Many of the skills needed for effective international operation will be similar to those required for success in a national context,[1] for example, the ability to communicate, flexibility or a willingness to learn and change. Here is a list of the qualities sought by interviewees:

- understanding of business environment
- sensitivity to customer requirements
- commitment to vision and mission
- open-mindedness
- self-awareness and self-confidence
- communication skills
- teamworking and networking skills
- willingness to take responsibility
- adaptability, flexibility and willingness to change
- tolerance of diversity
- ethical behaviour
- commitment to lifetime learning
- multiple activities and careers.

Table 7.1 shows how these management qualities were ranked by participants in the BIM *Flat Organisation* survey.[1]

Table 7.1   Ranking of management qualities

Management qualities in order of 'very important' replies	Percentages
Ability to communicate	67
Flexibility	55
Adaptability	52
Ability to handle uncertainty and surprise	47
Understanding of business environment	45
Broad perspective on the organization's goals	43
Ability to assume greater responsibility	38
Ability to contribute to teams	38
A balanced perspective	29
Commitment to ongoing learning	26
Awareness of ethics and values	24
Tolerance of ambiguity	14
Specialist expertise	12
Multiskills	10
Mobility	5

Source: Colin Coulson-Thomas and Trudy Coe, *The Flat Organisation: Philosophy and Practice*, British Institute of Management, 1991

The skill needs of each company will reflect its own activities and the requirements of its customers. In some cases, the number of those who require new skills and competences as a result of international expansion may be relatively small. In other cases, what is needed may be a refinement or modification of an existing skill base rather than the acquisition of a new one.

Many management techniques may be less relevant and applicable in the international market-place than is the case in the national context. In a domestic environment it may be possible to see sufficiently far ahead to apply the decision making approaches learned at a business school. In the international environment, where there is greater uncertainty, traditional and rational approaches to decisions may be less applicable than an understanding of crisis decision making.[2] In crisis situations, information is likely to be incomplete and there will be additional and relentless pressures of time, so a full and leisurely analysis may not be possible.

To deal confidently with operations in the global business environment, managers may need additional and distinct qualities:

- identifying and understanding challenges and opportunities in the global business environment
- understanding the key actors in international society, including relevant international institutions
- awareness of contemporary international business, economic, political, social, technical, financial and trade issues
- understanding the major sources of international risk and analysis
- understanding and assessment of the major sources of power and influence, including that of corporations, in international society
- appreciation of religious and cultural factors influencing international business decisions
- ability to manage international projects
- understanding the distinguishing features of crisis decision making
- international communication, bargaining and negotiation skills
- sensitivity to different national perspectives and requirements
- understanding the relationship of technology and skills to national economic and business development
- understanding the major political, economic and social issues in particular areas or regions.
- awareness of the different attitudes towards corporate objectives and policies that can exist at national, regional and international level.

Some of these relate to the dynamics of international society, others to a corporation's own activities and responses.

Expertise relating to contributions to, or the management of, multinational teams, projects, arrangements or joint ventures could be required as a result of an increase in international activity (project management skills are considered later on in this chapter).

Negotiation with those from other countries can often benefit from an understanding of their business cultures and negotiating practices. For example, in some cultures people like to bargain. They may feel that they have not done their job if they have not managed to improve upon the terms of an initial proposition in some way. In such cases an opening negotiating position may need to be some way ahead of the outcome that is sought.

At many levels in an organization, internationalization may be primarily a question of attitude and perspective rather than of specific skills. In some companies, considerable effort is devoted to the acquisition of language and other skills thought relevant to international operation, while little effort is devoted to broadening the international perspective of those involved. Brandon Gough, Chairman of Coopers and Lybrand Deloitte recognizes that internationalization requires a change of attitude and perspective: 'Much is already underway to internationalize the thinking of our partners and staff'.

International skills in the value chain context

Customer needs and preferences may dictate skill requirements. Certain customers may prefer a unified and consistent international approach. They may demand the same product or service wherever it is supplied around the world. The extent of tailoring or modification for reasons of national culture may be minimal. A company in a different business sector may find it difficult to operate without people on the ground who are fully immersed in local national cultures. The greater the requirement for local tailoring and adaptation, the more the discretion that may need to be given to local operations and the stronger the argument may be for local staff recruitment.

The Japanese market is one that is demanding of local cultural awareness, Johji Sato is a Japanese partner of Coopers and Lybrand who has been based in London in order to serve Japanese clients in Europe. He believes: 'We have got to be good at dealing with different cultures. It can be vital, particularly in Japan, where it is more important than technical expertise or professionalism'.

Organizations that are close to their customers should involve them in the discussion of skill needs. A supplier's need for new skills may be the result of the internationalization of one or more key customers or clients. In order to better respond, the supplier would benefit from an understanding of the customer's international development strategy. The successful implementation of such a strategy may depend upon the cooperative efforts of a number of organizations participating in a value chain. Skill requirements could be determined and developed jointly with other players in the value chain. Managers who were interviewed from several companies expressed an interest in developing joint management education programmes with other organizations that were not direct competitors.

A company may need to respond to the mergers and acquisitions of both suppliers and customers. When ASEA of Sweden merged with Brown Boveri of Switzerland, Digital Equipment quickly merged its account teams for the two companies and responded with an assessment of their new requirements.

Skills and strategies

Much will depend upon a company's own strategy for internationalization:

- will overseas operations be set up by expatriate staff and, thereafter, will they be allowed to grow organically and through local recruitment – the Japanese company Brother, in the office products field, has based its international expansion policy upon the organic development of a relatively modest initial arrangement or investment and an emphasis upon localization has required a minimal commitment of Japanese staff
- will overseas expansion be achieved through joint ventures or the acquisition of local companies – ICL has used joint ventures in what was the Soviet Union and Eastern Europe to secure access to relevant local skills and the international expansion strategy of the UK-headquartered public relations company Shandwick was largely based upon the acquisition of local companies
- alternatively, should greater use be made of local dealers, agents and other third party distribution channels – within the office equipment sector, in recent years the major suppliers have made greater use of third party distribution channels to cover remote areas, smaller businesses and lower margin commodity products, the companies' own skill development programmes being focused upon the higher margin business with major companies
- could resources be shared by some form of alliance – this was the question asked by the two German companies Krupp and Hoesch in response to the prospect of the single market and another factor leading to negotiations between these steel producers was the recognition that an enterprise needed to be of a certain size to operate successfully in a competitive international market.

Which route to internationalization is chosen, and how a local operation is to be managed, might significantly affect skill requirements.

The prospect of a single market has resulted in experimentation with various forms of collaboration:

- an opening up of the European financial services market-place has confronted insurance companies with the need to develop or acquire skills relevant to potential customers in other member states if they are to develop pan-European operations, so four insurance companies, AVCB of the Netherlands, Friends Provident of the UK, Topdanmark of Denmark and Wasa of Sweden, formed a strategic alliance, Eureko, to create a collaborative framework in which further companies could participate and the new framework was designed to handle the international business of the participants

– Rover, the UK car producer, has formed a strategic partnership with Honda of Japan and, through a family of arrangements, Honda is securing a route to the European market-place, while Rover is obtaining from its partner the expertise to improve its performance as a producer; Rover staff will secure access to Honda plants in the US and Japan in order to develop the skills and understanding to improve the company's production processes

– some strategic alliances have occurred across sectoral boundaries, for example, the Italian car maker Fiat and the French engineering and telecommunications company Compagnie Générale d'Electricité (CGE) have taken a shareholding in each other and exchanged some business units – such exchanges can enable a company to build upon areas in which it has a critical mass of resources and skills and to shed those activities that are not strong enough to compete internationally

– component sourcing is extending across national borders as the EC Commission has adopted a policy framework for the encouragement of closer supply chain collaboration and particular emphasis has been put upon transnational sub-contracting.[3]

All the above forms of arrangement can make heavy demands upon those with relevant bargaining and negotiation skills. Those able to handle cross-border negotiations – with the qualities of both the diplomat and the trader – are increasingly in demand.

Arrangements and mergers to pool or acquire skills also take place within countries. In Japan, for example, smaller family businesses often overcome succession problems by means of a merger or acquisition. Small as well as large companies may now need the skills to handle arrangement negotiations.

Companies are now using a variety of ways of securing access to expertise through various forms of relationships with other organizations. The Xerox Corporation of the US, for example, has made a major commitment to benchmarking. All Xerox managers are encouraged to learn from non-competing companies.

The qualification 'non-competing' could be significant when a benchmarking collaborator or arrangement partner also turns out to be a competitor. The essence of what is distinctive about some companies lies in their know-how and in the skills and competences of their people.

Care sometimes needs to be taken to ensure that core skills are not lost to a competitor through a collaborative link.

In some sectors, to become a global player a company may need to conclude a range of alliances and arrangements. Human resource issues may be of considerable importance in assessing potential business partners. Securing access to certain skills could, therefore, be a prime motivator of an arrangement. Fujitsu, as we have noted, acquired the UK company ICL in part to obtain access to European software development skills.

The prime 'assets' of many organizations are the expertise and experience of their people and this resource needs to be understood. Key staff might leave shortly after an arrangement is concluded so some contact with those involved might be desirable during the course of arrangement or acquisition negotiations.

Just as internationalization creates new shortages of some skills, it can result in a surplus of others. Where acquired skills are not needed, rationalization may be found to be relatively costly as a result of local legal requirements relating to redundancy.

For one US-owned high-tech company, a major justification of small-scale joint ventures with overseas companies is the international development opportunties they provide for senior executives. They are able to learn through involvement in a real project. The investments involved are generally modest, some of the joint ventures falling below the minimum threshold set for the normal consideration of strategic investment opportunities. A Danish company has constructed an international network in order that the partners might better learn about each other's national markets.

7.3 International managers

There are almost as many definitions of the European or international manager as there are companies. A common element is an international or global awareness and perspective:

- Rhône-Poulenc is encouraging its managers to adopt a broader world view beyond a purely French perspective on international events
- companies with 'British' in their names, such as British Steel and British Gas, are trying to get their managers to become more internationally aware
- Ford believes that an international perspective should *precede* international responsibilities, rather than be left to emerge as a *result* of them.

The international manager should be able to work, and communicate, with both as individuals and in groups, people from a variety of cultures and of different nationalities. It is difficult for those who are narrow-minded, chauvinistic, biased or bigoted to become international managers. Sensitivity to local political, ethical and religious issues and a willingness to travel and relocate are also qualities that are sought in international managers.

Some of those interviewed for the surveys cited in Appendix 1 (especially 4) consider that they employ international managers, while others claim that they have yet to meet one. The distinction between national and international manager is often regarded as a question of degree. The characteristics that may need to be possessed to a greater degree by international managers are:

- international awareness and perspective
- tolerance of cultural and life-style diversity
- cross-cultural awareness and sensitivity
- willingness to be geographically mobile
- willingness to assume local responsibility
- ability to handle time zone differences
- ability to handle loneliness and separation from family and friends
- stamina in respect of international travel
- ability to achieve a rapport quickly
- ambassadorial or representational qualities
- ability to command respect and engender trust.

The criteria that need to be satisfied to become an international manager vary between companies:

- within some management teams, the international managers are those who have served in more than one country and expressed a willingness to be internationally mobile, while this mobility may or may not be associated with specific training and development for international operation
- in other companies the label 'international' is applied to jobs involving responsibilities that extend across a number of countries, whether or not this requires relocation
- some companies establish a separate cadre of international managers with considerable experience of living and working abroad
- other companies, rather than create a corporate equivalent of the international civil servant, seek to identify the strengths and qualities of individual managers, the distinct attributes of whom might include national characteristics, and this understanding enables these companies to put together teams of those with complementary qualities, the result of which could be a mixture of nationalities.

A period of service abroad can help a manager develop international awareness. The optimum length of an assignment from the point of view of helping to build an international perspective may differ from that required to make a significant contribution to a local operation. In such cases, there may be a trade-off between development objectives and current business requirements.

While resident in a home country, a manager can take steps to become more aware of the international dimension:

- service on international taskforces and teams can help a person become more sensitive to national and cultural differences
- for those able to receive them, tuning in to foreign radio and TV programmes can broaden cultural awareness
- reading foreign or international newspapers can also broaden an executive's perspective.

In some smaller countries, such as Finland, a relatively high proportion of the population speak English. In part this is because television programmes and films are shown in their original versions or with subtitles rather than dubbed with the local language. (Preparation for international operation will be considered in greater detail in Chapter 13).

Changing international requirements

In-depth knowledge of one or more countries will not necessarily equip a manager to operate effectively in other parts of the world. The skill requirements in respect of a particular country can also change substantially as a result of political upheavals. In what was the Soviet Union and Eastern Europe, prior to the dramatic political changes of 1989–90, many Western companies were represented by local managers who, over many years, cultivated contacts within Communist bureaucracies. Overnight these same individuals found themselves dealing with emergent entrepreneurs and free-marketeers who were suspicious of their previous connections.

Many of the new businessmen of Eastern Europe have a preference for dealing with freer spirits rather than the cautions of the bureaucratic intriguer. On occasion they are prepared to sail close to the wind, in contrast to their predecessors who avoided risks.

An ability to engender trust is very important in environments in which survival and advancement have depended upon keeping one's thoughts to oneself and being wary of others. Recruitment decisions and appointments of representatives are not easy when the choice may be between the discredited and unimaginative bureaucrat and the 'wide boy' with a finger in many pies. Those with relevant language skills returning in 1990 to Eastern

Europe from the West often demanded and command salaries that would seem excessive in other regions.

Conditions in many countries, for example, those in Eastern Europe have been chaotic and uncertainties have been rife. Business decisions can be in the nature of a gamble. In such a situation, the golden rule should be to avoid becoming locked in to what might prove to be an unsatisfactory arrangement.

One international professional firm finds it difficult to prepare pro-actively for international operation in areas such as Eastern Europe as the individuals likely to be involved in, and the circumstances of, future assignments are difficult to predict. Every effort is made, however, to encourage staff to review and learn from each major task they have completed. A record is made of the experience and any new skills or insights acquired. The database records what it is felt has been learned rather than courses attended. The firm hopes that through this process of periodic reassessment, the skills of its staff will evolve to match the changing business environment.

The need to develop managers in Eastern Europe has resulted in the establishment of new business schools and a growing range of exchanges and collaborative links between East and West: the European Business School has established a business school in Prague, they quickly followed political changes in Bulgaria and Hungary, one was also established in Yugoslavia in 1986 and they have been set up in what was formerly the Soviet Union.

7.4 International representatives

Many of the key international appointments that need to be made do not involve contracts of employment. The personnel department or human resource function might not even be consulted. For these distributors, agents and other forms of local representative are appointed.

Whether or not to appoint an agent or distributor may be primarily a marketing consideration. However, these local representatives are people and, when people decisions are to be made, a personnel professional ought to be able to add some value. This is particularly so when the professional concerned focuses on the questions of motivation and commitment.

Lists of possible agents can be obtained from the British Overseas Trade Board, local Embassies, commercial consuls, Chambers of Commerce, customers and suppliers and potential agents and useful contacts can also be approached at trade fairs and international conferences. The local trade press can reveal those who have experience of handling particular categories of goods and services.

Typical criteria used in the selection of agents are:

- understanding of vision and mission
- commitment to quality and customer satisfaction
- sensitivity to customer requirements
- trade connections, market coverage and knowledge
- knowledge of product
- degree of product competition and compatibility
- ability to provide local service and support
- representation experience and track record
- ethical conduct
- quality of management
- financial and other references
- compatibility of objectives
- degree of overlap of territories
- personal empathy and rapport
- flexibility and willingness to learn
- breadth of experience and perspective
- degree of motivation and commitment.

There may be a trade-off between certain of these qualities. For example, breadth of experience could result from an agent handling such a wide range of goods that relatively little attention may be devoted to any particular product, whereas a smaller firm with less experience may have a higher motivation to succeed with a new product.

Relationships with overseas representatives

Senior operating managers should be encouraged to equip themselves with the necessary skills to appoint and manage agents in those countries for which they are responsible. However, a sensible manager, especially one new to an appointment, will wish to learn from the experience of others. This is more likely to occur in the network organization that records experience and expertise and enables and encourages it to be accessed as and when required.

A successful relationship with a distributor or agent will depend upon whether a vision is shared and his or her drives and needs and the extent to which these are compatible with those of the company. Other factors will need to be considered. For example:

- there will be contractual arrangements and business objectives to agree
- an effective method of working will need to be established
- advice and training are likely to be needed in the early stages of a relationship
- the agent will need to be supported, motivated, evaluated and managed.

The role of the personnel function is likely to be greatest where an agent is considered as a business colleague, a member of the international network community. In such an environment, agents may participate in the training and development activity of the network. Assistance could be provided to support local training and on a range of human resource issues as required.

A company's own staff may need to be equipped to work more effectively with agents and distributors. Specific matters that may need to be addressed include:

- whether to assess performance in terms of their own domestic experience or local market conditions
- whether the objectives that have been set are realistic
- whether problems are analysed jointly and whether an arrangement is properly managed
- in particular, whether home-based staff communicate effectively with those who are at work abroad.

7.5 Senior management team qualities in practice

In this chapter we have examined some of the skill requirements for effective international operation, but what qualities are companies seeking in practice? Some clues emerge from the 1990 Adaptation Ltd. survey for SEMS entitled *Human Resource Development for International Operation*.[4]

The survey findings suggest that certain qualities which have traditionally been linked to international operation, such as transnational confidence and perspective, rank behind the qualities associated with operations in general. In recruitment decisions these general qualities may be given priority.

The responses to the survey question concerning the qualities for effective international operation that are sought in members of a senior management team are summarized in Table 7.2 in order of 'very important' replies. The most important quality sought is 'strategic awareness', followed by 'customer focus', 'individual responsibility' and 'communication skills'. These specific findings relating to senior managers are consistent with the general HRD requirements presented at the start of this chapter (see Table 7.1).

Some respondents made the point that the importance of qualities relating to international and European operation vary according to function and/or discipline. It emerged from discussions that these qualities are perceived as most relevant to those people within the organization concerned with international operations, whereas the other qualities were

Table 7.2 Ranking of qualities a senior management team require for effective international operation

Senior management team qualities ranked in order of 'very important' replies	Percentages
Strategic awareness	76
Customer focus	61
Individual responsibility	59
Communication skills	52
Creativity	43
Perspective	40
Team player	35
Objectivity	34
Self-discipline	34
International awareness and perspective	28
Breadth	28
Transnational confidence and effectiveness	21
European awareness and perspective	18
Language ability	7

Source: Colin J Coulson-Thomas, *Human Resource Development for International Operation*, a survey sponsored by Surrey European Management School, Adaptation, 1990.

considered as important for the organization as a whole. Europeanization is, in many cases, yet to be regarded as an issue for the total organization.

Overwhelmingly 'language ability' is the quality ranked least in importance. The Price Waterhouse Cranfield Project has also found that, in spite of the single market, languages are one of the lowest ranked training needs of organizations across Europe.[5]

In the survey undertaken for SEMS,[4] only one person from a UK company ticked the 'very important' box, and then qualified this with 'in theory', putting another tick in the 'not very important' category qualified with an 'in practice' comment. About a half of the UK company respondents feel that 'language ability' is 'not very important' as a 'quality'.

'Individual responsibility' ranks fourth as a quality sought by UK companies, but ranks first in terms of 'very important' replies from UK professional firms and associations. This reflects the traditional importance placed by professionals upon individual professional autonomy and responsibility. It is closely followed by 'strategic awareness'.

European and international company respondents give 'international awareness and perspective' a significantly higher importance rating than is the case with respondents from UK companies. 'Language ability' is another 'quality' that is ranked significantly more highly by European and international companies. All but one of these respondents consider it to be either 'important' or 'very important'. 'Transnational confidence and effectiveness' is also ranked more highly by European and international companies than is the case with UK companies.

Survey participants[4] were also asked what 'other qualities' they seek in members of a senior management team. The abilities to lead, motivate and develop others, both individuals and teams emerge at the head of these 'other qualities'. Significantly, even in a survey explicitly concerned with internationalization, the qualities listed in Table 7.3 are not international specific.

Overall, personal qualities and attributes appear to rank ahead of technical expertise. Little importance is attached to 'qualifications', these being only mentioned by two respondents. These findings are consistent with those of a 1991 survey of senior personnel professionals.[6] The criteria for boardroom and related senior appointments are dominated by personal qualities.

7.6 Internationalization in practice

Given that many of the general qualities sought in senior managers are not specifically associated with international operation, how in practice are major companies building international awareness and perspective? This is also a question that was asked in the SEMS sponsored survey, *Human Resource Development for International Operation*.[4]

Over four out of ten of the survey respondents develop a European and/or international awareness and perspective and a capacity for transnational effectiveness in senior managers by means of international work secondments, exchanges, transfers or assignments (see Table 7.4):

- Coopers and Lybrand relies upon overseas secondments to build 'an awareness of other cultures and a sense of internationalism'
- the Xerox Corporation and Rank Xerox move high-flyers into and out of overseas assignments to encourage an international outlook and the board of a national operating company such as Rank Xerox (UK) might be drawn from four nationalities.

Three out of ten of the survey respondents cite work or work-related participation in international projects or taskforces or participation in international activities, including conferences and meetings, as a means of building international awareness:

- 3M consciously develops its staff by allocating them to project groups and multinational teams and, within Europe, upwardly mobile managers will be expected to join one or more European taskforces

Table 7.3 Other qualities sought in members of a senior management team

Qualities	Number of organizations
Leadership/motivational skills	16
Development of others/team building	10
Ability, intellect and 'other' personal qualities	9
Awareness and sensitivity	8
Financial understanding and awareness	7
Interpersonal skills	6
Flexibility	6
Communication/presentational skills	5
Ethics, values, trust	5
Strategy/planning	4
Technical expertise/qualifications	4

Source: Colin J Coulson-Thomas, *Human Resource Development for International Operation*, a survey sponsored by Surrey European Management School, Adaptation, 1990.

Table 7.4 Means of developing a European and/or international awareness, perspective and capacity for transnational effectiveness

Method	Number of organizations
International transfers/assignments	23
Secondments/exchanges	17
International activities, conferences, contacts, meetings, etc.	15
International projects/taskforces	12
Total: Part of normal job	67
Internal courses	22
External courses	10
Other training and experience	8
Total: Training	40
Note: Does nothing	5

Source: Colin J Coulson-Thomas, *Human Resource Development for International Operation*, a survey sponsored by Surrey European Management School, Adaptation, 1990.

– one insurance company operates an extensive network of secondments and exchanges between its major subsidiaries and senior UK managers are expected to have completed assignments in both North America and the Pacific Rim area.

Questioning reveals that many of the staff engaged in international transfers and assignments are working primarily on particular projects. They are more likely to be working in a team or group context when drawn from operating units, while those in staff positions travelling abroad to undertake specific investigations are more likely to work alone.

In the main, preparation for international operation appears to be undertaken as a part of ongoing work. In less than half of the organizations covered by the SEMS survey does specific training occur. Where training does occur, internal courses are cited more than twice as often as external courses.

Improving the internationalization process

A wide range of responses were received in the SEMS survey[4] to an open-ended question concerning how the process of internationalization of senior management might be improved (see Table 7.5). Over a half of the respondents feel that some improvement could be made.

The responses suggest that, in the main, what is being sought is incremental improvement to current practice. There is little, if any, evidence of any perception that there is a new or different 'external' solution that might be employed to better equip managers for international operation. Some complacency was detected among a few North American companies: a US multinational thought that it did not require its senior managers to have international awareness as its international business operated through national companies that recruited locally.

Further questioning confirms that preparation for effective international operation is far from simple and requires subtlety and complexity. Even companies with extensive experience of international operation acknowledge that there is usually room for improvement. As circumstances change, individuals and organizations must continue to learn from their experience.

7.7 International project management

For many organizations, the major vehicle for the internationalization of senior members of a management team is their involvement in international projects, taskforces and teams. Some international projects can involve people from a number of separate organizations with different cultures, styles of management, conditions of employment and operating procedures and processes. If success is to be achieved, it is important that the distinct nature of project management competences are understood.

Some of the distinguishing aspects and features of project management are:

Table 7.5 Improving the effectiveness of internationalization of senior management

Method	Number of organizations
More of current activities	8
Improvements to training, courses, etc.	7
Greater formality and structure	6
Targetting, focus on individual needs	6
Greater use of international secondments, exchanges, taskforces, projects, etc.	6
Satisfied with current approach	6
Greater focus/awareness on international dimension	6
More planning	3
Clearer objectives	3
Improved evaluation and feedback	3
Self- or action learning	3
Allocation of greater resources, time, etc.	2
Others	4

Source: Colin J Coulson-Thomas, *Human Resource Development for International Operation*, a survey sponsored by Surrey European Management School, Adaptation, 1990.

- matches desire for flexible organization
- roles and responsibilities = tasks and projects
- teamwork-based
- focus on output and human skill
- speeds and allows access to scarce skills
- matches preferences of individuals for accountability and responsibility
- multilocation, multifunction, multinational
- can be supported by facilitating technology
- consistent with organization as portfolio of projects.

It will be seen that these are consistent with the changing nature of organizations and organization for international operation as outlined in Chapter 6.

A project normally involves the achievement of defined outputs, within an agreed timescale and at a budgeted cost, but this combination of requirements is not present in much management activity. It should not be assumed that good managers will necessarily make good project managers. Several German companies referred to the need for improved skills in joint venture and joint project negotiation and management.

Project management competences and qualities

In 1989, Adaptation undertook a survey[7] for the Association of Project Managers (APM) to help determine the nature of project management competences (see Appendix 1). Participants in the survey *The Role and Status of Project Management* were asked to distinguish and prioritize the major project management competences. This ranking of project management competences in terms of both 'very important' replies and when 'very important' and 'important' replies are added together, is presented in Table 7.6.

The first column in Table 7.6 ranks the 'competences for project management' in terms of 'very important' responses. Understanding the anatomy of a project and communication top the list of competences. Management of contracts is regarded as a very important competence by only 36 per cent of respondents. All the other competences listed are regarded as 'very important' by over a half of the respondents.

The second column of Table 7.6 summarizes the position if one adds together the 'very important' and 'important' responses. Four of the competences achieve a 100 per cent response. In the case of the lowest ranking competency, management of contracts, 87 per cent of respondents rank it as either 'important' or 'very important'.

In the APM survey,[7] respondents were also asked to identify the qualities thought to be particularly desirable in project management. Their responses are given in Table 7.7 and provide further insight into the priority ranking of relevant qualities. Communication skills emerge clearly as the number one requirement. In general, human relations skills rather than technical skills are those that are thought to be most important.

APM survey respondents felt that, with increased emphasis being given to team and project work, the setting of more specific objectives and a greater focus upon tangible and discrete outputs, management in general is becoming more like project management. Terms such as 'tending together' and 'convergence' were used by interviewees. However, project management is still considered distinct. The existence of a finite timescale, multidisciplinary teams, greater dependence on others and a lack of traditional line authority were the most mentioned features that distinguish project management from general management.

International project teams

The establishment of an international project team is a means of handling cross-border collaboration between companies of similar standing. Each participant might be a national champion within its own country. In the case of a major project, for example in the aerospace industry with Panavia or Airbus Industrie, such a venture could be incorporated and might become a substantial company in its own right. The various parties

Table 7.6 Competences for project management

Competences	Ranking of 'very important' in percentages	Ranking of 'very important' and 'important' together in percentages
Understanding the anatomy of a project	88	100
Communication	81	100
Decision making	69	100
Control of change	62	100
Planning and scheduling	60	99
Cost-planning and control	55	93
Management of contracts	36	87

Source: Colin J Coulson-Thomas, *The Role and Status of Project Management*, an Adaptation survey for the Association of Project Managers, Adaptation, 1989.

Table 7.7 Qualities desirable in project management and project managers

Qualities	Project management percentages	Project managers percentages
Communication	31	
Motivation/leadership		30
Understanding the anatomy of a project	13	
Decision making	10	
Cost-planning and control	8	
Control of change	8	
Team building		8
Determination/persistence		8
Management of people		7
Planning and scheduling	6	
All-round experience/ability		6
Diplomacy		3
Humour		3
Confidence		3
Seeing beyond the obvious		3
Self-motivation		2
Dynamism		2
Being computer literate		2
Being technically proficient		2
Management of contracts	1	

Source: Colin J Coulson-Thomas, *The Role and Status of Project Management*, an Adaptation survey for the Association of Project Managers, Adaptation, 1989.

involved will need to agree not only a set of common objectives, but also trade-offs between time, budget and quality as a project unfolds.

A degree of self-awareness is an advantage in those who are putting together international project teams. The more that is known about the attitudes, style and interpersonal skills of those involved, the easier it will be to put together teams made up of those with complementary skills.

At all stages of a career, individuals should be encouraged to refine and deepen their understanding of themselves. Development activity should be designed to help individuals to better understand their own capability and potential as learners, communicators and team workers.[8] Groups should also be encouraged to identify their own areas of weakness in order that these might be covered by the qualities of new team members.

Project teams and the network organization

Individual managers need to consider their various roles and activities as an integrated whole. Groups and teams are only able to act in an integrated way to the extent that individuals can interact, sharing information and understanding. When separated by barriers of function and location, information technology needs to be used to provide the interaction that is required. Those working on individual tasks within a team also need to ensure that they retain some understanding of the overall picture. The network organization provides the supporting technology that is required.

Managers often have a limited amount of time for individual inputs and may prefer oral rather than written communication. The understanding and perspective of many managers is internal to *them*; it is held within their heads rather than expressed formally in documents that can be shared with others. For effective teamworking, this internal information may need to be shared. This suggests that a teleworker, or team member, in another location who largely communicates with others by means of formal documents that require time to absorb may be cut off from access to, and the benefits of, a prevailing informal network of communications.

Active participation in a network can allow individuals to assess the relevance of each other's competences to particular project roles. While completing one project, some individuals will be searching for their next role. Looking ahead can help to avoid down time between projects.

Some slack is likely to occur and some means may need to be found of occupying individuals between project assignments. One possibility is to encourage them to think about what they have learned from their previous assignments and what could be done to improve their future performance in similar situations.

Check-list

- Does your company understand the distinct human resource requirements for effective international operation?
- In particular, are the requirements of significant customers, or groups of customers, taken into account when skill needs are identified and defined?
- Is your company taking adequate steps to develop international managers and ensure effective local representation?
- Do the directors of your company have a shared perspective on international issues or are the concerns of the board largely domestic, the views of individual directors reflecting their functional hats?
- Does the management team of your company share the vision of the board and have an international perspective?
- Are the people consequences of international issues fully understood at all levels of your company?
- Is your company and its managers equipped to successfully manage international projects?
- To what extent should your company be working more closely with customers and suppliers in determining skill needs?
- Does your company's internationalization strategy demand a more diverse team of people, for example, are particular nationalities and cultures under-represented?

References

1. Coulson-Thomas, Colin, and Trudy Coe, *The Flat Organisation: Philosophy and Practice*, British Institute of Management, 1991.
2. Coulson-Thomas, C, 'Is the traditional executive programme obsolete?', in S J Paliwoda and A C Harrison (Eds), *The Association of MBAs Guide to Business Schools* (seventh Edition), Pitman, 1988.
3. Commission of the European Communities, *Enterprise Policy Framework*, adopted by the Council, 18 June, 1991; and Office for Official Publications of the European Communities, COM (90) 528 final, 18 December, 1990.
4. Coulson-Thomas, Colin J, *Human Resource Development for International Operation*, a survey sponsored by Surrey European Management School, Adaptation, 1990.
5. Price Waterhouse Cranfield Project on International Strategic Human Resource Management, The, *Annual Report 1990*, Price Waterhouse and Cranfield School of Management, 1990.
6. Coulson-Thomas, Colin, *The Role and Development of the Personnel Director*, an Adaptation Ltd survey undertaken in conjunction with the Institute of Personnel Management Research Group, Institute of Personnel Management, 1991.
7. Coulson-Thomas, Colin J, *The Role and Status of Project Management*, an Adaptation survey for the Association of Project Managers, Adaptation, 1989; 'Project

Management: A Necessary Skill?' *Industrial Management and Data Systems*, pp 17–21, Vol. 90 No. 6, 1990.
8. Coulson-Thomas, C J, 'Breaking Through the Information Barrier: Management Development and IT', *International Journal of Computer Applications in Technology*, pp 269–71, Vol. 3, No. 4, 1990.

Further reading

Barham, Kevin and David Oates, *The International Manager*, Business Books, 1991.
Barston, R, *Modern Diplomacy,* Longman, 1988.
Citron, Richard, *The Stoy Hayward Guide to Getting into Europe*, Kogan Page, 1991.
Guy, Vincent, and John Mattock, *The New International Manager*, Kogan Page, 1991.
Jacobson, Gary, and John Hillkirk, *Xerox: American Samurai*, Macmillan, 1986.
Liston, David, and Nigel Reed, *Business Studies, Languages and Overseas Trade*, Pitman Publishing and The Institute of Export, 1985.
Manpower PLC, *Employment and Training*, Mercury Books/CBI Initiative 1992, 1990.
Mole, John, *Mind your Manners: Culture and Clash in the Single European Market*, Industrial Society Press, 1991.
Moran, Robert T, *Cultural Guide to Doing Business in Europe*, Butterworth/Heinemann, 1991.
Petersen, Donald, and John Hillkirk, *Teamwork: New Management Ideas for the 90s*, Victor Gollancz, 1991.
Raffia, H, *The Art and Science of Negotiation*, Harvard University Press, 1982.
Young, George, *The New Export Marketer*, Kogan Page, 1991.

8
Culture and cross-cultural communication

Perspectives

Don't forget to listen. People spend far too little time on listening to foreign languages. All the emphasis is on speaking them. Getting your message across may be of little value if you miss the response.

Director of Australian aerospace company

In England they take me to be a Greek peasant. In the US they take me to be a success because I have made a lot of money.

Greek owner of travel companies

My American colleagues are convinced I am buying up their culture. My view is that I am buying what you would call 'software' to be used with our consumer products.

Representative of a Japanese company acquiring film rights

All my visitors try to speak Portuguese. I don't like this because I try to learn English. I send my children to St Paul's School to learn English. I want to learn about English ways.

Owner Director of Brazilian construction company

Cultural adaptation of itself is not enough, but on top of all the other things you need to get right it can be a differentiator. That was easy to say, but how do I adapt what is generally perceived to be a 'commodity' product to tribal cultures?

International Director with responsibilities covering Africa

Empathy with the local culture doesn't help me when our interest rates are out of line. When the competition offers an extra half point off the interest, we lose the business.

US banker

Localization of both operations and management is a key objective. Our aim is to avoid conflict and become an insider.

General Manager, Japanese plant in Europe

193

Our corporate language of business is English, but it is not your English or my English before I joined my present company. We use words that have a special meaning to us. The words may mean different things outside of the company.
Director of Corporate Affairs of German engineering company

8.1 Introduction

In Chapter 7, tolerance of cultural and life-style diversity and cross-cultural awareness, together with sensitivity, were among the key identifying characteristics of the international manager. In this chapter we will examine in more detail the question of national culture and the impact it can have upon international operation.

An international organization may evolve its own distinct corporate culture and many of its staff will need to develop cultural awareness and language skills in order to communicate effectively across cultural barriers.

8.2 Culture

Whenever a team of managers is asked to identify the major sources of the differences between countries, 'culture' will generally appear on the resulting list. Some managers might use a term such as 'cultural structure', which hints at greater complexity, the existence of a number of aspects of culture and the possibility of there being more than one distinct culture within a country. The internationally aware manager understands that the many sources of differences between countries are interdependent. Such factors as the political structure, legal framework and economic development impact upon culture and each, in turn, will be influenced by culture.

Many of those working in domestic and multinational companies operate in a single-culture environment. Even when the country concerned is a multicultural society, many companies only recruit from those with similar cultural characteristics. In some countries this is possible without the need to be concerned about labour market legislation or regulations aimed to prevent such discrimination. Internationalization can result for the first time in a need to work more closely with those of different cultural backgrounds. The development of cross-cultural skills that can result may help a company to be more effective at recruiting from domestic minorities.

There are many determinants and elements of national culture that influence each other:

- shared historical experiences and attitudes
- traditions and customs
- social, political and religious values
- education and process of socialization
- degree of homogeneity or presence of minorities
- perception and knowledge base
- physical environment
- economic and social infrastructure
- built-environment
- life-style pace and quality
- language, communication and interaction
- media and communications infrastructure
- behaviour patterns, customs and habits
- speed of adoption of new ideas
- consumption of food, clothing, etc.
- work ethic
- leisure pursuits, entertainments, etc.
- literature, music and art
- interdependence with outside world and other cultures.

Some of the explicit distinguishing attributes of a culture can have their roots in underlying values and beliefs. A predominant religious faith, for example, can have a profound influence upon values, life-style, behaviour, architecture, dress, diet and work and business practices. The attitude of an Arab manager, say, towards wife and family may differ significantly from that of an expatriate colleague from the US or UK. He may not wish to discuss the health of his children and may fill available management positions with various relatives, while the American manager may consider that asking after the health of his children is a normal social courtesy and that staffing positions with relatives is outrageous nepotism.

The importance of work, business and consumption and the nature of human relationships and attitudes to time and place, as we have seen, can vary significantly between cultures. Here are some more examples:

- *time:* Japanese managers may appear slower than their American equivalents because they look at all the aspects of a problem, whereas Americans have been encouraged to make quick decisions; a public official in Italy may be reluctant to arrange a meeting in the afternoon
- *life-style:* whereas a European manager might work to support a life-style, the life-style of the Japanese manager could be designed to support work; the European might stress advancement by merit, job change and 'looking after number one', while, in comparison, a Japanese colleague might expect that more weight would be given to loyalty and long service

– *human relationships:* in a group, a Japanese colleague might appear overly defferential to a US manager with a penchant for plain speaking, while the American, in turn, might appear brash, if not rude, to the Japanese manager.

Steretypes abound: are Japanese managers too nice and 'naturals for groups', while those from Germany too disciplined and British managers invariably eccentric individualists?

Certainly particular behaviour patterns can be popularly associated with particular cultures, giving rise to such descriptions of people as being 'Westernized' or 'Oriental' in attitudes or perspective. Generalizations can be dangerous. Managers developing international businesses need to be aware of cultural differences between regions of the world and variations of culture that may exist within individual states:

– Marks and Spencer found that it had to incorporate changing rooms into the designs of clothing departments for its stores in France, even though the company offered a refund in the event of customer dissatisfaction, as French customers were reluctant to buy off the peg
– a manager travelling from Milan to Southern Italy may encounter a very different attitude towards timekeeping and the conduct of meetings – in the south it may not be possible to fit as many appointments into the day as would be the case in the north because of the long lunchbreak
– Japanese companies like Sharp have put effort into understanding local life-style differences and reflecting these in product design, major Japanese corporations moving their R&D operations closer to customers in Europe and Japan and market research is being done on the ground rather than by a head office unit in Japan
– Honda has recognized the need to give its operating units abroad a greater degree of autonomy, which can require a greater sharing of responsibility with locally recruited staff.

The gulf between the cultures of national companies operating in the same business sector can be profound:

– in Japanese companies, many suggestions arise from within the organization and travel around it in search of refinement and support, so such proposals for change may reach senior management when a consensus has been accumulated
– in a US company, the prime responsibility for decision making and initiating change may well be seen as the prerogative of senior management, the same degree of trust not necessarily being shown to those further down the organization.

It is clearly not easy for two such dissimilar cultures to work together within the framework of a joint venture. One comparative study of enterprises in the US and what was the USSR concludes that success with joint ventures requires mutual understanding and teams 'drawn from both cultures who are committed to work together and integrate the essential elements of the two management systems'.[1]

The impact of culture

How people interact in different cultures can be important for an organization that encourages work to be undertaken in groups and teams. In some cultures, more emphasis is put upon the individual than in others. Returning a favour or deferring to age or seniority, may be given a higher value in some countries than working together to achieve a 'best' solution.

In some cultures there may be both majority and minority views. The negative and positive attitudes towards older people were identified in *Too Old at 40?*[2]

Negative views of older people are that they:

appendix

- are set in their ways and tend to be inflexible
- are a brake on innovation
- block promotion of the young
- have out-of-date skills and are not so willing to train
- have often run out of steam and are not so willing to travel
- tend to look for a quieter life
- have a more cynical attitude
- are more conscious of their rights
- do not work so well in groups and teams
- are more likely to have health problems
- require more expensive pension arrangements
- can be resentful of younger bosses.

Positive views of older people are that they:

- deserve and command respect
- have more experience and patience
- often have more developed social skills and are socially acceptable
- can be more tolerant and can calm troubled waters
- are self-confident and less apprehensive
- distinguish between results and activity
- are happy to work part-time
- will do jobs younger people see as dead ends
- have got enthusiasms out of their systems

- know who they are and say what they think
- think more about the team, less about themselves
- can be more financially secure
- can handle detail and are more accurate
- are more aware of down side risks and think before they rush in.

The negative attitudes could be said to be the majority UK and US view, but, elsewhere in the world, for example in the Far East, the more positive view might be taken by the majority.

Interpersonal conduct, for example the amount of emotion that is displayed in group situations, or people's sense of personal space, can also vary across cultures. People of different cultures can annoy each other without realizing it. For example:

- warmth, a willingness to display emotion and form close personal relationships may be appreciated in some cultures but frowned upon, when too explicit, in others
- interruptions or more than one person speaking at once are more prevalent in some countries than others
- those from the US often prefer to have a greater degree of personal space around them than do many Central and South Americans
- Germans can sometimes appear relatively stiff when greeting each other and, in comparison with those from the Middle East, can avoid close physical contact.

A sense of what is the 'done thing' varies greatly between cultures. For example:

- the English gentleman who demonstrates traditional social values by holding open a door for a lady would be taken as a doorman in Tokyo and could outrage a feminist in New York
- the Japanese are brought up not to eat in the street, but an American colleague might consider it natural when busy, to have a snack *en route*.

The sources of status vary across cultures. In one context, family, tribal or educational background can be of crucial importance, while, in another, the abilities of the individual and a current role may be of greater significance. Education is not just valued in developing countries; in France and Japan the secondary and tertiary education received by some individuals can largely determine their future life chances and career options.

Managers can travel to a corporate event from various points on the globe with very different expectations. A German or French manager might consider a group or team to be primarily a forum of communication. A US manager at the same meeting might consider it a decision making body. The German might have been invited to attend on account of his or her status, while colleagues from the US and UK could have been selected primarily on account of the relevance of their experience.

Attitudes to time, as we have already seen, vary across and between countries:

- Dutch and German managers may exhibit a reluctance to interrupt a meeting for lunch, while, to a French colleague a meal could represent an opportunity to really get down to business
- the German executive may attend promptly at an agreed time, whereas Southern European colleagues may use a stated time as a rough guide and arrive late and it is not uncommon in Africa or the Middle East to keep people waiting for a few hours – this is not taken as a snub as might be the case in the US or the UK.

While significant differences remain, there is some evidence of a convergence of leisure habits in different parts of the world.[3] Activities such as driving, eating out, listening to music, reading or swimming are increasingly popular in many countries.

Of course, not *all* executives from a particular country will exhibit similar characteristics and attitudes and behaviour are often modified by working for an international company. Equally, some companies themselves develop strong corporate cultures. When groups of executives need to work together it may be important that they understand each other's attitudes towards such matters as time keeping or delivering what has been agreed.

Misunderstanding some local customs could have significant consequences. For example, in many countries, shaking hands is a simple courtesy at the conclusion of a meeting, while in others, shaking hands at the end of a meeting could be taken to indicate that the parties have reached agreement on a deal.

8.3 Managing in the context of cultural diversity

A company may need to take account of cultural differences when making relocation decisions and expatriate appointments. The bureaucratic organization that has a standard and fixed view of the qualities a senior manager should have may find it difficult to staff positions in those cultures that ascribe status on the basis of *different* criteria. For example, the company that puts great emphasis on youth may find that in certain countries older managers would be more acceptable. Fewer problems are likely to be encountered with those who share a common understanding of vision and mission, are open-minded and willing to learn and who judge others on the basis of their current contributions.

A company that is more tolerant of diversity may find it easier to staff international operations. The more varied the qualities, attributes and characteristics of members of the senior management team, the more likely it will be that one or more people may be identified to meet a local requirement. Rather than impose *uniformity*, a company may be better advised to consciously build in *diversity*. One beneficial result can be a wider range of choices when seeking to put together the members of international project groups and teams.

The US corporation Du Pont considers that, 'Europe in the 90s represents the largest economic region and absolute growth opporunity in the world'. For 'Du Pont to be a successful global company it must be strong in Europe', where more than one third of the company's sales have been generated. The corporation recognizes the need to 'increasingly commit more resources to respond promptly to the specific needs of the European market'.

In developing its people, Du Pont is 'capitalizing on the diversity of their talents and cultural backgrounds. In Europe, the company 'is continuing down the road towards a new global corporate culture . . . in which European employees are expected to play an increasing role'. Du Pont recognizes that 'The corporate culture of a long-established company is a complex phenomenon made up of value judgements, behaviour patterns, traditions, precepts and expectations, all interrelated. Corporate culture reflects the personalities of a company's employees'.

Ricoh, the Japanese supplier of office automation equipment, employs some 2400 in Europe and its products are manufactured in both France and the UK. Hiroshi Hamada, President of Ricoh, acknowledges that operating in Europe represented a considerable challenge to the Ricoh corporate culture: 'Many years ago we had no idea that we would be conducting operations in Europe on such a large scale. Europe appeared to be too diverse a region in which to conduct unified business, with so many different languages and cultures'.

To cope with the cultural diversity of Europe, Ricoh introduced a policy of localization. Managers were encouraged to put themselves in the positions of local employees and customers. Hiroshi Hamada explains: 'We see it as essential to keep working hard to understand the needs of the local community, to keep changing and improving our service as a member of the community and, above all, to be able to put ourselves in the shoes of the local community'.

Too much diversity, though, can be counter-productive: it may quickly become apparent in a group context that some of those present prefer to quickly come to the point, while others may consider this impolite unless there is first some general conversation to set the scene and establish rapport; certain individuals may concentrate upon achieving one major objective at a time and tackling one issue may be thought to be sufficient for a particular meeting, while other people may regard the same meeting as an opportunity to move forward on a number of fronts simultaneously.

A company intent on becoming more flexible and responsive may have to accept that flexibility is achieved more easily in some countries than in others. Consistency, predictability and a degree of rigidity may be highly valued at a local level. In another context, what may be seen as flexibility and openness may, in fact, be a reluctance to focus and concentrate and a greater susceptibility to distractions and changes of mind. Those who put a premium upon plain speaking may not appreciate that the word 'no' does not feature in the local vocabulary.

The attitudes of Japanese managers need to be understood against a background of two and a half centuries of relative isolation. Their distinct perspective and negotiating style, appreciation of sincerity and how they listen and demonstrate agreement and understanding can be deep rooted. In certain contexts these cultural features can represent great strengths.

Cultural attributes can also be a source of weakness when they are not accompanied by a degree of flexibility. Honda sought to capitalize upon its attitudes and technological strengths in large volume production with the concept of the 'global car'. However, the company failed to appreciate the full extent of market differences. A culture that had put a high value upon integration and standardization also had to come to terms with the growing requirement for customized products and services.

Although acknowledging significant differences between individual companies, the UK's Department of Trade and Industry has identified[4] 'seven signposts', or, qualities that need to be understood by those seeking to build relationships with Japanese customers:

1. meticulous and thorough preparation
2. patience and sustained commitment
3. focus upon quality
4. flexibility in meeting requirements
5. cost reduction
6. cooperation, understanding and teamwork
7. open communication.

The continuation of what may appear core cultural attributes should not always be assumed. For example:

- will the Japanese continue to show such a commitment to work as their standard of living continues to rise and the people become more conscious of the lack of time they have to enjoy the many consumer goods they have acquired?
- will the Japanese educational system put more emphasis upon individual values in order to encourage the diversity that is increasingly required if companies are to meet the growing demand for empathy with, and tailoring to, individual customers?

Many people tend to place a higher value upon the attributes of their own culture than on those of others. Internationalization is viewed in terms of overcoming cultural barriers and inhibitors. On occasion, those from other cultures may be more receptive to what a company is seeking to achieve. The high-tech company wishing to introduce some 'fun' into a corporation may find that little persuasion is needed in Brazil where, according to one interviewee, the managers may 'work for some of the day and play for most of the night'.

UK and US managers may persist in seeing life in terms of a series of steps up a career ladder to an eventual goal that will justify the hard work and commitment of the intervening years. The company, however, may be intent on replacing functional chains of command with a flatter organization composed of teams and taskforces working on various projects. This may match the aspirations of those in other cultures who see life as a journey between situations, each of which should be handled and even enjoyed, but that do not inevitably lead to a certain destination.

8.4 International corporate culture

Head office staff of multinationals can overlook the fact that their own attitudes, behaviour and business practices, many of which may be imposed upon operating companies around the world, will reflect the peculiarities of their own home or domestic culture. Hence, a multinational will frequently be distinguished by a national adjective as an American or Japanese multinational.

The objectives of companies and their management styles can reflect their corporate nationality , as it were:

- the management team of a UK company might be expected to place considerable emphasis upon profitability and shareholder returns as UK companies are well represented in the league tables of the most profitable European companies
- in contrast, the senior management of a German company might be assumed to put more emphasis upon the growth of turnover and meet-

ing the requirements of the employees or social partners as German companies are relatively highly placed in international comparisons of the remuneration of engineering staff
- many Japanese companies put great stress upon an underlying business philosophy, so sustaining and sharing the attitudes that underlie such a philosophy may be regarded by senior managers as more important than tactical production and marketing considerations.

Some national differences emerged in the Adaptation survey carried out for SEMS, *Human Resource Development for International Operation*.[5] For example, non-UK companies appear to be more concerned than UK companies with internationalization as an issue. UK professional firms and associations appear to attach greater importance to it than do UK companies. UK government organizations, even those departments with international links, attach less significance to internationalization than do UK companies.

The culture of a corporation may be recognized from a variety of symptoms:

- a mission statement
- values, concerns and business ethics
- terms of employment
- form of organization
- importance of network relationships
- approach to decision making
- location or pattern of authority
- communication practices
- sharing of information
- criteria for assessment
- delegation of responsibility
- emphasis on teamwork
- focus on quality
- degree of specializaion
- tolerance of diversity
- speed of action
- method of control
- extent of mutual trust
- commitment to learning and development
- openness to outsiders
- sensitivity to values and feelings.

A number of these aspects of corporate culture will be taken for granted by most staff, and so many are not noticed until individuals change jobs.

when they then realize that their new employer has a different way of doing things.

An induction programme or settling in period can be an important part of the process of initiation into a different culture. Some new entrants will, inevitably be unable to adjust to a fresh corporate culture, just as some immigrants fail to settle in certain countries.

The values that companies with strong cultures seek to inculcate in their long-serving managers may not necessarily be those that are prevalent in the home country or other countries in which it operates. It may be more relevant to compare internal corporate culture with the cultures and values of major overseas corporate customers rather than the general attributes of domestic corporate cultures.

Cultural barriers have to be understood if they are to be bridged. The Japan Travel Bureau undertook a survey of its office staff in London that revealed that: 'There was a lack of empathy between Japanese managers and local staff, caused by cultural misunderstandings and language difficulties'.[6] The exercise was repeated across Europe and a pan-European programme of workshops was introduced to bring European and Japanese managers together to explore corporate values. Facilitators were used and, to ensure their full involvement, the participants were encouraged to use their native languages. As a result of the programme, 'in all offices there is much greater appreciation of different values and customs'.

Corporate culture and corporate cooperation

Compatibility of corporate cultures can be a key factor in determining whether or not arrangements, alliances and joint ventures will succeed:

- the logic of market-place requirements and relative technical capability might suggest that Apple and IBM should form a joint company to develop new systems software, but the challenge for those managing the relationship is the extent to which the relatively open, free and flexible approach of Apple can be reconciled with the relatively greater emphasis IBM has put upon hierarchy, structure and operating according to standard procedures
- strategically it made sense for Sony to acquire Columbia Pictures from Coca-Cola in 1990 as a link between the past and future output of Californian creativity at producing software with Japan's traditional hardware manufacturing strengths could be forged, but the 'ad-hocracy' and flair of the film making culture was so different from the discipline and sustained incrementalism of manufacturing as to put great strain on the management of Columbia under Japanese ownership and so the acquisition was followed by some expensive termination payments

- as a combination of both hardware and software has increasingly become the electronic product, so Matsushita Electric of Japan also bought a US entertainments company in 1990: Matsushita acquired MCA and, again, a degree of 'culture clash' occurred
- when the Japanese computer manufacturer Fujitsu acquired the UK company ICL in 1990, an attempt was made to put a 'management ring fence' around ICL in order to preserve its cultural identity and standing as a European company – it was agreed that ICL would operate as an autonomous entity, raising its own finance in Europe and seeking continued participation in European collaborative programmes, and, to preserve their complementary qualities, Fujitsu and ICL agreed to treat each other as trading partners
- Nestlé, following its acquisition of Rowntree in 1988, took action to preserve Rowntree's autonomy and standing in the city of York, so certain of its headquarters' functions were transferred from Switzerland to the UK.

The local firm that achieves an initial rapport, perhaps as a result of being able to speak the language, may not necessarily be the best long-term partner. A local representative may paint a very selective picture of what is happening on the ground so companies need to avoid overdependence on those who offer a bridge to a relatively inaccessible culture.

Corporate culture change

Corporate cultures can change over time in response to an extensive commitment to international operations. As a consequence, the attitudes and values of management teams in different countries may reflect the company's geographic distribution of interests. Executives in a company whose business and trade is overwhelmingly with Hong Kong or South East Asia may have a different perspective from those in other companies whose overseas business relationships are predominantly with Africa or the Middle East.

The international company recognizes that the attitudes and practices of one culture will not necessarily be the most appropriate in another. Effective international operation may require tolerance and acceptance of a number of different and co-existing approaches. Central ways of doing things will not necessarily be better than those preferred at a local level. Indeed, the latter may be more suitable for, and acceptable in, the national context.

A growing number of consultants appear to make a living advising companies of the national characteristics of managers. Such stereotyping can give rise to myths and attitudes that can prejudice a realistic assessment of managers as individuals. Stereotyping can also apply to the characteristics expected of companies registered in certain countries.

Japanese companies, for example, are expected to possess certain characteristics:

- taking a long-term view
- increasing market share
- having a mass-market orientation
- keenness on the application of R&D
- exploiting strategic windows
- an incremental product and market adaptation
- aggressive marketing tactics
- competing on price and features
- employee involvement
- lifetime employment
- the dedication of their top management.

The forces of international competition apply as much to Japanese companies as they do to others. The demand for those with scarce skills is such that more Japanese managers are aware of their market value. In some sectors people are becoming noticeably more individualistic so one's expectations need to be kept up to date.

Most organizations throughout history have been composed largely of those with nationality and other characteristics in common. There have been many exceptions, including religious orders and other organizations, that have drawn their members from many countries and have lasted for hundreds of years. Even in these cases, however, key members have generally been drawn from a few countries and a strong central mission or purpose has been necessary to hold them together.

The major determinants of corporate culture are its:

- company history and traditions
- corporate vision and mission
- culture associated with its business sector
- culture of its headquarters' nation
- culture of its leadership team or professional groups
- culture of its key networks/relationships
- external attitudes and expectations
- form of organization and method of operation
- homogeneity of beliefs and values
- critical success requirements.

A manager should seek to understand the changing corporate cultures of those organizations with which he or she deals. Advancement may depend upon the demonstration of this understanding. Empathy with the culture of a customer, supplier or business partner can help to build a working relationship.

A corporate culture also needs to be understood in order that it can be changed. A company may be seeking to move from a directive culture to an approach based more upon involvement, discussion and consensus. In the EC, staff used to taking orders may need some encouragement to fully participate. In contrast, those operating in Asia may find that the new approach is considered natural by local staff who may be unfamiliar with the practice of issuing and responding to direct commands.

8.5 Communication and the network organization

In some companies too much emphasis is put upon national cultural barriers to communication and too little upon other barriers – for example, those relating to the use of information technology. An example of such a barrier would be the incompatibility of PTT standards at national borders. This can frustrate attempts to create an international network.

When messages cross national borders in the form of cryptic telephone calls, fax sheets or electronic mail notes, the risk of misunderstanding due to cultural differences may be greater than in face-to-face meetings as people who are together in the same room can provide each other with various non-verbal clues. While in the US, UK and Scandinavia, great emphasis may be attached to precise wording and drafting, in certain cultures meaning and understanding may be communicated to a greater extent by non-verbal means. Body language and the context in which communication takes place may assume a vital significance in relation to the form of words used.

The way messages themselves are constructed will not be the same in all countries. A group made up exclusively of those from one country may have become accustomed to working together by electronic mail and they might overlook the need to be aware of possible sources of misunderstanding when those of different nationalities are introduced into a team.

Barriers to effective international communication need to be identified and understood if they are to be successfully tackled. The nature and relative importance of technical obstacles to communication will vary according to the purpose of communication. Is it to secure a piece of information or to exchange views? How much time is there in which to respond? Is communication likely to be on a continuing basis? Where visual clues are important, telephone conferencing could be replaced by video conferencing.

Technology can help those who are aware of its limitations to overcome barriers of distance, language and culture. Its drawbacks may be more than compensated for when its many advantages are taken into account. Network organizations distinguish themselves by the extent to which they harness the potential of converging information and telecommunications technologies.

In a corporate culture in which views are exchanged by means of text-dominated memos, individuals may require access to translation facilities before they are able to respond. The introduction of workstations with a relatively user-friendly graphical interface can enable messages with a higher visual element to be sent by electronic mail:

- within Ford, some 2000 knowledge workers can access a central design database so that when design changes occur, they can be communicated to relevant staff throughout the world and exchanges of views can be almost instantaneous
- Northwest Airlines has been a pioneer in the use of workstations linked to local and wide area networks – by using scanners and artificial intelligence technology, the Northwest network has enabled data from documents around the world to be 'captured' and this has meant that both the response to customer needs and management reporting can now take place on a 24-hour basis.

Diagrams and charts can aid electronic communication, clarification can be sought, and elucidation given, a number of times in the course of an afternoon and elements of an incoming communication can easily be shared with, or 'bounced around', colleagues in order to obtain their comments and views.

Electronic messages tend to be relatively short and to the point so contributions can be fed directly into final documents without the necessity of re-typing. Managers in geographically distant locations may be only seconds away in terms of exchanges of electronic mail.

Many managers make greater use of visual images when communicating with multinational audiences. As a result of being able to visualize the nature of their inputs into documents, they may feel more involved and focusing on and clearly presenting key points can be a useful discipline.

Document management is a key corporate task when the cost of producing and handling documents can absorb a tenth of the turnover of many businesses. A supplier such as the Xerox Corporation is able to design and install global document management systems and processes that have a multilingual capability. For example, Chinese and other characters can be handled by the document network, enabling managers to work in their first languages.

8.6 Culture and international communication

Culture may, but need not, be a significant factor in international communication:

- in some specialist fields, the language of greatest value in international communication may be a computer language or the language of mathematics or a science and many such languages employ symbols that are recognized internationally so a computer program or mathematical problem, therefore, may, in essence, lack any particular nationality
- functional and specialist groups may find common ground in the language of their profession – whether this be the principles of engineering or international accounting conventions – so it may be advisable to encourage managers to attend international meetings of their professions in order to broaden their perspective.

Companies that have their own international policies, practices and processes may find that these create a shared approach and a bond between employees independent of nationality. In some cases a corporate culture can take on the attributes of a particular national culture. Other and very strong corporate cultures might even take on a distinctive existence of their own.

Operating within a 'differentiated' corporate culture may not be incompatible with the preservation and observance of behaviour patterns based on national cultures. The truly international company goes beyond tolerance and acceptance of national differences and preferences, it actively seeks to encourage and understand them and will apply them elsewhere as appropriate.

Greater diversity and variety can and should be sought among those who share the vision as learning and change are more likely to occur where views are continually challenged and there is tension between alternative viewpoints. Debate can be more important than a consensus that is based upon uncritical acceptance.

Different ways of doing things should be actively encouraged within an international network organization, so that different elements of the network may learn from each other. The drive for a shared understanding of certain ground rules for effective intercultural communication can itself strengthen a distinct corporate culture. Effective international communication involves:

- understanding conventions concerning greetings, interruptions, listening, giving tips, treatment of staff, etc.
- being aware of and observing local sources of respect and status
- not infringing upon personal space

- avoiding gestures, value-laden judgements or comments that may cause offence
- being prepared to accept that differences of values and opinions can exist
- appreciating that knowledge and what is right or best may be relative to context rather than being absolutes
- trying to understand the perspectives of the other parties involved
- adjusting expectations regarding outputs, timescales, etc., to suit local circumstances
- being patient and avoiding emotional reactions to frustrations and disappointments
- aiming to refine understanding and practice with experience
- not over-estimating linguistic understanding
- appreciating that to *understand* a point that has been made is not necessarily to *agree* with it.

There are also few companies that cannot learn from others – even the most formidable of competitors have areas of weakness. The Japanese company that excels at efficient volume production may well need to be more flexible in tailoring products to local markets. Indeed, a number of Japanese companies appear to be finding it difficult to move closer to their customers in overseas markets because of a lack of home-grown managers with international experience. The development of Japanese managers on assignments abroad is limited in some companies because of their reluctance to devolve responsibilities away from centres in Japan.

A disadvantage of centralized international planning is that head office staff will interpret the meanings of communications in terms of their own experience and culture. The meaning of words can vary between cultures, so different shades of meaning and subtle differences of emphasis can be lost when inputs from various countries are aggregated by national planning staff.

When in doubt, one should always check an interpretation with the source of the information. In an issue monitoring and management exercise, for example, draft summaries and reports could be circulated to those who have provided inputs to ensure that consolidations are an accurate reflection of their views.

8.7 Culture and international teams

When selecting members of international teams, thought should be given to the extent of any culture gaps between individuals. How relevant are these to the content of discussions and form of interaction that is sought? Will there be time, and is there a capacity, for cultural adaptation?

A mature executive should be able to handle such differences as the US preference for informality and the use of first names as compared with the German insistence on formality and the sensitive executive would not arrange a breakfast meeting if this would be regarded as an imposition by one or more of the team members. Participation in international taskforces and teams can increase a manager's awareness of differing national attitudes towards such matters as the recording of decisions, humour, status, dress, punctuality, entertainment and teamworking itself.

Within the management team, a Japanese manager might feel obliged to observe the consensus that emerges, while, in contrast, an Italian or French manager may be reluctant to implement a decision with which they do not personally agree. Local staff may observe a number of religious and traditional practices at work locations that can affect their relationships with colleagues. These could range from offerings to Gods to consulting a lunar calendar to determine whether or not it is a good day to negotiate business.

The greater the number of dimensions of difference – whether of linguistic ability, function, company or level of seniority – the more difficult cultural adaptation may become. If a group or team is to function effectively, there must be a sufficient area of common ground. This could lie in the strength of commitment to an objective, a shared technical understanding or common ways of thinking and learning.

A focus upon *differences* between national cultures can obscure the *similarities*. Self-aware executives understand the weaknesses as well as the strengths of their own culture. For example, impatience and a desire for instant and tangible results, qualities praised within the US corporate culture, may not be the best attributes for successful penetration of the Japanese market.

The more superficial aspects of culture can also mislead. One should avoid the temptation to have an unjustified faith in one person rather than another just because of a better command of the English language – linguistic ability may not be matched by business competence or commitment to a corporate mission.

8.8 The importance of languages

It could be argued that the learning of one or more foreign languages should be part of the preparation of any citizen for life in today's world. In some countries this is, to some degree, the case, with a significant proportion of the population being able to speak and understand an international language such as English. In such cases, people do not wait until they join a company with international operations before undertaking language studies.

UK nationals do not have a good reputation for a willingness and ability to learn a foreign language. One defence of the UK approach is that, in many sectors of business, English is the language of international commerce. However, in most countries of the world it is a *second* language. Within the EC, German, not English, is the most widely spoken language.

The arguments in favour of being able to converse and negotiate in the language of the customer have been well rehearsed. However, language skills of themselves may not be enough. Understanding the local culture, as we have seen, is an essential pre-condition of business success in many parts of the world.[7]

Language skill matched with cultural awareness demonstrates commitment, improves understanding and helps to achieve a rapport. Importantly, it can enable direct contact to take the place of communication through intermediaries. The dangers of an inadequate language facility leading to misunderstanding are also widely appreciated. In those sectors in which goods and services are increasingly tailored to the requirements of individual customers, an ability to enter into a dialogue with them in their own language tends to become more important.

In some such cases language training may not be needed, for example where the interface with customers is undertaken by local nationals. The customers may speak, or at least understand, the language of the company. In some business sectors, such as information technology, most of the available literature and many of the programs used are in English.

Some foreign language requirements do not come so immediately to mind so they may be overlooked and, yet, they can be of considerable importance. They are understood by the international company. These requirements are:

- answering incoming calls and letters
- understanding foreign technical requirements and regulations
- product documentation, labelling and manuals for foreign markets
- foreign advertising and marketing materials
- monitoring the activities, messages and dcoumentation of competitors
- entering into foreign agreements and arrangements
- drafting contracts and other legal documents
- negotiating, bargaining and selling
- communicating with one's own suppliers, customers and staff
- securing access to foreign expertise and know-how
- consolidating information from various national operating companies
- satisfying foreign legal and reporting requirements
- participating in international discussions and disputes.

Language policy

The languages that a company's staff should be encouraged and helped to acquire will depend upon the pattern of its business. A knowledge of German may be of value in Eastern Europe, while Spanish and Portuguese will be of greater importance if the priority is developing business opportunities in Central and South America.

Language policy should reflect customer requirements. It is not unknown for companies to train sales staff in local language skills, but *not* those who may actually be required to provide customers with ongoing support. Once sold, products may need to be serviced or updated. This can involve liaison and much contact between technical staff. Those who may receive technical enquiries from foreign customers need to be equipped to respond.

A number of multinational and transnational companies have adopted English as their 'corporate language'. The English used in such companies, particularly by those for whom it is not a native language, has been called 'offshore English'.[8] This offshore English can vary from company to company and, while it may on occasion seem strange to a native English speaker, it gives those of other nationalities a common base for communication.

In general terms, an international company should employ staff with language skills appropriate to their jobs. Where this is not possible, one may be able to utilize the language skills of business partners such as local distributors. The key requirement is access to relevant language skills as and when needed.

The requirement for particular language skills is not always easy to predict. For example:

- for some companies, the need for a general programme to increase language skills may not arise – *ad hoc* access to skills may be sufficient
- in other cases a new development, such as a decision to enter a particular market or conclude a strategic alliance, may overnight create a new requirement for language skills
- a need for a wider understanding of foreign languages could arise as a result of organizations or groups in additional countries joining an international network.

The first step in preparing for the future may be to understand the present. A company undertaking a significant expansion of its international operations is likely to require some form of 'language audit'. This will establish a database of existing language skills and determine what, if any, further language skills are needed by each individual. Such an audit should distinguish between listening, reading, speaking and writing skills. The more detailed an audit, the easier it will be to tailor language training to the needs of particular functions or groups.

The prime requirement may be an understanding of the foreign terminology relating to one's own job. This may involve an understanding of foreign practice and conventions as well as foreign vocabulary. Such specific preparation may well be of greater value than general language training. It may also secure greater commitment on the part of those learning, because the relevance of what is being learned is clear.

The results of a language audit should be recorded. The language skills of individuals may be an important consideration when selecting the members of an international project group or team. A database of language skills can also allow customer enquiries to be routed, and responded, to by those with the most appropriate language skills. In the case of the network organization, this routing can occur automatically and regardless of location through the use of call forwarding arrangements.

Learning languages

The best way of learning a foreign language will depend upon the people involved. What is the level of their existing knowledge? What is their learning potential? There may be some areas of possible sensitivity to consider: how, for example, will a senior manager react to being outshone by a junior with a greater facility for languages?

Often it is those who may be regarded as more junior within an organization, such as secretaries and telephonists, who may have the greatest need for language skills as a result of being the first point of contact for those calling from abroad. Wherever possible, learning groups should be composed of those with similar levels of skill, learning potential and seniority to avoid unnecessary conflict and, therefore, facilitate learning.

The acquisition of language skills can be time-consuming and costly. Some of the investment may be recouped as a result of lower expenditure on translation and interpretation services. These tend to be relatively expensive and their use can sometimes make significant inroads into profit margins. The most significant commitment is likely to be that of management time. This is more likely to be given freely and energetically when the individuals concerned perceive the relevance and value of language skills to their own jobs and careers.

First encounters with learning a language can have a lasting impact. One approach involves a period of total immersion in the country whose language is to be acquired. This can also allow some understanding to be gained of the local culture and the distractions of the office environment can be avoided. The base established can then be built upon by means of lunchtime, evening or weekend courses. Jaguar Cars uses full-time and total immersion language courses to prepare its staff for service abroad.

One airline operates a programme of total immersion cultural weekends to prepare selected staff for service abroad. Many other companies interviewed do not provide any induction into the social, cultural and business context within which their managers are expected to operate abroad, preparation often being limited to just learning the language.

At little incremental cost, a company could arrange country weeks in its various catering establishments at which national or ethnic cuisine could be offered. Alternatively, national tables could be set up for those who might wish to practise a particular language over lunch. Many of these initiatives can add some variety to the working lives of those involved. Once the initial concept has been accepted, this sort of initiative can be self-sustaining.

The full support of the family can also encourage the person learning the language. Where a relocation overseas is planned, it may be sensible to offer a course to the spouses or partners. A period in an overseas company could be regarded as a development opportunity for the whole family. This is important because, while some executives will be motivated primarily by their own career objectives, others may be more concerned with the interests and views of the family as a unit.

Check-list

- Is your company sufficiently aware of the cultural dimension in so far as it relates to its international operations and the requirements of particular customers?
- Does your company take cultural factors into account when bringing together international taskforces and teams, defining roles and allocating responsibilities for activities and tasks?
- Are your company's managers properly equipped for cross-cultural communication and multicultural teamworking?
- Does your company have a distinct corporate culture and how appropriate is it in relation to its vision and international strategy?
- Do any skills audits that are undertaken in your company pay sufficient attention to cross-cultural skills and sensitivity to cultural diversity?
- Is the possession of, or a lack of, cross-cultural and other international skills assessed, recorded on your company's personnel records and considered when career move and location decisions are taken?
- Is there an international skills database that can be accessed across the

network and consulted when multinational teams have to be formed?
– Does your company's language skills assessment and training distinguish between listening, speaking, reading and writing skills, and does the training reflect the particular requirements of the individuals and groups concerned?

References

1. Lawrence, Paul R, and Charalambos A Vlachoutsicos, *Behind The Factory Walls – Decision Making in Soviet and US Enterprises*, Harvard Business School Press, 1991.
2. Coulson-Thomas, Colin J, *Too Old at 40?*, British Institute of Management, 1989.
3. Henley Centre for Forecasting and Leisure Development Centre of Japan, *Leisure Futures*, Henley Centre for Forecasting, 1991.
4. PA Consulting Group, *Power in Partnership, Building Business with Japanese Electronics Manufacturers*, UK Department of Trade and Industry, 1991.
5. Coulson-Thomas, Colin J, *Human Resource Development for International Operation*, a survey sponsored by Surrey European Management School, Adaptation, 1990.
6. Fitzgerald, Janet, 'A Japanese Lesson in European Togetherness', *Personnel Management*, pp 45–7, September 1991.
7. Guy, Vincent, and John Mattock, *The New International Manager*, Kogan Page, 1991.
8. Young, George, *The New Export Marketer,* Kogan Page, 1991.

Further reading

Barham, Kevin, and David Oates, *The International Manager*, Business Books, 1991.
Jacobson, Gary, and John Hillkirk, *Xerox: American Samurai*, Macmillan, 1986.
Jervis, Robert, *Perception and Misperception in International Politics*, Princeton University Press, 1976.
Jones, Stephanie, *Working for the Japanese*, Macmillan, 1991.
Liston, David, and Nigel Reed, *Business Studies, Languages and Overseas Trade*, Pitman Publishing and The Institute of Export, 1985.
Little, R, and S Smith, *Belief Systems and International Relations*, Basil Blackwell, 1988.
Mole, John, *Mind Your Manners: Culture and Clash in the Single European Market*, Industrial Society Press, 1991.
Moran, Robert T, *Cultural Guide to Doing Business in Europe*, Butterworth/Heinemann, 1991.

9
Labour markets and international operation

Perspectives

The labour market is what we and our competitors decide it is to be. The extent to which we compete, and for what, decides how wide the net is cast.

Director, Human Resources, UK company

What is a national labour market in Africa, or in parts of the world such as the Balkans where states are breaking up? You need ethnic and cultural rather than political maps.

Chairman, UK multinational corporation

The arrangements for military service are very important for us. This is the age at which we recruit, and the gap between university and work, and how people are treated, has a strong influence on their attitudes.

Personnel Director, German chemical company

Our obligations are ultimately to our owners. We owe them good returns, and we are not in the social welfare business. If it costs more to employ people in Europe, then we will move the manufacturing jobs somewhere else, perhaps to the Pacific Rim.

President, US multinational corporation

If the free market came to China, we would be looking for technical staff not in China, but in US Universities. These are the people who will be familiar with our processes.

Director, Australian industrial company

In some cities in Brazil we measure the risk of being 'done over' if you walk down the street. You travel light and poor. Labour market conditions are a matter of staying alive.

Director, international hospital products group

You don't know a labour market until you understand the factors that are going to affect it. Japanese companies are going to source more of their products in Taiwan, Singapore and South Korea. This will have a significant impact upon the market for skilled labour.

Director, European technology group

9.1 Introduction

The personnel experience of a company without significant international operations may be largely limited to its domestic labour market. However, even a company without any international activities may find that the labour market of its home country is influenced by developments at regional level. For example, a company operating exlusively in the UK may need to keep a close eye on the progress of those EC directives that are likely to have a direct or indirect impact upon its activities.

Companies with more extensive international operations will be aware of material differences between national labour markets. We will consider these in this chapter. We will also examine some of the distinguishing features of HRD and labour market research in an international context. Finally in this chapter, we will examine trade unions and the extent to which their acitivities might influence international operations.

9.2 National and international labour markets

As a result of internationalization, many companies are encountering a wider range of languages, of differences of culture, attitudes, habits and tastes, business practices and legal requirements. While the marketing team will be primarily concerned with the impact of such differences upon purchase and consumption decisions, the personnel professional will need to consider their implications for various aspects of employment, such as recruitment and remuneration.

In most companies, the great majority of people are likely to be employed on *local* conditions of employment and, hence, a great variety of such conditions may be encountered. The extent to which differences will concern those at the centre will depend upon the division of responsibilities between staff functions and operating units.

In Chapter 7 we examined desirable qualities in international managers. Many companies are able to support significant international operations without recruiting and developing a cadre of international managers. The internationalization of managers may be limited to those being prepared for management positions, requiring them to have an understanding of operations in a number of countries or those with specialist professional or technical skills who may be required to support operations in different countries. Such individuals may be employed on international terms. Otherwise, many companies take the view that there is no reason why someone employed on local conditions of employment should not have international responsibilities.

Mobility (a topic we will consider more fully in Chapter 12) can vary greatly across different categories of staff. A 'high price' labour market for senior international executives, for example, has been created by professional headhunters, while the willingness of 'top researchers' to move is causing research centres to be moved to those locations likely to attract such migrants. However, among managers in general there may actually be some reluctance to move.

An international perspective on labour market issues

The personnel practitioner with global responsibilities in an international company needs to understand human resource issues in an international context. Unemployment or the availability of young people with appropriate aptitude or skill may be concentrated at certain points around the globe. The extent to which people are willing to be mobile or are self-employed also varies significantly between countries. For example, a Dutch, Irish or UK manager might be more willing to relocate than a French or German manager.

At the global level, there are significant differences between regions on major demographic indicators:

- for some years, unemployment in the EC has been roughly one and a half times that in the US and four times that in Japan
- the labour force of the EC is expected to grow by 2 per cent by the year 2000; that of Japan and the US is expected to grow by 8 per cent and 17 per cent respectively; in the decade to the year 2000 the labour force of the developing world is expected to grow by 45 per cent
- the population of the EC is ageing: between 1990 and 2020, the proportion of those in the total population aged over 65 is expected to *rise* from 14 to 20 per cent, while the proportion of those under 15 *falls* by 3 per cent; in contrast, in Africa 45 per cent of the population is under 15 years of age and this segment is expected to increase still further.

A significant source of untapped human potential lies outside the 'triad' of the developed world.

Japan faces severe skill shortages. The Japanese Ministry of Labour has calculated that, continuing at present growth rates and with current practices, there will be a labour shortage of 2.6 million people by the year 2000 and over 9 million by the year 2010. Given that Japan has tightened rather than relaxed its rules on immigration, much greater use will need to be made of female skills and new technologies. The internationalization of many Japanese companies is, in part, a search for overseas sources of skill.

In the developed countries, whole populations may be ageing, at various rates, while, in other parts of the world there may be an overwhelmingly larger number of *younger* people. Even within the EC, the participation rate of women in the labour market in Denmark is over twice that in Spain. Compared with Greece and Italy, more than four times as many of the women employed in the UK work on a part-time basis.

There are many special circumstances that can inhibit a full contribution from individual employees:

- access to higher level skills at lower cost
- multilocation teams
- one-off tasks
- uneven workload
- staff shortages
- specific skill requirements
- relocation/disruption
- maternity teleworking
- management development
- 'step' expansion
- overhead/headcount reduction
- plateaued managers.

It is surprising how many of these situations are encountered by most managers at some point in their career. They will also be present to a greater extent in some cultures than in others.

A corporate programme to encourage the greater participation of women might encounter severe difficulties in much of the Middle East, indeed, the objections could prevent its application. Greater respect is given in some cultures than others to those who are older, as we have seen, and this could impact on employment. Also attitudes to the family vary greatly between different countries and could, therefore, influence attitudes to employment in different ways.

A regional perspective on labour market issues

Significant differences can exist between labour markets in the *same* region. For example, at the level of major economic indicators within the EC, the gross domestic product per head in 1991 for the UK, while not the highest of the member states in the EC, is about twice that of the lowest.

The gross domestic product per head in Luxembourg was two and a half times that in Greece.

There are also significant variations within the EC in the areas of education and training:

- the proportion of Germans in part- and full-time education at the age of 18 is twice that in the UK
- the proportion of the labour force receiving some training in 1989 varied from less than 2 per cent in Greece and Portugal to more than 15 per cent in Denmark and the Netherlands.

In May 1991 unemployment within the EC exceeded 12.5 million, or 8.7 per cent of a labour force of some 140 million.[1] About half of these had been unemployed for over a year. In all member states other than Belgium, the unemployment rate of women was above that of men – women are twice as likely to be unemployed as men in most member states.

Within the EC, the rate of unemployment in 1990 ranged from 1.5 per cent in the Grand Duchy of Luxembourg to 28.9 per cent, or, approaching three out of ten, of those in the Spanish region of Centa y Melilla. The rate of unemployment in the Republic of Ireland and Spain was over ten times that in Luxembourg. In the south of the EC, particularly in Greece and Italy, there is considerable under-employment or concealed unemployment among those working less than full-time on small farms.

Other differences between the North and South of the EC are apparent in industrial employment. Manufacturing employment in the EC fell during the 1980s. Whereas in 1987 high-growth industries accounted for over 45 per cent of manufacturing jobs in many regions of France and Germany, the proportion was under 25 per cent over most of the South of the EC. The situation is reversed in the case of low-growth labour-intensive industries.

Considerable variation can also occur in basic labour market factors, such as the age of retirement:

- within the EC, this has varied from 60 to 67 years for men and from 55 to 67 years for women (see Table 9.1), although in 1991 the Italian government announced a review of the age of retirement
- in the UK, many companies have raised the retirement age of women to that of men following a 1990 ruling of the European Court in the case of Barber v Guardian Royal Exchange to the effect that employees cannot be given differential occupational pension benefits on the basis of age
- in comparison, in Japan, the retirement age of those working for large companies is 55, but thereafter many go on to work for smaller companies and, as a consequence, some 70 per cent of Japanese men in their early sixties are still working

– in Eastern Europe or what was the Soviet Union the age of retirement has depended upon such factors as the nature of the work undertaken or the number of children a person has had, so that in the former Soviet Union, men have retired between 55 and 60, while the age of retirement of women has varied between 45 and 55.

There are wide variations in the number of foreign employees in different countries. Over half of the non-Community employees in the EC work in Germany and France. An affluent area such as the EC faces growing pressure from those trying to emmigrate from North Africa in the South and what was the Soviet Union and the emerging democracies beyond its eastern border. A company establishing operations in certain EC cities, or indeed in California or Florida, could find itself operating in a multicultural and multilingual environment.

Labour practices can vary, even between adjacent countries. For example, the extent to which a labour force is unionized can vary significantly between countries (we will be examining trade unions later in this chapter).

The status of professionals, and the route to professional qualifications, can also vary greatly between different states. Hence the importance attached to the mutual recognition of professional and other qualifications within the EC.

Some categories of workers and professionals, as we have seen, will be more willing to be internationally mobile than others. Trade unionism and professionalism can both stand in the way of mobility. In many cases, the most mobile are those at each end of the skill spectrum – those without skills and the very highly skilled. Those in between become caught by the various institutional mechanisms and by social, cultural and language differences, that reduce mobility.

Within the EC, labour mobility from one area to another actually decreased during the 1980s. There has been a return drift from the North of those who previously migrated to Germany, back to countries of origin in the South.

In certain areas apparent differences can conceal similarities:

– for example, there might appear to be a more significant variation in the approach to, and calculation of, working time among EC member states than is actually the case because, if account is taken of overtime, the average hours of full-time work are generally in the range of some 40 to 41 hours per week across the Community
– in some respects there has been some convergence in the level and pattern of social protection across Europe, but significant national differences still remain,[2] because this has mainly resulted from increases in member

Table 9.1   Ages of retirement in the EC

Sex	B	DK	D	GR	E	F	IRL	I	L	NL	P	UK
Men	65	67	65*	65	65	60	66	60	65	65	65	65
Women	60	62	65*	60	65	60	66	55	65	65	62	60

*Between 63 and 67, at the person's discretion.
Source: European Commission, 1990

states such as Greece, Portugal and Spain with lower levels of protection and, in 1989, the proportion of gross domestic product in these countries devoted to social protection was only just over half that in the Netherlands and Denmark.

A national perspective on labour market issues

To examine the extent to which national labour market characteristics can persist within the EC, let us consider one member state. The UK under a Conservative government has opposed elements of the EC's Social Dimension and favoured the retention of diversity within the EC. Differences have been viewed as a healthy source of competitive advantage.

Other member states stress the extent to which national differences can distort competition or undermine the commitment of organized labour to the single market process. Labour representatives in a country such as Germany have sought to protect an erosion of the relatively high levels of social protection they have secured.

The UK has a fairly flexible labour market. For example, some five million people, or over one in five of those employed, work on a part-time basis and this proportion is expected to increase. The UK proportion, while four times that in Italy, is below that in Denmark, where approaching a quarter of those employed work on a part-time basis.

Between 1987 and 1989, part-time employment in the UK increased by 7 per cent, more than twice the rate of increase in France. In the UK and Denmark over one in five jobs are part-time. Some three out of ten of those at work in the Netherlands are part-timers. In contrast, in Greece, Italy and Portugal, it is unusual for people to work on a part-time basis. On the other hand, in Greece, Portugal and Spain, about one in five are employed on a temporary basis, whereas in the UK, Belgium and Italy the proportion is only about one in twenty.

People in the UK appear more willing than those in other member states to become economically independent:

– between 1980 and 1987, the number of people who are self-employed in the UK grew by over 800 000, which accounted for the whole of the increase of self-employment in the EC during this period, and the number of self-employed women in the UK has more than doubled since 1979
– the UK has been the leader in Europe in the area of management buy-outs, accounting for over a half of those occurring in Europe in 1990.

The experience of one member state, such as that of the UK, can influence developments elsewhere in the EC. There is some evidence, for example, that managers in larger companies in other member states are increasingly willing to leave the security of multinational corporation employment to set up their own businesses.[3] Trends elsewhere should be monitored.

Experiences can transcend regional boundaries as well as national borders within regions. The UK car company Rover had adopted a variety of 'Japanese' labour practices. Its New Deal proposals are designed to learn from benchmark practices, such as *continuous improvement*, *single status* and *single grade* employment, which are used by Japanese companies, including its strategic partner Honda.

A corporate policy on such matters as teleworking or the use of skills on a part-time basis, may need to take account of wide variations in practice and these may be related to the existence of legal restrictions.

9.3 The regional HRD framework

Personnel specialists need to remain up to date with changing legal requirements in the international human resource environment. Access to relevant expertise on a continuing basis may be required.

National requirements frequently change as new laws and regulations are introduced and new precendents are established. Additionally, within regional groupings of states such as the EC, there may be programmes and measures, including EC Directives, Regulations and Recommendations, that might influence developments in a number of countries.

Within a region there can be various forms of diversity:

– in some areas, the EC Commission has recognized the likely continuation of a significant degree of diversity among member states – for example, in the summer of 1991, the Commission adopted a proposal for a Recommendation to promote employee participation in profits and 'enterprise results', including equity participation, and it acknowledges, and is not seeking to reduce, the variety of financial participation schemes in use across the EC, but the Commission announced its intention to

investigate the difficulties being experienced in the operation of cross-border schemes
- within the EC, there has been some discussion of the prospect of a 'two-tier' or 'two-speed' Europe and, in the area of border checks, some member states have already indicated a willingness to move more quickly than others – under the Schengen Agreements, the three Benelux countries, France, Germany and Italy, agreed to end checks at the common borders of the signatory states from 1 January 1992.

New regions can emerge. For example, the signing of a Treaty for an economic community in Moscow in October 1991 could be said to have transformed the former Soviet Union from a single state into an economic region composed of a commonwealth of independent states.

The boundaries of a region can also change. The countries of Eastern Europe, Poland, Czechoslovakia, Hungary, Yugoslavia, Romania and Bulgaria have all been developing economic links with the EC and, in 1991, EC external affairs Commissioner Frans Andriessen pointed out that EC institutions might have to cope with as many as 24 member states.

The EC HRD framework

Progress towards the creation of a single market within the EC continues to be made. Of the 282 proposals in the 1985 'Cockfield' White Paper,[4] three quarters had been adopted by the end of 1990. By the summer of 1991, 89 measures were still to be approved by the 12 member states,[5] only 17 of these being considered by the Commission to have a reasonable prospect of adoption by the end of 1991. Outstanding issues tend to be those that are more sensitive and intractable.

Member states vary in the extent to which EC measures are translated into national law and enforced so the Commission has increasingly focused upon implementation and measures to allow for the prompt institution of infringement proceedings. By the end of 1990, only the UK had implemented *all* the 18 legislative measures in the social affairs field that had been agreed by the EC. Germany had implemented 16 measures, France 15 and Italy only 9. One of the measures that had not been implemented in Italy dated from 1975.

Within the EC there are several strands of developments of relevence to people management:

- there are measures concerning freedom of movement that are designed to encourage mobility of labour and questions such as rights of residence and work are also covered

- there are employment and employment rights measures, for example concerning equal pay, sex discrimination, disclosure and participation, patterns of work, proof of an employment relationship and transfer of undertakings
- there are measures to encourage the mutual recognition of professional qualifications, designed to make it easier for professionals who qualify in one member state to practice in others
- there are health and safety directives that affect the workplace and provisions and proposals relating to product safety to protect people as consumers
- there is also an Action Programme of measures and initiatives to implement various proposals of the Social Charter.[6]

On ratification of the 1991 agreement between the EC and EFTA, from 1993 free movement, the right to live, work and offer services and such measures as the mutual recognition of professional qualifications would apply across the European Economic Area. Some exemption is provided for Switzerland with its strict immigration policy, but the Swiss have five more years to come into line.

Those concerned with human resources should keep a close eye on health and safety developments as these can be of concern to companies in a wide range of sectors. An example is the Directive on the control of asbestos that was adopted by the Council of Ministers in June 1991 for implementation by 31 December 1992. Another proposed Directive that was under consideration at the same time, namely that on construction sites, is an example of a proposal that might have a significant impact upon one particular sector.

The EC Charter of Fundamental Social Rights was adopted by all member states with the exception of the UK on 9 December 1989.[7] While it does not create binding legal rights or obligations, the Commission brought forward on 29 November 1989 a complementary and non-binding Action Programme that identifies over 40 areas in which it believes steps need to be taken in what is termed the Social Dimension.[6] Within the Social Charter there are measures concerning a range of matters of some importance to human resource professionals:

- living and working conditions
- freedom of movement
- employment and remuneration
- social protection
- freedom of association and collective bargaining
- vocational training

- equal treatment for men and women
- information, consultation and worker participation
- health protection and safety at the work-place.

In many cases, and according to the principle of subsidiarity, it is proposed that the action required be taken by the individual member states or by non-binding opinions or recommendations of the Commission. Nevertheless, some Directives are proposed under the Action Programme. For example, four proposed Directives of relevance to the use of flexible patterns of work such as part-time and temporary employment are considered in Chapter 10.

Progress on the EC Social Dimension has been slower than most member states would have liked. A number of proposals from the Commission, brought forward under the Action Programme derived from the Social Charter, have been blocked by UK opposition.

The Commission has shown a particular interest in improving the participation of women, training and the encouragement of continuous training. At the start of 1991 there were proposals concerning, or with implications for, employee participation in the Draft European Company statute, the Draft Fifth, Ninth and Tenth Company Law Directives and the Vredeling Directive. There were other Draft Directives covering part-time and temporary work and parental leave.

During 1991 the Commission was expected to publish proposals concerning such areas as disabled workers, free movement, subcontracting, financial participation, protection of young people at work and an amendment of a Directive on collective redundancies. Measures in the pipeline covered such matters as contract compliance, pensions, training and young workers. Together these amount to a significant number of proposals that need to be monitored.

In Chapter 6 we looked at some of the management aspects of acquisitions, arrangements and joint ventures. In the EC there are particular legislative measures designed to protect the rights of employees when the ownership of a business is transferred or as a result of an arrangement there are collective redundancies or insolvency occurs. Examples of EC protection for the rights of employees with how they were introduced into the UK are:

- *Collective Redundancies Directive:*
  - requires advance notification of collective redundancies and consultation concerning the consequences
  - implemented in the UK as Part IV of the Employment Protection Act 1975

- *Insolvency Directive*
  - requires member states to establish a guarantee fund to cover the outstanding pay of employees in the event of employer insolvency
  - already covered in UK by the Employment Protection (Consolidation) Act 1978
- *Transfer of Undertakings Directive:*
  - requirements concerning the rights of employees when there is a transfer of ownership of a business; coverage has been widened by three decisions of the European Court of Justice
  - introduced in the UK by the Transfer of Undertakings (Protection of Employees) Regulations, effective from May 1982.

Other areas of EC legislation such as free movement, equality of treatment or health and safety could also be relevant in the context of an international joint venture within the EC.

The EC legal framework

Citizens of the EC already have rights under the 1957 Treaty of Rome to set up in business and provide services throughout the EC. An international company with a policy of making use of the most relevant skills regardless of nationality should not need to worry about provisions such as Articles 7, 48, 49, 59 and 60 of the EEC Treaty concerning discrimination on grounds of nationality. Article 7 prohibits discrimination on grounds of nationality, while Articles 48 and 49 give all EC citizens the right to live and work anywhere in the EC without discrimination for reasons of nationality, unless this can be justified on grounds of public policy, security or health.

Under Articles 59 and 60, which give EC citizens the right to establish a business or provide services anywhere in the EC without discrimination on grounds of nationality, an organization cannot specify that those undertaking work for it should employ local nationals.

The law of some countries, including that of several EC member states and that of the EC itself, is a civil law system. This is based upon legislation and, unlike the common law system of the UK, judicial decisions do not form precedents. In the absence of such precedents, the volume of detailed legislation can be higher in a civil law system.

Decisions of the European Court are binding upon all member states, although the Court itself need not be bound by its own past decisions. EC law prevails over the national laws of member states. EC legislation, unlike the literal interpretation applied in the UK to UK law, is interpreted according to its intended purpose.

In general, there is no common sanction across the EC in the event of a breach of EC law, whether a Directive or European Court of Justice Decision. It is left to the member states to determine the sanctions so the penalties in respect of the same circumstances could be stiff in one member state and derisory in another.

Proposals for Community legislation are drafted and agreed by the Commission and are then put formally to the Council of Ministers. The European Parliament has an input, but the final decision rests with the Council.

In the case of the EC, Directives once agreed by the Council of Ministers have to be implemented into national law by each member state. A Regulation of the commission has immediate legal effect within each member state without the necessity of changing national law. Recommendations do not have a binding effect, although they can have some moral authority in influencing future conduct. One can subscribe to a range of databases that give up-to-date information on the state of various measures.

A unanimous decision is required concerning proposed EC measures that relate to taxation, free movement and the rights and interests of employees. However, following the Single European Act, measures relating to health and safety protection or fair competition can be adopted by a qualified majority vote. It is likely that the Commission will seek to bring forward as many of its Action Plan proposals as possible in the form of measures to encourage fair competition or ensure health and safety.

EC monitoring

International companies need to take a view on developments at a regional level, such as those occurring within the EC, that impact upon their operations. Questions to ask might include:

- 'How much of what is being proposed could be said to represent good corporate practice?'
- 'Could a voluntary system of employee information and consultation be introduced that would satisfy the objectives of the Commission?'
- 'Are there new opportunities, for example, to widen the recruitment of professionals, or new burdens that will increase employment costs, to the extent that a review of the international allocation of activities may be justified?'

A company of some standing, or one that is significantly affected by a measure or particular proposal, may find it worthwhile to undertake some lobbying activity. There is sometimes much to play for. Even when it has been agreed between states, how a measure is implemented in practice can very much depend upon the outcome of negotiations between various interested parties.

In general, the earlier a company becomes involved in the discussion of a particular measure, the more likely it is that comments made will have some influence. It should not be imagined that representations are always resisted by officials. They may be welcomed, particularly practical points concerning implementation from those with direct knowledge of the areas concerned.

The Commission consults with employers, trade unions and other groups, which could include member state's governments, before finalizing a proposal. Since early 1991, the Commission has agreed that experts from the governments of the member states will be consulted before all social affairs proposals are finalized by the Commission. This commitment will cover proposals involving employment law and work practices.

Corporate representations

Representations can be put at the national and regional levels. The UK Government has adopted the approach of itself seeking the views of companies concerning proposed EC legislation. For example, in early 1991 it sent consultation documents to a wide range of organizations concerning the Commission proposals for a standardized Europe-wide written statement of employment terms and conditions and the proposed Directive on informing and consulting employees.

Reference has already been made in Chapter 5 to the possible financial impact of certain EC proposals. The proposed Directive on the protection of pregnant women at work would give rights to 14 weeks' maternity leave at full pay and two weeks' paid leave before the expected birth of a child, an absolute right not to be unfairly dismissed for reasons connected with a pregnancy and proposes changes in working arrangements on health and safety grounds. While the UK government is, in principle, supportive of proposals to protect the health and safety of pregnant women, it estimated in 1991 that the cost to UK employers of the proposed paid maternity leave provisions would be in excess of £400 million.

A company should be on the alert for opportunities to influence developments relating to its own sector. For example, the European Commission has planned a programme of work to examine the problems of the retail and wholesale sector 'to encourage self-regulation rather than imposing legal measures' and enable Community programmes to further developments in the sector.

Some major companies carry out extensive programmes of lobbying on their own account. Others seek to combine with others and work through their national trade, employers and Chamber of Commerce organizations. These national organizations tend to have links with others at the regional and international level. For example, in the UK, the CBI works with its equivalents in the other member states of the EC through the Union of Industrial and Employers' Confederations of Europe (UNICE).

Other European networks include the Permanent Conference of Chambers of Commerce and Industry (EURO CHAMBRES) and the European Centre of Public Enterprises (CEEP). These organizations and networks, and their sector or trade equivalents, can advise on whether or not an approach should be made to the appropriate Directorates General of the Commission, the European Parliament or the Economic and Social Committee. They maintain continuing contact with these institutions.

The need for monitoring and representation does not cease when a measure is agreed. For example, when a EC Directive is adopted by the Council, it then needs to be implemented into the national laws of each member state. Agreed directives of particular interest to personnel professionals include those concerned with collective redundancies, acquired rights, equal treatment and health and safety matters. The process of expressing their content in national laws proceeds at different speeds in various countries. Those with European responsibilities may find a different legal regime in force in a number of member states, even when the matter concerned has been covered by an agreed directive.

9.4 HRD requirements and labour market research

Within regions, labour market conditions can vary significantly between countries. We have seen some examples already and there are others. For example:

- Spain's rate of unemployment in the late 1980s approached four times that of neighbouring Portugal; in Scandinavia, the Norwegian rate of unemployment has been over three times that of Sweden
- statutory regulation of hours of overtime working have applied in Belgium, France, Germany, Greece, Ireland, Luxembourg, the Netherlands, Portugal and Spain, but in Italy and the UK no such legislation has applied and in Denmark, overtime has not been a matter for legislation, but instead has been governed by collective agreement
- the minimum wage in the Netherlands, or for a skilled worker in Luxembourg, has been over four and a half times that in Portugal, while, depending upon age and occupation, the minimum wage of a Belgian has been over seven times that of an agricultural worker in Portugal.

To understand a local labour market requires a combination of quantitative information and informed opinion and assessment. Before undertaking research it is necessary to determine what information is needed. A programme can then be drawn up to secure both qualitative and quantitative information at home and, where necessary, abroad. The information obtained will need to be analysed then conclusions reached and disseminated.

Where timescales run into years, comparative assumptions need to be regularly reviewed and trends closely monitored. For example, in the early 1980s, the French rate of inflation was above that of the US and UK, whereas in the late 1980s it was below. An examination of trends would have revealed a crossover point in 1987.

Labour market issues

An issue monitoring and management process should throw up, for each country, those issues of most concern to the corporation. These will not necessarily be the issues of interest to those who are working for the company.

Some of the differences between countries that may need to be brought to the attention of an employee prior to an assignment in the country concerned are:

- political structure
- legal framework
- economic strength
- consumption patterns
- cultural structure
- patterns of trade
- distribution system
- business practices
- commercial ethics.

The legal framework may be a significant issue if the company and its employees are not to break the law. A knowledge of the time it may take to secure a work permit may be of value in scheduling the timing of an activity.

An understanding of business practices and commercial ethics is also important. Many companies have their own corporate code of ethics, which may be more or less strict than the requirements of particular states.

There are companies that do not bother to understand, or that do not feel it is necessary to understand, their *own* domestic labour market, let alone those abroad. Smaller companies may feel that, as minor players, their own presence in the market-place will not be affected by macro issues. Some companies used to obtaining all the skills they need are surprised to find that in other countries such skills may not exist. In certain areas of Eastern Europe in 1990, for example, it was not possible to find local staff with experience of working in a commercial enterprise.

Labour market factors

Some of the factors that will need to be taken into account when carrying out a labour market assessment are:

- *labour market characteristics:*
  - size
  - structure
  - trends - volume, value, etc.
  - social factors - attitudes, demography, etc.
- *labour market position:*
  - market share
  - competition
  - corporate image/awareness
- *labour market practice:*
  - employment pattern
  - regulatory framework
  - recruitment channels/tools.

In certain parts of the world the labour market may be relatively mature and stable, while in others it may be in a state of flux. In the latter case it is important that any assessments that are made are kept up to date.

It is possible that some segments of the labour market may span a number of countries. Those with certain educational, economic, political, religious and cultural characteristics may have more in common, regardless of nationality, than those of the same nationality who are divided by caste, tribe, religion or politics. Nationality and location may not be important when the segment consists of those who understand a particular programming language and who can be reached by electronic mail.

There will also be countries in which one may find labour sub-markets rather than one, homogeneous labour market or a number of distinct segments of the market. Many countries are far from homogeneous in their make-up. Communities in the Lebanon, for example, have been torn apart by divisions that have proved to be irreconcilable. Differences can result in a formal divide, such as that between Singapore and Malaysia or the division of Cyprus into Greek and Cypriot enclaves. Overnight, a latent conflict between communities can become violently overt, as was the case in Yugoslavia in 1991.

Some parts of the world are bedevilled by ethnic tensions. An example is the struggle between Arab and Jew in the Middle East. Within religions there may be struggles between sects, schisms and doctrinal differences. A Shi'ite Muslim, for example, should not be confused with a Sunni Muslim. In some societies there may be a set of intergroup tensions and conflicts that become more apparent the greater the effort devoted to their analysis. In some cases there are restive minorities that seek recognition and a place in the sun. Commercial operation in such circumstances requires sensitivity and a light touch.

Labour market research

The major methods of labour market research are set out in Figure 9.1. 'Off the peg' research can be obtained in a variety of ways. The possibility that the questions to which one is seeking answers may already have been put is always present and there are regular updating services to which a company can subscribe to find out whether or not this is the case.

Tailor-made research can be internal or external and undertaken at home and abroad. The views of certain groups could be ascertained through group discussions or in-depth interviews. There are many quantitative techniques that can be employed, including face-to-face, telephone and questionnaire surveys.

A balance has to be maintained between the cost of gaining the information and its value. It should always be borne in mind that the object of the exercise is to increase understanding.

International research can be costly and time-consuming and, in some countries, collecting information is an expensive and fraught activity. The data may be complex and not compatible with that obtained elsewhere, or available statistics may be out of date and of dubious quality. Indeed, much country information is of questionable value.

In some countries, information is falsified for political or other reasons. Bias can also creep into survey results when non-respondents differ as a group from respondents. A question that is clear in one language or culture may not be comprehensible in another. The infrastructure to undertake a survey may not be available, as to do a telephone survey, for example, one requires access to a telecommunications system that functions to an acceptable degree.

Internal or external research?

Some companies undertake their own labour market research. This is because it might not be possible to find an external party with sufficient

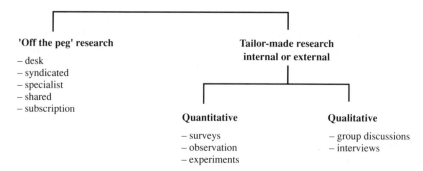

Figure 9.1   Labour market research methods

understanding of an organization's specific requirements or, where such external expertise *is* available, a view may need to be taken on the benefits of 'in-house' versus external agency research.

A company that does its own research is likely to have a realistic awareness of its own requirements. Information may be needed in a hurry and selecting an agency may take too much time. It is also sometimes helpful if a company itself obtains first-hand understanding of local personnel issues. On occasion it is a 'soft option' to sub-contract the process of investigation to a third party.

On the other hand, a company may have limited capability and little experience of undertaking the sort of investigation that is sought. There may be other higher priority claims upon the resources that are available or a general capability may not relate to the specific country under investigation.

In the case of a one-off exercise, it may make sense to go to a third party who 'knows'. Independence and objectivity may be easier to both achieve and demonstrate if a third party is used.

9.5 Works councils

Some companies have found that the establishment of operations abroad can create new opportunities to avoid the restrictive practices of heavily unionized domestic operations. In other situations, companies have been introduced to negotiation with employee representatives as a result of internationalization. In Germany, for example, a company is required to establish a works council once it has reached a certain size, but several US multinationals have encountered works councils for the first time as a result of a move into Europe.

Some form of works council or committee to represent the interests of employees is a legal requirement under certain circumstances in Belgium, Germany, the Netherlands, Portugal and Spain. Local laws may set out the information to which a works council is entitled. In some EC countries, quite small enterprises may be required to establish a works council, the threshold being as low as 20 in Germany and 35 in the Netherlands.

A Draft EC Directive on 'information and consultation of employees'[8] would require companies employing more than 1000 people and with at least two establishments or undertakings in at least two EC member states each employing at least 100 persons to establish works councils. The proposed '5th Directive' also provides for workers' participation in the decision making bodies of companies employing at least 1000 people, but limits itself to national undertakings and does not apply to European-scale undertakings or groups of undertakings.

The later (1990) proposal, though, would require European-scale undertakings and groups of undertakings to establish a European Works Council when requested by employees or their representatives or they assent to such an initiative from central management. The proposal gives central management the right to withhold information, the divulging of which would have harmful consequences for the company.

9.6 Trade unions

The proportion of the labour force within trade union memberships varies greatly by country. The number of paid workers who are members of trade unions in Belgium and Denmark is five or six times that of those in France, for example.

In some countries, such as France, Germany and Italy, trade unions are organized on an industry basis, whereas in Denmark and the UK, they operate on a trade or craft basis. In some countries, for example, France and Italy, there is an ideological basis to union organization. The number of trade unions also varies greatly by country – in Spain there are only two major unions.

The role of trade unions varies between countries. For example, in relation to a minimum wage within member states of the EC:

– the system in France, Luxembourg, the Netherlands, Portugal and Spain has been based on a statutory minimum wage
– in Belgium and Greece, the minimum wage has been established by national collective bargaining that establishes a general minimum wage
– in Denmark, Germany and Italy, industry-level collective bargaining has established specific minimum levels of pay

- in the United Kingdom, specific minimum wages have been established in some sectors by Wages Councils
- in Ireland, in certain sectors a specific minimum wage has been established by a Joint Labour Committee.

In Japan, unions tend to be company-based. Hence, there are over 900 times as many unions in Japan as in the UK. Although there is a legal right to strike, compared with the UK, relatively few days of work are lost as a result of industrial action.

Individual trade unions vary in their attitudes towards internationalization. Some may harbour suspicions that labour forces and their unions in different countries might be played off against one another. The threat of withdrawing investments or the prospect of making incremental investments, could be used by a company to support a 'divide and rule' policy.

Other unions might understand the need for international operation as some are themselves seeking to build international networks of like-minded unions with common interests. Such a network could cover a business sector or be established to coordinate dealings with a single international company.

Trade unions and 1992

The bargaining power of trade unions will reflect the state of supply and demand for certain skills in each labour market. In Europe, many unions were inititially suspicious of the single market programme, but a number now see debates concerning the implementation of the Social Charter as providing new opportunities to influence the emergence of a EC labour framework.

In response to 1992, trade unions themselves are having to internationalize. Some have 1992 strategies, the elements of which range from language audits to the establishment of direct contacts and working relationships with unions in other member states. The European Trade Union Confederation (ETUC) has recognized a number of industry committees that bring together groups of unions from various member states covering particular sectors.

Individual trade unions have established joint working groups with their equivalents in other member states. A number of transnational union committees and works or consultative councils have been established. Trade unions are also represented on Joint Committees composed of both trades unions and employers and established to discuss sector strategies with the Commission of the EC. The number of such linkages and arrangements is likely to increase.

The corporate response

As a consequence of internationalization, a company may need to establish machinery for relating to the representatives of trade unions in more than one country. Larger companies may prefer to make their own arrangements, while some smaller companies may be content to participate in organizations representing employers at the regional or international level. UK employers associations, like UK trade unions, are building networks of international contacts and relationships.

In 1985, the Social Dialogue between representatives of employers and trade unions was revived in order to provide within the EC a forum for the discussion of social and employment issues. It has now become part of the Commission's formal consultative process. National employers associations, such as the CBI in the UK, are direct participants. Article 118B of the Single European Act provides for the Social Dialogue to be extended to various industrial or business sectors where this is acceptable to the parties involved. To date, a number of 'joint opinions' have been issued as a result of the Social Dialogue.

In Holland, a form of social dialogue exists at the national level. Representatives of trade unions and employees are required to be consulted before changes in the law relating to employment matters can be made.

Not surprisingly, trade unions favour the various proposals of the EC Commission to encourage employee involvement. In general, companies would prefer to determine their own arrangements according to their own particular circumstances, rather than have a standard approach imposed upon them. Any company with operations in the EC needs to be aware of and monitor the status of Commission proposals concerning employee involvement.

Matters that in one country are covered by labour law may, in another country, be resolved by collective agreement. A company's issue monitoring and management system ought to flag up labour relations issues that might arise in certain countries. For example, will centralization of an activity at a single point to service a total EC market make a company more susceptible to trade union pressure? Should the size of a local unit be kept below the threshold that would force the establishment of a works council?

Check-list

– Does your company understand the major features of those labour markets in which it has significant operations and their relevance for customers, competitors and suppliers as well as itself?

- In particular, does your company have access to knowledge of relevant law and practice in those local, regional and international labour markets in which it recruits?
- Is your company fully prepared to implement, and comply with, any new local or regional legal requirements that may emerge?
- Are your company's domestic and international personnel policies compatible with emerging regional (such as, European) frameworks?
- Is your company's personnel community able to respond effectively to requirements for the assessment of local and regional labour markets?
- Is your company aware of, and monitoring the international activities of, those trade unions with which it may come into contact?
- In particular, is your company alert to interunion links across national borders and union responses to the emergence of a single European market?
- Do your personnel colleagues and other managers fully appreciate the significance of national and regional (such as, EC) measures relating to their roles and responsibilities?
- In particular, is your company aware of the likely impacts of national and EC measures relating to staff mobility, remuneration, recruitment and retention upon its operations and its comparative position in competitive labour markets?
- Is your company responding to and taking full advantage of any opportunities being created by changes in legal requirements and other developments at both national and regional (such as, EC) levels?

References

1. Commission of the European Communities, *Employment in Europe 1991*, third report of the Commission, Office for Official Publications of the European Communities, 18 July 1991.
2. EUROSTAT, 'Social Protection in Europe: Trends from 1980 to 1989, Population and Social Conditions', Rapid Reports, 1991 4, EUROSTAT, 1991.
3. Bannock, Graham, *Attitudes to Breaking Out in Europe*, 3i, 1990.
4. Commission of the European Communities, *Completing the Internal Market*, White Paper from the Commission to the European Council, Office for Official Publications of the European Communities, 1985.
5. Commission of the European Communities, *Completion of the Internal Market, Sixth Report of the European Commission*, COM (91) 237 final, Office for Official Publications of the European Communities, 1991.
6. Commission of the European Communities, *Communication from the Commission Concerning Its Action Programme Relating to the Implementation of the Community Charter of Basic Social Rights for Workers*, COM (89) 568, Office for Official Publications of the European Communities, November 1989.
7. Commission of the European Communities, *Community Charter of the Fundamen-*

tal Social Rights of Workers, Office for Official Publications of the European Communities, 1990.
8. Commission of the European Communities, *Employee Information and Consultation in EC-Scale Undertakings*, Draft Directive, COM (90/58), Office for Official Publications of the European Communities, 1990.

Further reading

Arbuthnott, H, and G Edwards, *A Common Man's Guide to the Common Market*, Macmillan, 1989.
Atkinson, John, *Corporate Employment Policies for the Single European Market*, Report No. 179, Institute of Manpower Studies, 1989.
Brewster, Chris, and Paul Teague, *European Community Social Policy*, Institute of Personnel Management, 1989.
Brown, Richard, and Tim Rycroft, *Involved in Europe*, British Institute of Management Discussion Paper No. 12, 1989.
Commission of the European Communities, *Directory of Community Legislation in Force and Other Acts of the Community Institutions*, Office for Official Publications of the European Communities, 1991.
Commission of the European Communities, Directorate-General for Employment, Industrial Relations and Social Affairs, *Employment in Europe*, Office for Official Publications of the European Communities, 1989.
Louis, Jean-Victor, *The Community Legal Order*, second completely revised Edition, Commission of the European Communities, 1991.
Manpower PLC, *Employment and Training*, Mercury Books/CBI Initiative 1992, 1990.
Séché, Jean-Claude, *A Guide to Working in a Europe Without Frontiers*, Office for Official Publications of the European Communities, 1988.
Teague, P, *The European Community: The Social Dimension – Labour Market Policies for 1992*, Kogan Page in association with Cranfield School of Management, 1989.

10
International recruitment and retention

Perspectives

I don't recruit there – at least, not yet. However, I visit and talk about recruitment and about the company. Those people are going to be important, and one day we will have to deal with them in one capacity or another. Now you try to cost justify that.

Director, International Recruitment, international management consultancy

We pick up bright youngsters who do not want to wait five years to move to a desk that is three feet closer to the boss in the corner.

Chairman of US-owned company operating in Japan

The company now has over 20 people who examine new patents all over the world. We can usually obtain people's ideas without having to recruit them.

General Manager, Japanese company

We retain people so long as there are interesting projects for them to work upon and they have opportunities to develop. We would be naive if we thought there was any long-term commitment to us. We assume we will lose good people, but each person lost is a potential client.

Senior Partner, international management consultancy

At a senior level one or two Austrians have done quite well, if that counts as international executive recruitment.

Personnel Director, German engineering company

Is there such a thing as international recruitment? We recruit locally. The international potential of some people emerges later, during the course of their careers.

Management Development Manager, UK headquartered retailer

There is no problem. São Paulo has a huge Japanese community. At one time every single person we employed locally was from the Japanese community.

Japanese banker in Brazil

We know our competitors all right – we trained most of them.
International Personnel Director, Canadian company

10.1 Introduction

We have seen in Chapter 4 that, for a growing number of organizations, human skill has become a critical success factor. We also saw in Chapter 6 that a key requirement of organizations is the ability to secure flexible access to relevant skills as and when required, and the maximum commitment and value added contribution from people. In this chapter we examine some aspects of recruitment and retention of particular significance to international operation.

10.2 Recruitment

The overriding requirement is access to those with relevant skills. This may or may not involve recruitment. In some cases, the skills that are needed might be secured by contracting them on a consultancy or other basis.[1] For example, Lewis Galoob Toys of the US sub-contracts almost all management activity beyond central coordination, management and strategy formulation.

It may also be possible to develop or better harness the skills of those that are already employed. Where the demand for skills exists on a local basis, mobility or the transfer of staff may be an alternative to recruitment.

Which course of action is the best will depend upon the particular circumstances of each case and legal factors. For example, the labour market of an individual state will be subject to national labour laws. It may only be possible to recruit certain categories of staff through government recruitment agencies, as has been the case in Italy. There may be restrictions on the employment of temporary or part-time staff. A company will need access to local knowledge concerning any such restrictions.

Some activities may need to be scaled down or closed. In times of recession and cutbacks a company should be aware of different national provisions relating to termination. These will have to be taken into account when the options are considered.

Local labour market knowledge will also be required (we saw how this might be obtained in the last chapter). Skills that are plentiful in one location may be unavailable in another, or the willingness of people to work for a particular company may depend upon whether or not it is perceived as a domestic or foreign organization. Equally, the same company may be more established in one location than another.

An international perspective can sometimes be reconciled with a largely national employment policy:

- the French company SCOR SA operates in the 'world reinsurance industry', its 1990 annual report and accounts abounds in global and surrealistic images commissioned from Japanese artist Tsunehisa Kimura and the company has a global vision and perspective, even though 'European business accounted for almost 80% of underwriting booked in 1990' and most of its senior executives are French nationals
- the UK National and Provincial Building Society recruits almost all its staff in the home market, its offices and operations have been confined to the UK and yet the Chief Executive, David O'Brien puts great stress upon an international perspective: 'While we only operate in the UK, people from all over the world live and do business in the UK. We need to understand their needs and build relationships with them.'

The recruitment process

The ease with which an opportunity can be brought to the attention of potential candidates can vary between states. For example:

- recruitment agencies can range from the passive or reactive to the aggressively pro-active
- the media that can be used to advertise a vacancy will also vary in quality and familiarity
- in France and Germany more use appears to be made of public sector job centres than is the case in the UK.

Those recruiting graduates in Europe may encounter considerable differences between countries:

- in France it is illegal to recruit on a university campus whereas in the UK some universities make elaborate arrangements to encourage potential employers onto their campuses for 'milk round' recruiting
- UK students generally attend a university some distance away from where they grew up, but elsewhere in the EC there is often a tradition of attending a local university and of living at or close to home
- a recruiter in the UK can make use of 'the milk round' to consider an annual 'crop' of people who graduate together, but in other countries people graduate throughout the year and so an *annual* labour market does not exist.

Questions of the comparability of qualifications and experience can also arise. The length of a degree course is typically three years in the UK, but between four and six years elsewhere in the EC. Those on the Continent who repeat a year or are required to undertake military service will join the labour market later than their UK colleagues.

Search and selection processes can differ in rigour between countries. For example:

- in Spain, a family connection can be of value
- in Germany, many companies use graphology (the study of handwriting) as a selection aid
- a French recruiter might pay considerable attention to paper qualifications as evidence of a logical mind
- a recruiter in the UK might pay more attention to sporting and other achievements as evidence that a person is a team player
- in Sweden, where there is a real labour shortage, companies have more of an incentive to keep track of people than would be the case in Greece or Turkey where labour is plentiful.

Expectations of the distance someone might be expected to travel to take up employment also vary. People in the UK and US are often prepared to travel further than those in Germany and Italy. What constitutes acceptable grounds for being absent from work also differs between countries. For example, under the social support system in the Netherlands, people are able to be psychologically unwell who would have to be available for work elsewhere.

A company that is not familiar with a particular labour market may need to make greater use of third parties, such as executive search and selection agencies. There are companies like Ricardo International that maintain extensive and up-to-date databases of engineers and specialist staff who are willing to undertake assignments at home and abroad. Greater use may also be made of other international networks, such as the alumni lists of certain business schools. At least those who belong to a network will have some characteristics in common.

More companies are now recruiting on an international basis. Usually, as in the case of Olivetti's No Frontiers programme, this is for certain categories of staff. ABN AMRO Bank has recruited graduates for its international management programme in Brussels, Dublin, Milan and Paris. The more specialist and clearly defined a target group, the easier it usually is to widen the geographic area of recruitment:

- the Spanish motor car producer Seat has advertised for skilled labour in the North East of England as the area has built up a body of relevant

skills as a result of a major local investment by the Japanese car maker
Nissan
- a company recruiting young engineers may find it relatively easy to
identify the world's leading engineering schools as a number of listings
and rankings of business schools are produced on a regular basis
- many professional associations and institutes are able to provide the
names, addresses and telephone numbers of their equivalents overseas
and, in some cases, representatives of these associations may come
together from time to time at regional or international level
- some national bodies publish lists of members or maintain career registers, educational institutions sometimes maintain alumni registers and
lists and, in many countries, alumni associations of both home and
overseas institutions are active, so identifying potential recruits in these
cases may be no more difficult than uncovering a new and local source
of possible employees.

While international recruitment has increased, many international programmes appear to have been experimental in nature and modest in
scope. Particular companies might face local shortages or be planning an
overseas expansion, which has caused them to look further afield. Only a
handful of people are recruited on an international or pan-European
basis in the case of many organizations. In general, those recruited from
another country appear to be a very small proportion of the total number
of people employed.

The locations in which a company recruits should reflect the nature of
its skill needs. The company seeking highly creative individuals may put
a higher priority upon recruitment in the UK than another corporation
that puts more emphasis upon teamwork. The latter company might
favour recruitment in Japan. A company seeking a location within the
EC with good prospects of a flow of young people might select Turkey.

In Chapter 8 we considered national cultural differences and these can
be very relevant in recruitment decisions. Japan, as a nation state, has a
reputation for its openness to, and willingness to absorb, external ideas.
However, while there is a considerable commitment to education in
Japan and teachers have a high status, the teaching methods used can be
relatively inflexible and an emphasis upon rote learning can inhibit individual creativity.[2] Those who recruit should seek to understand the likely relative strengths and weaknesses of those drawn from different cultures.

Selection criteria

A selection process can introduce an unconscious national bias into a
company's recruitment. In some countries weight may be attached to

social standing and charm, while elsewhere more attention may be given to actual performance. A particular requirement may lead to the over-representation of nationals from those countries with a higher proportion of people who are likely to be able to satisfy it.

As the focus of emphasis in assessment and remuneration shifts to various measures of output, it is important that potential recruits are assessed upon output rather than input factors. Past job titles held in bureaucratic organizations in a quite different market context may be a poor guide to their potential to contribute to groups and teams in today's network organization. There follow lists of questions from the 1989 BIM report *Too Old at 40?*[3] that show the difference in focus that is required to elicit appropiate information from candidates.

Input-focused questions include:

- 'What qualifications do you have?'
- 'What have you done?'
- 'What was your job title?'
- 'Who did you report to?'
- 'What was your salary?'
- 'How did the move benefit you?'
- 'Why do you want this job?'
- 'Did you have a company car?'
- 'For how long were you a director?'
- 'What would you most like to be?'
- 'What golf clubs do you belong to?'

Output-focused questions, on the other hand, include:

- 'What are your key competences?'
- 'What did you learn?'
- 'What did you achieve?'
- Who did you work with?'
- 'What value did you create for the company?'
- 'What is the greatest benefit the company obtained from you?'
- 'What can you contribute?'
- 'What qualities and experiences did you acquire?'
- 'What were your major accomplishments during this period?'
- 'What would you most like to do?'
- 'What project groups or taskforces do you belong to?'

Companies seeking recruits with particular academic or professional qualifications need to understand that education and training practices vary greatly between states. The proportion of young people attending and completing a university education can vary significantly, even between member states of the EC at a similar stage of development. The differences can be even more noticeable when comparing developing countries with those that are already industrialized.

The existence of military service or degree programmes that take longer to complete, as we have seen, delay the entrance of young people into the labour market in many countries, so a recruitment programme aimed at the 21-year-old graduate may be appropriate for the UK, but not for Germany, say, where many students may graduate 5 or 6 years later.

In the UK, many employers express a preference for the generalist, for example the individual with an arts degree. Elsewhere within the EC there is often a strong preference for a relevant degree. Those with aspirations to go into marketing would, therefore, first obtain a marketing degree. The Continental graduate is, in comparison with the UK equivalent, both educated *and* trained.

Many of the professions are Anglo-Saxon phenomena. Certain types of professionals may simply not be available in some countries. In other countries, the route to professional standing may be via a university course or on-the-job training, rather than through the membership of a professional association.

Successful recruitment

To access possible recruits, it may be necessary for those responsible for recruitment to travel abroad. Senior staff of local operations could be encouraged to speak to local audiences. Companies that have educational liaison programmes could extend their geographical scope from national to international centres of excellence. For example:

- some of the educational institutions with which a company is in contact in its home market may well have links and exchange arrangements with their overseas equivalents and many existing programmes may cover an international student body
- a company could establish guidelines for its educational liaison or support programmes, for example, that funding should only be given to programmes involving exchanges between institutions located in two or more countries or having a minimum number of overseas students upon them.

In a growing number of knowledge businesses, competition for the talents of those with scarce skills is every bit as intense as it is for customers. In some cases, the competition for recruits may be even more vigorous. In times of economic prosperity many consultancy-type organizations are supply constrained, unable to take on new assignments as a result of a shortage of consultancy staff.

The concentration of high-tech- or R&D-based companies at a particular point can exhaust the supply of local skills. The Swiss company Sandoz has found it difficult to recruit locally qualified specialists such as physicians, pharmacologists and computer scientists. Over certain periods 'a high percentage of such vacancies were therefore filled by candidates from other countries'. Sandoz has sought to tap a wider pool of expertise through research centres in Japan, the UK, and the USA.

To succeed in recruitment, many companies are having to become both more focused and more imaginative. Managers in line positions can no longer afford to leave recruitment to staff specialists. They are having to become directly involved in defining their requirements and assessing potential recruits. Such involvement is likely to become the norm rather than the exception.

More effort will need to be devoted to distinguishing one opportunity from another. Questions should be asked such as:

- What is so special about a job opportunity with one company?
- How does it differ from the alternatives available?
- To what extent can the opportunity be tailored to the needs of a particular prospect?
- Can any such tailoring be achieved at acceptable cost?

Companies in Germany and the UK are becoming more open-minded when defining recruitment targets. A willingness to tailor recruitment to meet the needs of individuals and certain groups can also be the key to widening the normal catchment area for recruitment. For example, specific appeals may need to be made to women returners or to those who are older.[3] Tapping those within these groups who are seeking work opportunities, particularly on a part-time or temporary basis, is a core element of the business strategy of the Swiss services company Adia.

Approaches to recruitment

Many companies devote considerable effort to the evaluation of proposals for the purchase of an item of capital equipment or the introduction of a new product or service. In contrast, much less effort may be devoted to the question of a new recruit who, over a period of years, may have a much more significant impact upon both costs and revenues. The employment costs of retaining a senior executive for a number of years can run into hundreds of thousands, if not millions of pounds. Where human skill is the key to generating added value, for example through individual tailoring, the revenue contribution of a key person over a number of years may greatly exceed that of an item of capital equipment.

In general it would appear that major companies are devoting more effort to the recruitment process than in the past. For example, within Europe there is a greater willingness to introduce flexibility into employment contracts and various inducements are offered to potential recruits, such as the prospect of training.[4] Even strong labour market competitors should not assume that they will continue to meet their recruitment needs:

- the German company VEBA has introduced a programme of 'open house' events and corporate presentations aimed at students, has increased its participation in trade shows and offers short-term practical experience placements to students in order 'to give young people an opportunity to get to know the working world of VEBA'
- the Netherlands headquartered chemical company DSM has recognized that it will 'encounter greater difficulty in recruiting a sufficient number of well-trained people' and that 'under these circumstances' it 'will have to strengthen its position on the labour market and devote greater attention to training'
- the initial training of non-MBA graduates that Citibank Europe offers those who join its management associate programme lasts between 18 months and 2 years and is aimed at those seeking international careers and although the length of training provided may seem a significant commitment by the standards of many companies, as many as 10 000 applications have been received across Europe for the 100 places that are available.

10.3 Career prospects

In the bureaucratic organization, it is relatively easy to discern ladders of advancement:

- career paths can be planned so that, traditionally, those who work hard and exhibit loyalty in good times and bad can expect some reward
- some positions in the organizations are highly prized and individuals compete against each other and compare their progress towards career objectives with others of a similar age.

In the network organization, paths to advancement are not so easy to identify:

- steady upwards progress is not assumed so that working today for future rewards may be less a motivating factor than contributing towards, and learning from, current projects
- the future is more uncertain so elaborate career and succession plans are replaced by a search for the next project or task when the last has been completed
- there tends to be less emphasis upon looking over one's shoulder at others and, instead, more effort may be devoted to identifying those roles that best make use of particular skills and attributes, so opportunities for personal growth may exist independently of such notions as level, grade or status.

The goal in the bureaucratic organization tends to be an impressive job title, but in the network organization it may be remaining up to date and being in a position to make a continuing contribution. It is more difficult to take wrong turnings, miss the boat or become permanently plateaued in the network organization. Each situation needs to be experienced and savoured on its own merits. Unlike the bureaucracy, there may be few sinecure positions that can be enjoyed for long periods of time without successful adaptations to change.

10.4 Expatriate or local national

Many companies face the choice of whether to recruit locally or to make use of expatriate staff. In the case of a new operation, the employment of expatriates may bring greater flexibility. A local recruit, while having less knowledge of the company and its products and services may have greater local market and customer awareness. Much will depend upon the intended nature and scale of a local operation. While the balance of the argument may, in the short term, support the use of expatriate staff, over the longer term it may favour local recruitment. The latter can demonstrate a greater commitment to a local market-place.

If an expatriate is selected, a company should be open about any particular drawbacks associated with the assignment. The individual and his or her family will need to be prepared for a move, with all the problems of adjustment that this can bring, at both the beginning and at the end of a tour of duty abroad.

The Japanese company Brother puts great emphasis upon the localization of recruitment. The local knowledge the corporation acquires through its employees helps it to penetrate local markets. In Germany, Harold Rudloff, the German CEO of Brother International GmbH claims, 'We have no Japanese staff members except myself'.

In the case of international sales staff, there may be a choice between travelling sales people who move from territory to territory, locally based expatriates or local recruitment of foreign nationals. A selection of the advantages and disadvantages of each of these alternatives follows, but these are for the purpose of illustration only as the advantages and disadvantages for any particular company will vary according to a number of factors.

Travelling sales staff have the following advantages:

- economic because of limited involvement
- understanding of vision and mission
- product and company knowledge
- demonstrated commitment to company
- close company control possible
- customer relations benefits of direct contact
- less threatening to distributors
- allows wider learning, including from the market.

The disadvantages of travelling sales staff are:

- limited local cultural empathy
- limited availability for lengthy negotiation
- high absolute costs, for example, travel
- spread too thinly
- low morale where approach does not match customer requirements
- no local base for future expansion.

With expatriate sales staff, there are the following advantages:

- understanding of company, its objectives and products
- known commitment and competence
- better cultural empathy
- time to establish relationships
- possible cost savings *vis-à-vis* travelling sales staff
- post sale support and service.

Expatriate sales staff have the following disadvantages:

- less company contact than with travelling sales staff
- less able to learn from experience of other markets
- host government interference
- shortage of suitable recruits
- high absolute costs
- inhibit career opportunities of local nationals.

Foreign nationals have the following advantages:

- extensive cultural empathy
- meet local customer requirements
- possibly lower salaries *vis-à-vis* expatriates
- possibly lower travel costs
- more local customer contacts
- future supply of local national recruits
- visible local presence.

The disadvantages of foreign nationals are:

- limited direct company contact and understanding
- loose company control
- incompatible management style
- local recruitment problems
- could be poached by local competitors
- motivation and communication
- limited ability to learn from the experience of customers in other territories.

In the case of all three options regarding the appointment of sales staff, involvement and communication can be problems, particularly for the more bureaucratic organization. Both travellers and expatriates can become lonely, isolated and culturally insecure, while foreign nationals, too, can feel isolated as a result of geographic distance and cultural barriers.

These problems are addressed to a degree by the network organization as it facilitates continuous interaction within the network community. The individual with access to a compatible terminal can, regardless of location, secure flexible access to the people, information and resources of the network.

10.5 A presence on the ground

The value of a presence on the ground will vary according to the nature of the market-place. In the case of a complex high-technology product, the visit of a travelling specialist might be preferred to the attentions of a local generalist. A company should be led not by a check-list of theoretical advantages and disadvantages but by the precise requirements of existing and potential customers.

Returning to our example of sales staff, the advantages of a person on the ground as identified by one company are:

- direct customer contact
- can demonstrate product

- physical presence throughout sales cycle
- direct distributor contact
- quick follow-up of leads and references
- demonstration of commitment
- cultural empathy/requirement
- incremental market learning
- alternatives, such as advertising, are limited
- low salaries and living costs in less well-developed countries
- regional travel problems.

In this case, personal selling has been found to be particularly effective within the export promotions mix (again, this list is for the purposes of illustration only as quite different factors could be relevant to another company).

One option for a company with limited resources that is eager to move quickly because of customer or competitive pressures is to appoint a local national to mastermind a move into a particular market or region. Where appropriate, the individual concerned, colleagues and local investors could be given a stake in the enterprise. Local incorporation could eventually lead to quotation upon a local stock exchange and minority shareholdings.

While Eastern Europe was under the grip of Communism many Western companies were limited to a representational office and were not allowed to enter into local trading relationships as the *state* used to be the employer. With the transition to market economies, direct employment has become possible and companies such as ICI have established local companies.

Those who have experienced the rigid and impersonal nature of Communism have relatively high expectations of inward investing companies. This enthusiasm, desire to learn and technical competence has to be weighed against a lack of commercial experience. A local work-force may need to be run by an expatriate who is accustomed to the ways of the market-place.

10.6 Employer appeal

The extent to which a new overseas operation can be staffed will depend upon a number of factors. These include the relative attractiveness of the country concerned and the competitive appeal of the company *vis-à-vis* other employers in terms of the ability to meet the needs of existing or potential employees (see Figure 10.1). For example:

- in the case of a company with high competitive appeal moving to a

Competitive appeal

	High	Low
High	Willing expatriates Eager local recruits	Willing expatriates who could be lost to competitors Recruitment difficulties
Low	Reluctant expatriates Eager local recruits	Reluctant expatriates Recruitment difficulties

Country attractiveness

Figure 10.1 The opportunity/attractiveness matrix

highly attractive country, it may be relatively easy to attract both expatriates who are willing to move *and* local recruits
– in the 'worst case' scenario – a company is not able to match the appeal of other employers in a country that is not attractive to those who would otherwise be willing to be internationally mobile – the company may experience difficulty in local recruitment and in persuading mobile managers to relocate.

The competitive appeal of a company may reflect favourable or unfavourable views of what is perceived as its home country. It may also relfect the image associated with its customers, which may vary country by country. Entrenched attitudes can be difficult to shift. A particular attitude may be the result of a mixture of historic, economic, social and cultural factors. The time and cost it may take to improve an image should not be underestimated.

Competing for talent

The extent to which a company is able to sustain competitive appeal in recruitment and retention will depend largely upon the reactions of competing employers.[5] Competing companies may find themselves in a zero-sum game situation (see Figure 10.2).

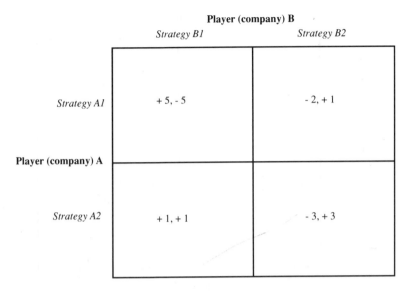

Player (company) B

	Strategy B1	Strategy B2
Strategy A1	+ 5, - 5	- 2, + 1
Strategy A2	+ 1, + 1	- 3, + 3

Player (company) A

Gain of one = loss of another

Figure 10.2 The theory of games (duopoly – the zero-sum game)

If company A increases the benefits to potential employees and company B does not, then company A may benefit or recruit at the expense of company B (A1, B1). Alternatively, if company A does not match the benefits of company B it may experience greater difficulty in recruitment.

In a duopoly situation in which two companies are competing for the same talent, a company may experience the dilemma of many states on the question of whether to 'arm' or 'disarm' (see Figure 10.3).

The consequences of failing to match a competitor's appeal may lead to the loss of much-needed skills. Alternatively, a competitive spiral, with each company seeking to match the extra benefits offered by the other, can lead to an escalation of employment costs. This can erode the profitability of *both* players, particularly when they are fishing in the same pool for talent. However, any attempt to reach some common understanding to avoid a competitive 'bidding up' of the cost of skills could, in some countries, lead to charges of market collusion.

Retention

Just as it is easier to retain an existing customer than win a new one, so the retention of existing staff may be more cost-effective than recruitment.

		State B	
		Arm	*Disarm*
State A	*Arm*	- 5, - 5	+ 10, - 10
	Disarm	- 10, + 10	+ 5, + 5

Positive sum outcome?

Figure 10.3 The arm and disarm dilemma

This assumes that a company wishes to retain its existing staff, but in certain cases there may be no option but to retain. The recruitment option may not be available as a result of local skills shortages.

In general, a balance has to be struck between recruitment and retention. There is little point being aggressive and active on the recruitment front, only to lose a high proportion of new entrants within a few years as a result of passively accepting the poaching by competitors of key staff. Such poaching is likely to be directed at the more valuable staff who will be difficult to replace.

The extent of poaching varies across countries. In Japan, although many able executives are increasingly willing to change jobs, there is still a widespread tradition of life-time employment with a single company. Many occupational pension schemes are not transferable and total remuneration often increases steadily with length of service and seniority. These practices are now under challenge. However, in a number of sectors and for some time to come, retention is likely to be less of a problem in Japan than it is in, say, the UK.

Continuing allegiance should not be assumed. Too many companies have taken it for granted that the overwhelming majority of their staff will wish to remain employed and dependent on them. The emphasis that is being placed upon delegation and the giving of greater discretion to line and junior staff can result in greater self-confidence and a sense of self-worth. This can awaken a desire for even greater control over one's life. Continuing relationships between people and organizations will depend upon a partnership of common interests.

RETENTION FACTORS

Discussions with international companies suggest that the relative importance of various retention factors is changing. In particular, it is thought that with younger managers less emphasis should be placed upon pay and conditions. More weight may need to be given to articulating clear values and a vision that 'grabs'. A wide range of retention factors now need to be considered:

- empathy with goals and values
- belonging to a network
- individual recognition and standing
- assessment criteria
- reward and remuneration
- career and development opportunities
- life-style options
- individual tailoring
- personal responsibility and discretion
- involvement and participation
- continuing contribution
- extent of supporting/facilitating processes and technology
- working environment and conditions
- health and safety considerations
- team and project activity
- flexibility of working options
- social and recreational facilities.

In many cases a combination of factors rather than one particular factor will be important. The weighting attached to different factors may also need to be adjusted to meet the distinct needs of different people and groups. Many of the items listed may be necessary but not sufficient retention factors in themselves. A certain minimum level may need to be achieved if dissatisfaction is not to arise, but incremental improvements beyond this threshold level will not necessarily bring about corresponding increases in employee satisfaction.

Retention factors cited by international companies include:

- *empathy with goals and values*: this is becoming more important as larger numbers of middle managers inherit or acquire property and achieve a degree of financial independence; such individuals can choose to work on those projects they feel happy with or consider important – a positive concern for the environment, for example, could be an important factor in retaining the services of those who are environmentally aware

- *belonging to a network with standing and laudable purpose*: it may be a plus that the network is international as this can enable people to feel that they are a part of something that is larger than national institutions and that they have a bond with like-minded people around the world
- *individual recognition and standing*: research undertaken for the 1988 BIM report *The New Professionals*, suggests that a growing number of younger staff are not attracted by the prospect of being a piece on some-one else's chessboard,[6] they are seeking a greater degree of control over their own lives and prefer to be regarded as individuals in their own right, rather than as holders of corporate job titles, so such individuals are attracted by opportunities to make a mark and secure personal recogni-tion for what they have done
- *assessment criteria need to be seen as both fair and relevant to the goals and self-image of individuals*: increasingly, there is a desire for forms of assessment that relate to output, achievement and tangible results, rather than to rank or position in the corporate hierarchy, so being able to identify an individual contribution to a final output can itself be a positive retention factor
- *reward and remuneration*: certain categories of sales staff may be strongly motivated by the competitive struggle to achieve high commission earn-ings *and* may retain this drive while a company is seeking to encourage them to become team players within account teams – the two perspec-tives may need to be reconciled; in other companies attempts are being made to link reward and remuneration with tangible output and cus-tomer satisfaction
- *career and development opportunities*: so long as many managers think of life in terms of advancement and steady upward movement, these will be retention factors, but such opportunities will need to be deliverable and this may become increasingly difficult in the flatter organizations that are being achieved, so *new* forms of development and opportunity that involve movement around the network organization rather than up bureaucratic ladders may need to be stressed
- *life-style options*: there will be those for whom savouring life-style options may be more important than continuing and incremental career development and, given the limitation of a single biological life, there is a natural drive to experience as many different career lives as possible, but movement between organizations to achieve a 'new life' may not be necessary if the network organization provides a continuing

flow of opportunities to join new project groups or taskforces and, where each team is allowed to determine its own way of working, such moves could involve a period of service in a culture that has not been experienced before

- *individual tailoring, flexibility and a willingness to accommodate the particular requirements of each employee*: these are becoming more important, but some give and take may be necessary to sustain a relationship – for example, the company may feel its own interest would be best served by employing an individual in the same role at a new location, while the preference of the individual may be for a different role at the same location – so some negotiation may be necessary to achieve an outcome that is acceptable to both parties

- *personal responsibility and discretion*: this is very important for many people, indeed, individuals often leave bureaucratic organizations to set up their own businesses or to work for a smaller company in order to secure a greater freedom to decide how work should be done to achieve an agreed output – people like to feel that they are making an individual contribution

- *for others, involvement and participation are very important*: these people may perceive independence as isolation, as not being at the centre where things are happening, and, indeed, being able to work and interact with those who one respects and from whom one can learn is a powerful retention factor and being an active participant rather than a passive passenger is also important for many people

- *the prospect of being able to make a continuing contribution*: as more work is undertaken by project groups for delivery within an agreed timescale, the question 'What next?' inevitably arises and networks that are able to supply a continuing flow of projects will have an appeal, while membership of those networks that do most to develop their people will be in the greatest demand

- *access to facilitating processes and supporting technology to enhance performance and learning*: individuals who are well supported by appropriate knowledge and able to secure flexible and speedy access to the information and understanding they need may be reluctant to leave a network to work in a less supportive environment – this will become an increasingly important factor

- *the working environment and conditions of work*: individuals can be strongly influenced by their working environment and may be attracted by the prospect of having greater control over it, so something as simple as allowing managers to choose their own office decor can be a positive retention factor

- *health and safety considerations*: these should also not be overlooked and,

while satisfying minimum legal requirements may seem a bureaucratic chore, looking at it as the positive promotion of health and well-being is edifying
- *opportunities to obtain project management experience*: reference has already been made to involvement and participation, but, as more work is done by project groups and teams, more managers are expected to positively seek out such opportunities, so the provision of these will, increasingly, be a retention factor
- *flexible working options*: this can create variety, meet a personal need or allow a pattern of working to be matched to the requirements of a particular task, but it should be remembered that a pattern of work, while it may be enjoyable, is a means to an end rather than an end in itself
- *social and recreational facilities*: work does provide an opportunity to meet people with whom one may have some interests in common and, when all else is the same, a recreational option could be a deciding factor (social and recreational facilities feature strongly in the recruitment and retention activity of military organizations)
- *development for international operation*: a Dutch company considers that its international development programme is 'a major staff retention tool'.

The retention mix

In practice, a number of the above retention factors are likely to be interrelated. For example, social and recreational facilities can improve health and working conditions and the working environment and working options can be important elements of life-style. Managers need to understand which retention factors score with each individual and group.

A similar mix of retention factors will not score the same in all locations, especially when different nationalities are involved. The international company needs to understand which elements of the mix are more appropriate in one context rather than another and how the mix may need to be changed over time.

Some elements of the mix will be more expensive than others. Changes in the relative importance of different elements will not necessarily lead to an increase of employment costs. A retention programme could be self-financing.

The elements selected for inclusion in a retention policy need to reflect the reasons why people leave the organization concerned. While the relative significance of these will vary from company to company, a number of them appear to be relatively common among leavers:[7]

- the reality of a job may be very different from the rhetoric of the recruitment process, so expectations should not be raised above the ability of a company to deliver
- change can breed uncertainty, insecurity and stress and many people have a fear of being unable to cope when placed in a new situation
- an individual may not have been fully prepared for a new role or may feel that there is a lack of support, which is the 'thrown in at the deep end' syndrome
- a job may not match the qualities, competences and aspirations of the individual so some people just get bored
- unfulfilled ambitions or a failure to progress can breed disappointment and this can lead to resentment when people feel that they have been treated unfairly
- personality clashes can make office life a burden and those who do not relate to an immediate boss can feel trapped
- disillusionment can result from a lack of respect for those above; more junior staff can feel a range of emotions from being unloved and unrecognized, to being duped or betrayed.

International retention policy

An effective retention policy is likely to involve 'disaggregation', that is, breaking down large groups of employees into those with particular requirements. For example, the retention of women wishing to start or enlarge a family might be assisted by the provision of childcare facilities or work breaks. In some countries state-funded childcare provision is available and in Belgium, France and Italy most children will be receiving some form of full-time public education by the age of three. Companies can, of course establish a range of childcare facilities, from nurseries and play centres to a variety of schooling arrangements, but this is at their own discretion.

Maternity and paternity arrangements could also be considered. Relatively few companies appear to have introduced career break or other child support schemes. Law and practice in this area vary between states. Paternity leave is a statutory right in certain countries and the law of some countries also recognizes the responsibilities that parents can have for children who are unwell, so that in Germany and Denmark it is possible to obtain paid leave for pressing family reasons.

In competing against a larger competitor, a small company might wish to stress the advantages in terms of visibility of working for a smaller enterprise or the possibility of acquiring an equity stake. Such a competitive appeal will need to be varied between countries. In the UK, for example, the practice of employee shareholding is more widespread than is the case in other EC states.

Retention policies should not be developed in isolation, the staff should be involved. For example, the views of parents could be taken into account when determining the most desirable form of childcare arrangements.

A variety of options exist for securing flexible access to skills[1] and we will shortly be examining a few of the possibilities. Flexible patterns of work could be devised to meet the circumstances of particular employees. It is not easy for employees to understand why a company that puts so much emphasis upon satisfying the requirements of individual customers cannot display similar flexibility when meeting their own needs.

In some countries, under certain conditions, a company may have no choice but to retain staff. For example, in the Netherlands a company that is profitable is not allowed to make employees redundant after a merger. Such provisions need to be borne in mind in cases of cross-border mergers and acquisitions.

10.7 Flexible access to skills

An organization could develop the skills that are required in existing staff rather than recruit new staff with the skills that are sought. Access to needed skills might also be secured on a contract or consultancy basis or through some arrangement with another organization.[1] Such factors as the speed of response required, the duration of a need or the level of skill demanded will influence which option is selected.

In the UK many companies resort to executive leasing or temporary contracts of employment in order to secure access to those skills they may require for a defined period of time. GMS Consultancy, for example, maintains a separate executive register of those with European and international experience. Such a course of action is not always as freely available as in the UK. Within the EC there are legal restrictions upon temporary work in Belgium, Denmark, France, Germany and the Netherlands and these can inhibit flexible access to skill.

However, in spite of such restrictions, the cost of full-time employment is such that there is likely to be an increasing use of flexible patterns of work. There is a large number of ways in which it is possible to secure access to skills:[3]

– single function/location *or* multiple functions/locations
– full-time *or* part-time
– employee/one employer *or* contractor/multiple clients

- home-based *or* neighbourhood office
- stand alone *or* networked
- individual only *or* team/sub-contracted colleagues
- self-employed *or* own company
- compulsion *or* choice
- temporary *or* permanent.

This situation could favour those with specialist expertise who reside in countries that are relatively free of labour market constraints. The development of global networks enables a far wider geographic access to such skills.

Assessing the options

Depending upon the nature of the assignment, those whose skills are accessed upon a flexible basis may also need certain of the qualities that were identified as desirable in an international manager in Chapter 7. On occasion, companies contract skills on a flexible basis without asking the questions relating to their international awareness and experience that would be posed in the case of a full-time appointment or internal staff transfer.

The relative merits of whether or not to contract externally rather than employ an internal skill resource will vary according to the nature of the task. Some of the arguments will be similar to those for or against external input in respect of domestic market activity. As an example, some of the arguments for or against using an external agency to research international market opportunities are set out next.

For say, international market research a company would weigh up the pros and cons of carrying this out in-house versus contracting an agency to do the work. Factors favouring an external agency are:

- access to, availability of, and quality of relevant skills
- company's own limited internal capability
- company's own resources are already committed
- internal resource lacks understanding of culture and business environment in the particular market
- the external 'endorsement' is more acceptable to data users
- commercial secrecy considerations, for example, being seen to have an interest in the market
- a one-off job, that is, developing in-house expertise, is not justified
- objectivity and independence is required
- an additional third party opinion is sought.

Factors favouring an in-house handling of the task are:

- availability and cost
- lack of suitable agencies covering the particular market
- company has available and suitable internal capacity
- company has good understanding of the local market
- company needs to build its own understanding of the market for longer term reasons
- opportunities for direct contacts
- selection and appointment could lead to delay
- communication problems might arise between the company and an external agency
- task is a relatively straightforward one and will help to develop a company's internal capability.

A company without experience of international operation may put more emphasis upon external contracts in the early stages of an internationalization programme. Later, in the light of experience, the company could be better equipped to determine the nature and quantity of its own internal skill needs.

The overhead costs of a new operation might be reduced by telecommuting where this is compatible with local labour market conditions, and it can be supported by appropriate technology.[8] Some of the typical office tasks that might be handled by a telecommuter are those that can be defined as the supply of a specified piece of work with fixed parameters of cost and time such as:

- computer programming
- data entry
- form processing
- bookkeeping/accountancy
- invoicing
- estimating
- planning/budgeting
- financial modelling
- report preparation
- article/press release writing/mailing
- research analysis
- graphic design
- word-processing
- offering specialist/professional opinions.

Skill and experience records

If skills are to be rapidly accessed as and when required, they will need to be recorded. A company may be advised to construct a database of relevant expertise that is available internally and externally. This could be supplemented by access to relevant external databases. Such sources of information on skills will become more important as increasing use is made of project groups and teams.

Those seeking to put together a taskforce could search the database for individuals with relevant characteristics. Many consultancies adopt this approach. The value of the database will depend upon the extent to which it is kept up to date. It may be more important to record service on, and contributions to, recent project teams than historical data on past job titles within bureaucratic structures that are being steadily eroded.

As greater use is made of flexible access to skills, so there may be independent contractors and part-time employees who should be considered for training and development. The existence of such training could itself make it easier to attract part-time staff.

10.8 International skill management strategy

The purpose of skill recruitment, retention and access is to add value for customers. An international skill management strategy[3] (see Figure 10.4) should be rooted in the added value vision and mission of a company, its basic purpose and reason for existence.

Too many management teams begin with an existing organization and seek ways of keeping it alive for a further 12-month period. When this approach is adopted, decisions on such matters as headcount reductions, overhead savings, advertising programmes and new control procedures, tend to relate to the company's own needs for survival rather than the external requirement of its customers.

Some form of roles and responsibilities exercise should be undertaken to determine to whom the company is responsible for what. A strategy and objectives will need to be determined. Once these have been expressed in terms of output goals, tasks can be determined and matched to project groups and teams.

At this point, the company will be able to formulate skill requirements within a framework of agreed vision, mission, strategy, objectives, roles and responsibilities and specific tasks. The company can then consider the most appropriate sources of skills, whether internal or external, and, if external, which source is most appropriate. Where an existing skill does not exist it may need to be developed.

At this point, the questions of patterns of work, facilitating processes and supporting technology arise. If human skill is the critical success factor, then the potential contribution of people should not be constrained by any of these. For example, a standard pattern of work should not be

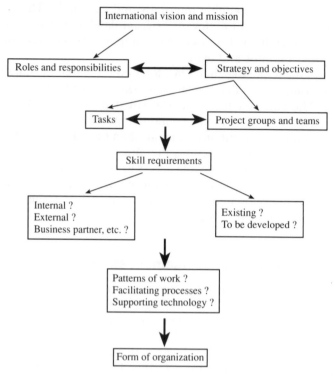

Figure 10.4   International skill management strategy

imposed. Individuals and teams should be encouraged to adopt whatever patterns of work allow them to give of their best.

Management processes and supporting technology should be the servants of people, *not* their masters. Processes and technology used should be those that best enable people to effectively harness their individual and joint potential in order to add value for customers. The form of organization should evolve out of what is necessary in terms of patterns of work, processes and technology to maximize the contribution of human skill.

Customers could be involved at all stages of the process and representatives of customers could be involved in the refinement of a vision or mission. There will be responsibilities to customers to take account of and roles, or aspects of certain roles, that could be allocated to both customers and suppliers. Representatives of both could be invited to join teams and project groups, providing access to customer and supplier skills and know-how.

The need for customer or supplier participation could suggest that a certain pattern of working be adopted and that appropriate telecommunications links be installed. If this wider involvement is advantageous from the point of view of adding value for customers, it must be facilitated and supported.

Relevant EC proposals

Companies seeking to make greater use within the EC of such flexible means of securing access to relevant skills as part-time and temporary work should be aware of certain proposals that have been brought forward by the European Commission under its Action Programme. These are designed to tackle what the Commission considers to be the risk of companies 'exploiting' differing national standards of social protection by moving work to those member states with the lowest standards.

On 13 August 1990, the European Commission published three proposals to extend the rights of part-time and temporary employees to give them comparable treatment, pro rata, to that enjoyed by full-time staff. The proposals (which are considered in an Appendix to this chapter) cover part-time employees working more than eight hours a week, including temporary employment through job agencies, and other employees working on fixed-term contracts.

There are over 14 million part-time employees and some 10 million temporary employees in the EC. The rights covered by the EC proposals include access to education and vocational training and health and safety protection.

Proposals such as those being developed by the EC should be regarded with more than academic interest. A growing number of professional people are backtracking on the corporate escalator and are being attracted to patterns of working that enable them to lead more rewarding lives.[9]

Check-list

- Does your company have an effective international recruitment and retention strategy and does this take sufficient account of the requirements of customers?
- Does the mix of nationalities among your company's employees match the international distribution of its business or are certain nationalities significantly under-represented?
- Has your company established criteria for deciding whether or not to employ local or expatriate staff?

- Does your company's commitment to the recruitment and development of local staff match its international aspirations?
- How successful is your company at retaining staff in comparison with its major international competitors and how might it achieve a better retention of staff?
- Does your company have an effective international skill management strategy for securing flexible access to needed skills?
- Does this strategy take account of the specific requirements of particular national groups and categories of potential staff such as women returners?
- Has your company analysed the main obstacles to more effective international recruitment and how might these be removed?
- Does your company actively seek to understand, and is it responsive to, the attitudes, aspirations, concerns and preferences of its employees?
- Why do some staff leave, become disinterested or plateaued, while others stay, learn and develop?

References

1. Coulson-Thomas, Colin, 'IT and New Forms of Organisation for Knowledge Workers: Opportunity and Implementation', *Employee Relations*, pp 22–32, Vol. 13, No. 4, 1991.
2. HMI, *Aspects of Upper Secondary and Higher Education in Japan*, a report by HMI, Her Majesty's Stationery Office, 1991.
3. Coulson-Thomas, Colin, *Too Old at 40?*, British Institute of Management, 1989.
4. Price Waterhouse Cranfield Project on International Strategic Human Resource Management, The, *Annual Report 1990*, Price Waterhouse and Cranfield School of Management, 1990.
5. von Neumann, John, and Oscar Morgenstern, *Theory of Games and Economic Behaviour*, Princeton University Press, 1944 and 1953; and Thomas C Schelling, *The Strategy of Conflict*, Oxford University Press, 1963.
6. Coulson-Thomas, Colin, *The New Professionals*, British Institute of Management, 1988.
7. Bevan, Stephen, *Staff Retention: A manager's guide*, Report No. 203, Institute of Manpower Studies, 1991.
8. Coulson-Thomas, Colin, and Susan Coulson-Thomas, *Implementing a Telecommuting Programme: A Rank Xerox guide for those considering the implementation of a telecommuting programme*, Adaptation, 1990.
9. Saltzman, Amy, *Downshifting – Reinvesting Success on a Slower Track*, Harper Collins, 1991.

Further reading

Atkinson, John, *Corporate Employment Policies for the Single European Market*, Institute of Manpower Studies, Report No. 179, 1989.

Brewster, Chris, and Paul Teague, *European Community Social Policy*, Institute of Personnel Management, 1989.

Commission of the European Communities, *Communication from the Commission Concerning Its Action Programme Relating to the Implementation of the Community Charter of Basic Social Rights for Workers*, (COM (89) 568), Office for Official Publications of the European Communities, November 1989.

Commission of the European Communities, *Positive Action: Equal Opportunities for Women in Employment, A Guide*, Office for Official Publications of the European Communities, 1988.

Incomes Data Services and the Institute of Personnel Management, *1992: Personnel Management and the Single European Market*, Incomes Data Services and the Institute of Personnel Management, 1988.

Manpower PLC, *Employment and Training*, Mercury Books/CBI Initiative 1992, 1990.

Pearson, Richard, *Recruiting Graduates in Europe: What is happening?*, Institute of Personnel Management, 1991.

Price Waterhouse Cranfield Project on International Strategic Human Resource Management, The, *Annual Report 1991*, Price Waterhouse and Cranfield School of Management, 1991.

Turner, Ian, *The Living Market: The Impact of 1992 on Europe and Work*, Sanders and Sidney PLC, 1989.

Appendix to Chapter 10: EC part-time and temporary work proposals

This Appendix considers three proposals published on 13 August 1990 by the European Commission. You may well find that these proposals have been debated and amended since this book was written, but they are considered in order to illustrate the potential impact certain EC developments can have upon national labour markets.

First proposed part-time and temporary work Directive

The first proposed EC Directive would require part-time and temporary employees to be considered in any thresholds relating to worker representation or consultation. Unions would need to be informed when part-time or temporary employees are to be taken on. Where a business employs over 1000 people, regular reports would be required on the use and numbers of part-time and temporary employees in relation to the total work-force.

Where part-time or temporary employees are used, their contracts of employment would need to include a statement explaining why this form of employment has been opted for. All part-time employees would have to be brought within both national social security schemes and any company schemes, such as private occupational pensions. This would probably extend to a whole range of perks and benefits, such as Luncheon Vouchers and loans for season tickets, though this would be in proportion to the actual hours worked or the length of any fixed-term contract.

The proposal also seeks to regulate certain aspects of the employment of part-time and temporary employees through employment agencies, that is, where there is no direct relationship between the employee and the firm in which he or she is working. These employees would generally be entitled to exactly the same protection under the Directive as if they were employed *directly* by the firm. States would be required to outlaw clauses in any agency contract that prohibit the firm offering the agency employee a permanent position.

At the end of 1990 it was planned that the Directive would be based on Article 100 of the EEC Treaty. This means that it can only be adopted by a unanimous vote of the member states, thus allowing for its possible blockage in the face of United Kingdom opposition.

Second proposed part-time and temporary work Directive

The second proposed Directive tackles 'external aspects' of the use of part-time and temporary staff. It aims to prevent a business enjoying an unfair competitive advantage because it operates either in a member state where part-time staff are cheap (in terms, for example, of wages, social security and national insurance costs) compared with other member states; or where a business saves money by employing part-time or temporary staff while its competitors operate with a full-time work-force.

Member states would have to ensure that part-time and temporary employees are entitled to full pro rata benefits from, and must make contributions to, national social security schemes. At present many part-time employees working more than eight hours make no national insurance contributions in the UK. Legislation would be required in the UK to change the qualifying threshold for contributions so that it will in future be linked to hours worked and to the level of pay.

Similar changes would be required to ensure that part-time and temporary employees can qualify under each country's employment protection, redundancy and maternity rules. At present in the UK, full-time staff acquire rights after two years' employment with a particular firm, while part-timers will only acquire rights at the end of five years' employment.

The Commission proposals do not attempt to establish the same qualifying period in each member state for protection from unfair dismissal and so on, but, instead, they simply seek to ensure equal treatment for full- and part-time employees within each member state's national rules. The Directive would seek to give part-time employees the *same* entitlement to annual holidays, dismissal allowances and seniority allowances as the full-time work-force. These rights and entitlements would be on a pro rata basis, that is, in proportion to the actual hours worked by that employee or the length of any fixed-term contract.

The proposals would regulate the ability of firms to rely on a part-time or temporary work-force. Limitations would be imposed on the length of a short-term contract with the aim of forcing employers to make the position permanent. In addition, employees on fixed-term contracts would be entitled to some form of 'equitable allowance' in the event of early termination by the employee.

At the end of 1990, the proposed Directive was expected to be based on Article 100a of the EEC Treaty. This means that it can be adopted by a qualified majority of member states, so that the important changes introduced by the measure can be introduced in the face of UK opposition.

Third proposed part-time and temporary work Directive

The third proposed Directive seeks to ensure that part-time and temporary employees are treated equally with regard to health and safety protection and related training. Employment agencies would be required to clearly state the health and safety risks for temporary employees and to set out details of the nature of the work to be undertaken and the qualifications required.

The proposal, when announced, was expected to be based on Article 118a of the EEC Treaty. This allows health and safety legislation to be adopted by a qualified majority vote of member states.

Proposed working hours Directive

A further Directive has been proposed on working hours for all employees, providing, on the grounds of health and safety, maximum limits for the number of hours worked over defined periods, including overtime. The proposed Directive on certain aspects of the organization of working time aims to create uniform minimum rules for rest periods and maximum hours worked within defined reference periods throughout the Community. The rules would apply to all employees, including, as appropriate, part-time and temporary employees, and contains particular provisions relating to shift- and nightworkers.

If adopted, the consequences of these proposals would vary by member state. They would have a major impact on UK work patterns, introducing regulations in many industries where agreement on working hours and shift patterns has been a matter of agreement between the employer and the work-force. It is likely that new legislation would be required to introduce the relevant changes in the UK. Many other member states would be able to implement changes through their system of collective industry agreements.

When announced, the proposed Directive concerning working hours was expected to be based on Article 156a of the EEC Treaty. This allows for its adoption on the basis of a qualified majority vote of member states.

11
International
remuneration

Perspectives

The people that stay put are large groups. You know what you need to know and can plan for them. The internationally mobile are always special cases. The life-style of a whole family group – everything, even what to do with the dog – is at stake. Whatever the policy, there is always 'horse trading' between the local general manager and the centre. It depends on how much that particular person is wanted.

International Compensation Manager, Dutch company

We know what we want, which is to link remuneration to customer satisfaction. The problem is that customer satisfaction has to be measured. In some countries people will answer customer satisfaction surveys, but in others they won't.

Personnel Director, European-based multinational corporation

My problem is that all over the world people have different views of what is fair. I know what I want, which is to relate remuneration to output that adds value for customers. Local personnel management is largely about how much of what we want can we get away with.

Chairman, UK industrial group

We know the *cost* of our international managers, but not their *value*. I receive requests to commit expenditure rather than investment appraisals. I don't accept anyone on my team without a 'justification', that is, what will they do for the business?

General Manager, German subsidiary of Dutch company

I want to link remuneration to output, and, particularly, to customer satisfaction. But this seems about the lowest priority of our personnel people. I keep hearing about there being no tradition of this in certain countries, or that it won't be seen as fair by European trade unions. We innovate with products and technology, why not with remuneration? And customers are people too, what's fair for them?

European Regional General Manager, US-based services company

11.1 Introduction

In Chapter 10 we considered the comparative appeal of companies when they seek to recruit and retain staff for international operations. Remuneration is likely to be an important element of relative attractiveness in a competitive situation and in this chapter we will consider some international issues relating to remuneration policy and practice.

11.2 International remuneration in perspective

It is important to retain a balanced and objective perspective on international remuneration. Judging from their behaviour and practice, in some companies there would appear to be an automatic assumption that 'if it's foreign it's expensive'. Staff who happily hitch-hiked around the world in their youth, surviving for months on the loose change left over from a student grant, now demand and receive as a matter of course salary supplements that can more than double their remuneration. In return many of them get to live in attractive, if not always exotic, locations.

Companies should challenge the premise that people need to be compensated for overseas or foreign service. Terms such as 'disruption', 'penalties', 'dislocation', 'rigours', 'challenge' and 'readjustment' are used to describe what are perceived as burdens that need to be sweetened by additional compensation. These burdens may not be so easily understood by the local nationals alongside whom the expatriates and travelling staff may work.

In reality there are many benefits of foreign service, positive factors that need to be stressed more often. Just a few of the ways in which an individual might gain from an international assignment are:

- a chance to broaden, grow, develop, learn, etc.
- opportunity to experience new life-styles and values
- ability to test and challenge assumptions
- better climate and physical environment
- direct contact with culture, such as art, music, etc.
- more palatable diet
- closer proximity to leisure and sporting facilities
- a new adventure for the whole family
- direct contact with colleagues in other countries
- working more closely with customers
- a way of getting out of a rut or avoiding boredom
- a respectable alternative to being a plateaued manager.

This list of advantages to the individual is not exhaustive – what is a benefit for one individual may be a burden to another. The point is that many individuals positively welcome and enjoy international assignments. In many companies staff who would willingly undertake them at an existing level of remuneration receive an additional benefit of a salary supplement.

Approaches to international remuneration

The most sensible course of action is often to be sufficiently responsive to take each case on its own merits in terms of matching remuneration to added value contribution. Just as incremental costs and revenues are compared when deciding whether or not to acquire or retain a capital asset, so a similar calculation could be undertaken in respect of people skills.

The individual concerned could participate in an assessment of their own costs and contributions. Such involvement could encourage people to raise or improve their ouputs or lower their remuneration. Few companies seek to include their staff in the discussion of such trade-offs as that between lower remuneration and a higher probability of having a continuing employment relationship.

In some cases it might be advantageous to ask employees to put their own valuation upon their expected contribution in a new role. Employees at the Brazilian manufacturing company Semco determine their own salaries and hours of work. Semco's Chief Executive Ricardo Semler has created a flatter organization and relationships are based upon mutual understanding, commitment and trust rather than hierarchical authority.

Matching the competition

Aiming to match the higher levels of remuneration awarded by the more successful of a company's labour market competitors can lead to a steady escalation of remuneration when a group of players adopt the same practice. The risk of this has dampened enthusiasm for creating Euro-markets for certain categories of staff.

The impacts of growing practices upon competitive positioning in the labour market need to be considered. For example:

– there would appear to have been a trend in Europe in favour of variable and company-specific pay and the use of profit sharing as an incentive, so shifting the emphasis to a link between pay and long-term profitability can result in a loss of staff to those companies offering

higher current rates, although the risk of such a loss will, of course, vary between countries and companies
- there has been a steady increase in the range of extras that are offered as a part of the remuneration package in Europe: as companies seek to match the best being offered by competitors in tight labour markets, mobile managers seek to preserve past benefits and, as those in each market seek to acquire the benefits available elsewhere, a creeping inflation of remuneration can occur, benefits may drift upwards, in each case to the highest available levels, and there is an element of fatalism in the way some managers accept such upward trends as if market forces are taking matters entirely out of their hands.

A manager always has a choice of whether or not to acquire or retain a skill. There is little point hanging on to a skill if its price exceeds the value of its contribution and the gap cannot be bridged by development activity at an acceptable cost.

Paying more can be a soft option when it does not lead to extra value for customers. Few managers are likely to refuse incremental remuneration, but automatic increases on the basis of past practice should be questioned.

At the end of the day remuneration comes from customers. They should only be expected to contribute to the costs of employing, or otherwise securing the services of, those who benefit them in some way. In some companies, the establishment of remuneration policy has become an arcane science far removed from the concerns of customers.

Remuneration and the customer

The starting point in any consideration of remuneration should be the customer. In the survey for the 1990 BIM report *Beyond Quality*,[1] participants were asked to rank in importance three methods of making management more customer oriented, namely, linking remuneration to the level of sales, account profitability or customer satisfaction. The results in terms of both 'important' and 'very important' replies are shown in Table 11.1. The responses are both encouraging and worrying:

- over six out of ten respondents consider it 'very important', and nine out of ten believe it is either 'important' or 'very important', to link remuneration to an external measure, namely, customer satisfaction: this is encouraging from the point of view of the requirements for longer term survival in competitive markets
- when the 'important' and 'very important' replies are added together, however, it can be seen that a high proportion of companies still attach importance to motivating staff to achieve such internal measures as

'account profitability' and the 'level of sales': these can lead to actions that impact *negatively* upon customer satisfaction.

CEOs in particular who were interviewed during the course of this survey expressed a strong preference for linking remuneration to objective measures of customer satisfaction as a means of making management more customer oriented. A proportion of the income of members of an international account team could be linked to improvements in customer satisfaction. Rank Xerox has adopted this approach.

Asea Brown Boveri is, according to Percy Barnevik, President and Chief Executive Officer, 'putting in place the mechanisms to integrate our businesses to address the customer's total needs and to be more responsive to those needs. Our performance measurements define success from the customer's point of view, and we are focusing more closly on these "report cards" from our customers'. Barnevik makes the point that 'customer satisfaction is not just another improvement program, but an effort to permanently change our value system and to orient the entire ABB family in the direction of the customer'.

Linking pay to profit or customer satisfaction creates a dilemma for some international companies. In certain countries, such as the UK, there is a tradition of profit-related pay while in other countries there is not. Similar considerations apply to executive share option schemes. These are more prevalent in the UK than elsewhere in Europe. In some cases the question of whether or not to participate may need to be left to each manager to decide.

A company may also need to decide at what level contribution to profit or customer satisfaction should be measured. It could be done at individual, account team, sectoral, local, national, regional or international level. The levels chosen should make sense for those involved. If the contribution to value for the customer largely occurs as a result of collective effort at one level, this should be chosen as the area for remuneration.

An approach to international remuneration could reflect future intention

Table 11.1 Methods of making management more customer oriented

	'Very important' responses, percentages	*'Very important' and 'important' responses together, percentages*
Customer satisfaction	62	90
Account profitability	28	82
Level of sales	11	57

Source: Colin Coulson-Thomas and Richard Brown, *Beyond Quality*, British Institute of Management, 1990.

rather than past reality. Thus, linking remuneration to performance at the pan-European or international level could precede a conscious policy to provide European or international solutions to customer problems.

Factors influencing remuneration

Starting from the perspective of the customer, there are a number of factors influencing remuneration to take into account. A selection of these includes:

- value added contribution
- customer relationships
- skill supply and demand
- complementary skills
- alternative cost of skill development
- retention factor
- operating/employment costs
- living costs
- relocation/support costs
- associated technology requirements.

For example:

- skill needs derive initially from the requirement to add value for customers so the quality of the relationship with a customer is also important, but many companies continually reorganize and change people's jobs without ever considering the consequences from the point of view of the customer: when managing an operation or activity, assessment and remuneration should be MACRO, that is, Measured According to Customer-Related Outputs and not MICRO, or, Measured in terms of Internal Company-Related Outputs
- it would be naive to assume that the interests of customers and employees will *always* coincide, so a balance may well have to be achieved between employee fulfillment and productivity: Saab, for example, has found that giving work teams the responsibility for more added value per car improves employee satisfaction, but at the cost of a longer production cycle per car.

There will be other factors to consider in determining which individuals to employ in generating value for customers:

- the supply and demand for the skills in question will need to be considered, as well as the cost of developing rather than buying them, but the development of skills may not be an option if insufficient time is available
- as more work is undertaken in teams, the individual who better comple-

ments the other skills available in a group becomes more valuable, so, in some cases, a retention factor can operate in that fears of losing someone may lead to more being paid than would otherwise be the case
- when deciding for or against the employment of a particular individual in an international role, various extra items of cost may also be influencing factors, for example, there may be a need to offer compensation for very expensive living costs or relocation and support costs could be high for certain moves.

It should also be remembered that administrative support costs can equal a salary, while the additional costs of employment such as state social and health costs and pensions and other benefits might be anything between a half and a full salary.[2] The total cost of employing an executive can be up to three times the basic salary cost.

Finally, attention needs to be given to technology and other support costs. For the network organization, telecommunications and other communication costs can be a significant element of total operating cost.

11.3 Remuneration and labour markets

Some countries are relatively self-contained as labour markets. In other parts of the world, for example the EC, regional labour markets exist for certain skills. In the case of certain categories of staff, an international labour market could be said to exist. The minimum levels of remuneration tend to be set by the forces of supply and demand in the relevant labour market at local, national, regional or international level. The more willing individuals are to be geographically mobile, the larger the area covered by a particular labour market.

Where local and national labour markets exist, a company may find wide variations in the rates of pay for particular jobs. Hourly average rates of compensation in Germany at the start of the 1990s were some 80 per cent above those in the UK.[3] The 'social costs' of employing people in Germany are also significantly above those in the UK. There may also be differences of living costs, labour law, taxation provisions and remuneration practices to take into acount.

How remuneration is determined can also vary between countries. For example:

- in some countries, legally binding minimum wage and wage and benefit indexation provisions exist, while in other states pay is left to the outcome of collective bargaining, thus a company can have greater freedom to determine pay in one context than in another
- the extent to which pay bargaining is centralized or decentralized can

also differ greatly between countries: in France and Holland many industry-level negotiations have a significant influence upon corporate pay levels

- in Italy, national industry agreements between unions and employers are enforceable in law and these agreements frequently run for a period of three years, which can prevent the degree of flexibility that an international company may have become accustomed to in a more flexible labour market such as that of the UK
- in Japan, while pay bargaining tends to take place at the company level, it occurs within the framework of a national discussion (involving unions, employers and the government) of what can be afforded given the state of the national economy and the national norm that emerges is discussed by an industry's unions and employers, who may recommend that the industry norm should be above or below the national level, so the outcome of company-level negotiations tends to be very close to the industry norm
- the process of bargaining for most industries and companies in Japan tends to occur at the same time of the year and discussion tends to be based upon a shared set of expectations regarding business prospects, so it is more difficult to engage in the leap-frogging-type discussions to improve on earlier settlements that are found in, say, the UK.

Remuneration policy

A company that has traditionally operated in a relatively free and flexible labour market in which the discretion to conclude local arrangements is delegated to line managers may find it lacks the skills to undertake centralized collective bargaining in another country. Some means may need to be found of reconciling international policy preferences with such local differences as the importance that is attached to experience.

In countries as widely spread as Brazil in South America and France, Holland and Spain in the EC, many employers pay an extra month's salary. In some cases, 14 or more monthly salaries are paid. This practice needs to be borne in mind when fixing rates of monthly remuneration in these countries.

A company should have a view on the question of whether it should offer the prevailing local rates of pay or create a cadre of international managers who are offered international rates of pay. Achieving comparability and matching previous living standards may encourage staff mobility, but they can also make it more difficult for a company to take advantage of lower operating costs in certain markets. Much will depend upon the approaches of competitors and the relative importance of the skills in question.

There is some evidence that the pay and benefits packages of directors and senior managers across Europe are converging,[4] but generalization should be avoided:

- a narrowing of differentials between countries at a similar stage of development has occurred in the case of some relatively mobile categories of staff, such as senior managers and certain specialists
- for other and less mobile levels and categories of staff, particularly those located outside of major cities, significant national differences may persist.

General levels of remuneration are likely to be higher in some sectors than in others. Differentials between countries are likely to be less in those sectors in which skills are relatively easily transferable across national borders.

The preferred international remuneration policy is:

- consistent with the company's vision or business philosophy, with strategy and business objectives and longer term compensation plans
- clear, easily understood in different national contexts and relatively simple to administer
- perceived as fair and supported not just by head office or home base staff, but also by local operating units
- sufficiently flexible to cope with change and a diversity of local situations
- sufficiently appealing to attract, retain and motivate, to induce mobility and encourage good candidates to take up overseas assignments.

Remuneration practices should be periodically questioned and reviewed. If this is not done, they can acquire a life of their own. For example:

- why does length of service carry more weight in one country rather than another?
- are more experienced operatives that much more productive?

Remuneration and mobility

Some people require a greater inducement to become internationally mobile than others. The relative cost of living will be just one of many possible sources of variations in the remuneration offered to similar groups in different countries. For example:

- labour market conditions and the balance between supply and demand or the willingness of staff to change employers will not be the same in all countries
- an occupational group may have a higher status in some countries than

in others: in a particular business sector, an engineer in Germany or Scandinavia may be paid more than his or her equivalent in the UK.

Differences in social security arrangements are another barrier to international mobility and some compensation could be provided for those who lose benefits because of an international move. The level of benefits provided and the contributions expected from both employees and employers vary across countries. In many cases, a simple course of action is to keep an employee under a home country scheme, where this is acceptable to both the home and the host country. Difficulties may sometimes arise in respect of payments made in the host country.

Pension arrangements can represent a significant constraint upon mobility and flexibility. The levels of state benefits that are paid, and the average age of retirement, differ between states. Under a typical French scheme, today's employees pay for the benefits of past employees, while most employees in the Netherlands and the UK pay into a pool or common fund that is invested to meet expected future commitments.

Within the EC, efforts are being made to ensure that individuals do not become worse off in state benefit terms as a result of moving between member states. As the situation evolves, proper professional advice should be sought. While it is possible through a life assurance route to operate a cross-border scheme, areas that need to be tackled at the EC level include:

- obstacles to the cross-border membership of pension funds
- restrictions on cross-border pension fund management
- requirements that a certain proportion of a pension fund be invested in certain ways or domestically.

Companies can themselves reduce the extent to which pensions and other benefits are a disincentive to mobility by encouraging contracting out or linking benefits to company service rather than to age. Some companies operate a separate international scheme for those who are internationally mobile.

The complexity of inter-country transfers of pension rights can be avoided when mobile executives remain in a home country scheme or an equivalent number of years are credited to a home country scheme for time spent abroad.

Certain nationalities may become under-represented in a cadre of international managers due to a reluctance to be mobile. For example, a number of companies have found Spanish managers difficult to relocate. A greater inducement to mobility may therefore need to be offered. Because Spanish law provides an extremely lenient treatment of benefits in kind, many Spanish managers receive a range of extras that are paid for by their employers and that could only be equalled in, say, the UK at a very high cost.

A company should not expect to always shoulder the full burden of coping with differences of living costs and taxation provisions between countries as these are difficult to compute and compare. The variations can be very significant:[5]

- on moving from New York to Tokyo, an executive may experience an increase of approaching 50 per cent in the cost of living
- an executive moving to Spain may be delighted with a relatively attractive salary, only to find that 45 per cent of this is paid in tax
- the cost of living in the UK is similar to that in Spain, but, while salaries appear modest, relatively low taxation in the UK means that a higher proportion of what is earned is retained
- managers in the USA benefit both from relatively high levels of salary and comparatively modest levels of taxation, so, if the policy is to maintain the living standard of mobile executives, transferring an American manager could impose a heavy cost burden upon a small operating company in, say, Africa
- an administrator or secretary on moving from Lisbon to Geneva might complain about a 'massive' increase in living costs, but with the higher salaries paid in Switzerland the individual might find that his or her 'real buying power' has increased two or three times
- other factors, such as hours of work, the tax treatment of a spouse and the extent of holidays, tax deductions and other benefits, also vary between countries.

Organizations that operate as international networks may sometimes find that value can be added from almost any location so long as access to the network exists.[6] Where each individual lives may be a matter for them to decide. Where this is the case, and differences exist in, for example, the tax treatment of benefits, it could be left to the individual to move when the balance of advantages versus discomforts justifies it.

In other cases, staff may need to be at particular locations as customers may demand their physical presence. In such circumstances, a company may have to take responsibility for compensating employees for the adverse effects of national differences if it is to secure access to all the skills that it needs.

It needs to be remembered that remuneration is but one aspect of mobility and other considerations will be examined in the next chapter. Whatever policy is adopted should be carefully documented and clearly explained.

11.4 International remuneration issues

Only those companies that are new to international operation will approach the determination of international remuneration with a clean slate. In other cases freedom of action may be constrained by past practice. In particular, staff will have developed expectations concerning a number of aspects of remuneration, such as:

- quantity
- quality, such as variability, predictability, etc.
- pattern of earnings
- comparative aspects
- performance element
- currency of payment
- location of payment/remittance arrangements
- timing of payment
- relation to cost of living
- proportion under control of the individual
- proportion linked to individual/team/unit assessment
- relationship to pension arrangements
- foreign supplement
- relocation allowance
- benefits
- taxation regime.

The weighting each individual attaches to various aspects of remuneration is likely, to a degree, to be unique: one person may be more concerned with the current level of remuneration, another with how secure this is or the prospects of its future growth; some welcome a performance-related element, while for others this may be a source of concern. Where remuneration is related to performance there will be the question of the extent to which this is linked to individual or group performance.

In an international context, the currency in which a payment is made may be an important issue. Some individuals may prefer payment to be made to a bank or other financial institution at a location other than in the country in which they are operating. When relative currency fluctuations become significant, the timing of payments or protection against adverse movements may become a major concern. Then there are the traditional questions of whether or not a foreign supplement should be paid or a relocation allowance offered. These may need to be addressed.

Cost of living comparisons can be significantly influenced by exchange rate movements and relative rates of inflation. For example, within the EC in the year to August 1991, the rate of inflation in Greece was over eight times that in Denmark. When assessing likely future costs, particular attention should be paid to those items that could form a significant element of expenditure in the cases under consideration. For example, short-term rental accommodation could account for a significant proportion of the budget of an executive on assignment.

Some cost of living comparisons do not include those items of cost that are difficult to compute. How does one value the relatively generous holidays that are given in Germany? Comparative housing costs are not easy to calculate either. In some countries, a significant proportion of expatriate executives live in accommodation provided or subsidized by their employers.

One issue facing a growing number of companies is that of the dual-career family. An international move could result in the loss of the income of a partner or spouse. While companies are reluctant to compensate for such a loss in earnings, some organizations offer counselling and other services as an element of their partner programmes. BP seeks to help an accompanying spouse or partner with practical matters such as work permits.

International remuneration practice and the individual

There appears to be a trend towards the individualization of remuneration. Greater use is being made of bonuses and merit awards that link remuneration with performance.[7]

Individuals vary enormously in their financial and taxation situations. Within a small group of managers at a similar level in the organization, one may find some whose assets have been substantially reduced by a messy divorce, while others have suddenly inherited a parental home and other assets. Given such differences, it may not make sense to treat all such managers as if they are the same. In one case, the key priority may be assistance with a house purchase, while for another a change of lifestyle may be sought rather than a salary increment.

While desirable in a national context, individualization can cause problems internationally. Expatriates on assignment and drawn from different national contexts may compare their packages and the reactions can range from feelings of unfairness to demands for a levelling up to the best.

Many companies use general cost of living indices that may not reflect the consumption habits of individual managers. If such indices are used, they must be representative and kept up to date. They should also reflect differing tax regimes. There is some evidence that within the EC some convergence of living costs is occurring. There are companies which expect that the emergence of regional trading blocks around the world will equalize living costs within these blocks.

Special arrangements may need to be made for those people who can command prevailing global rates of pay. In some sectors, companies have to accept that relating remuneration to value added contribution is likely to result in a widening of earnings differentials. The superstars are likely to pull further ahead of those who are average performers.[8]

In network organizations, individuals, particularly those who are more visible, such as senior management, will face greater pressure to prove their worth. It will not be possible to justify a high level of remuneration by pointing to a position high up the organization chart of a bureaucracy.

Those on boards may need to demonstrate an independent and objective assessment of their added value contribution. The principle of independent assessment – perhaps groups and teams assessing each others' contributions – should be extended as far as possible through the corporate network. In the UK's National and Provincial Building Society, the competences and contributions of individuals are evaluated in a team context.

Certain market contexts may require special treatment. For example in Eastern Europe and what was the Soviet Union:

- in the past, a state agency might have been paid for the use of local labour
- the employer may have traditionally paid a range of social security costs
- in some countries, because of past underfunding, it has been necessary to pay a relatively high proportion of remuneration into state social security systems
- staff might expect help with basics like food, holidays and travel
- the weakness of the local currency may have resulted in demands for hard currency payments for foreign travel or hard currency supplements to cover periods abroad
- a portion of a local salary may have been paid in a hard currency when a company would have preferred to have paid it in a local currency
- the official rate of inflation would sometimes be 'understated' or simply not be relevant in the case of goods that were not available
- the exchange rate applicable to foreign companies engaged in local commercial operations has sometimes been different to that available to local organizations and individual tourists
- more recently, some staff became disgruntled on learning of the disparities between local and overseas salaries.

Taxation considerations

To actively compete in the international recruitment market, a company needs to understand the normal basis of remuneration in targeted sectors in each country. Total remuneration may well reflect a variety of bonuses and special payment practices.

Some local practices may result from legal provisions relating to whether or not particular items are tax deductible. For example, in France a number of family or social costs, such as childcare, are deductible from income tax and a benefit that is given there for a period of three years becomes a permanent entitlement. This needs to be borne in mind when the purpose of a payment is an initial inducement or relocation sweetener.

The company car is a good example of how benefit practice can be influenced by tax treatment:

- in France, company cars are not as common as in the UK because they are relatively highly taxed
- in Holland, company cars are more widespread, petrol being fully tax deductible
- in Spain, in many companies, *every* executive will have a company car 'on expenses'.

A company could aim to equalize before or after tax salaries or living standards for equivalent jobs. An approach that is understood to be fair and appears not to discriminate between different groups of employees may better survive the test of time. It may also provide an acceptable base for the payment of additional increments depending upon individual performance and contribution rather than mobility per se. Over a period of time, as barriers between countries in regions such as the EC are reduced, one may see a greater approximation of taxation arrangements and some further convergence of remuneration.

A means of achieving flexibility and of avoiding both the distortions of differing tax treatments *and* an upward drift of benefits is to increase the proportion of remuneration that is paid in cash:

- this allows each individual to decide how to spend the money in question so that, instead of operating relatively expensive benefit arrangements, a company could concentrate instead upon matching cash payments to valued added contributions
- a switch to a cash approach could benefit those who are making significant contributions to generating value for customers because those who fight for a retention of standard benefits are likely to be people

in overhead or staff positions who find it difficult to relate what they do to benefits for individual customers.

Many companies are finding it increasingly difficult to guarantee an equivalent job at the end of a period abroad. Taxation considerations might also apply to a decision to terminate employment at the conclusion of an overseas assignment. This can prove more expensive in some countries than in others.

Overseas assignment remuneration practices

International remuneration systems tend to be based upon either home base or host country salaries. Their relative popularity varies in different parts of the world. For example:

- many US and UK multinational corporations adopt a home base approach for executives on overseas assignments
- companies in Scandinavia and other countries with relatively high tax rates have tended to prefer a host country approach.

The host country approach can discourage moves from high pay locations to those where levels of salary are significantly lower. A company could pay a host country salary in some locations and for certain jobs and a home country salary, with or without cost of living adjustments, at others. Shell has tended to use salary levels in the Netherlands as a base and offers its managers the option of joining an international remuneration category.

Typically, when an executive is moved abroad, a home salary is 'grossed up' with a cost of living adjustment and any location and expatriate allowances. The foreign salary will normally reflect the local levels of taxation that are applicable. The final remuneration may be paid in more than one currency:

- some elements of the package, such as the allowances and housing costs, might be paid in the currency of the home country
- other elements, such as those that cover local living costs, might be paid in the local currency.

While the payment of an adjusted home salary enables an expatriate to maintain a similar standard of living and can facilitate further mobility or reintegration to the home country at the end of an assignment, it can have disadvantages:

- the home salary, and other elements of a remuneration package, may bear little relationship to normal local practice and local conditions and circumstances and too big a gap can divide staff on the ground into local and expatriate categories

– when there are considerable differences between remuneration levels and practices in the various home countries from which expatriates are drawn, people doing similar jobs at the same location may enjoy noticeably different standards of living – this, too, can be divisive.

Differences between people can be reduced by seeking greater harmonization of incentive payments, using local discretion or by relying upon a composite level of remuneration. However, companies that offer a composite salary tend to face pressure for levelling up to remuneration levels at the higher end, such as those in Switzerland. Average and composite salaries can prove very difficult to calculate.

Some companies pay a monthly supplement to staff on overseas assignment. Increasingly, companies are replacing such payments with lump sums to cover the costs of movement and settling in, which are made available at each end of an assignment. The more committed a company is to internationalization, the less willing it may be to pay an extra amount for relocation.

A significant relocation premium can distort the relative attractiveness of an opportunity to the expatriate as opposed to a local candidate. It can result in a higher proportion of mobile managers than might otherwise be the case. This may be beneficial when operations are being built up in certain parts of the world, but it may not be desirable when operations have reached an optimum size as higher overall employment costs and reduced opportunities for local managers can be the result.

Preserving certain aspects of the benefit package can cause resentment in a new location. An English executive moving from London to Zurich would probably assume the continued use of a company car, but such a benefit has been rare among Swiss managers. A car on top of a Swiss-level salary could also be an expensive combination for an employer.

Some companies, for example, British Steel, adopt a dual salary solution. Executives on assignment overseas are paid according to local conditions and practices. However, a parallel or 'ghost' salary is indicated and periodically reviewed. This gives the overseas executive some idea of the sort of salary he or she would obtain on returning to the UK. Pensions and other benefits could be paid on the basis of the parallel home salary. This practice can make it easier for mobile executives to assess the relative merits of a further or extended assignment overseas in comparison with a return to the UK.

As we have seen, resentments can arise when expatriate staff are paid more highly than locally recruited staff. For this reason some companies have a policy of paying local or host country rates of pay. It is then for the international manager to take a broader view of how a period of service in a relatively low-paid environment might enhance future career prospects.

Employees can have a strong sense of fairness where remuneration matters are concerned. For example, when BP introduced an international salary package for its senior executives, the more junior staff wondered why they had been excluded from the scheme.

Housing considerations

Where assignments overseas are on a short-term basis, a company may encourage its mobile executives to retain a residence in their home country. The incremental costs of overseas housing could be paid as a supplement. However, where periods of service overseas are of longer duration and, in any event an employee may move on retirement, then help with relocation might be provided. This may or may not be linked with a housing supplement.

The mature international company, for which mobility is the norm and with a choice of candidates for most assignments, could take the view that housing is a private matter for the individuals concerned. The individual manager will then need to take relative housing and other costs into account when deciding for or against a move.

Housing is more of a problem for some nationalities than it is for others. A Belgian executive might expect to live in a rented appartment, while, in contrast, an English colleague might expect to be an owner occupier (we will consider the impact of housing and other factors upon mobility in the next chapter).

Performance-related pay

A move to performance-related pay is likely to find greater favour in some countries than others:

- general attitudes towards assessment, measurement and testing vary between countries, for example, psychometric testing could be the norm at one location and yet unheard of at another
- levels of familiarity with performance-related pay also vary: performance-related bonus payments are popular in France, relatively common in Holland, but have been rare in many industrial sectors in Spain
- the attitudes of trade unions towards performance-related pay can vary widely across countries, so the effort that will need to be devoted to discussing a proposed scheme with staff representatives will vary between locations
- the extent of employee shareholding also varies between countries and

reference has already been made to the fact that within Europe the use of share options is most widespread in the UK.

As more work is undertaken in project groups, teams and taskforces with a membership drawn from different functions and locations, comparability questions become difficult to avoid:

- to those undertaking similar roles and working together as a team, an accident of location may not seem an acceptable or fair reason for paying some people significantly more than others
- a focus upon output can also make differences of remuneration upon the basis of where one lives, length of service and past background less acceptable.

Some companies employ different criteria for establishing each element of a total remuneration package. Thus, a proportion of remuneration could reflect international performance and policy, while other elements could reflect regional performance and local factors.

Over time, a company could have a conscious policy of seeking to increase the proportion of total remuneration that is set at the regional (such as European) or international level. This is more likely to occur where the location of staff has little bearing on the benefit achieved by a final customer.

The linking of remuneration to value added contribution or customer satisfaction may make it easier to reconcile the divergent views that can arise between central, local, sectoral and functional management. Independently measured changes in customer satisfaction can provide a common standard that may be acceptable to each of these groups.

The acceptability of performance-related pay is likely to reflect the perceived fairness of the link between performance and remuneration. Preferable measures are those that:

- are tangible and objective
- relate to customers and are consistent with vision and strategy
- use simple and relevant indicators that can be readily understood
- establish a clear base from which developments can be judged
- enable benchmarks and priorities and timescales for their achievement to be set
- allow for steady, noticeable and continuing improvements over time
- enable progress to be monitored and reported
- provide scope for management intervention.

The approach that is adopted must be communicated and understood as insufficient involvement of those concerned may result in a scheme that fails to motivate.

11.5 The employment and treatment of women

The employment of women can be an issue of social, political and economic importance. Women make up a significant element of many national labour markets. For example, over two and a half million women have entered employment in the UK since 1983, the number of women working on a full-time and part-time basis increasing by a quarter and approaching a third, respectively.

In the UK the labour force is expected to grow by 800 000 between 1989 and 2000; women are expected to account for 95 per cent of this increase. Companies that have not already done so will need to introduce new patterns of work such as job sharing, career breaks and voluntary parental leave in order to make work more compatible with family life.

Law and practice relating to the recruitment, employment and remuneration of women varies greatly across countries. For example:

- in Muslim countries, women would not be expected to undertake certain activities and occupations that are effectively reserved for men
- in contrast, 1990 saw the European Commission proposing a third 'equal opportunities for men and women' action programme covering the period 1991–1995.

Within the EC, by the autumn of 1990 five Directives on equality of opportunity for men and women had been adopted and a further Directive concerning the protection of pregnant women at work and of women who had recently given birth was awaiting adoption by the Council:

- *the first Directive 75/117 (OJ L 45/75)*: created the obligation to apply the principle of 'equal pay for work of equal value' and provides judicial guarantees of the enforcement of this right and the protection of workers against dismissal resulting from the application of this principle
- *the second Directive 76/207 (OJ L 39/76)*: on equal treatment in employment, prohibits all sex-based discrimination at work and, by implication, it guarantees equal treatment with regard to recruitment, vocational training and promotion
- *the third Directive 79/7 (OJ L 6/79)*: on equal treatment in social security matters, is aimed at achieving equal treatment in statutory social security schemes
- *the fourth Directive 86/378 (OJ L 225/86)*: is on equal treatment in occupational social security schemes
- *the fifth Directive 86/613 (OJ L 359/86)*: on equal treatment in self-employment, applies the principle of equal treatment to women who are self-employed, including those in agriculture.

The purpose of this third EC action programme is to support implementation of the measures agreed and progress further proposals concerning the burden of proof, parental leave (paternal as well as maternal) and statutory and occupational social security schemes (to supplement Directive 86/378). The programme also embraces initiatives to promote the occupational integration of women by such means as qualifications, training, advice and childcare facilities, and to improve the status of women.

Check-list

- Does the international remuneration policy of your company result in a sufficient focus upon the customer?
- In particular, does your company relate remuneration to the tangible output of individuals and teams and to their contributions to improved customer satisfaction or value for customers?
- Is your company's international remuneration policy a facilitator of, or barrier to, international mobility?
- Is the policy sufficiently flexible to take account of the particular characteristics of local labour markets and the distinct needs of individuals and groups?
- Does your company actively seek the views and opinions of its staff regarding compensation issues and its remuneration and benefits policy?
- Is your company aware of the extent to which its approach to remuneration encourages commitment, flexibility, contribution and so on in comparison with other factors?
- Does your company monitor international remuneration developments, trends and practices, particularly pension arrangements, compensation for mobility and relevant taxation provisions?
- In particular, within Europe, is your company taking account of the possible impact of the EC Social Dimension upon its remuneration policy and employment costs?
- Ought your company to put more emphasis upon cash within compensation packages so as to reduce the distortions caused by varying national requirements and differing practices regarding benefits?
- Do any of your company's benefits discriminate against particular forms of staff, for example, should company pension scheme benefits be related to the number of years of service rather than to age?

References

1. Coulson-Thomas, Colin, and Richard Brown, *Beyond Quality: Managing the relationship with the customer*, British Institute of Management, 1990.

2. Judkins, Phillip, David West and John Drew, *Networking in Organisations: The Rank Xerox Experiment*, Gower, 1985; and Colin Coulson-Thomas and Susan Coulson-Thomas, *Implementing a Telecommuting Programme: A Rank Xerox guide for those considering the implementation of a telecommuting programme*, Adaptation, 1990.
3. Business International, *Business Europe Annual Survey of Comparative Labour Costs in Europe*, Business International, 1991.
4. Monks Partnership, *Management Remuneration in Europe*, Monks Partnership, 1991.
5. P E International, *International Taxation and Cost of Living*, P E International, 1991.
6. Coulson-Thomas, Colin, 'IT and New Forms of Organisation for Knowledge Workers: Opportunity and Implementation', *Employee Relations*, pp 22–32, Vol. 13, No. 4, 1991.
7. Price Waterhouse Cranfield Project on International Strategic Human Resource Management, The, *Annual Report 1990*, Price Waterhouse and Cranfield School of Management, 1990.
8. Coulson-Thomas, Colin, *The New Professionals*, British Institute of Management, 1988.

Further reading

Atkinson, John, *Corporate Employment Policies for the Single European Market*, Institute of Manpower Studies, Report No. 179, 1989.
Brewster, Chris, and Paul Teague, *European Community Social Policy*, Institute of Personnel Management, 1989.
EUROSTAT, *Earnings in Industry and Services*, Rapid Reports, Population and social conditions, No. 5, EUROSTAT, 1991.
Income Data Services and the Institute of Personnel Management, *1992: Personnel Management and the Single European Market*, Incomes Data Services and the Institute of Personnel Management, 1988.
Manpower PLC, *Employment and Training*, Mercury Books/CBI Initiative 1992, 1990.
Price Waterhouse Cranfield Project on International Strategic Human Resource Management, The, *Annual Report 1991*, Price Waterhouse and Cranfield School of Management, 1991.

12

International mobility

Perspectives

As a result of our approach to total quality, all of our managers worldwide have been equipped with a common set of tools and approaches. This makes our people more mobile – they all share a common approach to problem solving. You can see the same techniques in use all over the world.

Vice-President International Operations, US multinational corporation

We looked at Brazilia as an office location because of the government relations aspect. However our local staff were the problem. We could not persuade any of them to live there. They all wanted to come home to Rio or São Paulo for the weekends.

Brazilian Representative Director of Dutch multinational coporation subsidiary

I travel south in winter in order to see some daylight. We are a short trip company, not a long-term assignment organization.

Owner Director, Finnish high-tech company

We stay put, but our customers are mobile and they spread the word. They move around campuses and you see them with knapsacks on their backs. They like to speak English, so that is the language we use.

Publisher and Producer, German-based media company

Mobility experience takes time to acquire and is expensive. Our managers creep around the world, rather like snails with expensive shells on their backs.

Personnel Director, UK bank

Whatever you do, put down shallow roots. Changes take time and can be very expensive. People and property are like lead boots. Show me our local office and I'll give you the termination payments, the penalties on leases and rents and all the rest of it, we will pick up when we move on.

International real estate consultant, European chemical multinational corporation

Several people who left Hungary in 1956 have been tempted back. Although they have been out of the country for a generation, one or two of them are treated like heroes because of their opposition to Communism. They also have experience of working in a market economy. You don't get that in those who stayed in Hungary.

General Manager reponsible for Eastern Europe, US multinational corporation

12.1 Introduction

Internationalization tends to be associated with mobile people, foreign travel and the life-style of the expatriate. However, the extent to which these occur might, in some cases, be limited. Most major companies appear to rely largely upon local recruitment, supplemented by a relatively small cadre of international managers.

The proportion of a company's labour force that is employed overseas will depend upon a number of factors, especially the business it is in:

- a major international contract may involve relatively few employees: in 1990, only just over 4 per cent of the total number of employees of The Celsius Group of Sweden, which owns the shipbuilding group Kockums, worked in Australia, where, through a 50 per cent share of the Australian Submarine Corp., six Kockums Type 471 submarines were being constructed, but the order, worth SEK 20 billion at 1991 prices, represented over 2½ times the total 1990 group sales
- other sectors, though, are more labour intensive: another Swedish company SCA is in forest products businesses, an area traditionally associated with Scandinavia, but over a half of the company's 30 000 employees are located outside of the EC. However, these are overwhelmingly local rather than mobile employees.

The drive towards internationalization originates in the widening geographic scope of the customer requirements that the enterprise is seeking to satisfy. The corporate desire to add value for customers and their needs and preferences should determine the nature and extent of staff mobility.

This chapter examines the reasons for mobility, the alternatives to it and the barriers to it. We will also consider how mobility might be encouraged and managed. The main focus of the chapter is upon living and working abroad, but we will touch briefly upon another aspect of mobility, namely travel, which is generally for shorter term visits.

12.2 Is mobility strictly necessary?

The physical mobility of people should not be assumed and there may be other options:

– using external sources of advice
– taking the work to the people rather than the people to the work
– using technology to access distant sources of information.

Jacobs Suchard uses a computerized network to allow a head office team of some 50 staff to communicate directly with its country general managers around the world. A smaller central bureaucracy enables a faster response to local requirements and takes expensive jet-setting executives out of the organization. Most people would prefer an answer by fax today to a visit from someone two days later to discuss the answer, by which time it may be too late.

Could people secure the information they need without travelling to it? Information that is stored electronically may be accessible from any point in an international network. When information and opinions need to be drawn from a variety of locations, it may not be possible to travel to all of them. When speed of response is of the essence, time-intensive travel may not be a feasible option.

Building international networks can be an alternative to mobility, as ideas and insights rather than people circle the globe:

– VEBA finds that the globalization of chemical products and services is 'requiring increasing internationalization in research', so the basic 'unit of research' is viewed as a network of people rather than as a building or centre
– a worldwide data network is being used at MEMC Electronic Materials Inc. to identify new developments and business opportunities in wafer technology – the world's second largest supplier of silicon wafers, it has a global perspective and the corporation has joined with two Korean companies to produce wafers in Korea
– global networks are increasing in scale and complexity, for example, Ford's global network is being expanded over 5 years to embrace 20 000 engineers and designers, with information on some 700 000 vehicle parts being maintained on the central computer, and the network can accommodate some 500 000 messages a day.

Rather than take people to the work, could the work be taken to where the people are?[1] In Chapter 10 we examined a number of ways in which it is possible to secure flexible access to skills and, in many cases there may be tasks and roles that could be performed by people in the comfort of their own homes. Similar considerations apply in the international dimension. For example, programming and software development of UK public and private organizations is being undertaken in places as far apart as India and the Philippines.

Telecommunications and computer technologies can provide an alternative to physical meetings and relocation:

- computer conferencing may be possible if workstations can be linked up: Northwest Airlines is not short of aircraft seats, yet it encourages managers to use its workstation network to secure instant access to the information they need
- business television can sometimes be used as an alternative to physically delivering a message as many audiences can be reached simultaneously: Federal Express understands the business of physical movement and is a major user of business television; in the US well over a thousand centres are on the Federal Express TV network
- developments in mobile communications and telephone points on boats, in cars and on planes are making it easier for the mobile executive to stay in touch and now time differences, a source of much frustration for many jet-setting staff, can be bridged by Voicemail, which is a service where a message can be left for someone on the other side of the world to be accessed when they wake up – travelling Coopers and Lybrand staff and those working on international projects make considerable use of Voicemail
- video conferencing could be another option: when the Nationwide Building Society merged with the Anglia Building Society in 1987, a video conferencing link was established between the three key locations to help facilitate the merger and has now become accepted as an integral element of working and communicating within the building society.

A range of telephone and computer conferencing services are available from commercial suppliers. The organization without its own video conferencing facilities could hire them for the day from an external supplier (we will be examining supporting technology further in Chapter 15).

In general terms, international travel is expensive and should only be undertaken when strictly necessary, especially now that so many excellent alternatives exist. A major company should have an international travel policy and travel arrangements should be regularly reviewed and closely managed.[2]

Alternatives to mobility

People require access to facilities, support and a working environment. Relative facilities costs and employment on-costs must be taken into account in location decisions. Many companies seek to recreate in all locations what they consider is a standard corporate environment without considering its relevance to the nature of the work being undertaken or the requirements of local customers. Some flexibility could yield significant savings in setting up costs.

On the other hand, a common standard of facilities worldwide could be regarded as an important element of the distinctive identity of the company concerned. Compatibility of technology allows for the closer integration of dispersed locations. Clients and staff of the professional firm Arthur Andersen, for example, have been encouraged to feel at home in any and all of its offices throughout the world from the moment they see the front door by the use of common and global design guidelines.

Where mobility involves significant cost and disruption, a company should, as we have seen, consider taking the work to the people rather than the people to the work. In many cases, as the cost of facilities in inner-city offices rises and information can be transmitted, worked with and exchanged at a falling real cost as a result of improvements in computing and telecommunications, a new pattern of work such as telecommuting might be preferable to physical relocation.[1]

Reference has already been made in Chapter 10 to the many ways in which it is possible to gain access to needed skills. A particular pattern of work should, therefore, not be assumed because how and where work can best be done will vary according to circumstances. For example:

- much will depend upon whether or not legal restrictions apply in a particular country context and executives may be more willing to adopt a new pattern of work in some cultures than in others – those in Germany and the UK, for example often being more open to the possibilities than colleagues in France or Italy
- a flexible pattern of work may be a more sensible alternative to relocation when a whole series of moves are envisaged or an assignment or duty is likely to be temporary as it may not be necessary to bring teams together when they can comment on each other's work and exchange documents by fax or electronic mail
- the disruption of the career of a spouse or partner or the schooling of one or more children due to a physical move might be avoided by teleworking or, it can enable other members of the family to be on hand to help out during pregnancy or allow a continuing contribution to be made by those who, for reasons of age, health or life-style, do not want the upheaval of another relocation
- on the other hand, one of the purposes of a projected move may be to give those concerned some experience of working and living in another culture and this broadening of a perspective may not be achieved by staying at home.

One should always return to basics. If the essential requirement is access to relevant skills as and when required, then the question should be 'How might this be most cost-effectively achieved?' A company should be prepared to use whatever patterns of work are most appropriate for the tasks in hand. Individuals should be allowed to work in modes that best tap and develop their competence and expertise – this being especially true of knowledge workers.

When deciding for or against relocation or to where an activity should be transferred, the focus should be upon the output that is required as there may be a number of ways of delivering the desired output. When choosing between them it is important not to forget the customer. A corporate network may well be able to support teleworking, but this pattern of work may not be advisable in a culture in which face-to-face contact is the preferred way of doing business.

12.3 Mobility in perspective within the EC

To put the issue of mobility into some sort of perspective, only just over 1.5 per cent of the labour force of the EC works abroad. Less than 1 in 250 of those at work commute across national borders, the total for the EC being significantly less than the number of people making lengthy and daily commuting journeys into many European cities.

Official statistics tend to understate mobility because of illegal immigration. There are some 5 million illegal immigrants in the EC and up to 1½ million of these could be in Spain.

There are flows of people from Eastern Europe to Germany, from Yugoslavia and Albania to Italy and from Morocco, Algeria, and Tunisia to Spain, France and Italy. This influx has changed the mix of local populations:

– over a quarter of the total population of Luxembourg is made up of EC immigrants and approaching three out of ten of those in Luxembourg are migrants when non-EC migrants are included
– in France in the early 1980s there were over 1½ million EC migrants and over 2 million non-EC migrants; a quarter of those at work in the French construction industry are migrant workers
– in Germany in the late 1980s, and before the 1989 inflow from the East, there were over 1⅓ million EC migrants and over 3 million non-EC migrants
– the number of non-EC migrants in Germany was over 5 per cent of the total population, which compares with over 1½ million non-EC migrants in the UK, approaching 3 per cent of the total population.

The emergence of a single market ought to increase labour mobility within the EC. However, a number of practical barriers to mobility remain, such as the reluctance of people to move, the lack of information concerning opportunities, psychological and cultural barriers and continuing vocational restrictions that are not covered by EC measures. Unfamiliarity with a local recruitment or selection process, problems of language and dual-career difficulties can all inhibit mobility.

1992 is not the only factor likely to increase mobility within the EC. For many years, only some 100 000 people per annum left Eastern Europe for the West. In 1989 as the iron curtain fell, 1.3 million people migrated from the East to the West. A growth of unemployment in Eastern Europe and the prospect of an economic collapse in what was the Soviet Union, are likely to cause more people to seek opportunities in the EC.

EC proposals concerning foreign secondments and assignments

The European Commission has monitored the growing tendency for companies to move employees between member states to work on temporary assignments or for other companies on a secondment basis and in June 1991 adopted a draft Directive,[3] 'Secondment of Workers to Another Community Country'. The purpose of the draft Directive is to coordinate the legislative frameworks of member states and establish a 'core of imperative rules' to ensure a minimum level of protection for a worker who is temporarily in, or on secondment in, another member state concerning:

- maximum working hours and rest periods
- minimum holidays and rates of pay
- the supply of labour by temporary employment agencies
- health, safety and hygiene at work
- protective measures for certain categories of employee
- equal treatment and the prohibition of discrimination.

The proposed arrangements would not affect the significant differences that exist between member states in such areas as working hours, minimum pay and holiday arrangements. The intention of the Commission is not to inhibit, through unnecessary costs, transnational work of short duration. The Directive would apply to three categories of business:

1. those that send employees to carry out a specific task on their behalf in another country in the EC for a limited duration
2. those that make available one or more employees to another establishment or another company in their group located in another member state

3. temporary employment agencies that provide the services of a worker to a company which employs the person concerned in another member state.

12.4 Mobility in an international context

Across the world, a tightening of borders against immigration could act as a counter to the trend towards reducing the significance of national barriers. Although the pattern of responses to immigration may change over time and in response to the scale of the flows, differing regional responses have emerged:

- the prospect of a surge of immigration into the Community has provoked responses as varied as Italy sending a ship load of refugees back to Albania, the threat of French Prime Minister Edith Cresson to 'repatriate people when French justice establishes that they have no right to be in our country' and the growth of extreme political groups in Germany, even though, in general, northern European countries have strict immigration policies
- Japan's response to immigration has been unenthusiastic but fatalistic; the traditional homogeneity of Japanese society is being challenged by an inflow of lower skilled workers from the Philippines and Thailand and, although immigrants make up a relatively small proportion of Japan's population, their sudden arrival has increased their visibility, plus illegal immigrants are arriving from as far afield as Africa and Iran even though Japan's immigration policy is tight.
- in North America, that the US is a nation of immigrants and pioneers has entered American folklore, so successive waves of immigrants from Europe have become integrated into American society, but the more recent flows of people from the South, from Mexico and Cuba, have resulted in the emergence of a 'twin culture' in areas of California and Florida and US policy has become more restrictive; an inflow of people from Hong Kong has resulted in a sizeable Chinese community in Canada
- in South America, Brazil has traditionally stood out as a racial melting pot, a range of cultures having become integrated through intermarriage, and overt discrimination and tensions between groups are less overt than in other parts of the world: within Brazil, an area larger than the Continental USA, there are varying concentrations of immigrant peoples, such as those from Africa in the north and from Central Europe in the South, and São Paulo boasts the largest community of Japanese descent outside of Japan.

– the continued growth of the Australian economy has been greatly assisted by a selective immigration policy that has attracted skills from Europe and whether or not, and to what extent, the country should open up the opportunities afforded by a relatively underpopulated continent to immigration from Asia has been a topic of intense political debate.

In the absence of national restrictions on immigration it is likely that there would be larger flows of people across national borders.[4] At the international level the labour market is imperfect.

Historical flows of people have occurred for reasons as varied as climatic change and economic necessity, to religious fervour and a thirst for gold or glory. The outcome is a diversity of peoples in multicultural societies that are linked, historically and culturally, in bewildering and, at times, surprising ways. These present the international company with operational challenges and marketing opportunities.

12.5 Reasons for mobility

In a corporate context, mobility tends to be linked with flexibility and it is generally thought to be desirable. However, it can be costly, time-consuming and disruptive – it can even involve the risk of kidnapping. It is more difficult in some countries than others. A business traveller to Taiwan, for example, will find that there are only a few countries in which it is possible to obtain a visa.

The proportion of executives who move through airport lounges and between homes each year may not be an accurate reflection of how international a company is – as we have seen, people in different parts of the world can work together using such means as the telephone, fax, electronic mail and video conferencing without having to travel, except for periodic meetings.

Mobility is challenging to some and a source of stress for others. One's attitude towards, and tolerance of, major upheavals can change over time. Some may have had enough of travel and the traumas of relocation after a time, while others retain their enthusiasm for opportunities to make a fresh start. The individuals concerned and their families must be taken into account as the family, lacking the cushion of work colleague support, can often bear the brunt of an overseas assignment.

The Japanese company Brother minimizes the extent of mobility across national frontiers through a policy of localization. This involves, as Kazuaki Tazaki, Chairman and Managing Director of Brother International Europe, explains, 'recognizing and building on the skills of local labour. Of a work-force of 2300 throughout Europe, only 40 are Japanese and these are concentrated in Ireland and the UK. All the Continental subsidiaries are run by local management'.

A selection of possible reasons for mobility are:

- *customer reasons:*
  - to determine requirements
  - meet needs, for example, after-sales service
  - build relationships
  - demonstrate commitment
- *individual reasons:*
  - broaden perspective
  - build skills
  - widen experience
  - provide variety
- *organizational reasons:*
  - staff mobility
  - team requirements
  - introduce changes
  - spread knowledge of best practice.

This list is not intended to be exhaustive; its purpose is to make the point that there may be reasons for mobility quite apart from customer requirements. Hidden agendas need to be understood.

Priority should be given to the customer-related reasons for mobility. For example, a particular skill may be needed to meet the requirements of local customers or a certain form of presence may be sought to demonstrate local commitment. Individual and organizational arguments for mobility should be tested in terms of the extent to which the potential to add value for customers is actually enhanced.

12.6 Mobility and the individual

Mobility may be sought by employees themselves. We saw in Chapter 10 how a period of service abroad can both benefit individuals and be enjoyed by them.

Those whose skills are in demand may set out on a career equivalent of 'the grand tour' of the centres of art and culture undertaken by the upper class of the eighteenth century. The knowledge worker may consider a life to be incomplete if it has not included periods of work in North America, Japan or another country of the Pacific Rim, not to mention two or three member states of the EC.

Job moves and career planning may need to take into account the desire of greater numbers of young people for life-style mobility. Individuals may join international networks *just* because such opportunities for mobility exist within them – they have but one life and mean to enjoy it.

Within the EC, the UK has taken the lead in proposing a new network of careers advice centres. These will help ensure that young people have access to careers advice on education, training and employment opportunities across national boundaries.

Life-style mobility could be encouraged by greater use of project groups and teams and job swaps. Employees with similar jobs could arrange swaps. When those involved stay in each other's houses, even send their children to each other's schools, little in the way of incremental expenditure may be incurred beyond travel costs that might, in any event, be spent on holidays to the countries concerned.

An organization could have its own reasons for encouraging staff mobility. These could relate to its general capacity to respond to external challenges and opportunities quite independently of the needs of individual customers. For example, mobile staff could be thought to be more receptive to new circumstances and willing to adapt. Moving people around an organization can spread knowledge of best practice and encourage change. Larger multinational corporations and international companies can create an internal or corporate labour market to overcome imperfections in the external and international labour market.[5]

The creation of a more open and flexible culture can increase the willingness of staff to be internationally mobile. The Roche Group links a greater willingness of staff to take up opportunities for international posting as evidence of 'growing openness towards new ideas and practices'.

A policy of localization can result in fewer executives spending longer periods of time in a smaller number of overseas operations. The Japanese company Brother aims to achieve a high level of integration between local staff and Japanese employees on assignment abroad. The latter are 'often committed to spending their whole working life in the host business culture'.

12.7 Regional labour market issues

In Europe, as we saw in Chapter 9, populations are ageing and pensions and healthcare costs are likely to impose a growing burden upon employers and those in work, but, in the less-developed world, populations continue to grow and in many developing countries young people are in abundance. A challenge for network organizations experiencing skill shortages in the EC, US and Japan is to access and build the talents of young people in developing countries without incurring the difficulties that large-scale migration might cause. These could include social, political and industrial relations problems. It may be wiser to find ways of taking work to people in the developing world, rather than uprooting them and bringing them to work in the developed world.

Within the EC a greater flow may occur of unskilled and semi-skilled workers from the South and periphery to the golden triangle; from Greece, Southern Italy, Spain and Portugal to the Benelux countries and Germany. The traditional migration from South to North may encounter a reverse flow of returners and another flow from East to West – a migration into the EC from the countries of Eastern Europe and what was the Soviet Union. As many as four million gypsies, for example, could have an interest in moving westwards.

Around this regional core there are wider concentric rings of countries, such as those in North Africa, from where the more mobile may be drawn by the promise of the single market:

– already there could be as many as three million people from the Mahgreb region in Italy alone
– approaching 1½ million people have moved from Turkey to Germany in search of work.

A major question mark is the extent to which people will be allowed to flow into the EC from what was the Soviet Union, creating a European equivalent of the migration from Mexico into the United States.

Reference has already been made to the exodus from the East. Since 1987 more than one million people have emigrated from what was the Soviet Union. As many again, or more, could be seeking to travel to the West. As concerns of 'brain drains' grow in Eastern Europe, Germany, which is a likely destination for many of those seeking to migrate, has started to negotiate 'guest worker agreements' with individual countries.

12.8 Local labour market issues

When considering flexible access to skills, it is important to check that local legal restrictions do not apply to certain forms of work. In Spain, for example, there is special protection for home-based employees. Whereas in one country the emphasis may be upon enabling employers to secure flexible access to skills, in another, priority may be given to protecting the interests of those individuals who are not employed on a regular full-time basis.

Local factors that inhibit mobility can vary from country to country, even between areas or regions within a country:

– an Italian manager may be reluctant to move from a home that has been occupied by members of the family for hundreds of years

- a German manager may not wish to prejudice a child's education by moving to an area with a different local school system that has its own syllabuses and set books, but in another country, equivalent managers may be quite happy to move house and a national curriculum may be in operation
- mobility between locations is often associated with changes of job or employer and attitudes towards such moves vary between countries – in the Netherlands, for example, a relatively high value has traditionally been placed upon loyalty and continuity of employment.

The sheer number of expatriates can alter the cultural nature of a particular location. Certain areas of some cities are taking on a decidedly international character. Over a fifth of the population of New York, for example, and approaching three out of ten of those living in Brussels are foreign born.

International executives are often more concerned than their domestic colleagues to send their own children to international schools. It is possible at all stages of education to be prepared for international operation. For example, instead of a conventional university, an institution like the European Business School could be considered. Its four-year programme has included periods of study at three of five centres, each in a separate EC member state. Students emerge from the programme understanding a minimum of three European languages.

The continuation of significant differences between countries in labour law and practice has been used as an argument against the mobility of personnel practitioners. A lack of mobility can hinder the spread of awareness of best practice and may make it difficult for personnel professionals to compete with colleagues from other more mobile functions for senior management appointments. Mobile personnel staff can help others to share a corporate culture and experience a distinct management style. Marks and Spencer uses this approach when new stores are opened abroad.

Particular incentives, such as profit-related pay, can also, as we saw in the last chapter, be affected by an international move. In the UK and also, to some extent, in France and Germany, the tax regime encourages employee share ownership. In Italy there are no such special incentives and hence profit sharing is not so widespread.

12.9 Barriers to mobility

There are various practical barriers to mobility, including issues such as pensions, housing and education. Within the UK, as more individuals contract out and make their own pension arrangements, pension rights might become less of an inhibitor to mobility. A company should examine its own pension arrangements to see what can be done to facilitate rather than discourage mobility. Instances have occurred of rights being granted to encourage staff retention that have subsequently acted as a considerable constraint upon mobility.

Different countries have adopted varying approaches to the transfer of pensions benefits abroad. Enrolling a mobile executive in a succession of local pension arrangements can put an individual at a disadvantage, as compared with those who build up benefits in a single plan. Under certain circumstances the use of some form of umbrella plan can be beneficial.

A move of an executive from one country to another could involve coming to terms with differences in employment and tax laws and of pensions, national insurance and social security arrangements. There could also be the question of work permits to consider (see below). In general, though, such questions as establishing the most tax-efficient remuneration package should be established *before* the move occurs. The use of offshore trusts and companies, for example, could reduce the tax impact of certain international moves.

Education, particularly schooling, has already been mentioned as a constraint upon mobility. At the higher education level, greater mobility of students is occurring within Europe as a result of such EC programmes, as COMETT, LINGUA and ERASMUS. The increase in the number of students from other member states entering the UK in 1989, as compared with 1988, was some three times greater than the increase for students from abroad as a whole.[6]

Housing also remains a significant barrier to mobility. Suitable housing is not always available, and renting for short periods can be expensive. House prices can vary significantly between countries and between regions within countries. The purchase of a property can be a relatively straightforward matter in one country, but a minefield of legal issues involving protracted delays in others. In the UK there is a tradition of home ownership, while in other countries a higher proportion of managers may prefer to rent. When house prices rise rapidly, people may be reluctant to spend a period off the property ladder.

Reference has already been made to factors that may apply in particular labour markets. In some countries restrictions apply to work that is undertaken in or for the public sector. There may also be restrictions relating to those who work on certain public contracts, especially when national security is involved.

Minimum wage legislation may restrict the mobility of the lower paid or inhibit the employment of staff on a part-time basis. In the Netherlands, for example, minimum wage requirements apply to all those who are employed for more than a third of the normal working week, while in Spain, part-time workers already have the same rights on a pro rata basis as full-time employees.

Work permits

Within the EC, with the exception of Spain and Portugal, which chose to retain work permit barriers until 1993, people have been free for some time to travel between member states in search of work. Those who do so are entitled to equal treatment in terms of employment and working conditions, income tax and social security and trade union rights. Immediate dependants also secure considerable rights. Even so, not all qualifications have secured mutual recognition and the traditional barriers to mobility, such as housing and pensions, may still result in a reluctance to move.

Elsewhere in the world and within the EC for non-EC citizens, the work permit remains as a barrier to mobility. When planning an overseas assignment, full account should be taken of the time that may be required to obtain a work permit as in some countries this can be a protracted process.

There may be both a regional and a national dimension to consider. For example, the UK will still require work permits in the case of those who are not UK and EC nationals after completion of the 1992 process. In 1990, 47 201 applications for work permits were made in the UK and 34 611 work permits were issued. Over a six-year period, the volume of work permit applications in the UK has increased by 125 per cent.

In the UK, work permits are generally restricted to posts requiring highly qualified and skilled people where there are no suitable UK or EC nationals available. They are generally issued for strictly limited duration, related to the essential needs of the employer. Only in exceptional circumstances are permits given for the four-year period that can qualify an overseas national to apply for indefinite leave to remain in the UK.

Following consideration of the responses to a consultation paper issued in May 1989, the UK government early in 1991 announced an easing from March 1991 of the formalities required of employers seeking to bring essential staff to the UK. Employers are no longer required to advertise vacancies in the UK and EC if they can demonstrate that such advertisements would be inappropriate or unproductive for the post in question. All applications for work permits can now be sent to a single point of contact at the Department of Employment. Work permits are no longer restricted to those overseas nationals who have gained their qualifications and experience outside the UK.

12.10 Mobility as normal service

A manager joining an international company should expect the occasional move between countries as a normal aspect of a career. International mobility should not be regarded as something that is different in kind from other forms of relocation. In many companies more effort could be devoted to encouraging mobility by reference to the enhancement of experience and career prospects, rather than by expensive benefits that are not available to other staff making similar contributions to customer satisfaction.

A company that is genuinely intent on becoming an international organization, open to all those with talent irrespective of nationality, should question whether foreign service should continue to be an opportunity for some people to make more money than would otherwise be the case. Other approaches can be less costly and not so divisive between local and expatriate staff. For example, the occasional period of overseas service could be regarded, for those concerned, as normal employment at local rates of pay, rather than as something out of the ordinary that requires special remuneration arrangements.

Different approaches to service abroad could reflect the extent to which organizations have developed from a multinational corporation to an international network form of organization:

- for a multinational company operating abroad through relatively self-contained business units in each country, relocation can be the exception rather than the norm, but in the mature multinational, it may be largely limited to new or start-up operations, giving head office staff some experience of an operating unit and ensuring that senior operating unit staff spend an assignment at head office at some point in their careers
- in contrast, staff of an international company may move between countries as part of a normal process of ensuring that the optimum use of available expertise and experience occurs across the organization as a whole and relocation may also occur as priorities change so that when cutbacks occur and operations are reduced in some countries, a conscious effort may be made to identify staff who could be redeployed elsewhere.

12.11 The management of mobility

A decision to relocate either an individual or an operation should not be made lightly. There are many factors to take into account. Some will relate to customers and job responsibilities while others, such as housing, education and even shopping arrangements relate to the individuals involved. Managers who are moved may need support staff and are likely to require access to communications and other facilities.

The relative importance of such factors will vary depending upon the company. Within the same organization crucial considerations for one department may be irrelevant to another. Transportation facilities, for example, may be vital for the service function but largely immaterial to those in finance. Location decisions are rarely taken in isolation – there may be customers, suppliers, business partners and competitors to take into account.

Not everyone within a company will have the same attitude towards mobility so a conscious effort should be made to understand the life-style aspirations and preferences of each member of staff. A larger company could itself operate as a labour market, bringing opportunities to the attention of those most likely to be interested and then entering into negotiations with a view to concluding an agreement that is likely to be acceptable to all the parties involved.

The extent to which a relocation move is supported by an employee's family can be the key to his or her performance in a new role, so the family should be involved in a decision to relocate and the families of mobile employees may need to be prepared for the changes that they are likely to encounter.

For some employees there may be a dual-career situation to address and those concerned may need to agree which is the main one. Care should be taken to avoid the experience of one Scandinavian company, offering as it did both a husband and wife overseas assignments, but in different locations.

Employees themselves will need to consider their personal situations and those of their families when contemplating moves abroad. The harmonization of personal taxation is not currently envisaged as a part of the single market programme and this is an important factor in their decision making. Whereas a company tends to think in terms of gross remuneration and the total costs of employment, individuals tend to concentrate upon their earnings after tax and how much this will buy in terms of local goods and services.

Compensation for mobility

In the last chapter we considered how companies vary in their approach to compensating staff for moves across country borders, but why should a move across a national border be treated differently from a move within a country? A policy frequently adopted, and an expensive one, is to pay for the cost of moving *plus* whichever is the higher of a home or foreign level of remuneration. The result may then be further adjusted to preserve living standards. Other approaches concentrate on making sure staff are not worse off as a result of a move even though they may not be better off.

Many companies automatically make generous provisions relating to housing and the education of children, even when the staff concerned would not necessarily make the same arrangements if the cost were to be found from their own pockets. When expatriate employment costs can be between one and a half and two and a half times that of a home country executive, it is difficult to justify a continuation of practices that give such favourable treatment to those who happen to cross national borders in the course of their careers.

A company may be reluctant to change how it remunerates those of its staff who are internationally mobile for fear of losing them to competitors. This risk of loss of key staff will need to be weighed against the consequences of an escalation of employment costs as a higher proportion of staff are required to be mobile. Within regional groupings of states, such as the EC, national borders are becoming less significant. It follows that moving a person or a job location across such a barrier ought to have a correspondingly lower impact upon remuneration.

Settling in problems

The management of a relocation does not end with an appointment. The settling in of an executive during the first year of a move should be monitored. An initial honeymoon period may be followed by an adverse reaction – the vision of mountains, sea and sand being replaced by the reality of crime, disease and telephones that do not work. The efforts of an executive to settle may be undermined by an unhappy spouse or partner who has little to do and few friends for most of the day. Help may need to be provided on such matters as securing local accommodation and arranging transportation.

Openness should be encouraged as an executive may be tempted to conceal misgivings and regrets in order to appear positive and committed, the expressions of anger being left for the family in the evenings. Such an individual may soldier on and survive without ever achieving his or her expected potential in a new role. A realistic assessment might need to be made of whether such an individual should be allowed to battle on in the hope of eventual adjustment or an assignment terminated.

Those familiar with mobile executives should be able to recognize the danger signs of a failure to adjust to a new cultural environment. Such sensitivity, however, will not always be present where there is less experience of international operation. The tell-tale symptoms might not even be recognized. For example:

- the unhappy appointee may hang around national (such as, English or American) clubs, grasping at anything that is familiar or reminds them of home
- many of those who fail to adjust exaggerate and play up aspects of life in the home country that were taken for granted and hardly noticed prior to the trip abroad
- some individuals can become almost paranoiac, fuming over the dangers lurking in food and water or interpreting any bodily change or symptoms, however minor, as a reaction to a local climate, so considerable psychological support may be necessary.

When such a situation occurs can be important. A period of deflation is quite common following the initial excitement of a relocation, but it is when this persists for an excessive period that remedial action should be taken. Equally, attention needs to be given to the problems of readjustment that can arise on return to the home country at the conclusion of a foreign assignment.

Overall, it has to be recognized that the successful management of expatriates presents particular problems and especial awareness and sensitivity are required.[7] Hence, from time to time, a company should review its use of expatriate staff in the context of the alternatives that are available.

12.12 Mobility and staff development

Some companies that largely satisfy overseas customers by direct export from a home base may have relatively few staff employed in overseas locations. They may have correspondingly few opportunities to broaden the international perspective of selected staff by sending them on overseas postings. In some cases, overseas placements of limited duration with selected customers may be an alternative.

Spending time overseas in order to analyse the requirements of an individual customer can increase an executive's understanding of a particular national market. Joint projects could also be established with overseas customers to develop new products or adapt existing products and services to local conditions. A company should always be alert to opportunities to learn from its customers. One Japanese motor manufacturer has established a small design bureau in California in order to be close to an important group of customers for whom its cars are designed.

Formal management education and development can encourage or inhibit mobility depending upon the arrangements made and the extent to which these tie staff to a particular location:

– for some mobile executives, greater mutual recognition and transferability of credits or course modules would be an inducement to formal management education and development and, indeed, a number of universities have established overseas programmes or distance learning options to cope with the needs of mobile staff and expatriates
– some distance learning programmes can appear relatively expensive due to the cost of developing distance learning materials, but once the initial investment in setting up costs has been made, unit costs can fall as more students join the programme or the development costs could be shared with non-competing companies on a consortium basis or with customers or other members of a value chain.

One international network of business schools is the International Management Programme (PIM), which is supported by the ERASMUS programme of the EC. Each of the participating institutions exchanges a certain number of students for periods of six months or a year. The credits earned abroad count towards the award of a home qualification. A number of institutions have their own networks of bilateral links with overseas institutions and the number of such relationships is expected to increase.

International exchanges

A company that operates its own training programmes should consider the extent to which these could be made more international. Many larger companies maintain a number of training centres at various locations around the world. In most cases these primarily serve local managers and offer courses and programmes that are very similar to those available at other centres of the same companies. At the cost of some incremental travel, national operating companies could swap participants on each other's programmes in order to encourage the informal interaction of staff at all levels. In the SEMS survey of HRD for international operations,[8] a Belgian, Dutch and a US company took the view that all internationalization development activity should be undertaken abroad.

Exchange programmes can be extended to other organizations:

– exchanges of staff could take place with other companies in a supply chain and this could enable customers and suppliers to obtain a better understanding and closer relationship
– exchanges of people between non-competing companies could occur as part of a benchmarking exercise and a period of time spent within an

area of interest could enable implementation issues to be more fully explored
- exchanges of personnel could be set up between alliance, arrangement or joint venture partners, for example, Renault of France and Volvo of Sweden have exchanged sales and other staff as part of a longer term programme to increase cooperation between the two companies, following an exchange of shareholdings in 1990.

Within an international company, regular international meetings of staff in particular functions or at a certain level could be rotated so that they can take place at a different location on each occasion. The local national operation concerned could play host. A visit to a local establishment of interest or an opportunity to meet local customers could be built into the programme.

The outcome of such arrangements could be a network of staff and course student exchanges. In some cases these exchanges could be on a regional basis. For example, European units only might be asked to participate where customer requirements demand greater cooperation across Europe. Operations around the Pacific Rim could be brought together in a similar way. Other exchanges could be on an international basis or involve business partners, suppliers or customers.

Exchanges of staff need not be limited to those at managerial level. In many companies shop-floor staff or technicians could also usefully spend time at overseas plants. Perhaps group or team visits could be arranged. Exchanges of this nature can enable knowledge of best practice to be spread around an international network.

Working overseas and spending time in another national operating company may not of itself lead to an international overview and perspective, but the outcome might be an understanding of two national markets rather than one. It is important to remember that for many companies an objective of internationalization is to give more people some understanding of the global market-place as a whole and of the forces that may impact upon any or all national operating companies. The general question of preparation for international operation will be considered in the next chapter.

Check-list

- Are your company's human resources sufficiently mobile to be able to respond flexibly to the needs of its international customers?
- What are the main external barriers to, and internal inhibitors of, the international mobility of your company's staff and what could be done to reduce their impact and facilitate mobility?

- In particular, is your company aware of national and regional (such as, European) developments and measures that might restrict mobility and flexibility?
- Which individuals and groups should be the most mobile between your company's various international activities and interests and what should be done to encourage this?
- Does your company understand the particular requirements of certain mobile categories of staff and positively identify, actively attract and successfully retain them?
- Is sufficient consideration given in your company to the question of whether work or people should be mobile, that is, work taken to people or people taken to work?
- Does the company take sufficient steps to ensure that its customers and work colleagues learn, and secure the maximum of benefit, from those who are internationally mobile?
- Is your company sensitive to the views and preferences of its staff and those of their families and does it take these into account in decisions regarding relocation?

References

1. Coulson-Thomas, Colin, and Susan Coulson-Thomas, *Implementing a Telecommuting Programme: A Rank Xerox guide for those considering the implementation of a telecommuting programme*, Adaptation, 1990.
2. Rock, Stuart, *Director's Guide to Travel Management*, Director Publications, 1991.
3. Commission of the European Communities, draft Directive 'Secondment of Workers to Another Community Country', COM(91) 4 Final, Official Journal of the European Communities, C 185, 17 July 1991.
4. Bohning, WR, *Studies in International Labour Migration*, Macmillan, 1984.
5. Teague, P, *The European Community: The Social Dimension – Labour Market Policies for 1992*, Kogan Page in association with Cranfield School of Management, 1989.
6. Department of Education and Science, *Students From Abroad in Great Britain 1980 to 1989*, Department of Education and Science Statistical Bulletin No 20/91, August 1991.
7. Brewster, Chris, *The Management of Expatriates*, Kogan Page, 1991.
8. Coulson-Thomas, Colin J, *Human Resource Development for International Operation*, a survey sponsored by Surrey European Management School, Adaptation, 1990.

Further reading

Atkinson, John, *Corporate Employment Policies for the Single European Market*, Institute of Manpower Studies, Report No. 179, 1989.
Cox, R, *Production, Power and World Order: Social Forces in the Making of History*, Columbia University Press, 1987.

Incomes Data Services and the Institute of Personnel Management, *1992: Personnel Management and the Single European Market*, Incomes Data Services and the Institute of Personnel Management, 1988.

Manpower PLC, *Employment and Training*, Mercury Books/CBI Initiative 1992, 1990.

Ohmae, Kenichi, *The Borderless World: Power and Strategy in the Interlinked Economy*, Collins, 1990.

Schioppa, FP (Ed), *Mismatch and Labour Mobility*, Cambridge University Press, 1991.

Séché, Jean-Claude, *A Guide to Working in a Europe Without Frontiers*, Office for Official Publications of the European Communities, 1988.

Turner, Ian, *The Living Market: The Impact of 1992 on Europe and Work*, Sanders and Sidney PLC, 1989.

13
Preparation for international operation

Perspectives

Participation in international taskforces and multinational groups is mandatory. We stress the international dimension rather than knowledge of particular countries.

Manager, Human Resource Development, European headquarters of US
multinational corporation

We've defined the requirements [for international managers], we think we know what we are looking for. Every division has added one or two items to the list. However we have not yet done anything new to develop these qualities. I keep looking and I have the world's biggest collection of prospectuses and brochures.

Head Office Manager, Human Resources, Finnish company

Sometimes it's best to listen, particularly when you first arrive. Spend time finding out if your assumptions are correct or out of date before you jump in. On the ground things do change.

Director of Australian aerospace company

The preparation of some people is like a coat they put on when they go out to meet foreigners. What is important is to think and feel your local market when you are in the office with colleagues, your own culture is all around you and there are decisions to be made.

International Director for Latin America of Canadian company

While we do encourage our people to understand the international business environment, they are currently spending most of their time watching their backs. They should do both, but when you are reorganizing and there is uncertainty, the business environment – even our customers – can seem a long way away.

Director, UK-headquartered international financial institution

I'm surrounded by people who can tell me what it was like when they were there. I need to get a feel for what may happen next year.

Chairman of UK-based multinational corporation

13.1 Introduction

In Chapter 7 we examined a number of the skills and competences required for effective international operation. In this chapter we examine some of the ways in which these could be developed and how, in practice, companies are preparing their staff for international challenges and opportunities.

13.2 Internationalizing the board

Internationalization should start in the boardroom. Companies that devote a great deal of effort to internationalizing their management teams often spend little time considering the internationalization of the board. A number of multinational corporations have not exploited their full potential as a result, in part, of the limited vision of their main boards.

The composition of many boards would be improved by the inclusion of one or more foreign directors. A company could establish guidelines to the effect that every subsidiary board or management team should contain a minimum number of non-nationals.

An international board is more likely to have an international perspective, yet the overwhelming majority of corporate boards consist of members of the same nationality. Some companies have made a conscious effort to develop an international board. For example:

- the main board of Rank Xerox contains a mix of nationalities, as do the boards of several Rank Xerox operating companies in Europe, directors from Europe and Japan serve on the main board of the Xerox Corporation and the historical structure of the group is based upon strategic joint ventures involving companies in the US, Europe, Japan and Asia
- following the acquisition by Fujitsu of an 80 per cent stake in the UK computer company ICL, a need was perceived to demonstrate European credentials: ICL valued its participation in EC collaborative programmes and in 1991, Viscount Davignon, a former Commissioner and Vice-President of the European Commission from 1977 to 1984, was appointed to the main board of ICL, while other international directors on the ICL main board included Koshiro Kitazato who was with

Fujitsu, the head of Finland's Nokia Corporation and two individuals who were formerly with Northern Telecom.

In many cases, for a fraction of the cost of a consulting project relating to internationalization, a company could bring an international business leader of standing on to the board as a non-executive director. Where the size of the board is a matter for the discretion of the chairman, a number of non-executive directors could be recruited.

In the US, a substantial majority of members of the boards of most major companies are non-executive directors whereas in the UK the non-executive director is in the minority on all but a very few boards. Discussions with European company chairmen suggest many of them find it difficult to identify candidates with directorial attributes. Extending the field to non-nationals might make it easier to identify appointees.

An international group board could rotate its meetings around different international locations in order to facilitate the inputs of its various members. Meeting overseas can, of itself, broaden awareness and allow contacts to be made with local business partners and government representatives. The boards of US companies such as Motorola meet periodically in Europe.

Given that a board does not need to be physically together in order to constitute a meeting, a directors' network could be installed comprising telephone, fax, electronic mail or video conferencing links with all board members. The cost and difficulties of travel as well as physical distance need no longer be a barrier to active participation as a director.

Directorial qualities and internationalization

Members of boards should be selected according to their directorial qualities and competences. Given that the role of the director relates to the company as a whole, the possession of directorial qualities or attributes that complement those of other members of the boardroom team should take priority over considerations of nationality.

According to a survey[1] of company chairmen carried out for the Institute of Directors (IOD) in 1990, strategic awareness and planning, the abilities to be objective, see the company as a whole and look ahead are ranked at the top of the qualities that are thought to distinguish direction from management. The top ten qualities cited are:

- strategic awareness and planning
- objectivity - the ability to see the company as a whole
- long-term vision
- taking ultimate responsibility for the company

- commanding respect/leadership
- decision/policy making
- anticipating changing trends
- delegation
- lateral thinking
- responsibility to shareholders.

In the case of an international company, the board requires a global perspective. Directors need an understanding of international operations and the factors in the business environment that are likely to affect them.

Participants in the survey were also asked to rank the qualities they seek in new appointments to the board. Their responses, in order of percentages of 'very important' replies, are given in Table 13.1. A similar ranking of directorial qualities, headed by strategic awareness, has emerged from a more recent survey of senior personnel professionals.[2] If you remember from Chapter 7 (see Table 7.2), strategic awareness, communication, skills and individual responsibility also rank as the top four qualities sought in senior managers within large organizations.

When a multinational corporation has an international cadre of managers, but its directors are drawn from one or two nationalities, a significant proportion of the other employees may feel that their career aspirations do not extend to the boardroom. In some cases this may result in a conscious career plan to spend some time working in the company concerned in order to obtain experience of working in a corporation of a particular nationality before moving to a national or domestic company. It is sometimes thought that there may be fewer barriers to securing senior and board appointments in the home country.

Developing directors

A company does not necessarily need to bring extra directors on to a board in order to internationalize it, effective though this can be. Alternatives include a conscious attempt at both formal and informal learning. The chairman should assume active responsibility for reviewing and developing the competences of individual directors and the effectiveness of the board as a team.

Another survey for the Institute of Directors[3] has revealed the extent to which directors learn informally from each other. For example, the main way in which directors keep up to date is through discussion with colleagues, (see Table 13.2). The popularity of this informal interaction means that all directors would broaden their perspective as a consequence of non-nationals joining the senior management team or the board itself.

Table 13.1   Ranking of directorial qualities

'Very important' qualities sought in new appointments to company boards	Percentage
Strategic awareness	48
Objectivity	47
Communication skills	46
Individual responsibility	45
Customer focus	42
Self-discipline	38
Team player	37
Creativity	33
Perspective	33
Breadth	19

Note: Some respondents considered more than one quality to be 'very important'
Source: Colin Coulson-Thomas, *Professional Development of and for the Board*, Institute of Directors, 1990.

Table 13.2   Ways in which directors keep up to date

Ways in which directors keep up to date	Percentages
Discussion with colleagues	80
Professional journals	77
Courses, seminars, workshops	71
Newspapers	62
Books/journals	33
Television	22
Radio	14

Source: Alan Wakelam, *The Training and Development of Company Directors*, Report for the Training Agency, Management Centre of Exeter University, October 1989.

A chairman could schedule a number of board workshops or other activities designed specifically to help members develop a broader international perspective. These could be used to build a bridge between the main board and key executives:

- General Electric of the US has established a Corporate Executive Council that brings together board members and the heads of the company's various business units and it has been used to achieve a better mutual understanding, and closer integration, of various international activities
- Scottish and Newcastle Breweries of the UK operates a Chairman's Forum, attended by the board and selected executives, and this has been used to address international issues.

Directors could be encouraged to take and read international newspapers and magazines. They could also be required to attend in-company and external international events or to visit overseas customers.

A chairman could establish international development objectives for each individual director. Such objectives could include learning a language, an overseas visit, responsibility for an international project or representing the company at an international meeting. Every main board director could be expected to adopt a supervisory role *vis-à-vis* a particular geographic region or a mentoring role with the general manager of a significant operating company. ICI, for example, has a triad of regional coordinators for the Americas, Asia-Pacific and Europe.

While many directors define their roles in terms of an external focus and a long-term view, their day-to-day executive responsibilities often subject them to conflicting pressures (see Figure 13.1). For example, the priority being given to creating more flexible and responsive organizations is forcing directors to concentrate upon internal transformation.[4]

While divisional management teams concentrate upon building longer term relationships with customers, holding company boards of quoted companies may feel compelled to pay considerable attention to the impact upon the share price of short-term fluctuations in performance.[4] The demands of analysts are considered by many UK and US companies to be particularly insidious. A focus upon international issues can act as a welcome counterweight to these pressures.

A careful watch needs to be kept upon differences of perspective and potential conflicts of interest, such as those suggested in Figure 13.1. In many international companies arenas of conflict have arisen between holding company or group boards and those responsible for running operating units or subsidiaries. An operating unit team can become disillusioned when faced with head office actions that are perceived as incompatible with the requirements of a longer term vision (we will return to the need for communication and shared understanding in the next chapter).

Involving the board

Involving the board in an international exercise such as an issue monitoring and management process (such as suggested in Chapter 3) could also broaden their perspective. To recap, national operating companies or business units could be requested to identify the major political, economic and social trends in the country or business sector concerned, their likely impacts upon the company and the actions they feel it ought to take in response.

Such a process can bring distinct national or sectorial perspectives to

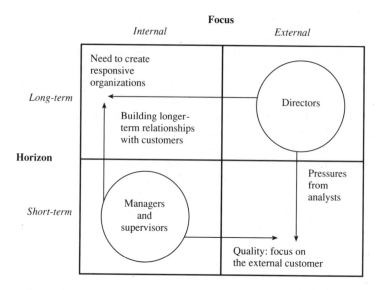

Figure 13.1 The conflicting pressures of directors' day-to-day executive responsibilities
Source: Coulson-Thomas and Wakelam, 1991

the attention of the board. Selected operating or business unit general managers could be invited to main or group board meetings to give a presentation and discuss it afterwards. Incompatibilities between global, regional and local business strategies could be highlighted in the course of such exchanges.

A similar interactive process could be used to refine the vision and mission of the corporation. Inputs from operating and business units could reveal differences of national perspective, of cultural barriers to communication and of attitudinal factors that might limit the degree of unity of purpose and action. At the international level, a shared vision may be found not to exist. A mission statement might require modification.

A major multinational corporation may feel that it is necessary to develop a host country strategy for each of the countries in which it has significant operations. The purpose of these may be to demonstrate that it is a good corporate citizen and avoid the discrimination that can be applied to foreign companies. The implementation of a host country strategy could involve contacts with governments at a senior level. This is another area in which the board might become involved, for example, in reviewing such strategies. Individual directors could be appointed to act as, in effect, ambassadors to particular countries. A corporate ambassadorial appointment could be made on an ad hoc, term or roving basis.

A company negotiating with others should remember that the role and purpose of the board can vary greatly across countries. In some countries the board determines strategy and may act in a general supervisory capacity. In others its main purpose could be legal, to technically approve accounts or to appoint a chief executive to whom wide powers are delegated.

Some boards exist to tap expert advice, to lend prestige or authority by drawing upon big names or to give the appearance that certain interests are represented. Then there are subsidiary and supervisory boards to consider. The degree of influence exerted by a board and the importance of its individual members may not be easy to determine.

Within the EC, discussion concerning employee involvement has tended to focus upon the board. It should be remembered that the main board may be but one decision making forum within a company. It may not be the body whose decisions relate most, or directly, to many of the immediate concerns of local employees.

13.3 Internationalizing senior management

So far in this chapter we have considered internationalization of the board. This focus is necessary as surveys undertaken in both 1989[3] and 1990[1] have revealed that nine out of ten directors do not receive any formal preparation for their boardroom roles, let alone preparation for international operation. A board that does not recognize its *own* development needs is less likely to understand the development needs of senior management.

One reason why few of the directors surveyed had received specific formal preparation for their boardroom appointments is that at the time these were made this was not widely available. This deficiency is now being remedied. In the UK, for example, Henley Management College offers programmes at director and general manager level. Also Surrey European Management School has established a programme of short, board-level courses in European company direction. Those who complete the programme and satisfy the requirements are entitled to the Diploma in Company Direction of the Institute of Directors. This diploma is also available at various other centres.

The internationalization of managers is assuming a higher priority for those companies that are most committed to international operation:

- Asea Brown Boveri recognizes the global dimension – according to Percy Barnevik, its President and Chief Executive Officer, 'Beyond the traditional management abilities, many Group management positions require unique "cross-border" skills – managers must be able to operate and communicate effectively in a variety of national and cultural environments'

– the Netherlands-headquartered chemical company DSM has recognized that, in its 'training and education programmes, more and more emphasis will be placed on enhancing employees' international knowledge and experience. The recruitment and career guidance policy, too, will assign greater weight to international orientation'

– ITT Flygt is one of three operating divisions of ITT Fluid Technology Corporation, which is headquartered in the USA and operates in over 100 countries, and it has 'identified the importance to its worldwide operations of bringing on new managers with international experience' – the company has introduced a new international management programme to supplement existing training, with subsidiary managers being the key target group for this programme, and the company will be 'taking advantage' of its 'international structure to give future managers valuable experience of working for subsidiaries in different countries'

– ICL has introduced an international management development programme that 'reinforces the company's global values and beliefs and demonstrates ICL's commitment to staff development on a worldwide basis, 'elements of the programme being tailored to the needs of particular roles and specific country issues and the country manager module being aimed at newly appointed or potential country managers

– British Gas has developed an international development programme that is designed to equip managers to understand international social, economic and political issues, plus distinct national cultures, so managers learn how to operate effectively within a particular national context, including building relationships with host country governments at both political and administrative levels.

Modes of study preferences

In Chapter 7 we examined the relatively low priority being given by many companies to the formal development of the skills and competences that are particularly associated with international operation, the evidence for this being taken from a survey concerning developing HRD for international operation.[5] The participants in this survey were also asked for their views regarding the relevance of various modes of study to their organizations' management development needs. The relevance attached by the respondents to various modes of study is presented in Tables 13.3 and 13.4. In Table 13.3 the responses are ordered according to the percentage of 'very relevant' responses, while in Table 13.4 they are ranked in order of the percentages of 'very relevant' and 'relevant' responses added together.

The most relevant modes of study are thought to be the tailored company-specific programme, with a project component and in-company delivery. Issue-based, modular and open programmes are also thought to be relevant, while a period of study in another EC country, a study visit abroad and block release are not thought to be very relevant. Full-time study is ranked last in order of relevance when the 'very relevant' and 'relevant' replies are combined (see Table 13.4).

Some differences emerged between various categories of respondent. For example:

- compared with UK companies, the replies from professional firms and associations give a significantly higher 'relevance rating' to the portability of credits/qualifications within the UK, and the mutual recognition of qualifications within the EC – the recognition of their professional qualifications clearly being a matter of some concern to professionals, over seven out of ten of these respondents believing mutual recognition and over three quarters of them believing portability to be either 'relevant' or 'very relevant'
- compared with the replies from UK companies, the European and international respondents put a higher 'relevance rating' upon issue-based programmes and a period of study in another EC country, less relevance being attached to distance learning, block release, portability of credits/qualifications within UK (perhaps not surprisingly) and mutual recognition of qualifications within the EC, than was the case with respondents from UK companies.

Location of learning preferences

In a further question, the participants in the above survey[5] were asked to rank their preferences regarding the location of learning. Their responses in terms of 'very appropriate' replies are ranked in order of preference in Table 13.5. The most appropriate location for learning chosen, by a considerable margin, is a 'place of work'.

This is interesting because the most effective training and development is that which is integrated with working. Other factors in effective learning are that:

- the relevance, purpose and context are understood
- learning is through doing rather than learning at institutions
- team activity and group learning are involved
- individuals learn in different ways

Table 13.3   Relevance of various modes of study in order of 'very relevant' replies

Modes of study	Percentages
Tailored company-specific programme	52
Project component	36
In-company delivery	30
Open programme	24
Modular programme	23
Self-managed	21
Issue-based	21
Part-time day release	20
Evening	19
Distance learning	18
Portability of credits/qualifications within UK	14
Mutual recognition of qualifications within EC	14
Joint programme/joint validation	13
Residential element	13
Period of study in another EC country	13
Full-time	13
Study visit abroad	11
Discipline-centred	11
Industry-specific programme	11
Block release	3

Source: Colin J Coulson-Thomas, *Human Resource Development for International Operation*, a survey sponsored by Surrey European Management School, Adaptation, 1990.

- it is tailored to the learning potential of each person
- it is supported by appropriate tools, techniques and processes
- the environment is conducive to, and supportive of, learning.

Learning should not be regarded as something apart from normal work, but as an essential component of it:

- the Swedish chemical company Perstorp operates an international management programme and it creates opportunities to 'discover' and rotate qualified personnel from one business area or division to another, which 'facilitates the overall planning of management resources across a highly decentralized form of operation'
- Hawker Siddely, a UK company, has introduced an international management development programme to encourage an international perspective among its managers – accustomed to working in a national context, they are also being required to focus upon market sectors that cross national borders and so it is hoped that learning and working can be integrated.

As we saw, when those involved understand its relevance and purpose, effective learning occurs. Group and team learning, too, at the place of

Table 13.4. Relevance of various modes of study in order of 'very relevant' and 'relevant' replies together

Modes of study	Percentages
Tailored company-specific programme	90
Project component	81
Modular programme	80
Issue-based	79
In-company delivery	77
Self-managed	74
Open programme	71
Distance learning	71
Part-time day release	69
Evening	69
Portability of credits/qualifications with UK	62
Mutual recognition of qualifications within EC	60
Discipline-centred	60
Industry-specific programme	58
Joint programme/joint validation	56
Residential element	54
Block release	40
Study visit abroad	37
Period of study in another EC country	36
Full-time	13

Source: Colin J Coulson-Thomas, *Human Resource Development for International Operation*, a survey sponsored by Surrey European Management School, Adaptation, 1990.

Table 13.5 Preferences regarding the location of learning

Location	Percentage
At place of work	40
Country house or specialist executive centre	23
Convenient hotel	11
University environment	8

Source: Colin J Coulson-Thomas, *Human Resource Development for International Operation*, a survey sponsored by Surrey European Management School, Adaptation, 1990.

work can be more successful than the learning of individuals at a location separate from normal life that is designated as an institution of learning. This is understood by those companies that seek to broaden their managers by involving them in international project groups and teams.

Increasingly, as competing companies seek to 'differentiate', they are developing distinct cultures. Understanding of their unique features needs to be shared. For example:

– Nissan's development programmes at all levels reflect its concern with such concepts as total quality, continuous improvement and 'just in

time' and it is thought that these need to be understood by all employees
- Rank Xerox has pioneered a range of approaches and techniques designed to achieve continuous transformation and all employees, as individuals and in teams, are equipped to understand and employ them; in some areas, managerial productivity has improved by a factor of ten as a result of using the new tools
- a commitment to developing people can be a significant element of a company's philosophy of business. Kiyoshi Ichimura, the founder in 1936 of Ricoh, a Japanese producer of office automation products, believed: 'Business is people. Business starts with people and ends with people', so, for Hiroshi Hamada, President of Ricoh, 'realizing the full potential of every company member is the company's most important aim'.

Approaches to learning need to reflect local circumstances. For example, in Eastern Europe:

- prior to the transition to a market economy, groups such as accountants did not exist, so job swaps and overseas assignments have been used by ICL to develop those who in other countries would have learned locally
- what is taken for granted elsewhere may not apply – ICI found that its employees in some countries needed to learn what job evaluation was before it could be applied locally
- as is the case in much of the developing world, multinational corporations and international companies are playing an increasingly important role in the transfer of technology, commercial awareness and business skills.

Different people learn in a variety of ways. This view is instinctively acceptable to those interviewed and it also accords with what is being discovered at research centres about how people learn. The most effective approaches are those that can be tailored to the way in which individual people naturally build their understanding.

One UK manufacturer endorses the need to consider each person as a unique individual. The company sends its staff to personality assessment centres and the independently assessed personality profiles are then matched with what it is thought would best meet the requirements for effective performance in a certain capacity abroad.

Preparation for international projects

Many companies still operate hierarchical management development programmes designed to offer those perceived as having the potential for advancement a succession of courses at supervisory, junior management, middle management and senior management levels. National initiatives, such as the UK Management Charter Initiative, seem set to entrench still further this model, which does not match the likely evolution of many organizations.

For the flexible network organization, a more relevant approach would recognize that movement between projects rather than up functional ladders is likely to become more prevalent.

The training and preparation required by people prior to their joining a project team should reflect the distinct nature of project management[6] and will depend upon a number of factors:

- *the project task*: for example, whether the responsibility is at the national, market sector or product division level, or it is technological, financial or multi-functional
- *the role the individual will play*: whether as a member of the team or in a coordination, liaison or project management role
- *the location or market context*: for example, whether at home or abroad
- *other team members*: for example, whether inter-cultural communication issues might arise
- *the context*: for example, whether it is a single company or joint venture project.

Special preparation could be required in any combination of these areas (see Table 13.6).

Formal frameworks for the development and assessment of project management competences have been established. For example, in the UK the Association of Project Managers has agreed a matrix of project management competences and introduced a competence-based assessment process. A national team of assessors has been formed and individual project managers can seek certificated status.

13.4 Formal training and development

Training is not necessarily desirable; it depends both upon the training and the trainer. Many trainers continue to teach out-of-date ideas or jump aboard the latest bandwagon without thinking through the consequences for an individual company. Many of the notions that can appear the most compelling on the trainer's slide, and are delivered with the panache and confidence that comes from frequent repetition, have limited application in the work context. Those who teach sometimes themselves find it very difficult to learn.

Education and training can involve between a fourth and a fifth of those living in a developed country. Overall investment in training and

Table 13.6   Projects and special preparation

	1	2	3
Task	Overseas market plan	International product management	Joint venture negotiation
Role	Team member	Coordinator	Liaison
Location	Overseas	International HQ	Home
Team	Mainly local management	International	Multinational organization
Context	Single company	Single company	Multinational company
Preparation	Local cultural familiarization Marketing planning/research	Project management Inter-cultural communication Product knowledge	Bargaining and negotiation skills Business sector induction

development in the UK, for example, is some £20 billion per annum. A similar sum is spent on state education. To this one could add the expenditure and activities of people themselves to acquire new qualities and experiences. Within a few years the total annual investment of the UK in HRD may reach £50 billion.

Expenditure on training and development, and its quality, varies greatly across countries:

- the UK may have a lower proportion of its young people at university than some other EC member states, but a relatively high proportion complete their courses and obtain degrees
- trade and technical training in many cases is much more extensive in France and Germany than in the UK.

The relationship between management development and career progression also differs between countries.[7]

- almost all Japanese managers in major companies are likely to have degrees or other formal qualifications, whereas these may be possessed by a minority of equivalent UK managers
- the work and training experience of the Japanese manager is likely to be limited to that of a single company, whereas the UK or American manager may participate in the training programmes of several corporations during the course of a management career and, such moves as are made by the Japanese manager are more likely to be within a single function, while the American manager is more likely to move between functions

– UK and US managers may have participated in middle and senior management programmes at a younger age than would be the case with many Japanese managers.

Key questions are how flexible are the skills created and how relevant are they to a company's needs? For example, does the concentration upon rote learning and teamwork in Japan encourage individual creativity?[8]

People in some countries are more willing to take the initiative and assume responsibility for their own personal training and development than those in others. This needs to be borne in mind by those operating international corporate training programmes. Managers from certain countries may be under-represented on courses if positive steps are not taken to encourage their involvement.

In the UK today there is less reliance upon the paternal employer, less confidence that the company knows best what training is needed, by whom and when. Instead younger individuals are becoming more pro-active, demanding development opportunities. This trend may not be so apparent elsewhere. We will examine later in this chapter who takes the initiative in respect of the participation of managers in MBA programmes.

Training priorities

Training priorities may need to be flexible in order to reflect sudden changes in the international business environment such as those that occurred in Eastern Europe in 1990. The German industrial and energy group VEBA operates a special development programme in Eastern Germany with a focus 'on the teaching of the basics of business economics and advancing the occupational qualifications so that the people working there will acquire the level of knowledge needed to work to West[ern] German standards as quickly as possible'. 'Motivated by social responsibility', VEBA has offered a range of vocational training opportunities across Germany that are 'beyond its own requirements'.

Participation in training can also vary by such factors as age and level in an organization. Traditionally, the training and development of junior and supervisory management has been largely concerned with the internal dimension, equipping them for their role in the corporate bureaucracy (see Figure 13.2). Only at the level of senior management has there been a significant increase in external input.[4]

In the bureaucratic organization the route to the boardroom tends to be via progress up vertical and functional ladders, but in the network organization, the route to the boardroom is likely to encompass movement around the various elements or partners of the network (see Figure

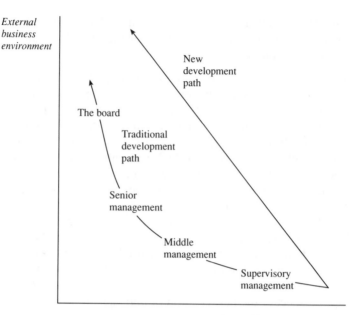

Figure 13.2   Management education and development – the internal and external balance
Source: Coulson-Thomas and Wakelam, 1991

13.3). Experience is sought of various forms of relationship rather than of different functions.[4]

In the international network organization, staff at all levels need to understand key features of the external business environment and the requirements of customers. This is recognized by participants in the survey concerning HRD for international operation.[5] Executive programmes for senior managers and directors, diploma programmes for middle management and certificate programmes for supervisory and junior management were all thought to be important (see Table 13.7). Certificate and diploma programmes for supervisory and junior managers, and middle managers respectively, were ranked ahead of masters degree programmes for senior management.

The European and international respondents appear to attach greater importance to *all* forms of education and development than those from UK companies. The difference is noticeable in the case of diploma-level programmes for middle management, at the masters degree level for senior management and at the executive programme level.

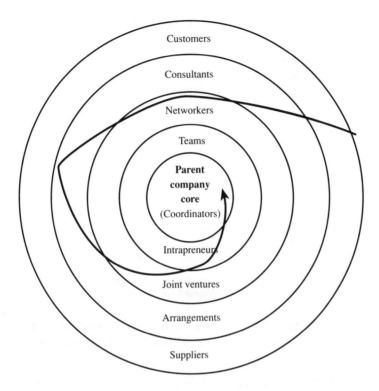

Figure 13.3   The network organization – the route to the boardroom
Source: Coulson-Thomas and Wakelam, 1991

Subject preferences

Let us consider how MBAs might be made more relevant to the needs of international companies. Although MBA programmes were not ranked high in priority compared with certificate and diploma-level programmes, the responses that the survey[5] participants gave to a question that asked them to rank in importance various core MBA subjects confirms the primacy of human resources. In Table 13.8 the various subjects are ranked in order of prevalence of 'very important' questionnaire replies.

Of all the subjects, human resources also emerges as the most important for those who were interviewed. Only one person thought it neither 'important' nor 'very important'; over three quarters of those interviewed considered it 'very important' that human resources be included in the core of an MBA programme.

Next in order of importance comes marketing. Again, only one person did not consider it to be either 'important' or 'very important' that the

Table 13.7   The relative importance of education and development at various levels of formal qualification

Qualification	'Very important'	'Important'	'Not very important'	'Unimportant'	NA
Executive programmes (senior management/directors)	24	48	17	1	2
Diploma (middle management)	12	49	28	1	2
Certificate (supervisory/ junior management)	13	42	32	3	2
Masters degree (senior management)	8	39 1 (tomorrow)	38 1 (today)	5	1

Source: Colin J Coulson-Thomas, *Human Resource Development for International Operation*, a survey sponsored by Surrey European Management School, Adaptation, 1990.

subject be included in the core of an MBA programme. Over six out of ten gave it a 'very important' rating. Throughout the preparation of this book two priorities emerged:

1. the external priority of understanding and satisfying customer requirements.
2. the internal priority of people and, in particular, of harnessing human talent.

Human resources subjects and topics are those mentioned most often (see Table 13.7) in responses to the open-ended questions in the questionnaire concerning whether there were particular subjects that the organizations the respondents work for would like to see as both core and optional subjects in an MBA programme. Human resources is followed by marketing/distribution and strategy/planning. The management/operations categorization of responses covers a wide range of topics.

The broad categorization of responses in Table 13.7 conceals the fact that over 70 different subjects and topics were mentioned by respondents. In only three cases, namely marketing, human resources and strategy were the same words used by them to describe a subject area on three or more occasions. The wide range of topics cited suggests a diverse set of requirements and is consistent with the preference for courses tailored to the requirements of individual companies.

Little emphasis was given to language skills. The responses suggest that

Table 13.8   MBA programme subjects

The relative importance of core MBA subjects, ranked in order of 'very important' replies

Subjects	Percentages
Human resources	81
Marketing	62
Business policy	42
Corporate planning	35
Finance and accounting	31
Information technology	31
Operations management	15

Respondents' preferences for MBA programme subjects

Subjects	No. of respondents as core subjects	No. of respondents as optional subjects
Human resources	13	5
Management/operations	11	3
Strategy/planning	9	3
Marketing/distribution	8	5
Financial aspects	6	1
International aspects	5	5
Quality/service	4	2
Manufacturing/production	3	3
Leadership	3	1
Business environment	2	2
Information technology	2	–
Learning	1	1
Others	6	2

Significance of a European element in various subjects in order of 'very significant' replies

Subjects	Percentages
Marketing	54
Business policy	51
Corporate planning	45
Human resources	24
Information technology	13
Finance and accounting	11
Operations management	10

Source: Colin J Coulson-Thomas, *Human Resource Development for International Operation*, a survey sponsored by Surrey European Management School, Adaptation, 1990.

language skills are not sought per se, but that those with strong technical or professional skills who also happen to speak one or more foreign languages may be preferred to those who do not. As one respondent put it, 'Why should we try to teach people to speak German? There are plenty of people who speak German fluently in Germany'.

The responses to a question concerning the significance of a European element in various subject areas are ranked in order of 'very significant' replies in Table 13.7. Marketing, business policy and corporate planning are the subject areas in which a European element is thought to be the most significant.

Entry and assessment criteria

Appropriate experience is the preferred criterion for entry onto an MBA programme and some two-thirds of the survey[5] respondents consider it to be 'very important' (see Table 13.9) The greatest divergence of views occurs over assessed competence as an entrance requirement. Few of those spoken to thought it could be done effectively and all of those giving assessed competence a 'very important' rating, and a majority of those giving it an 'important' rating, qualified their responses along the lines of 'assuming an effective means is found of assessing competence'.

A combination of continuous assessment and project work on one or more real management problems is overwhelmingly the first choice of those interviewed as a means of assessing performance on a programme at the post-graduate (MBA) level (see Table 13.9). Some seven out of ten interviewees gave continuous assessment a 'very important' rating and over a half gave project work a 'very important' rating.

Responses relating to assessment of competence were qualified with doubts and assumptions concerning whether or not it could be effectively done. Interview conversations suggest that assessment of competence would find significantly greater support as an overriding or single assessment criterion if those concerned were persuaded that it could be done fairly and effectively.

Training and who takes the initiative

In the *Human Resource Development for International Operation* survey,[5] 90 organizations responded to an open-ended question concerning who takes the initiative in respect of participation in MBA programmes. In some cases more than one response was given according to circumstances. For over a third of these respondents the individual employee is generally responsible for taking the initiative, while in about a half of the organizations participating, the individual employee generally or sometimes takes the initiative (see Table 13.10).

The organization is cited as generally taking the initiative regarding participation in MBA programmes in the case of two thirds of the respondents. The personnel and human resources functions take the ini-

Table 13.9 MBA programmes

Relative importance of MBA entrance requirements, ranked in order of 'very important' replies	Percentages
Appropriate experience	65
Other specified (potential to benefit from the course)	46
Assessed competence	27
First degree	23
Professional qualification	8
Completion of internal courses	4

MBA programme performance assessment, ranked in order of 'very important' replies	Percentages
Continuous assessment	69
Project work	58
Dissertation	19
Assessment of competence	19
Formal examination	8

Source: Colin J Coulson-Thomas, *Human Resource Development for International Operation*, a survey sponsored by Surrey European Management School, Adaptation, 1990.

Table 13.10 Who takes the initiative in respect of participation in MBA programmes

Individuals	No. of individuals
Generally individual	36
Sometimes individual	9
Total:	45

Functions	No. of organizations
Personnel/human resources	22
Training/management development	15
Operating units	9
Other functions	7
Personnel and line manager jointly	6
Total:	59

Source: Colin J Coulson-Thomas, *Human Resource Development for International Operation*, a survey sponsored by Surrey European Management School, Adaptation, 1990.

tiative in a quarter of cases, the training or management development function in a sixth of cases. Operating units or a line manager jointly with the personnel function, takes the initiative in a further sixth of the organizations covered by the responses.

Time and timing considerations

In the same survey,[5] 78 respondents answered a further open-ended question concerning how much time they felt a senior manager could reasonably commit per annum to preparation for a post-graduate degree. The most common response, which accounted for a quarter of these replies was from 20 to 30 days. Two thirds of respondents felt that less than 40 days per annum could be committed. The two respondents from UK professional associations citing 100 plus days per annum thought MBA study should be on a full-time basis (see Table 13.11).

Interviews suggest that in practice managers do not spend the time on their development that the questionnaire respondents felt they could commit. Motorola, a winner of the US Baldrige National Quality Award, requires all its staff to undertake a minimum of one week's training. A similar commitment is expected by Xerox, another winner of the Baldrige Award. These companies share a concern with both training and quality and both operate integrated training and quality programmes.

Fewer than six out of ten of the respondents answered a question concerning how much time during a post-graduate degree programme, the main purpose of which is to build European and/or international awareness and perspective, should be spent abroad. For those who did answer it, the most common response was 10 to 20 days (see Table 13.12). One global trading company links short-course and other personal development activity with periods of home leave.

All those citing over 100 days abroad referred to periods of either 4 or 6 months within the framework of a full-time MBA programme. The 'not relevant' replies all mentioned a period of foreign service, working and living abroad, as part of a typical career to be a preferred option.

A varied set of responses was obtained to a final open-ended question about MBA programmes. This concerned the point in the year at which it was thought a formal MBA programme should commence (see Table 13.13).

Over a third of the respondents did not have a preference, while a number specified more than one month as a preferred starting point. The most frequently cited month, but mentioned by under a quarter of the 76 respondents answering this particular question, was September.

The responses concerning commitment of time and programme commencement dates are consistent with the desire of companies to integrate learning and working. As many organizations 'scale down,' those managers who remain often find themselves under greater pressure to perform and in these circumstances, it is difficult to justify lengthy periods of time away from the office. While people are on external courses, there are also

Table 13.11   Time a senior manager could reasonably commit per annum to preparation for a post-graduate degree

| No. of days | No. of respondents | | | |
	UK companies	UK professional firms and associations	European and international companies	Total
100+	3	2	1	6
80⟩100	–	–	–	–
60⟩80	3	1	–	4
40⟩60	4	2	1	7
20⟩40	18	6	1	25
10⟩20	5	3	5	13
0⟩10	1	1	2	4
Varies	6	3	1	10
None/not relevant	7	2	–	9
Total	47	20	11	78

Source: Colin J Coulson-Thomas, *Human Resource Development for International Operation*, a survey sponsored by Surrey European Management School, Adaptation, 1990.

Table 13.12   Time that should be spent abroad during an MBA

| No. of days | No. of respondents | | | |
	UK companies	UK professional firms and associations	European and international companies	Total
100+	1	2	–	3
80⟩100	–	–	1	1
60⟩80	1	–	–	1
40⟩60	2	–	1	3
20⟩40	5	1	1	7
10⟩20	12	5	1	18
0⟩10	4	2	2	8
Varies	1	1	1	3
None/not relevant	5	1	2	8
Total	31	12	9	52

Source: Colin J Coulson-Thomas, *Human Resource Development for International Operation*, a survey sponsored by Surrey European Management School, Adaptation, 1990.

fewer colleagues in slimmer and flatter organizations to whom work can be delegated.

Two or three days has emerged as the preferred length of an individual training module or seminar.[3] A company could require that a certain minimum number of nationalities be present at every corporate seminar.

Table 13.13   Point in the year at which a formal MBA programme should commence

Month	No. of respondents
January	6
February	3
March	4
April	6
May	7
June	6
July	5
August	6
September	18
October	10
November	7
December	1

Source: Colin J Coulson-Thomas, *Human Resource Development for International Operation*, a survey sponsored by Surrey European Management School, Adaptation, 1990.

Indeed, the short seminar is used by a variety of companies to bring international participants together:

- within Asea Brown Boveri, Percy Barnevik, President and Chief Executive Officer, explains that, 'To further internal cohesion and understanding, some 400 upper-level managers from all business segments and countries attended [in 1990] three-day seminars in small groups, discussing critical issues and strategy implementation with Group executive management. A similar series of seminars is underway for 1991/92. The goal of the programme is to communicate and build acceptance for a common set of values throughout ABB'.
- a major priority for Jack Welch, the Chairman of the US company General Electric, has been to develop a shared global perspective across what remains of historic departmental and national boundaries, so some 5000 people per annum have attended seminars and courses at the company's Crotonville Management Development Institute – participation in these events aids the integration process.

Financial considerations

Inevitably in the case of a survey[5] undertaken at a time when companies were expecting, or experiencing, an economic recession in certain important national markets, reference was made to the need for the cost of training to be justified. A significant number of companies, while accepting the value of management education and development for individuals, questioned the extent to which their employing companies benefited. They accepted the strategic need to invest in order to tap more of the potential of their people, but their concern was rooted in a desire to invest more wisely and establish criteria that would enable people investments to be considered alongside other priority claims upon corporate resources.

The fixed cost of establishing a new training programme can represent a higher entrance barrier for the smaller firm than for the large company. This is recognized by the Commission of the EC which has developed a Community Action Programme aimed particularly at small- and medium-sized enterprises wishing to establish in-service training. The Commission has also proposed a Directive that would give all employees the right to continuous training.

There are a number of EC programmes designed to broaden awareness of the European dimension and equip people with the skills likely to be in demand in the single market. For example, there is:

- the Youth For Europe programme, to encourage European exchanges of young people
- the ERASMUS programme, concerning student exchanges
- the COMETT programme, aimed at developing technological cooperation between higher education and industry
- the PETRA programme, to improve the preparation and training of young people
- the FORCE programme, which aims to improve the training of those in employment
- COMETT and EUROTECNET, which have encouraged technology training
- the LINGUA programme, which is concerned specifically with linguistic skills
- the EC Executive Training Programme (ETP), which offers young businessmen and women an opportunity to acquire a detailed understanding of Japanese language and business.

Significant numbers of people are now participating in EC programmes:

- COMETT projects accepted in 1991 involve nearly 3000 European enterprises, 1000 universities and other institutions of higher education and 1000 other organizations such as chambers of commerce and professional associations
- in 1991–92 some 73 000 students were participating in exchange arrangements under the ERASMUS programme.

The expense of a training programme for an individual company could be reduced by sharing its development costs with other suppliers in a value chain or with customers. A spin-off from such an approach could be a greater understanding of each other's requirements and the establishment of informal contacts along value chains.

The importance of training is recognized by governments, too. For example, in the UK, the government has sought to encourage more people to take responsibility for their own training. It announced in the 1991 budget, relief at source on training paid for by individuals that leads to National Vocational Qualifications (SVQs in Scotland) up to and including Level IV. Career development loans were already available in the UK and, by early 1991, had encouraged individuals to invest some £50 million in their own vocational training. During 1991, initially on a pilot basis, the UK introduced training credits, which give young people the purchasing power to undertake training of an approved standard.

International relations programmes

In Chapter 2 we examined a number of distinguishing features of the global business environment. While business schools are devoting considerable effort, some more successfully than others, to making their MBA and other programmes more relevant to this international environment, around the world there are other institutions and university departments whose *raison d'être* is understanding international affairs. Organizations such as the UK Centre for International Briefing at Farnham Castle, the US Graduate School of International Management and the Japanese Institute of International Studies offer courses and facilities to prepare staff for overseas postings.

There are also the departments of international affairs and international studies. Indeed, in many cases their degree and other programmes would appear more suited to the development needs of the international business executive than the traditional MBA. Certain of these programmes are available to busy managers on a flexible evening basis.

The challenge to traditional approaches

Intense global competition, financial uncertainties, dumping and protectionism, crises and tensions, alliances and joint ventures are the reality of today's business world. Successful managers in this challenging international environment are increasingly called upon to make decisions in situations of high risk and uncertainty, very often under crisis conditions. This raises some fundamental questions:

– do traditional executive programmes prepare management for this turbulent environment?

- do they provide the multicultural skills and sensitivity examined in Chapter 8?
- do they offer the multidisciplinary skills and the analytic, communication and decision making capabilities needed to cope with surprise and new realities?
- do they equip participants with the international orientation and perspective needed to confront and handle revolutionary change?

The CEO of one US bank takes the view that, 'while MBAs tend to focus managers on the internal workings of the company, senior managers taking international relations programmes devote much more attention to the external business environment'. The bank now encourages its senior staff to obtain international relations rather than business degrees.

Defenders of traditional approaches to management education can claim that the MBA has facilitated career advancement within some large and functionally organized corporations. However, as we saw in Chapter 6, while functional tools and techniques will remain important, their usefulness is being eroded by the adoption of new patterns of work, new forms of organization as well as new management processes and supporting technology.

Few of today's MBA graduates will become general managers, leading a team composed of heads of functional departments at the top of a corporate bureaucracy. As companies change to accommodate a more demanding and international business environment, new management skills and competences are required.

Traditional executive and MBA programmes continue to address some corporate needs. However, their limitations are being increasingly recognized. As the changing business environment puts additional pressures on managers, a broader perspective, political sensitivity, fresh insights, multidisciplinary tools and techniques, cross-cultural awareness and different decision making approaches are sought.[9]

Executive programmes in international relations

Some of the benefits that can be provided by an executive programme which draws upon the subject matter of international relations rather than business studies are:

- a contemporary overview of the international political, economic, legal and institutional system
- an understanding of how nation states and international companies can make and conduct foreign policy

- an appreciation of how international companies can interact with, and influence, governments
- a systems framework for identifying and anticipating change in the global environment
- an awareness of contemporary international economic, financial and trade issues
- an appreciation of international risk analysis
- an assessment of the sources of corporate power and influence
- an understanding of crisis decision making
- international bargaining and negotiation skills
- relevant area and political studies
- guidance on corporate planning in a regional and international context
- greater awareness of the particular problems of international communication.

I, in fact, designed such a programme for the London executive centre of the University of Southern California (USC) School of International Relations in 1987–88. It provided management with tools to deal both with developments in the global environment *and* changes in the nature of the corporation itself.

The philosophy underlying the USC programme is that the study of international relations offers a rich pool of experience, cases and insights concerning global confrontation and competitive behaviour, cross-cultural communication, power and influence, international bargaining and negotiation, alliances and joint ventures and decision making in conditions of uncertainty and stress.[9] The executive programme applies the insights of international relations to the attainment of corporate change in an international context.

An international executive programme or workshop should give participants an overview of the international business environment and help them to identify the key international issues facing their corporations. The subjects discussed should include decision making, crisis communication, the sources of power and influence and the negotiation of arrangements and joint ventures. Course participants should be exposed to case studies and group exercises and these could include crisis decision making and contemporary cases dealing with such issues as international trade and dumping, global alliances and responses to regional conflicts.

A company might have an *ad hoc* need to orientate a group of managers to a new area or era of international operation as some companies have significant business interests in certain parts of the world. Area studies specialists could offer background briefings covering contemporary issues in particular regions or workshops on particular countries or situations. A US bank operating internationally invites all its European senior managers to a regular one-day briefing on major international political and diplomatic developments.

An executive programme should be developed *in conjunction* with corporate management to ensure that it benefits both the participants and a sponsoring company. Thus, team exercises could focus on actual international issues facing a company. In interactive sessions, groups could rank and discuss challenges and opportunities and assess their possible impacts upon corporate power and influence. Competitive strategy options could be explored through games and simulations.

Executive programme participants could be given the task of drawing up, along the lines suggested in Chapter 3, a corporate foreign policy in support of overseas operations or a global competitive strategy. A management team could be asked to formulate a programme for the implementation of such a corporate foreign policy.

Masters degrees in international relations

The benefits shown in Figure 13.4 could also be achieved by means of a Masters-level degree programme. One international construction company requires a proportion of its senior managers to have international relations degrees because, as its CEO says, 'International wars and crises create significant new business development opportunities and it helps to consider where these are likely to occur and what the outcomes might be'.

A number of formal postgraduate degree programmes are available that allow students to select a combination of courses of relevance to international business. The University of Kent, for example, offers an MA degree programme in international relations at the London Centre of International Relations.

Some international relations courses are also available on a flexible basis by means of distance learning and evening or weekend study. USC, for example, prior to the establishment of the London Centre of International Relations offered an evening MA programme in Europe. After 1975, when the USC Masters programme had been operating in the UK for ten years, it began to attract increasing numbers of mid-career executives and, by 1980, business personnel from more than 40 multinational companies had joined the programme.

The content and approach of the USC programme was then adapted to meet the distinct needs and interests of mid-career executives in their 30s and 40s. The USC curriculum now reflects 20 years' experience of the particular demands of mid-career students. The programme recognized that many mid-career students have practical experience of international

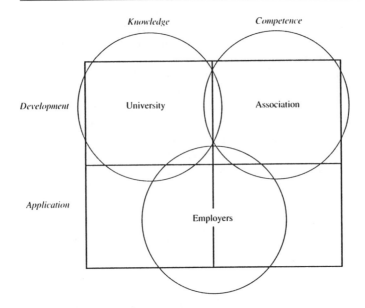

Figure 13.4 Knowledge and competence – the roles of universities, associations and employers
Source: Coulson-Thomas and Wakelam, 1991

operation and are specifically seeking to secure a better understanding of their own business environment and to carry out their duties and functions more effectively.

A general survey has been undertaken by GP Nielsson of over 200 of the USC UK Masters programme alumni who graduated in the period August 1967 to August 1977. Its purpose was to determine their overall assessments of the programme and its contribution to their careers.[10] Among the findings are some interesting points, including that:

- half the Nielsson survey respondents felt that completion of the MA programme was of some relevance to their performance in their current job, while nearly half felt that it had been instrumental in subsequent career advancement and almost a quarter expected it to be so in the future
- almost a third of the survey respondents believed that the MA had been instrumental in a subsequent change of career
- over 86 per cent of respondents believed that participation in the USC programme had affected their process of thinking and method of evaluating information in general and over 72 per cent had been affected 'very much and directly'.

An international relations programme tends, as one would expect, to attract people with an international orientation. Such individuals, therefore, may not be representative of the total population of those seeking systematic management development. On the other hand, the international orientation of many managers is often latent rather than explicit. Many of those undertaking international relations executive and Masters programmes have considerable background knowledge derived from the media and work experience and are seeking some means of structuring this experience in order to draw out insights and understanding of relevance to their international careers.

Sources of relevant management development expertise

To whom do companies turn for advice on management development matters? Companies can obtain management development services from internal departments or externally from professional associations, business schools and other educational institutions, as well as from management and other consultants, and each has its advantages and drawbacks. Their relative positioning can change according to whether individuals or teams need to be developed or whether the emphasis is to be placed upon development or application of either knowledge or competence. One traditional assessment[4] of the relative positioning of three of these sources of services is shown in Figure 13.4.

The various sources of development services could be viewed as either competitors or arrangement partners. Whatever the source, any provider of development services has to establish a priority focus, differentiate itself from other providers and determine its organizational requirements.

In the course of two of the surveys cited in this book,[1 and 5] the participants were asked to whom they turned for advice on relevant management development issues. Such a question was put in the survey *Human Resource Development for International Operation*.[5] The most commonly cited sources of advice are internal human resources, personnel or training specialists, followed by external consultants and advisors (see Table 13.14). Some respondents mentioned more than one source of advice.

Sources of expertise relating to directors and boards

Who do companies seek advice from concerning competent directors and effective boards? In the survey *Professional Development of and for the Board*,[1] the participants were asked to rank in terms of relevance a number of sources of professional development services. The results are shown in Tables 13.15 and 13.16.

Table 13.14   Sources of authoritative advice and information on management development issues

Source	No. of organizations
Internal HR/personnel/training specialists	41
External consultants/advisers	25
Business schools	16
Professional and national/international associations	8
Other educational institutions	6
Various/others	5

Source: Colin J Coulson-Thomas, *Human Resource Development for International Operation*, a survey sponsored by Surrey European Management School, Adaptation, 1990.

Table 13.15   Services for the development of individual director's competences, ranked in terms of 'very relevant' and 'relevant' replies added together

Services	Percentages
Functional professional associations	70
Institute of directors	63
Specialist consultants	60
In-company trainers	57
Postgraduate business schools	52
Open/distance learning	41
Management consultants	39
Consortium participation	38
Individual academics	33

Source: Colin J Coulson-Thomas, *Professional Development of and for the Board*, Institute of Directors, 1990.

Starting with the development of the competences of individual directors, the relevance respondents attach to services from various sources are given in Table 13.15. This presents the 'very relevant' and 'relevant' replies added together. Professional associations, whether the Institute of Directors (IOD) other functional associations, head the list.

Over six out of ten respondents ranked the IOD's services for the development of competences of individual directors as of relevance. The IOD offers a range of courses, workshops, conferences, publications and other services and many of these are also available to non-members.

Turning to the development of the competences of the board as a whole, the relevance respondents attach to services from the various sources are given in Table 13.16. Again the ranking is of 'very relevant' and 'relevant' replies added together. The IOD itself is regarded as the most relevant source.

Table 13.16 Services for the development of the whole board's competences, ranked in terms of 'very relevant' and 'relevant' replies added together

Services	Percentages
Institute of Directors	58
Specialist consultants	56
Functional professional associations	50
In-company trainers	40
Management consultants	39
Postgraduate business schools	36
Consortium participation	36
Open/distance learning	29
Individual academics	28

Note: Some respondents considered more than one service to be of relevance.
Source: Colin Coulson-Thomas, *Professional Development of and for the Board*, Institute of Directors, 1990.

Some six out of ten respondents consider the services of the IOD for the development of the board as a whole to be of relevance. So far as this is concerned, the IOD ranks some way ahead of functional professional associations and significantly ahead of management consultants and postgraduate business schools. Indeed, postgraduate business schools only just rank ahead of individual academics. The business schools do not appear to be regarded as a 'relevant source' so far as the development of the competences of the board as a whole is concerned. Over half of the respondents consider postgraduate business schools to be either 'not very relevant' or 'irrelevant' as a source of services.

It was pointed out in Chapter 7 that where greater use is being made of international taskforces and teams, specific training may be needed in project management skills and competences. These have been defined and details of the related programmes of certification can be obtained from the UK Association of Project Managers mentioned earlier in this chapter or from the international umbrella organization INTERNET.

Check-list

- Is your company's preparation for international operation pro-active or reactive?
- Is it compatible with the qualities and capabilities needed to succeed in your company's market-place?
- Has your company fully explored how its preparation for international operation might be assisted by collaborative arrangements with its customers and suppliers?

- Does your company belong to collaborative education and training networks, participate in exchange programmes and tap related sources of national and regional support?
- Has its search for productive relationships and partnerships extended to sources of expertise that may be especially relevant to internationalization, such as international relations or project management?
- Is your company linked up to relevant national, regional and international learning networks that provide access to the competences, technology and processes needed to support the development of staff through their involvement in work-place projects?
- Is your company fully aware of national and regional (such as, European) education, development, and exchange programmes, initiatives and sources of funding?
- Does your company benchmark, that is, actively seek out instances of best practice and learn from other non-competing companies?
- In particular, do your company's employees swap insights and compare their experience with those holding similar responsibilities in other organizations?

References

1. Coulson-Thomas, Colin, *Professional Development of and for the Board*, Institute of Directors, 1990.
2. Coulson-Thomas, Colin, *The Role and Development of the Personnel Director*, an Adaptation Ltd survey undertaken in conjunction with the Institute of Personnel Management Research Group, Institute of Personnel Management, 1991.
3. Wakelam, Alan, *The Training and Development of Company Directors*, report for the Training Agency, Management Centre of Exeter University, October 1989.
4. Coulson-Thomas, Colin, and Alan Wakelam, *The Effective Board*, Institute of Directors, 1991.
5. Coulson-Thomas, Colin J, *Human Resource Development for International Operation*, a survey sponsored by Surrey European Management School, Adaptation, 1990.
6. Coulson-Thomas, Colin, 'Project Management: A Necessary Skill?', *Industrial Management and Data Systems*, pp 17–21, Vol. 90, No. 6, 1990.
7. Story, John, Lola Okasaki-Ward, PK Edwards, Ian Gow and Keith Sisson, 'Managerial Careers and Management Development: A comparative analysis of Britain and Japan', *Human Resource Management Journal*, pp 35–57, Vol. 1, No. 3, Spring 1991.
8. Stephens, Michael D, *Japan and Education*, Macmillan, 1991.
9. Coulson-Thomas, Colin, 'Is the traditional executive programme obsolete?', in SJ Paliwoda and AC Harrison (Eds), *The Association of MBAs Guide to Business Schools*, Pitman Publishing, 1988.

10. Nielsson, Gunnar P, 'Student perspectives on the UK programme', in RC Kent and Gunnar P Nielsson (Eds), *The Study and Teaching of International Relations*, Francis Pinter, 1980.

Further reading

Barham, Kevin and David Oates, *The International Manager*, Business Books, 1991.

Coulson-Thomas, Colin, *Creating Excellence in the Boardroom*, McGraw-Hill, 1993.

Groom, AJR and CR Mitchell, *International Relations Theory: A bibliography*, Frances Pinter, 1978.

Guy, Vincent, and John Mattock, *The New International Manager*, Kogan Page, 1991.

Light, M, and AJR Groom, (Eds), *International Relations: A Handbook of Current Theory*, Frances Pinter 1985.

Liston, David, and Nigel Reed, *Business Studies, Languages and Overseas Trade*, Pitman Publishing and The Institute of Export, 1985.

Manpower PLC, *Employment and Training*, Mercury Books/CBI Initiative 1992, 1990.

Price Waterhouse Cranfield Project on International Strategic Human Resource Management, The, *Annual Reports 1990 and 1991*, Price Waterhouse and Cranfield School of Management, 1990 and 1991.

Taylor, Trevor (Ed), *Approaches and Theory in International Relations*, Longman Group, 1978.

14

Internationalization: achieving the transition

Perspectives

I can't think of a single manager who has not been on a communication skills course. And yet no one really understands what we are trying to do. The memos float across in-trays and are passed on and the videos are circulated, but our managers don't discuss them with their people. Communication is an attitude of mind and wanting to share. It's not about being slick.

Director, Corporate Communications, international transportation company

Honesty and openness is very important. If you tell the truth, at least you will gain respect. Try to be smart and it becomes a battle of wits.

Former Director, international chemical company

They are cynical and distrustful. There is such a large gap between what we *say* and what we *do*. Every move is seen by our social partners as a way of cutting costs.

General Manager, Human Resources, German industrial company

More and more responsibilities are being heaped on people who are not being equipped to cope with them. They are dying out there. You can't keep on asking them to do more and more with less and less. Those guys need help.

Vice-President, International Operations, US company

My problem is that all I've got to do is raise the question and people rush all over the place talking about what I plan to do and worrying about how it will affect them. How does one raise issues and get colleagues to actually discuss them, think about them, critique them . . . ?

Chief Executive, UK materials supplier

So far, all we have got are words on paper – nothing has happened out there. And nothing is going to happen unless we equip people to cope with change.

Chairman, UK financial institution

14.1 Introduction

Internationalization presents each and every company with unique challenges and opportunities. The various parts of a company will not all be affected in exactly the same way. Advice in one context may not be relevant in another. Each significant element of a corporate network should determine its own response and yet there may need to be some consistency between activity at the local, national, regional and international levels.

Coordination and consistency appears in some companies to be pursued for its own sake. If this involves additional procedures and processes, along with the staff and other resources to operate them, it may be legitimate to ask the question, 'So what if consistency is not achieved?' Consistency should only be sought where it is relevant to the profitable delivery of value to customers.

In earlier chapters we have examined the forces for change. We saw in Chapter 6 that corporate transformation is not just being discussed, it is being actively sought. Internationalization can result in further pressures for change – the breaking down of national barriers between states, such as is occurring within the EC, creating new challenges and opportunities, for everyone, including those organizations that are already operating internationally:

– activities may have been dispersed in order that a corporation might appear a good corporate citizen in as many countries as possible, but within a single market it may make more sense to centralize an activity like distribution at a single point
– perhaps production should be rationalized or national operating companies replaced by sector groups or account teams able to produce European solutions to customer problems
– a distinction may need to be made between cosmetic change in order to appear European and the reality of evolving customer requirements – as Paul Allaire, Chairman and Chief Executive Officer of the Xerox Corporation has put it, 'our commitment to Europe is not just rhetoric. We are investing heavily in the critical areas . . . research, development and high-tech manufacturing'.

To achieve a successful transition to an international network organization, it is very important that all those involved understand the need for change, have a shared vision and agreed goals and understand what needs to be done to achieve them. We will explore these issues in this chapter.

14.2 Focus upon the customer

Any consideration of what to do next should begin with the customer. Participants in the surveys cited in this book (see Appendix 1) have left little doubt about the importance of the customer:

- in the survey *Professional Development of and for the Board*[2] in 1990, the number one business issue in terms of 'very important' replies was satisfying customers, followed closely by delivering quality. Over nine out of ten of the respondents thought that satisfying customers and delivering quality were very important
- in the survey *Beyond Quality*[3] in 1990, the number one management issue in terms of 'very important' replies was building longer term relationships with customers, followed closely by introducing a more customer-oriented culture. Over seven out of ten of the respondents thought that building longer term relationships with customers and introducing a more customer-oriented culture were very important, while *every* respondent thought the latter to be either 'very important' or 'important'.
- in the survey *The Flat Organisation*[1] in 1991, 97 per cent of the respondents felt customer focus to be either a 'very important' or an 'important' factor in the creation of a new philosophy of management.

Determining customer requirements

The relevance of the international dimension will depend upon the current and likely future requirements of a company's customer base. For example, a supplier of information systems may find that the evolution of its customers from national companies to global organizations is matched by a migration of their technology requirements from 'boxes' to integrated and international networks (see Figure 14.1). This evolution needs to be matched by a supplier's capability to install, support and service integrated global networks. The global customer will be likely to demand global service. AEG, for example, has offices in 111 countries and operates a global customer service network in order to respond flexibly to its customers' requirements across the world. Companies such as Chrysler and IBM are restructuring in order to match evolving customer requirements.

Not all customers are the same. We observed in Chapters 1 and 2 that they are increasingly demanding tailored products and services. It may be advisable, therefore, to draw up a hierarchy of customers:

- personal
- unincorporated business
- local company
- single-activity company

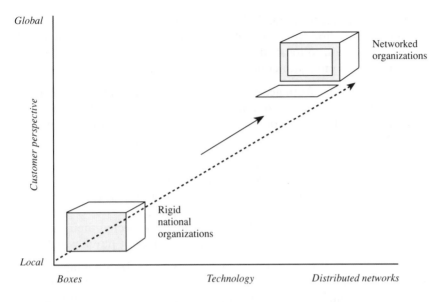

Figure 14.1 Customer and technology trends

- sub-national company
- local office of national operating company
- national company
- diversified company
- national champion company
- regional (such as, European) company
- joint venture company
- multinational company
- international company.

Against each category of customer could be put a profile of their interests and needs and the current and a target volume of business with them. The basis of classification might vary from company to company, but such an exercise can give a company a clearer perspective concerning the level at which future demands from customers are likely to arise, that is, at the national, regional or international levels. Of course a company need not respond to requirements at all levels, but tracking movements in the results of this sort of analysis over time can enable trends to be identified that may demand a corporate response.

Internationalization should be led by customer requirements. For example:

– are customers centralizing their procurement at fewer points?
– does differentiation from competitors require that more rather than less attention be paid to local differences?
– are there local environmental criteria that need to be satisfied?

This last point is far from academic. The environment has become a significant international issue that may need to be monitored through a corporate issue monitoring process. A survey[4] of major companies in 1990 found that:

– over eight out of ten respondents thought that 'organizations should investigate the environmental impact of goods and services they use'
– over seven out of ten respondents thought that 'organizations should only buy from environmentally sound suppliers'
– within five years a majority of the respondents expected their organizations to have formal policies concerning sources of purchasing.

Suppliers that do not meet the requirements of environmental policies established by customers are likely to lose their business. This creates problems for some companies, but opportunities for others. While recognizing that the Netherlands may have a more rigorous approach to the environment than Brazil, some companies, such as the Xerox Corporation, have global environmental initiatives to exceed *all* local requirements.

Some customers insist that the same environmental standards apply to their purchases worldwide. Internationalizing companies may, therefore, force internationalization upon those of their suppliers who wish to maintain a continuing relationship.

Responding to customer requirements

A company should not assume that the focus of its employees is upon its customers. Disturbing answers can be obtained to such basic questions as:

– 'Who in the company is responsible for the customer?' – in some areas where the response should be everyone, it may be no one
– 'Who in the company adds value for customers?' – administration, service, finance and a variety of other functions can all do things to improve customer satisfaction, yet too often people in these areas produce work for each other rather than for an external customer[5]
– 'Who could or should add value for customers?' – a function such as personnel and other sources of overhead to operating units should be asked to justify their cost to the business
– 'How much time and resource is devoted to the customer?' – the supplementary to this one is, 'Why do you need the rest?'

- 'Are people motivated to respond to customer requirements?' – in some companies, customer satisfaction appears to be an incidental rather than a core purpose of the objectives established for many employees.

A clear majority of CEOs interviewed in one survey[3] expressed a preference for linking remuneration to measures of tangible outputs and, preferably, to those that add value for customers. Remuneration policy should be used to facilitate change:

- to encourage more of a European perspective – the largest share of bonuses paid to senior Unilever managers is linked to Europe-wide performance
- Rank Xerox links a proportion of the remuneration of its senior managers to independently assessed measures of customer satisfaction
- IBM (UK) has also adopted a pay incentive scheme that depends upon *customer* assessments of performance
- Avis undertakes mail surveys of over 100 000 customers each year, spread across 15 countries and over 1100 monthly reports are sent to various Avis offices and departments around the world, then, according to the country, bonuses or other incentives are linked to performance as measured by the customer.

A company's assessment and reward system should reflect outputs and added value contributions of relevance to international customer requirements and so training and development may need to be reviewed in the light of these requirements. Also individual managers may need to acquire greater sensitivity to the feelings and values of customers from other cultures.

International customer issues and problems may not fit naturally into an existing departmental or divisional allocation of responsibilities. A more integrative approach may be needed to achieve their solution. In the process, flexible access will be required to relevant internal and external support services. Appropriate technology for the support of multifunctional, multilocational and multiorganizational teams will also be needed as cooperative effort along value chains is demanded to satisfy customers.

Corporate reorganizations too often reflect internal needs for cost savings rather than external customer requirements. However, customer-led reorganizations are occurring:

- Hoechst is one of many companies seeking to pull together resources to form group-wide business units to meet customer requirements
- the Harvester division of Deere and Company of the US has turned its back on a matrix form of organization and introduced a team-based approach in order to respond more quickly to opportunities to add

value for customers and, to speed up the product delivery process, teams stay together from the product concept to marketing stages

- Rank Xerox has embraced quality, European account management and developed a whole family of tools, processes and techniques to ensure that all managers are working on projects that add value for customers

- Philips has divested itself of non-core businesses and reduced its worldwide work-force by nearly a sixth and, in order to create a more customer-oriented organization, a corporate customer taskforce has been established and customer centres are being established in all business units; Jan Timmer, President of Philips, believes that a 'mental transformation' must preceed corporate transformation.

Organization should begin with the customer, the locations of activities that are best able to provide the customer with service and support.[5] A supplier should not be perceived to be remote from its customers. Front-line assistance may need to be provided on a local basis, but, beyond this, the location of back-up services and specialist support will depend upon likely customer requirements.

Where demands are made frequently and do not involve high levels of skills, support services may be located relatively close to the customer. Where calls for support arise less frequently, but involve higher level expertise, it may make sense to centralize support operations at fewer points so that individual members of staff can develop greater expertise by specializing in particular types of customer problem. A customer or client may prefer to wait until an international authority can be flown to the location of the problem.

An example of an international commercial network set up in response to changing customer requirements is The Pacific Rim Advisory Council, a network of professional law firms. Members of the network can gain access to each other's specialist skills.

In some business sectors, suppliers are engaged in a competitive race to improve their speed of action, whether of product-to-market or response to a customer request. Companies such as Hewlett-Packard have reduced the time it takes to develop and bring new products to the market-place to a small fraction of what used to be the case.[6]

While speed may be of increasing importance in responding to individual customer requirements, it does not follow that a company should rush naïvely into international operations as the wrong action may be *worse* than no action. In some corporate cultures, actions, initiatives and developments are valued and encouraged as activities quite independently of their outcomes.

Many UK companies have come unstuck as a consequence of their overseas diversifications. In some business sectors more joint ventures and arrangements appear to fail rather than achieve their initial objectives so it is worth taking the extra time to look at all the angles and carefully plan a strategic move.

14.3 Experimentation: typical next steps

Some tentative steps towards 'true' internationalization are being taken. The companies for which it is potentially most significant are often those that are exercising the greatest caution. Organizations are feeling their way.

We have seen already in Chapter 6 that certain organizational changes are perceived to be necessary for survival in a competitive market, whether or not this is international – the emerging organization, experiencing the following changes:

- need for flexibility and adaptability
- facilitating networks, rather than bureaucracy
- processes, rather than procedures
- delegation, devolution and decentralization
- flatter, leaner, tighter
- growth of teamwork
- integration of individuals into teams
- processes for continuous change
- continuous development and updating
- remuneration related to output and added value
- use of facilitating technology
- blurred boundary with customers, suppliers and partners
- greater accountability and responsibility.

Thus, harnessing human talent and the achievement of flexibility and responsiveness are high on the list of what is being sought.[1,7] There is also a feeling that permanency is giving way to more temporary arrangements, as processes for continuing change replace bureaucratic procedures, and that organic evolution is preferable to mechanistic reorganization.

A consensus appears to be emerging that effective responses are more likely to be those that involve groups and teams. Interdependence and cooperation is replacing compartmentalization. However, old habits are dying hard.

Teams and taskforces

Companies designating international accounts are reporting great difficulty in getting staff at the local level to participate in global initiatives.

The opportunity at the international account level may well be worth millions, but when it is broken down to the incremental business for offices as widely scattered as Singapore, São Paulo, Sydney, San Francisco and Sheffield, it may only be worth a few tens of thousands. In each of these offices local managers will have their own objectives and priorities and the international opportunity may seem remote, its benefits not worth the hassle and effort of international cooperation involved.

Another fairly typical institutional response to internationalization is to appoint a taskforce, unit, department or director with regional (such as, European) or international responsibilities. This can establish a focus and ensure that at least someone is concentrating upon the issues involved, but, on the other hand, it may encourage other members of a senior management team or board to conclude that internationalization does not concern them. When questions arise, they are passed to another group or to someone else who is thought to be responsible.

When a more general response is required and the perspective of the team as a whole needs to be broadened, an alternative approach may need to be adopted. For example, rather than appoint a director for international operations, one or more foreign nationals could be brought onto the board, perhaps as non-executive directors. Their participation in boardroom discussions, as suggested in the last chapter, might widen the horizons of the board as a whole.

Individual responsibilities

Another approach is to give *every* director *some* responsibility for overviewing activities in a particular region. Main board directors could serve as non-executive chairmen and senior executives as non-executive directors of certain overseas operating companies. These appointments could be rotated every few years so that, in the course of a career, those concerned are exposed to discussions about the company's operations in most parts of the world in which it has significant interests. This continuing and focused involvement may be preferable to spending one period of service in a single overseas operation or at a head office or international unit at one stage in a career.

Those with regional responsibilities could each pull together a group of executives to help them. Any support tasks could be undertaken in addition to the other responsibilities of those involved. This approach can help to broaden the perspectives of managers. However, it can also impose an extra workload upon those already suffering as a consequence of the slimming down of their organizations, so a balance must be struck.

Giving managers parallel home and international responsibilities can broaden them and secure the benefits of cross-fertilization between national operating units without establishing new heads in the organization chart and the costs and disruption of relocation. 3M is an example of a company that adopts this approach. Liaison can involve significant communication and travel costs and an already overloaded executive may face a conflict of loyalties between the two roles. Much will depend upon the understanding and support of immediate colleagues.

The composition of a board or management team can itself be an indicator of international orientation. In 1991, four European nationalities were represented in the first-line management team of Bernard Fournier, the French Managing Director of UK-headquartered Rank Xerox. As part of its Europeanization strategy, Unilever established Lever Europe. Establishing an effective board can be a key first step in successful internationalization.[8]

Systems and processes

Some companies are internationalizing their reporting and employee information systems and processes. A corporate reporting system may find it difficult to cope with national differences in employee consultation law and practice. For example, German employees will demand a higher level of disclosure of information, not to mention participation in certain decisions, than those in the US and UK.

A flexible approach, though, recognizes the need to respond to a diversity of requirements. A higher degree of openness may also be necessary when information disclosed to some staff can be passed on to colleagues in other locations. These other employees may be primarily interested in detailed information that relates to their own rather than other locations.

Greater openness could also be extended to external organizations. Companies need not, and should not, face the challenges of internationalization alone. There are competitors whose activities should be monitored. Some of these competing organizations will be new as the definition of the market a company is in is broadened. Suppliers may be internationalizing and there will be other non-competing companies with whom it may be possible to benchmark, swapping ideas and experience regarding best practice.

Companies should actively seek to learn from each other. This is particularly important in the case of customers. Account teams could enter into a dialogue with customers concerning how internationalization will affect them. They could be encouraged to jointly explore what new customer requirements might emerge. The company that plays a part in the articulation of customer requirements ought to be better placed to satisfy them.

14.4 Reviewing the organization

Some companies begin with a particular form of organization and then 'improve' it or reproduce it abroad, regardless of local circumstances. It was suggested in Chapter 10 that, rather than being constrained by the past, the form of organization adopted should emerge from skill requirements and pattern of work preferences.

The review of an organization must start with its purpose.[1] Vision, mission and strategy need to be defined so that they act as a guide to action. Ambiguity can lead to confusion and bland statements can result in a 'so what' response. People throughout the organization should be able to take a lead from corporate statements when responding to individual situations.

Once vision and mission have been established and roles and responsibilities agreed, a skill audit should be undertaken to identify the skills that are needed and whether they might be sourced internally or externally. Then the pattern of work and structure of the organization that should be used will be the one that best facilitates the contribution of those skills inherent in the company – an organization should serve its people rather than vice versa.

The patterns of work adopted must also be appropriate to the tasks to be undertaken and the individuals concerned.[9] Flexible patterns of work need to be managed. A company should – as British Telecom, IBM, ICL, Mercury Communications and Rank Xerox have done – consciously assess and review them in order to better understand the circumstances in which they do and do not work.

The importance of a clear vision

We have already seen in Chapter 4 the importance that is attached to a clear vision:

- *The Flat Organisation*[1] reveals that, 'Every respondent assessing it believes clear vision and mission to be important and about three quarters of them consider it "very important" ' and interviewees mentioned the need for a vision to be both compelling and shared, that it should, according to one director, 'grab' and not be 'anaemic' or bland
- another survey, *Communicating for Change*[10] in 1991, confirms the importance of articulating and communicating a clear vision: clear vision and strategy and top management commitment are jointly ranked as the most important requirements for the successful management of change, approaching nine out of ten of the respondents ranking these as 'very important'.

Why is so much emphasis being placed upon articulating and communicating a compelling vision? We also noted in Chapter 4 that *The Flat Organisation*[1] report goes on to reveal the relatively common phenomenon of a gap between vision and reality: 'While clear vision and mission are thought to be essential, in many companies both are regarded as just words on paper and they do not act as a guide to action'.

Points of departure

The existing organization will represent a point of departure and its form will have evolved over a period of time (see Figure 14.2). At some time most companies will have been new businesses, perhaps established by one or more entrepreneurs. At a certain stage of development, an organization tends to pass into the hands of a professional management team. Bureaucratic consolidation can occur.

Over a longer period, many organizations enter an era of decline, but downsizing in response to competitive challenges and pressures upon margins can prolong corporate life. Renewal can also occur, but its success will depend upon a number of factors, particularly the realities of the external market-place.

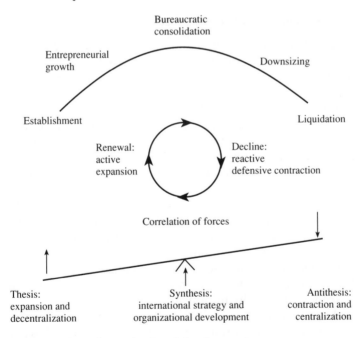

Figure 14.2 Models of organizational development

The motives for international expansion will be influenced by the stage of development of an organization. Is it the next stage of natural, evolutionary growth or is the purpose to stave off decline? A balance may need to be struck between conflicting pressures and viewpoints:

– internationalization could be perceived as an element of corporate renewal *or* as a search for less competitive market conditions during a period of decline, and within the company there may be those that favour expansion and investment in internationalization, while others would prefer a contraction, a pulling back into a more limited number of heartland markets – the international strategy of an organization can represent a shifting balance between these contending forces for expansion and contraction
– there may also be contending pressures for decentralization and centralization: decentralization should not be pursued for its own sake as what is generally sought is greater responsiveness and flexibility and so activities and responsibilities should be centralized or decentralized according to which option allows the organization to be most flexible and responsive[6] and, on occasion, an *excess* of delegation can make it more difficult for an organization as a whole to adapt quickly.

Involvement of people in the review process

As many people as possible among those likely to be affected should be involved in determining an approach to internationalization. A company's response is too important to be left to a few, however expert they may be. Adaptation is also likely to be a continuing process rather than a one-off exercise. For example, Sherwood Computer Services now operates as a flexible network organization, but the decision to adopt this form was reached after all employees were given an opportunity to participate in a fundamental review of the organization. As a result of the review processes, new client service teams and market coordination groups have been set up.

Each individual may be required to examine how internationalization and other fundamental developments in the external business environment will impact upon their own activities. During a transition phase it is not always easy to retain the commitment and loyalty of staff as naturally they will be concerned about the impact of changes upon their own prospects. It helps if the mystique of internationalization can be brushed away by keeping them fully informed.

A useful corporate party game, or exercise at management conferences and seminars, is to list the various perceived attributes of the bureaucratic and network organizations separately and contrast them:

- *bureaucratic organization:*
  - managers
  - departmental specialism/values
  - rivalry
  - rules and procedures
  - hierarchy, organization charts

  - committees
  - vertical communication

  - central direction
  - control
  - narrow specialism
  - strong head office
  - competition, office politics
  - points of view
  - continuity
  - loyalty
  - generalization and standardization
  - centralization
  - suspicion and monitoring
  - hoarding expertise
  - sophistication
  - inflexible
  - teaching

- *network organization:*
  - leaders/facilitators
  - shared vision and mission
  - interdependence
  - processes
  - roles and responsibilities, project teams
  - taskforces and teams
  - horizontal and all-channel communication
  - individual initiative
  - empowerment and support
  - general awareness
  - effective customer interface
  - cooperation, mutual trust
  - common interests
  - change
  - participation
  - responsive to individual
  - customers and employees
  - decentralization and delegation
  - trust and encouragement
  - sharing experience
  - simplification
  - responsive
  - learning

Being perceived as a 'good thing', the network organization tends to be associated with positive or desired qualities. Where an organization is making the transition to what it is hoped will be a more flexible form of organization, it is worthwhile from time to time running through such a brainstormed list to see if what is desired is actually being achieved.

Involvement of national operating companies in the review process

Developments in the multinational tend to proceed upon the basis of national plans agreed between each national operating company and the head office. In the global market-place, developments may need to be discussed on an international basis involving inputs from a number of geographic, functional and business units. The move to an international organization may be accompanied by less certainty, greater involvement of those who are affected and a more conscious attempt to reconcile and synthesize a wider range of viewpoints.

The traditional structures of many organizations stand in the way of internationalization. For example:

- in the traditional multinational, rather than organic and incremental development, the way forward often consists of larger steps that are planned from the centre, following detailed and rational analysis – the dramatic developments often being kept under wraps for reasons of commercial security, so that national operating companies are told of the outcomes rather than having been involved in the decision making process
- with a multinational (as opposed to an international) form of organization, it may be more difficult to redeploy resources from one country to another as customer requirements and business priorities change as national operating units tend to be relatively self-contained entities and, in times of recession, a marginal unit may be closed down without there being any mechanism for identifying and relocating talented staff whose services could be used elsewhere.

Whatever form of organization is established, it should not be set in concrete because arrangements may need to change as conditions and requirements evolve. For example, the arguments for or against centralization at centres of excellence may vary over time, as may the issues that determine whether an activity should be organizezd on a geographic, business sector or functional basis.

A policy of seeking greater added value opportunities may result in a shift away from a product-based to more of a customer-focused organization. Such changes are easier to accommodate in the more fluid network organization than in the bureaucratic organization. In any event, change may need to be accompanied by reorganization, the redrawing of organization charts and much concern about internal gainers and losers.

14.5 Building international networks

The creation of an international organization may be more important for an established multinational than a national company venturing abroad for the first time. Just some of the steps that can be taken to transform from a multinational to an international organization are:

- encourage international networking and cross-boarder all-channel communication

- create opportunities for informal international contact
- recruit to secure most relevant skills on an international basis
- replace national procedures with international project groups, taskforces and teams
- strengthen functional, business and sector units and customer account groups at the expense of national geographic units
- involve international participation in planning and issue monitoring and management exercises
- create mutual respect for, and build understanding of, cultural differences and variety
- encourage shared and joint use of resources and facilities on a regional or international basis
- build interfaces between national IT networks and develop a global computing and telecommunications network
- encourage organic growth and the shift of power and resources away from historic centres of bureaucratic influence and strength and to areas of greatest customer opportunity.

In the international network company there is freer and more open communication across the organization. In the multinational, national bureaucracies may be relatively self-contained. Each national operating company within a multinational corporation may recruit and remunerate its own staff, develop its own national plans and prepare its own accounts. It may retain its separate procedures and be supported by its own information technology, perhaps obtained from local suppliers. If resources are to be deployed to the best effect to meet the requirements of global customers and international access to relevant expertise secured, international planning and the integration of national systems into an international computing and telecommunications network may be needed.

Managing the transition

The Flat Organisation[1] report reveals that there is a clear commitment to change, which is seen as a necessity rather than as a matter of choice. However, in almost all of the organizations examined in the course of the survey, fundamental changes are taking longer to achieve than was first imagined.

While a consensus is emerging concerning the vision, that is, the form of international network organization that is desired, there is less certainty about how best to achieve the transition. There is a requirement for facilitating competences, facilitating processes and facilitating technology.

Some companies are achieving a more successful transition than others:

– *unsuccessful symptoms:*	– *successful symptoms:*
– working harder for longer hours	– working smarter in a more focused way
– change seen as headcount reduction and cost cutting	– change seen as improving service to customers
– insecurity and uncertainty	– confidence and commitment
– internal politics, competition and power struggles	– common customer focus
– keeping your head down and playing it safe	– assuming responsibility and getting it right
– frantic search for instant and final solutions	– frank discussion to build understanding of what is required
– repetition of slogans and production of motherhood videos and brochures	– each group responding according to context
– directed or instructed change	– shared desire to change

For example, taking out layers of management can lead to reduced barriers between customers and management in one company and, in another, to longer hours, as those who remain struggle to cope with the extra work left by those who have departed.[1] The experience of Ford suggests that change programmes themselves may need to be modified a number of times to have a significant, and the desired, effect.

The need for top management commitment

We saw in Chapter 4 that the gap between vision and conduct and rhetoric and reality that appears to have emerged suggests a lack of top management commitment in many companies. Let us review the evidence. *The Flat Organisation*[1] report and the *Communicating for Change*[10] survey reveal that:

– there is widespread awareness of the need to change, but that commitment to significant change is rarely matched by a confident understanding of *how* to bring it about
– simple and superficial change, such as shifting priorities or those involving the use of words, can and sometimes do occur overnight, but that fundamental changes of attitudes, values, approaches and perspectives usually take much longer to achieve
– the timescale to achieve fundamental change may extend beyond the lifetime of the change requirement.

In the *Communicating for Change*[10] survey, approaching nine out of ten of the respondents ranked top management commitment as a 'very important' requirement for the successful management of change.

The participants in a further survey, *Quality: The Next Steps*,[11] in 1991, were asked to attach varying degrees of significance to selected barriers to the successful implementation of a quality process. The main barrier, by a large margin, in terms of 'very significant' replies is a lack of top management commitment. Over nine out of ten respondents considered this to be a barrier to the successful implementation of a quality process.

The successful management of change, therefore, requires sustained top-level commitment:

- BP's Project 1990 had the full backing of the Chairman Bob Horton when it was launched – in April 1991, the company ran one-page corporate advertisements proclaiming its importance and outlining the progress that had been made, so, in the case of BP, the commitment has been consistent, explicit and public
- the commitment to transforming the organization and culture of ICI has been sustained through the chairmanships of Sir John Harvey-Jones and Sir Denys Henderson, so the process of transformation is accepted as continuing adaptation is needed to global market forces and competitor strategies that determine which core businesses have the potential to become or remain world leaders
- Nick Temple, the General Manager of IBM (UK), sees corporate transformation as the essence of his role and he has relied upon a combination of fundamental changes to secure the shift in attitudes that was sought – opinion surveys have been used to continuously track responses to change and the company's own computer technology has been used to monitor workloads and performance, to allocate priorities and resources
- Vern Zelmer, Managing Director of Rank Xerox (UK), strongly believes in the importance of equipping managers with the tools to successfully manage change and, drawing upon an experience with quality that by 1991 had secured nine national quality awards, the company has invested in the development of Policy Deployment, a range of approaches and techniques that collectively enables 'an organization that acknowledges the need for change to actually make it happen. Policy Deployment is the vehicle that turns intention into reality, it influences both thought and behaviour'.

Changing attitudes and behaviour at the level of the operating unit can take much longer than changing direction at the top of an organization. The direction of change may have to be reviewed and altered before it is possible for a particular change objective to be achieved; one is forever travelling but never arrives:

- while he was President of the Xerox Corportion, David Kearns made this point in relation to quality: 'Quality is a race without a finish line. A focus on quality has made Xerox a stronger company, but we know we'll never be as good as we can be because we'll always try to be better. We are on a mission of continuous quality improvement'
- according to George Labovitz, President of ODI International, 'The common element among winning companies is that they view continuous improvement as a never-ending journey'.

Complacency and satisfaction with a particular position may be the problem in a context in which change needs to become the norm. To achieve external customer satisfaction it may be necessary to consciously create dissatisfaction within. Satisfaction with the status quo can lead to complacency. According to Sir John Harvey-Jones, 'People must be dissatisfied in order to be motivated to do better'. Japanese companies such as Honda encourage their staff not to be satisfied and to continually seek to improve on whatever has been achieved. Dissatisfaction results where few opportunities to improve are identified.

The importance of people

The requirement for change needs to be rooted in opportunities to add value for customers in the market-place. Many of those interviewed in the surveys cited in Appendix 1 described their own reactions to changes in terms of impacts upon their own grading and status. The desire for change has to be shared throughout the organization and all employees should be equipped as well as encouraged to respond to change.

The role of the human resources professional during a period of transition needs to be an enabling and facilitating one.[7] Rather than tackle problems in isolation, practitioners should work with line managers to ensure that they have continuing access to the skills they require to respond to challenges and opportunities in the business environment.

In the transition to the network organization, the key management qualities, as we have seen, are communication skills, adaptability and flexibility, the ability to take risks and handle uncertainty and surprise.[1] A broad, balanced perspective and an understanding of the business environment are now essential in managers as well as directors. Also important is the ability to sustain and contribute to a variety of relationships with individuals, groups and teams located at various points around the corporate network.

In many cases, the qualities that are demanded are not so much techniques as attitudes and values. Greater sensitivity to feelings and tolerance of variety and ambiguity are likely to become more highly regarded. Personal qualities, such as balance, harmony, openness and a holistic perspective, will also assume more importance. Certain areas of management will need to be more subtle. For example, personal integrity and ethical conduct will need to be sustained in multicultural situations. Overall, individual managers will be required to make a significantly wider range of judgements.

The importance of corporate leadership

Top management commitment, so essential for successful corporate transformation, begins in the boardroom. We saw in Chapter 4 how the board itself may be partly to blame for the gap between aspiration and achievement, between rhetoric and reality that is found in many companies.[8]

The effective board is composed of a united team of competent directors who share and can communicate a common vision. To recap, it was suggested in Chapter 4 that the first step in formulating and communicating vision and strategy is for the chairman to ask the following questions:[8]

- 'Do the members of the board share a common international vision?' – if fundamental change is to occur, there must be an agreed vision of a better future
- 'Are they committed to an agreed international strategy?' – the directors should be committed to both a clear and compelling international vision and a common and realistic international strategy for its achievement
- 'How effective are members of the board at communicating with customers, employees and business partners, particularly across barriers of nationality and culture?' – a clear and compelling vision has to be communicated and understood if it is to be shared and to motivate.

14.6 Successful corporate transformation

The twin keys to successful corporate transformation are:

- vision and communication
- top management commitment.

These are of crucial importance in the management of change. If either is lacking, a change programme is likely to be built upon foundations of sand.

There is some consensus concerning what is important and what needs to be done to bridge the gap between expectation and achievement that is found in many companies.[1, 10, 11] To do what needs to be done within the context of one national market is challenging enough, but at the international level, even greater subtlety may be required:

- a compelling international vision is essential for both competitive differentiation and corporate transformation and the vision must be capable of generating commitment and understanding in a wide range of contexts
- the vision and the commitment must be sustained and be capable of accommodating the degree of change that is likely to occur in the international business environment
- this requires an effective board composed of competent directors and, in the context of the international business environment, the board itself should be international in composition and outlook
- the vision must be shared, the purpose of change communicated and employee involvement and commitment secured; those with whom an international vision must be shared may be drawn from many nationalities and cultures and each needs to understand the nature of his or her own contribution to the vision
- people need to be equipped to manage change – changes of attitude, approach and perspective are required and existing attitudes, approaches and perspectives may be significantly influenced by cultural factors, which will vary between locations
- communication skills are the greatest barrier to both internal and external communication,[10] so the ability to communicate is an essential management quality, the ability to do so internationally, across cultural and other barriers, a rare one
- two-way communication and mutual respect are the basis of relationships of trust so successful communication and sharing of a vision requires integrity, empathy and a tolerance of diversity and, ultimately, successful international communication is a question of approach, attitude and perspective rather than of specific technique or the technology of communication.

Check-list

- Does your company have an internationalization programme and are all relevant staff actively involved in its implementation?
- Will your company be able to achieve the transition that is required and, if not, what will you do about it?

- How relevant to the vision of your company is the concept of an international network organization?
- Has your company identified the likely barriers to effective internationalization and how they might be overcome?
- Has your company fully explored whether it could cooperate with other companies in developing and implementing an internationalization programme?
- Does your company work with its customer and supplier value chain partners in responding to the challenges and opportunities of internationalization?
- Could helping the company's customers and suppliers to internationalize represent a market opportunity for certain of its products or services?
- Could an existing corporate programme, such as one concerning empowerment, quality, or capacity to act, or a role review process, be modified to incorporate an internationalization dimension?
- Has your company done enough to identify best practice and learn from its own experience and the experiences of the others?

References

1. Coulson-Thomas, Colin, and Trudy Coe, *The Flat Organisation: Philosophy and Practice*, British Institute of Management, 1991; *see also* Colin J Coulson-Thomas, *The Change Makers: Vision and Communication*, booklet to accompany Sir John Harvey-Jones *et al. The Change Makers*, Didacticus Video Productions/Video Arts, 1991.
2. Coulson-Thomas, Colin, *Professional Development of and for the Board*, Adaptation survey for the Institute of Directors, Institute of Directors, 1990; and Colin Coulson-Thomas, 'Developing Directors', *European Management Journal*, pp 488–99, Vol. 8, No. 4, December 1990.
3. Coulson-Thomas, Colin, and Richard Brown, *Beyond Quality: Managing the relationship with the customer*, British Institute of Management, 1990.
4. Coulson-Thomas, Colin J, and Susan D Coulson-Thomas, *Managing the Relationship with the Environment*, a survey sponsored by Rank Xerox (UK) Ltd, Adaptation, 1990.
5. Coulson-Thomas, Colin, 'Customers Marketing and the Network Organisation', *Journal of Marketing Management*, pp 237–55, Vol. 7, 1991.
6. Smith, Preston, and Donald Reinertsen, *Developing Products in Half The Time*, Chapman & Hall, 1991.
7. Coulson-Thomas, Colin, and Richard Brown, *The Responsive Organisation: People Management – the challenge of the 1990s*, British Institute of Management, 1989; and Colin Coulson-Thomas, 'The Responsive Organisation' *Journal of General Management*, pp 21–31, Vol. 15, No. 4, Summer 1990.
8. Coulson-Thomas, Colin, *Creating Excellence in the Boardroom*, McGraw-Hill, 1993; and Colin Coulson-Thomas and Alan Wakelam, *The Effective Board: Current Practice, Myths and Realities*, an Institute of Directors discussion document, Institute of Directors, 1991.

9. Coulson-Thomas, Colin, and Susan D Coulson-Thomas, *Implementing a Telecommuting Programme*: A Rank Xerox guide for those considering the implementation of a telecommuting programme, Adaptation, 1990.
10. Coulson-Thomas, Colin, and Susan Coulson-Thomas, *Communicating for Change*, an Adaptation survey for Granada Business Services, Adaptation, 1991.
11. Coulson-Thomas, Colin, and Susan Coulson-Thomas, *Quality: The Next Steps*, an Adaptation survey for ODI International, Adaptation and ODI International, 1991.

Further reading

Campbell, Andrew, and Sally Yeung, *Do You Need a Mission Statement?*, Special Report No. 1208, *The Economist* Intelligence Unit, 1990.
Harvey-Jones, Sir John, *Making it Happen*, Collins, 1991.
Hermann, CF, *International Crises: Insights from Behavioural Research*, Free Press, 1972.
Jacobson, Gary, and John Hillkirk, *Xerox: American Samurai*, Macmillan 1986.
Jacobson, HK, *Networks of Interdependence*, (Second Edition), Knopf, 1984.
Johnson, Chalmers, *Revolutionary Change*, Little, Brown & Company, 1966.
Krasner, *Structural Conflict*, Berkeley University of California Press, 1985.
Kuhn, Thomas S, *The Structure of Scientific Revolutions*, University of Chicago Press, 1970.
Moss Kanter, Rosabeth, Barry A Stein and Todd D Jick, *The Challenge of Organizational Change: How People Experience It and Manage It*, The Free Press, 1992.
Ohmae, Kenichi, *The Borderless World: Power and Strategy in the Interlinked Economy*, Collins, 1990.
Pascale, Richard, *Managing on the Edge*, Viking Penguin, 1990.
Petersen, Donald, and John Hillkirk, *Teamwork: New Management Ideas for the 90s*, Victor Gollancz, 1991.

Appendix I

Source surveys

Coulson-Thomas, Colin, and Richard Brown, *Beyond Quality: Managing the relationship with the customer*, British Institute of Management, 1990.

Coulson-Thomas, Colin, and Susan Coulson-Thomas, *Communicating for Change*, an Adaptation survey sponsored by Granada Business Services, Adaptation, 1991.

Coulson-Thomas, Colin, *Human Resource Development for International Operation*, a survey sponsored by Surrey European Management School, Adaptation, 1990.

Coulson-Thomas, *Developing IT Directors*, an interim Adaptation report to the Department of Computing Science, Surrey University, 1990.

Coulson-Thomas, Colin, *The New Professionals*, British Institute of Management, 1988.

Coulson-Thomas, Colin, *Professional Development of and for the Board*, Adaptation survey for the Institute of Directors, Institute of Directors, 1990.

Coulson-Thomas, Colin, *The Role and Status of Project Management*, Adaptation Survey for the Association of Project Managers, 1990.

Coulson-Thomas, Colin, and Susan Coulson-Thomas, *Quality: The Next Steps*, an Adaptation survey sponsored by ODI International, Adaptation and ODI International, 1991.

Coulson-Thomas, Colin, and Richard Brown, *The Responsive Organization: People Management – the Challenge of the 1990s*, British Institute of Management, 1989.

Coulson-Thomas, Colin, *The Role and Development of the Personnel Director*, an interim. Adaptation survey in conjunction with the Institute of Personnel Management Research Group, Institute of Personnel Management, 1991. (Final report due 1992)

Coulson-Thomas, Colin, *Too Old at 40?*, British Institute of Management, 1989.

Coulson-Thomas, Colin, *Towards a New Philosophy of Management*, an Adaptation survey report for the British Institute of Management, revised and published as Colin Coulson-Thomas and Trudy Coe, *The*

Flat Organisation: Philosophy and Practice, British Institute of Management, 1991.

Coulson-Thomas, Colin, and Alan Wakelam, *Developing Directors: The Training and Development of Company Directors*, for the Training Agency, revised and published as Colin Coulson-Thomas and Alan Wakelam, *The Effective Board: Current Practice, Myths and Realities*, an Institute of Directors discussion document, Institute of Directors, 1991.

Wakelam, Alan, *The Training and Development of Company Directors*, University of Exeter, 1989.

Further information on any of these surveys can be obtained from Colin Coulson-Thomas, Adaptation Ltd, Rathgar House, 237 Baring Road, Grove Park, London SE12 0BE, Tel: 081-857 5907.

Further information on the primary survey *Human Resource Development for International Operation* 1990

The survey was carried out from May to July 1990. Those surveyed were predominantly larger organizations, but questionnaires were also sent to a number of professional associations and a selection of leading accounting firms.

The response rates varied by category of respondent, being 15 per cent for the 56 UK companies, 24.5 per cent for the 22 UK professional firms and associations and 26 per cent for the 13 European and international companies participating. This could suggest that UK professional firms and associations and European and international companies may be more concerned than UK companies with internationalization as an issue.

About half of the respondents were at chairman, CEO or director level. Half of the professional responses were from the chief executive or secretary of the organization concerned. Over a quarter of the responses from UK companies had 'training' or 'development in their job titles.

The turnover of 39 (or over four out of ten) organizations represented by returned questionnaires exceeded £1 billion. Over seven out of ten of the companies returning questionnaires had a turnover in excess of £500 million. All but one of the participating organizations with a turnover of under £10 million were professional firms or associations. In total, the survey covered organizations with a combined turnover of some £320 billion.

About a fifth of the organizations, and over a quarter of the companies, returning questionnaires had in excess of 50 000 employees, and 8 out of 10 of the companies employed over 10 000 employees. Again, organizations at the lower end of the scale were represented almost entirely by professional firms and associations. In total, the main survey questionnaire covered over 2.7 million employees. Over one million people are individual members of the professional associations participating in the survey.

The largest single category of corporate respondent is represented by the category manufacturing/production. Over a third of UK company respondents and over a half of the European and international respondents, gave manufacturing/production as the main activity of their organizations.

Appendix II

Source survey participants

This Appendix considers six organizational surveys, a survey concerning project management and four surveys concerning directors and board-room qualities, all of which have been drawn upon in this book. The work upon which the surveys are based was carried out over a three-year period from the summer of 1988 to the summer of 1991.

Organizational surveys

In the first organizational survey, the *Responsive Organisation* (Coulson-Thomas and Brown, 1989), a questionnaire was sent to some 300 individuals. The 136 written replies, including 102 completed questionnaires (of which 100 received prior to the cut-off date), were used. Of the questionnaire respondents 46 per cent indicated that they would be willing to be contacted to discuss their views regarding human resources management issues.

The returned questionnaires covered in excess of 2.97 million employees. Almost half of the responses were from organizations employing in excess of 10 000 people, while 46 per cent of the respondents identified themselves as from the manufacturing sector. Approaching two thirds of the responses were from organizations with a turnover in excess of £500 million, while 38 per cent of responses were from organizations with a turnover in excess of £1 billion. Some 38 per cent of the respondents were chairmen and over 60 per cent held the job titles of either chairman, chief executive or managing director.

In the second organizational survey, *Beyond Quality* (Coulson-Thomas and Brown, 1990), a questionnaire was sent to those most likely to have an overview of the relationships between an organization and its customers. Sufficient questionnaires were distributed to obtain 100 replies. A response rate of over 34 per cent was achieved. Of the respondents, 44 per cent were chairmen, chief executives or managing directors. The participants represented predominantly large organizations. Of the organizations, 43 per cent employed in excess of 10 000 people. Over half employed more than 5000 people and 85 per cent more than 1000 people. Overall, the survey covered more than 2 million employees.

The turnover of 60 per cent of the respondents' organizations exceeded £500 million. The turnover of about half of the organizations exceeded £1 billion, while the turnover of 17 of the 100 organizations participating in the survey exceeded £10 billion.

In the third organizational survey, *Human Resource Development for International Operation* (Coulson-Thomas, 1990), a questionnaire was sent to European and international companies. Those surveyed were predominantly from large organizations, a number of professional associations and a selection of leading accounting firms. The survey was designed to seek the views of about 80 organizations. This number was thought appropriate in relation to the size of the total population of major professions and of corporations with a turnover in excess of £1 billion. In the event, a slightly higher number of responses was achieved (91), a response rate of 17 per cent.

Of the respondents, 38 per cent were chairmen, chief executives or managing directors. Over a quarter of the companies returning questionnaires had in excess of 50 000 employees and 8 out of 10 employed over 10 000 employees. In total, the survey questionnaire covered over 2.7 million employees.

The turnover of four out of ten organizations represented by returned questionnaires exceeded £1 billion. Over seven out of ten had a turnover in excess of £500 million. In total, the survey covered organizations with a combined turnover of some £320 billion.

In the fourth organizational survey, *The Flat Organisation: Philosophy and Practice* (Coulson-Thomas and Coe, 1991), a questionnaire was sent to 422 major organizations and a response rate of 15 per cent was achieved. Over six out of ten of the respondents were the chairmen and/or CEOs of their organizations.

Approaching half of the organizations employed over 10 000 people. In total, the survey covered organizations employing 1.3 million people.

The turnover of over six out of ten organizations represented by returned questionnaires exceeded £1 billion. Over eight out of ten of the companies returning questionnaires had a turnover in excess of £500 million. In total, the survey covered organizations with a combined turnover of some £180 billion.

In the fifth organizational survey *Quality: The Next Steps* (Coulson-Thomas and Coulson-Thomas, 1991), a questionnaire was sent to 681 large organizations and follow-up and supplementary interviews were held. In total, 105 organizations participated in the survey, a participation rate of some 15 per cent. Over a quarter of participants were chairmen or CEOs of their organizations and approaching six out of ten of them directors of their organizations.

In total, and only taking into account the employees of those organizations for which employment figures were supplied, the questionnaire survey covers over 1.6 million employees. About a third of the organizations participating in the survey employ over 5000 people.

The combined turnover, of those organizations surveyed for which respondents provided turnover information, exceeds £84.6 billion. Of the participating organizations, 36 per cent have a turnover in excess of £500 million. Some 8 out of 10 of them have a turnover in excess of £100 million.

The sixth organizational survey *Communicating for Change* (Coulson-Thomas and Coulson-Thomas, 1991), involved a questionnaire and interview examination of 52 large organizations. A third of the participants are either the chairman, chief executive or managing director of their organizations, and a further quarter are directors of their organizations.

In total, the survey covers companies employing 1.2 million people. Some 3 out of 10 of the participants' organizations employ in excess of 20 000 people.

In total, the survey covers companies with a combined turnover of some £90 billion. Over 4 out of 10 of the respondents' organizations have a turnover in excess of £500 million.

PROJECT MANAGEMENT SURVEY

The questionnaire (Coulson-Thomas, 1990), The Role and Status of Project Management, was distributed to a random sample of the Association of Project Managers members and to companies that were major users of project management services.

The questionnaire was sent out in batches of 50 until 100 usable responses had been achieved. This number was reached when some 500 questionnaires had been distributed.

The main activities of the respondents' organizations were construction/engineering (31 per cent) and professional scientific or consultancy (20 per cent). Two thirds of respondents indicated that they would be willing to be contacted to discuss their views regarding project management issues.

DIRECTOR/BOARDROOM SURVEYS

The first director survey, *The Training and Development of Company Directors* (Wakelam, 1989), was undertaken by the Management Centre of Exeter University for the Training Agency. It is based upon a survey of Institute of Directors (IOD) members and non-members. Over 3266 question-naires were distributed and 373 of 390 responses were analysed. Approaching two thirds of the respondents held the job titles of chairman or managing director. The most common turnover of the respondents' companies was represented by the band of £1 to 10 million and this covered over 4 out of 10 respondents.

A parallel survey, *Professional Development of and for the Board* (Coulson-Thomas, 1990), undertaken by Adaptation for the IOD, involved a questionnaire and follow-up interview programme. A total of 2700 copies of the questionnaire were distributed to members of the IOD who were chairmen of the boards of companies. It is believed that the sample group selected is representative of the distribution of company size in the UK. Consequently, the most common company size was represented by a turnover in the range of £1 to 10 million.

Altogether 218 completed questionnaires were received and 134 of these respondents indicated that they would be willing to be contacted to discuss their views regarding professional development of and for the board. Three-quarters of the responses were from those holding the job titles of chairman or chairman and managing director. Over a third of the respondents' organizations were engaged in manufacturing or production as a main activity.

In order to relate the findings of the first survey mentioned above to the role and purpose of the board, a follow-on survey, *The Effective Board* (Coulson-Thomas and Wakelam, 1990), of the views of chairmen and CEOs was carried out jointly by Exeter University and Adaptation. Distributing 122 questionnaires elicited 56 replies, which covered 60 boards.

Appendix III

Sources of information

Copies of the British Institute of Management reports cited in this book can be obtained from:

Burston Distribution Services
Unit 2A
Newbridge Trading Estate
Newbridge Close
(off Whitby Road)
Bristol BS4 4AX
Tel: 0272 724 248

Further information on the research upon which these and other British Institute of Management reports are based can be obtained from:

Ms Trudy Coe
Head of Public Policy
British Institute of Management
3rd Floor
2 Savoy Court
The Strand
London WC2R 0EZ
Tel: 071-497 0580

Further information on the studies undertaken for the Institute of Directors can be obtained from:

John Harper, Esq.
Head of Professional Development
Institute of Directors
116 Pall Mall
London SW1Y 5ED
Tel: 071-839 1233

Further information on the response of Surrey European Management School to the findings of the survey it sponsored, *Human Resource Development for International Operation*, can be obtained from:

Professor Paul Gambol
Director
Surrey European Management School
University of Surrey
Guildford
Surrey GU2 5XH
Tel: 0483 571281

Details of the Association of Project Managers follow-up to the survey it sponsored, *The Role and Status of Project Management*, and its certification programme can be obtained from:

Mrs D Bevan
Association of Project Managers Secretariat
85 Oxford Road
High Wycombe
Buckinghamshire HP11 2DX
Tel: 0494 440090

Further information on the quality survey sponsored by ODI can be obtained from:

Robert J Evans
ODI Limited
Hill Place House
55 High Street
Wimbledon SW19 5BA
Tel: 081-944 8093

Further information on the Adaptation surveys and reports cited in this book and related research projects can be obtained from:

Susan Coulson-Thomas
Managing Director
Adaptation Limited
Rathgar House
237 Baring Road
Grove Park
London SE12 0BE
Tel: 081-857 5907

The strategic and marketing issues raised in this book can be discussed with the author at the Marketing Directors Workshop of the Chartered Institute of Marketing and certain of the Institute's international marketing programmes. Further details can be obtained from:

Harold Shilling, Esq.
Chartered Institute of Marketing
Moor Hall
Cookham
Maidenhead
Berkshire SL6 9QH
Tel: 06285 24922

The UK government departments most concerned with the issues raised in this book are:

Department of Trade and Industry
Ashdown House
123 Victoria Street
London SW1E 6RB
Tel: 071-215 6272

Department of Employment
Caxton House
Tothill Street
London SW1H 9NF
Tel: 071-273 6969

Other UK organizations that might be able to provide advice and information on matters concerning internationalization are:

Association of British Chamber of Commerce
Sovereign House
212a Shaftesbury Avenue
London WC2H 8EW
Tel: 071-240 5831/6

Confederation of British Industry
Centre Point
103 New Oxford Street
London WC1A 1DU
Tel: 071-379 7400

Information on the EC can be obtained from:

Directorate General X
Commission of the European Communities
rue de la Loi 200
B-1049 Brussels
Belgium
Tel: 010-32-2235 11 11

The EC press and information offices in the UK are located at:

8 Storey's Gate, London SW1P 3AT Tel: 071-222 8122
4 Cathedral Road, Cardiff CF1 9SG Tel: 0222 371631
7 Alva Street, Edinburgh EH2 4PH Tel: 031-225 2058
Windsor House, 9–15 Bedford Street, Belfast BT2 7EG Tel: 0232 240708

A series of basic information reports on the employment and training framework in each of the member states of the EC can be obtained from:

European Centre for Work and Society, Postbus 3073
NI-6202 NB Masstricht
Netherlands
Tel: 010-31-43 216 724

Information of particular relevance to small- and medium-sized enterprises can be obtained from:

Centre for European Business Information
Small Firms Service
11 Belgrave Road
London SW1V 1RB
Tel: 071-828 6201

An EC fact pack and updates on EC employment matters can be obtained from:

Department of Employment
Information 2, Ground Floor
Caxton House
Tothill Street
London SW1H 9NF

HMSO Books is the official UK sales agent for official EC publications. These can be obtained from:

HMSO Publications Centre
PO Box 276
London SW8 5DT
Tel: 071-873 8409

The main source of training information in the UK is the Training Agency. Information on Training and Enterprise Councils can be obtained from the TEC Project Team at:

The Training Agency
Moorfoot
Sheffield S1 4PQ
Tel: 0742 753275

Information on relevant UK educational programmes and language export centres can be obtained from:

Adult Training Promotions Unit
Room 212
Department of Education and Science
Elizabeth House
York Road
London SE1 7PH
Tel: 071-934 0888

Advice on language training requirements and how these might be met can be obtained from:

Centre for Information on Language, Teaching and Research
Regent's College
Inner Circle
Regent's Park
London NW1 4NS
Tel: 071-486 8221

Bibliography and further reading

This select bibliography suggests a mixture of background volumes on the international dimension and more recent books on managing in an international context. A continually updated list of both books and articles on various aspects of internationalization to suit individual requirements can be obtained from the Management Information Centre of the British Institute of Management, Management House, Cottingham Road, Corby, Northamptonshire NN17 1TT (Tel: 0536 204222).

Abe, Etsuo, and Yoshitaka Suzuki, *Changing Patterns of International Rivalry*, University of Tokyo Press, 1991.

Allison, Graham T, *Essence of Decision, Explaining the Cuban Missile Crisis*, Little, Brown & Company, 1971.

Arbuthnott, H and G Edwards, *A Common Man's Guide to the Common Market*, Macmillan, 1989.

Atkinson, John, *Corporate Employment Policies for the Single European Market*, Institute of Manpower Studies, Report No. 179, 1989.

Baldwin, D, *Economic Statecraft*, Princeton University Press, 1985.

Barham, Kevin, and David Oates, *The International Manager*, Business Books, 1991.

Barston, R, *Modern Diplomacy*, Longman, 1988.

Bartlett, Christopher A, Yves Doz and Gunnar, Hedlund, *Managing the Global Firm*, Routledge, 1990.

Bartram, Peter, and Colin Coulson-Thomas, *The Complete Spokesperson: A workbook for managers who meet the media*, Kogan Page, 1991.

Benson, Vince, and David Stoker, *1992: The Single European Market and The Business Start-up*, Trainer Resource Pack, Training Agency, 1990.

Bevan, Stephen, *Staff Retention: A managers guide*, Report No. 203, Institute of Manpower Studies, 1991.

Blau, PM, *Exchange and Power in Social Life*, Wiley, 1964.

Bohning, WR, *Studies in International Labour Migration*, Macmillan, 1984.

Bownas, Geoffrey, *Japan and the New Europe: Industrial Strategies and Options in the 1990s*, Special Report No. 2072, *The Economist* Intelligence Unit, 1991.

Bovard, James, *The Fair Trade Fraud: How Congress Pillages the Consumer and Decimates American Competitiveness*, St Martin's Press, 1991.

Brewster, Chris, and Paul Teague, *European Community Social Policy*, Institute of Personnel Management, 1989.

Brewster, Chris, *The Management of Expatriates*, Kogan Page, 1991.

Brierly, JL, *The Law of Nations*, (Sixth Edition), Clarendon, 1963.

Brown, Richard, and Tim Rycroft, *Involved in Europe*, British Institute of Management Discussion Paper No. 12, 1989.

Bull, H, and A, Watson, *The Expansion of International Society*, Oxford University Press, 1984.

Burgenmeier, B, and Jean-Louis Mucchielli, *Multinationals and Europe 1992*, Routledge, 1991.

Burstein, Daniel, *Euroquake: Europe's Explosive Economic Challenge Will Change the World*, Simon & Schuster, 1991.

Burton, John W, *World Society*, Cambridge University Press, 1972.

Burton, John, *Deviance, Terrorism and War: The Process of Solving Unsolved Social and Political Problems*, Martin Robertson, 1979.

Business International, *Business Europe Annual Survey of Comparative Labour Costs in Europe*, Business International, 1991.

Campbell, Andrew, and Sally Yeung, *Do You Need a Mission Statement?*, Special Report No. 1208, *The Economist* Intelligence Unit, 1990.

Casson, Mark (Editor), *Multinational Corporations*, Edward Elgar, 1990.

Cavusgil, ST, and PN Ghauri, *Doing Business in Developing Countries: Entry and Negotiation Strategies*, Routledge, 1990.

Cecchini, P, *The European Challenge: 1992, The Benefits of a Single Market*, Wildwood House, 1988.

Citron, Richard, *The Stoy Hayward Guide to Getting into Europe*, Kogan Page, 1991.

Commission of the European Communities, *Communication from the Commission Concerning Its Action Programme Relating to the Implementation of the Community Charter of Basic Social Rights for Workers*, (COM(89)568), Office for Official Publications of the European Communities, November 1989.

Commission of the European Communities, *Community Charter of the Fundamental Social Rights of Workers*, Office for Official Publications of the European Communities, 1990.

Commission of the European Communities, *Completing the Internal Market*, White Paper from the Commission to the European Council, Office for Official Publications of the European Communities, 1985.

Commission of the European Communities, *Directory of Community Legislation in Force and Other Acts of the Community Institutions*, Office for Official Publications of the European Communities, 1991.

Commission of the European Communities, *Panorama of EC Industry 1990*, Office for Official Publications of the European Communities, 1990.

Commission of the European Communities, *Positive Action: Equal Opportunities for Women in Employment – A Guide*, Office for Official Publications of the European Communities, 1988.

Commission of the European Communities, *The Single Act: A New Frontier for Europe*, Communication from the Commission (COM(87)100) to the Council, Office for Official Publications of the European Communities, 1987.

Commission of the European Communities, *The Single European Act 1986*, Office for Official Publications of the European Communities, 1986.

Commission of the European Communities, Directorate General for Economic and Financial Affairs, *The Economics of 1992: An assessment of the potential economic effects of completing the internal market of the European Community*, Office for Official Publications of the European Communities, 1988.

Commission of the European Communities, Directorate General for Employment, Industrial Relations and Social Affairs, *Employment in Europe*, Office for Official Publications of the European Communities, 1989.

Connock, Stephen, *HR Vision: Managing a Quality Workforce*, Institute of Personnel Management, 1991.

Coulson-Thomas, Colin, *Creating Excellence in the Boardroom*, McGraw-Hill, 1992.

Coulson-Thomas, Colin J, *Human Resource Development for International Operation*, a survey sponsored by Surrey European Management School, Adaptation, 1990.

Coulson-Thomas, Colin, *Professional Development of and for the Board*, Adaptation survey for the Institute of Directors, Institute of Directors, 1990.

Coulson-Thomas, Colin, *The New Professionals*, British Institute of Management, 1988.

Coulson-Thomas, Colin, *The Role and Development of the Personnel Director*, an Adaptation survey undertaken in conjunction with the Institute of Personnel Management Research Group, Institute of Personnel Management, 1991.

Coulson-Thomas, Colin, *Too old at 40?*, British Institute of Management, 1989.

Coulson-Thomas, Colin J, *The Change Makers, Vision and Communication*, booklet to accompany Sir John Harvey-Jones, *et al. The Change Makers*, Didacticus Video Productions/Video Arts, 1991.

Coulson-Thomas, Colin, and Richard Brown, *The Responsive Organisation: People Management – the Challenge of the 1990s*, British Institute of Management, 1989.

Coulson-Thomas, Colin, and Richard Brown, *Beyond Quality: Managing the relationship with the customer*, British Institute of Management, 1990.

Coulson-Thomas, Colin, and Susan Coulson-Thomas, *Communicating for Change*, an Adaptation survey for Granada Business Services, Adaptation, 1991.

Coulson-Thomas, Colin J, and Susan D Coulson-Thomas, *Implementing a Telecommuting Programme*, A Rank Xerox guide for those considering the implementation of a telecommuting programme, Adaptation, 1990.

Coulson-Thomas, Colin, and Susan Coulson-Thomas, *Quality: The Next Steps*, an Adaptation survey for ODI International, Adaptation and ODI International, 1991.

Coulson-Thomas, Colin, and Trudy Coe, *The Flat Organisation: Philosphy and Practice*, British Institute of Management, 1991.

Coulson-Thomas, Colin, and Alan Wakelam, *The Effective Board: Current Practice, Myths and Realities*, an Institute of Directors discussion document, Institute of Directors, 1991.

Cox, R, *Production, Power and World Order: Social Forces in the Making of History*, Columbia University Press, 1987.

Daniels, Caroline, *The Management Challenge of Information Technology*, The Economist Intelligence Unit, 1991.

DePorte, AW, *Europe Between the Superpowers* (Second Edition), Yale University Press, 1986.

Deutsch, Karl W, *Analysis of International Relations* (Second Edition), Prentice-Hall, 1978.

Deutsch, Karl W, *The Nerves of Government*, Free Press, 1963.

Dicken, P, *Global Shift*, Harper & Row,1986.

Dougherty, James E, and Robert L Pfaltzgraff, *Contending Theories of International Relations*, Harper & Row, 1971.

Dudley, JW, *1992: Strategies for the Single Market*, Kogan Page in association with the Chartered Institute of Management Accountants, 1989.

Eckley, Robert S, *Global Competition in Capital Goods*, Quorum Books, 1991.

Eli, Max, *Japan Inc.: Global Strategies of Japanese Trading Companies*, McGraw-Hill, 1990.

Employment Department Group (UK), *Labour Market and Skill Trends 1992/93*, Skills and Enterprise Network, 1991.

EUROSTAT, *Earnings in Industry and Services*, Rapid Reports, Population and social conditions, No. 5, EUROSTAT, 1991.

Evans, Paul, Yves Doz and André Laurent (Eds), *Human Resource Management in International Firms: Change, Globalization, Innovation*, Macmillan, 1989.

George, S, *Politics and Policy in the European Community*, Oxford, 1985.

Gilpin, Robert, *The Political Economy of International Relations*, Princeton, 1987.

Gilpin, Robert, *US Power and the Multinational Corporation*, Macmillan, 1976.

Groom, AJR and CR Mitchell, *International Relations Theory: A bibliography*, Frances Pinter, 1978.

Gross, B and E Gross (Eds), *The Great School Debate*, Simon & Schuster, 1985.

Guy, Vincent, and John Mattock, *The New International Manager*, Kogan Page, 1991.

Hafner, Katie, and John Markoff, *Cyberpunk*, Fourth Estate, 1991.

Halliday, F, *The Making of the Second Cold War* (Second Edition), Verso, 1986.

Halperin, Morton, *Bureaucratic Politics and Foreign Policy*, Brookings, 1974.

Harris, N, *Of Bread and Guns: The World Economy in Crisis*, Penguin, 1983.

Harvey-Jones, Sir John, *Making it Happen*, Collins, 1991.

Hermann, CF, *International Crises: Insights from Behavioural Research*, Free Press, New York, 1972.

Hochstrasser, Beat, and Catherine Griffiths, *Regaining Control of IT Investments: A Handbook for Senior UK Management*, Kobler Unit, Imperial College, 1990.

Holsti, KJ, *The Dividing Discipline*, Allen & Unwin, 1985.

Incomes Data Services and the Institute of Personnal Management 1992: *Personnel Management and the Single European Market*, Incomes Data Services and the Institute of Personnel Management, 1988.

Jacobson, Gary, and John Hillkirk, *Xerox: American Samurai*, Macmillan, 1986.

Jacobson, HK, *Networks of Interdependence* (Second Edition), Knopf, 1984.

Jervis, Robert, *Perception and Misperception in International Politics*, Princeton University Press, 1976.

Johnson, Chalmers, *Revolutionary Change*, Little, Brown & Company, 1966.

Jones, Stephanie, *Working for the Japanese*, Macmillan, 1991.

Keen, PGW, *Competing in Time: Using Telecommunications for Competitive Advantage*, Ballinger, 1986.

Kennedy, P, *The Rise and Fall of the Great Powers*, Unwin Hyman, 1988.

Kent, RC, and GP Nielssen (Eds), *The Study and Teaching of International Relations: A Perspective on Mid-Career Education*, Frances Pinter, 1980.

Keohane, R, *After Hegemony*, Princeton University Press, 1984.

Keohane, Robert O, and Joseph S Nye, *Transnational Relations and World Politics*, Harvard University Press, 1970.

Kobayashi, Koji, *The Rise of NEC*, Blackwell, 1991.

Krasner, *Structural Conflict*, Berkeley University of California Press, 1985.

Kuhn, Thomas S, *The Structure of Scientific Revolutions*, University of Chicago Press, 1970.

Laudon, KC, and J Turner (Eds), *Information Technology and Management Strategy*, Prentice-Hall, 1989.

Lawrence, Paul R, and Charalambos A Vlachoutsicos, *Behind The Factory Walls: Decision Making in Soviet and US Enterprises*, Harvard Business School Press, 1991.

Light, M, and AJR Groom (Eds), *International Relations: A Handbook of Current Theory*, Frances Pinter, 1985.

Lindblom, Charles E, *Politics and Markets: The World's Political–Economic Systems*, Basic Books, 1977.

Liston, David, and Nigel Reed, *Business Studies, Languages and Overseas Trade*, Pitman Publishing and The Institute of Export, 1985.

Little, R, and S Smith, *Belief Systems and International Relations*, Basil Blackwell, 1988.

Lodge, J, *The European Community and the Challenge of the Future*, Pinter, 1989.

Louis, Jean-Victor, *The Community Legal Order* (Second completely revised Edition), Commission of the European Communities, 1991.

Lynch, Richard, *European Business Strategies*, Kogan Page, 1991.

Manpower PLC, *Employment and Training*, Mercury Books/CBI Initiative 1992, 1990.

McDonald, Malcolm HB, and S Tamer Cavusgil (Eds), *The International Marketing Digest*, Heinemann Professional Publishing, 1990.

McGowan, William, G, *et al.*, *Revolution in Real Time: Managing Information Technology in the 1990s*, (*Harvard Business Review* collected articles), Harvard Business School Press, 1991.

Mitrany, D, *The Functional Theory of Politics*, Martin Robertson, 1975.

Mole, John, *Mind Your Manners: Culture and Clash in the Single European Market*, Industrial Society Press, 1991.

Moran, Robert T, *Cultural Guide to Doing Business in Europe*, Butterworth/Heinemann, 1991.

Morgenthan, Hans J, *Politics Among Nations: The Struggle for Power and Peace*, Knopf, 1978.

Moss Kanter, Rosabeth, Barry A Stein and Todd D Jick, *The Challenge of Organisational Change: How People Experience It and Manage It*, The Free Press, New York, 1992.

Ohmae, Kenichi, *Triad Power*, The Free Press/Collier Macmillan, 1985.

Ohmae, Kenichi, *The Borderless World: Power and Strategy in the Interlinked Economy*, Collins, 1990.

Olson, M, *The Rise and Decline of Nations*, Yale University Press, 1982.

Papp, DS, *Contemporary International Relations: Frameworks for Understanding*, Collier Macmillan, 1984.

Parkinson, F, *The Philosophy of International Relations: A study in the history of thought*, Sage Publications, 1977.

Pascale, Richard, *Managing on the Edge*, Viking Penguin, 1990.

Pearson, Richard, *Recruiting Graduates in Europe: What is happening?*, Institute of Personnel Management, 1991.

P E International, *International Taxation and Cost of Living*, P E International, 1991.

Petersen, Donald, and John Hillkirk, *Teamwork: New Management Ideas for the 90s*, Victor Gollancz, 1991.

Pinder, John, *European Community*, Oxford University Press, 1991.

Plenert, Gerhard Johannes, *International Management and Production: Survival Techniques for Corporate America*, Tab Books, 1990.

Price Waterhouse Cranfield Project on International Strategic Human Resource Management, The, *Annual Reports 1990 and 1991*, Price Waterhouse and Cranfield School of Management, 1990 and 1991.

Razvigorova, E, and G Wolf-Laudon, *East-West Joint Ventures*, Blackwell, 1991.

Raffia, H, *The Art and Science of Negotiation*, Harvard University Press, 1982.

Rank Xerox Ltd, *Marketing to the Public Sector and Industry*, Mercury Books/CBI Initiative 1992, 1990.

Rheingold, Howard, *Virtual Reality*, Secker & Warburg, 1991.

Ride, Tord, *How to Establish a Business in Japan*, Kluwer, 1991.

Rugman, Alan M, and Alain Verbeke, *Global Corporate Strategy and Trade Policy*, Pinter, 1990.

Saltzman, Amy, *Downshifting: Reinvesting Success on a Slower Track*, Harper Collins, 1991.

Scammell, W, *The International Economy Since 1945*, Macmillan, 1980.

Schelling, Thomas C, *The Strategy of Conflict*, Oxford University Press, 1963.

Schioppa, FP (Ed), *Mismatch and Labour Mobility*, Cambridge University Press, 1991.

Schonberger, Richard, *Building a Chain of Customers*, Hutchinson, 1990.

Séché, Jean-Claude, *A Guide to Working in a Europe Without Frontiers*, Office for Official Publications of the European Communities, 1988.

Somogyi, EK, and RD Galliers (Eds), *Towards Strategic Information Systems*, Abacus Press, 1987.

Spero, J, *The Politics of International Economic Relations* (Fourth Edition), Unwin Hyman, 1990.

Steinbruner, JD, *A Cybernetic Theory of Decision*, Princeton University Press, 1974.

Stephens, Michael D, *Japan and Education*, Macmillan, 1991.

Strange, Susan, *States and Markets: An Introduction to International Political Economy*, Pinter, 1988.

Sullivan, Michael P, *International Relations: Theories and Evidence*, Prentice-Hall, 1976.

Strassmann, PA, *Information Payoff*, Macmillan, 1985.

Swann, D, *The Economics of the Common Market* (Fifth Edition), Penguin, 1984.

Taylor, P, *The Limits of European Integration*, Croom Helm, 1985.

Taylor, Trevor (Ed), *Approaches and Theory in International Relations*, Longman Group, 1978.

Taylor, P, and AJR Groom (Eds), *International Institutions at Work*, Pinter, 1988.

Teague, P, *The European Community: The Social Dimension – Labour Market Policies for 1992*, Kogan Page in association with Cranfield School of Management, 1989.

Touche Ross, *Office Automation: the Barriers and Opportunities*, Touche Ross and the Institute of Administrative Management, 1991.

Tuller, Lawrence W, *Going Global: New Opportunities for Growing Companies to Compete in World Markets*, Business One, Irwin, 1991.

Turner, Ian, *The Living Market: The Impact of 1992 on Europe and Work*, Sanders and Sidney, 1989.

Urwin, DW, and WE Paterson, *Politics in Western Europe Today*, Longman, 1990.

Vasquez, John, *The Power of Power Politics: a Critique*, Frances Pinter, 1983.

Wallace, H, C Wallace and C Webb, *Policy-Making in the European Community* (Second Edition), Wiley, 1983.

Wallerstein, I, *The Politics of the World Economy*, Cambridge University Press, 1984.

Wenger, Etienne, *Artificial Intelligence Tutoring Systems*, Morgan Kaufman, 1987.

Woolfe, Roger, *Globalisation: The IT Challenge*, Amdahl Executive Institute, 1991.

Womack, James P, Daniel T Jones and Daniel Roos, *The Machine That Changed the World*, Rawson Associates and Maxwell Macmillan International, 1991.

Wight, M, *Power Politics*, Penguin, 1977.

Yergin, Daniel, *The Prize: The Epic Quest for Oil, Money and Power*, Simon & Schuster, 1991.

Young, George, *The New Export Marketer*, Kogan Page, 1991.

Index